FUNDAMENTALS OF
English
Grammar

FOURTH EDITION
WORKBOOK

PEARSON
Longman

Betty S. Azar
Rachel Spack Koch
Stacy A. Hagen

Fundamentals of English Grammar, Fourth Edition Workbook

Azar Associates: Shelley Hartle, Editor, and Sue Van Etten, Manager

Pearson Education, 10 Bank Street, White Plains, NY 10606

Staff credits: The people who made up the *Fundamentals of English Grammar, Fourth Edition, Workbook* team, representing editorial, production, design, and manufacturing, are, Diane Cipollone, Dave Dickey, Christine Edmonds, Ann France, and Amy McCormick.

Text composition: S4Carlisle Publishing Services
Text font: 10.5/12 Plantin

Illustrations:
Don Martinetti: 27, 38, 53, 57, 62, 66, 77, 89, 92, 112, 121, 125, 127, 130, 133, 142, 143 (top), 144, 148, 149, 162, 173 (bottom), 179, 182, 184, 199, 202, 203, 207, 208, 214, 222, 223, 229, 240, 244, 245, 249, 250
Chris Pavely: 4, 6, 7, 9, 11, 21, 24, 28, 30, 34, 43, 59, 79, 94, 97, 98, 104, 118, 126, 143 (bottom), 160, 173 (top), 192, 252

Printed in the United States of America

ISBN 10: 0-13-802212-7
ISBN 13: 978-0-13-802212-9

12 17

Contents

Chapter 6   NOUNS AND PRONOUNS

Chapter 7   MODAL AUXILIARIES

SPECIAL WORKBOOK SECTION

Appendix 1 PHRASAL VERBS

Appendix 2 PREPOSITION COMBINATIONS

Preface

The *Fundamentals of English Grammar Workbook* is a place for lower-intermediate and intermediate students to explore and practice English grammar on their own. It is a place where they can test and fine-tune their understanding of English structures and improve their ability to use English meaningfully and correctly. All of the exercises have been designed for independent study, but this book is also a resource for teachers who need exercise material for additional classwork, homework, testing, or individualized instruction.

The *Workbook* is keyed to the explanatory grammar charts found in *Fundamentals of English Grammar, Fourth Edition*, a classroom teaching text for English language learners, and in the accompanying *Chartbook*, a reference grammar with no exercises.

The answers to the practices can be found in the *Answer Key* in the back of the *Workbook*. Its pages are perforated so that they can be detached to make a separate booklet. However, if teachers want to use the *Workbook* as a classroom teaching text, the *Answer Key* can be removed at the beginning of the term.

Two special Workbook sections called *Phrasal Verbs* and *Preposition Combinations*, not available in the main text, are included in the Appendices. These sections provide reference charts and a variety of exercises for independent practice.

Chapter **1**
Present Time

► **Practice 1. Interview questions and answers.**
Complete the sentences with words from the list. A word may be used more than once.

am	do	is	meet	play	you
are	from	like	✓name	write	

KUNIO: Hi. My name ___is___ Kunio.
      1

MARIA: Hi. My ___name___ ___is___ Maria. I ___am___ glad to meet you.
            2   3   4

KUNIO: I ___am___ glad to ___meet___ you too. Where ___are___
        5   6   7
      ___you___ from?
            8

MARIA: I ___am___ from Mexico. Where ___are___ ___you___ ___from___?
        9   10   11   12

KUNIO: I ___am___ ___from___ Japan.
        13   14

MARIA: Where ___are___ ___you___ living now?
            15   16

KUNIO: On Fifth Avenue in an apartment. And you?

MARIA: I ___am___ living in a dorm.
        17

KUNIO: What ___are___ you studying?
            18

MARIA: Business. After I study English, I'm going to attend the School of Business
      Administration. How about you? What ___is___ your major?
                                          19

KUNIO: Engineering.

MARIA: What ___do___ you like to do in your free time?
            20

KUNIO: I play the guitar with a group.

MARIA: Really? Where?

KUNIO: We ___play___ together in a friend's garage on weekends. It's fun. How about you?
        21
      What ___do___ you do in your free time?
            22

MARIA: I like to get on the Internet.

KUNIO: Oh? What _____do_____ you do when you're online?
                      23

MARIA: I write a blog. I _____write_____ two or three times a week.
                              24

KUNIO: A blog! What _____do_____ you write about on your blog?
                          25

MARIA: The news. I _____try_____ to give my thoughts.
                        26

KUNIO: That's interesting!

MARIA: I have to _____write_____ your full name on the board when I introduce you to the class.
                      27

How _____do_____ _____you_____ spell your name?
         28   29

KUNIO: My first name _____is_____ Kunio. K-U-N-I-O. My family name _____is_____
                          30   31

Akiwa.

MARIA: Kunio Akiwa. _____Is_____ that right?
                        32

KUNIO: Yes, it _____is_____. And what _____is_____ your name again?
                    33   34

MARIA: My first name _____is_____ Maria. M-A-R-I-A. My last name _____is_____ Lopez.
                          35   36

KUNIO: Thanks. Well, it's been nice talking to you.

MARIA: I enjoyed it too.

▶ **Practice 2. Simple present and present progressive.** (Chart 1-1)
Circle the correct verb.

1. I (*sit* / *am sitting*) at my desk right now.

2. I (*sit* / *am sitting*) at this desk every day.

3. I (*do* / *am doing*) grammar exercises every day.

4. I (*do* / *am doing*) a grammar exercise now.

5. I (*look* / *am looking*) at Sentence 5 now.

6. Now I (*write* / *am writing*) the correct completion for this sentence.

7. Henry (*sits* / *is sitting*) at his desk now.

8. He (*works* / *is working*) at his computer.

9. He (*works* / *is working*) at his computer every day.

10. He (*checks* / *is checking*) his email right now.

11. He (*checks* / *is checking*) his email 20 times a day.

12. He (*writes* / *is writing*) more than 30 emails every day.

▶ Practice 3. Forms of the simple present. (Chart 1-2)

Complete each sentence with the correct form of the verb *speak*.

Part I: STATEMENT FORMS

1. I _____ *speak* _____ English.
2. They _____ speak _____ English.
3. He _____ speaks _____ English.
4. You _____ speak _____ English.
5. She _____ speaks _____ English.

Part II: NEGATIVE FORMS

6. I _____ *do not / don't speak* _____ English.
7. They _____ don't speak _____ English.
8. She _____ does not speak _____ English.
9. You _____ do not speak _____ English.
10. He _____ does not speak _____ English.

Part III: QUESTION FORMS

11. _____ *Do* _____ you _____ *speak* _____ English?
12. _____ Do _____ they _____ speak _____ English?
13. _____ does _____ he _____ speak _____ English?
14. _____ Do _____ we _____ speak _____ English?
15. _____ does _____ she _____ speak _____ English?

▶ Practice 4. Forms of the simple present tense. (Chart 1-2)

Complete each sentence with the appropriate verb from the list. Add *-s/-es* as necessary.

collect	cook	✓play	run	work
conduct	drive	program	train	write

1. Leon is a piano player. He _____ *plays* _____ the piano in a restaurant on weekends.
2. Akira is an orchestra conductor. He _____ conducts _____ the City Symphony Orchestra.
3. My grandparents are stamp collectors. They _____ collect _____ stamps from all over the world.
4. My sister is a computer programmer. She _____ programs _____ computers for a large corporation.
5. Ariel is a teacher trainer. He _____ trains _____ teachers for elementary schools.
6. Fred and Ted are marathon runners. They _____ run _____ in marathon races.
7. Gino is the cook in the governor's house. He _____ cooks _____ for the governor's family.
8. Two of my friends are post-office workers. They _____ work _____ in the post office.
9. Alex is a truck driver. He _____ drives _____ a truck up and down the interstate highways.
10. I am a travel writer. I _____ write _____ articles for a travel magazine.

► **Practice 5. The simple present tense.** (Chart 1-2)
Sentence a. is a statement with an incorrect fact. In Sentence b., write the negative of that statement, and then write the correct fact. Use the affirmative and negative forms of the verb in Sentence a.

1. a. The needle of a compass points south.
   b. No. The needle of a compass ___*doesn't point*___ south.
      It ___*points*___ north.

2. a. February comes before January.
   b. No. February _____ before January. It _____
      after January.

3. a. It snows in warm weather.
   b. No. It _____ in warm weather. It _____ in cold
      weather.

4. a. Bananas grow in cold climates.
   b. No. Bananas _____ in cold climates. Bananas
      _____ in warm climates.

5. a. Lightning follows thunder.
   b. No. Lightning _____ thunder.
      Thunder _____ lightning.

6. a. Whales fly.
   b. No. Whales _____. Birds
      _____.

7. a. The earth revolves around the moon.
   b. No. The earth _____ around the moon.
      The moon _____ around the earth.

8. a. Butterflies turn into caterpillars.
   b. No. Butterflies _____ into caterpillars.
      Caterpillars _____ into butterflies.

► **Practice 6. The simple present tense.** (Chart 1-2)
Complete the sentences with **do, does,** or **Ø**.

1. Polly and Scott ___*do*___ not work in an office.
2. They _____ own a small construction company.
3. The company _____ not build houses.
4. The company _____ repairs houses.
5. Polly and Scott _____ not do the same work.
6. They _____ do different kinds of work.
7. Polly _____ enjoys painting, but Scott _____ not like painting.
8. He _____ prefers to fix things.
9. They _____ spend 8 to 10 hours at work on most days.

10. They _____ not work at night or on weekends.

11. _____ they plan to work together for a long time? Yes, they're married.

▶ Practice 7. Forms of the present progressive. (Chart 1-2)
Complete the sentences with the correct form of the verb *speak*.

Part I: STATEMENT FORMS

1. I ___*am speaking*___ English right now.

2. They ___*are spea*___ English right now.

3. She ___*is*___ English right now.

4. You ___*are*___ English right now.

5. He ___*is*___ English right now.

Part II: NEGATIVE FORMS

6. I ___*am not speaking*___ English right now.

7. They ___*are*___ English right now.

8. She ___*is*___ English right now.

9. You ___*are*___ English right now.

10. He ___*is*___ English right now.

Part III: QUESTION FORMS

11. ___*Are*___ you ___*speaking*___ English right now?

12. ___*Is*___ he _____ English right now?

13. ___*Are*___ they _____ English right now?

14. ___*Are*___ we _____ English right now?

15. ___*Is*___ she _____ English right now?

▶ Practice 8. The present progressive. (Chart 1-2)
Complete each sentence with the present progressive form of the verbs in parentheses.

I'm looking around the classroom now. My classmates are not paying attention. Sally (*look*)

___*is looking*___ at her watch. Ali has his head back and he (*stare*)
    1

___*is staring*___ at the ceiling. Kiki and Ruth (*text*) ___*are texting*___
    2   3

each other. Janet (*file*) ___*is filing*___ her nails. Tanya and Olga (*listen*)
                                4

___*are listening*___ to something on their iPods. Spiro (*move*)
    5

___*is moving*___ around in his seat. Ana (*draw*) ___*is drawing*___ a
    6   7

picture of the professor. Dmitri (*sleep*) ___*is sleeping*___. I (*try*)
                                                8

___*am trying*___ to stay awake. The poor professor (*speak*)
    9

___*is speaking*___ very softly. He has a sore throat, and he (*lose*)
    10

___*is losing*___ his voice. I think that he (*fall*) ___*is falling*___
    11   12

asleep too.

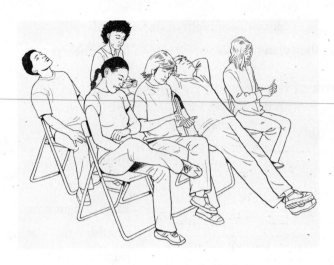

▶ **Practice 9. The simple present and the present progressive.** (Charts 1-1 and 1-2)
Choose the correct completions for each group.

Group 1

1. Jack __c__ .
2. Jack is __a__ .
3. Jack does not __b__ .

   a. working today
   b. work in an office
   c. works in a factory

Group 2

1. Nina __c__ .
2. She does not __b__ .
3. She is not __a__ .

   a. playing tennis now
   b. play tennis on weekdays
   c. plays tennis on weekends

Group 3

1. Leah and Hank are __b__ .
2. They ____ .
3. Leah ____ .

   a. chats on the computer every night
   b. chatting on their computers now
   c. chat on their computers a lot

Group 4

1. My roommate and I do not __b__ .
2. He __a__ .
3. I am not __c__ .

   a. watches the news at 11:00 P.M.
   b. watch TV in the afternoons
   c. watching TV right now

▶ **Practice 10. Present verbs: questions.** (Charts 1-1 and 1-2)
Complete the questions with **Does he** or **Is he**.

1. _____Is he_____ a student?
2. _____Does he_____ have good professors?
3. _____Is he_____ from Spain?
4. _____Is he_____ in the classroom?
5. _____Does he_____ like school?
6. _____Is he_____ a math major?
7. _____Is he_____ studying math?
8. _____Does he_____ study every day?
9. _____Does he_____ live on campus?
10. _____Does he_____ do homework every night?

▶ **Practice 11. Present verbs: questions.** (Charts 1-1 and 1-2)
Complete the questions with **Does she** or **Is she**.

1. _____Is she_____ at work?
2. _____Does she_____ have a good job?
3. _____Is she_____ working right now?
4. _____Is she_____ sitting at her desk?
5. _____Does she_____ come to the office every day?
6. _____Does she_____ like her job?
7. _____Is she_____ on the phone?
8. _____Is she_____ in a meeting?
9. _____Does she_____ work overtime often?
10. _____Is she_____ working overtime now?

▶ **Practice 12. The simple present and the present progressive.** (Charts 1-1 and 1-2)
Choose the correct completion.

1. Turtles, snakes, and alligators __b__ reptiles.
   a. do   (b.) are   c. is

2. Almost all reptiles __a__ eggs.
   a. lay   b. lays   c. are laying

3. A turtle __a__ eggs in the warmer months.
   a. lays   b. laying   c. is laying

4. __c__ frogs reptiles?
   a. Do   b. Is   c. Are

5. No. They __b__ amphibians.
   a. is   b. are   c. do

6. An amphibian __b__ in water and on land.
   a. live   b. lives   c. is living

7. __a__ frogs lay eggs?
   a. Do   b. Does   c. Are

8. Yes. Frogs __a__ eggs in the water.
   a. lay   b. lays   c. are laying

9. Do you ____ that frog on the rock over there?
   a. see   b. sees   c. seeing

10. __c__ it sleeping?
    a. Does   b. Do   c. Is

11. No, it __c__ sleeping.
    a. doesn't   b. don't   c. isn't

12. It is __c__ for insects to eat.
    a. look   b. looks   c. looking

► **Practice 13. Frequency adverbs.** (Chart 1-3)
Put the word in italics in its usual midsentence position. Write Ø if no word is needed.

1. *usually*   Ann ___usually___ stays ___Ø___ at night.
2. *usually*   Ann ___Ø___ is ___usually___ at home at night.
3. *always*   Bob _____ stays ___Ø___ home in the evening.
4. *always*   He _____ is ___usually___ at his desk in the evening.
5. *usually*   He _____ doesn't ___Ø___ go out in the evenings.
6. *always*   But he _____ doesn't _____ study in the evenings.
7. *sometimes*   He _____ watches _____ a little TV.
8. *never*   He _____ stays ___Ø___ up past midnight.
9. *never*   He _____ is _____ up past midnight.
10. *usually*   Does _____ Ann _____ study _____ at night?
11. *always*   Does _____ Bob _____ study _____ at night?
12. *always*   Is ___Ø___ Bob _____ at home at night?

► **Practice 14. Frequency adverbs.** (Chart 1-3)
Put the given adverbs in their usual midsentence position. Change the verb from negative to affirmative (i.e., statement form) as necessary.

1. *Sentence:* **Jane doesn't come to class on time.**

   a. *usually*   Jane ___usually doesn't come___ to class on time.
   b. *ever*   Jane ___doesn't ever come___ to class on time.
   c. *seldom*   Jane ___seldom comes___ to class on time.
   d. *sometimes*   Jane _____ to class on time.
   e. *always*   Jane _____ to class on time.
   f. *occasionally*   Jane _____ to class on time.
   g. *never*   Jane _____ to class on time.
   h. *hardly ever*   Jane _____ to class on time.

2. *Sentence:* **Jane isn't on time for class.**

   a. *usually*   Jane ___isn't usually___ on time for class.
   b. *rarely*   Jane _____ on time for class.
   c. *always*   Jane _____ on time for class.
   d. *frequently*   Jane _____ on time for class.
   e. *never*   Jane _____ on time for class.
   f. *ever*   Jane _____ on time for class.
   g. *seldom*   Jane _____ on time for class.

► **Practice 15. Frequency adverbs.** (Chart 1-3)
Use the given information to complete the sentences. Use a frequency adverb for each sentence.

Kim's Week	S	M	T	W	Th	F	S
1. wake up late	X	X	X	X	X	X	X
2. skip breakfast		X	X		X		
3. visit friends	X	X		X		X	X
4. be on time for class		X	X	X	X		
5. surf the Internet				X			
6. clean her room	X	X	X	X		X	X
7. do homework			X			X	
8. be in bed early							

1. Kim _____*always wakes*_____ up late.
2. She _____ breakfast.
3. She ___*frequently   visits*___ friends.
4. She ___*is   usually*___ on time for class.
5. She ___*is   seldom   surfs*___ the Internet.
6. She ___*usually   cleans*___ her room.
7. She ___*rarely   does*___ homework.
8. She _____ in bed early.

► **Practice 16. Reading comprehension.** (Charts 1-1 → 1-3)

Part I. Read the passage. Then circle eight more verbs in the simple present tense and one verb in the present progressive. <u>Underline</u> the three frequency adverbs.

Powerful Storms

Hurricanes and typhoons (are) powerful storms. They form over warm oceans. They have strong winds (at least 74 miles or 119 kilometers per hour), a huge amount of rain, low air pressure, and thunder and lightning. Scientists call the storms east of the International Date Line and north of the equator — for example, in Mexico and the United States — hurricanes. Storms west of the International Date Line and south of the equator — for example, in Indonesia and India — are typhoons.

Usually, about 100 of these tropical storms occur in the world each year. These storms travel from the ocean to the coast and on to land. On land, the wind, rain, and enormous waves often cause terrible destruction. People never like to hear the news that a hurricane or typhoon is coming.

Part II. Answer the questions according to the information in the passage. Circle "T" if the statement is true and "F" if the statement is false.

1. Hurricanes and typhoons have winds of more than 74 miles per hour.   T   F
2. These storms don't have rain.   T   F
3. There is often snow with hurricanes.   T   F
4. Hurricanes are bigger than typhoons.   T   F
5. In India and Indonesia, these big storms are typhoons.   T   F
6. Hurricanes and typhoons begin over land.   T   F
7. Hurricanes and typhoons rarely cause destruction.   T   F
8. People don't like to hear that a hurricane is coming.   T   F

▶ **Practice 17. Singular/Plural.** (Chart 1-4)
Is the final -*s* singular or a plural? Check (✓) the box.

	Singular	Plural
1. Flowers need water.		✓
2. The flower smells good.	✓	
3. Elephants live a long time.		✓
4. An elephant never forgets.	✓	
5. My brother works for an airline.	✓	
6. Pilots travel all over the world.		✓
7. Golfers play golf.		✓
8. A pianist plays the piano.	✓	
9. The mail carrier brings the mail in the morning.	✓	
10. The large packages arrive in the afternoon.		✓

▶ **Practice 18. Spelling of final -s/es.** (Chart 1-5)
Complete the second sentence with the correct form of the verb in **bold**.

1. I **eat** potatoes. Mary _____ eats _____ rice.
2. I **get** up early. Carl _____ gets _____ up late.
3. I **teach** English. Henri _____ teaches _____ French.
4. I **work** indoors. Mei _____ works _____ outdoors.
5. I **do** housework. My daughter _____ does _____ homework.
6. We **study** math. Paulo _____ studies _____ chemistry.
7. We **pay** bills by check. Yoko _____ pays _____ bills online.
8. We **have** a house. Maria _____ has _____ an apartment.

9. We **buy** magazines. Ali _____ buys _____ newspapers.

10. We **go** to the supermarket. Hannah _____ to a small grocery store.

▶ Practice 19. Final -s/-es. (Chart 1-5)

Underline the verbs. Add final **-s/-es** if necessary, and change **-y** to **-i** if necessary. Do not change any other words.

1. A kangaroo hop.

2. Kangaroos <u>live</u> in Australia. (No change.)

3. The mother kangaroo carry her baby in a pouch. She watch the baby closely.

4. This apple taste delicious. It come from a farm near here.

5. Apples are healthy. They contain vitamins.

6. Every Sunday, my grandma bake something. Usually she cut up some apples and put them in a pie.

7. Mauricio is a mechanic. He fix cars.

8. Lili work at a fast-food restaurant. She fry chicken and serve it to customers.

9. Harry and Jenny go to an Italian restaurant every weekend. Fred go to a Japanese restaurant.

▶ Practice 20. Simple present: final -s/-es. (Charts 1-4 and 1-5)

Read Sam's paragraph about his typical day. Then rewrite the paragraph using **he** in place of **I**. You will need to change the verbs.

Sam's Day

I leave my apartment at 8:00 every morning. I walk to the bus stop and catch the 8:10 bus. It takes me downtown. Then I transfer to another bus, and it takes me to my part-time job. I arrive at work at 8:50. I stay until 1:00, and then I leave for school. I attend classes until 5:00. I usually study in the library and try to finish my homework. Then I go home around 8:00. I have a long day.

Sam ____leaves____ his apartment at 8:00 every morning. ____He walks____ to the bus stop
      1   2

and _____catches_____ the 8:10 bus. It takes him downtown. Then
            3

_____He transfers_____ to another bus, and it takes him to his part-time job.
            4

_____arrives_____ at work at 8:50. ____He stays____ until 1:00, and then
       5   6

_____leaves_____ for school. ____He attends____ classes until 5:00.
       7   8

_____He_____ usually _____studies_____ in the library and _____tries_____ to finish
       9   10   11

his homework. Then ____he goes____ home around 8:00. ____he has____ a
                         12   13

long day.

► **Practice 21. Non-action verbs.** (Chart 1-6)
Circle the letter of the correct sentence in each pair.

1. a. The professor wants an answer to her question.
   b. The professor is wanting an answer to her question.

2. a. A student knows the answer.
   b. A student is knowing the answer.

3. a. Look! An eagle flies overhead.
   b. Look! An eagle is flying overhead.

4. a. It's over that tree. Are you seeing it?
   b. It's over that tree. Do you see it?

5. a. I believe that Tokyo is the largest city in the world.
   b. I am believing that Tokyo is the largest city in the world.

6. a. I think that São Paulo is the largest city in the world.
   b. I am thinking that São Paulo is the largest city in the world.

7. a. What do you think about right now?
   b. What are you thinking about right now?

8. a. I need to call my family.
   b. I am needing to call my family.

9. a. This is fun. I have a good time.
   b. This is fun. I am having a good time.

10. a. I like to meet new people.
    b. I am liking to meet new people.

► **Practice 22. Simple present and present progressive.** (Charts 1-1 → 1-6)
Complete the sentences with the simple present or present progressive form of the verbs from the list. Use each verb only once.

✓belong	✓need	rain	✓snow	✓understand
✓drive	✓prefer	shine	✓take	✓watch

1. Look outside! It _____is snowing_____. Everything is beautiful and white.

2. My father _____takes_____ the 8:15 train into the city every weekday morning.

3. On Tuesdays and Thursdays, I walk to work for the exercise. Every Monday, Wednesday, and Friday, I _____ my car to work.

4. A: Charlie, can't you hear the telephone? Answer it!

   B: You get it. I _____ my favorite TV show. I don't want to miss anything.

5. A: What kind of tea do you like?

   B: Well, I'm drinking black tea, but I _____ green tea.

6. I'm gaining weight around my waist. These pants are too tight. I _____ a larger pair of pants.

7. Thank you for your help in algebra. Now I _____understand_____ that lesson.

8. This magazine is not mine. It _____ to Colette.

9. I see a rainbow. That's because it _____, and at the same time, the
   sun _____.

▶ **Practice 23. Simple present and present progressive.** (Charts 1-1 → 1-6)
Complete the sentences with the simple present or present progressive form of the verb.

Rosa is sitting on the train right now. She (*take, not, usually*) _____usually doesn't take_____
                                                                                    1
the train, but today her son (*need*) _____ her car. She (*enjoy*)
                                                    2
_____ the ride today. There (*be*) _____ so many
               3   4
people to watch. Some people (*eat*) _____ breakfast. Others (*drink*)
                                                    5
_____ coffee and (*read*) _____ the newspaper. One
               6   7
woman (*work*) _____ on her laptop computer. Another (*feed*)
                              8
_____ her baby. Two teenagers (*play*) _____
               9   10
computer games. Rosa (*know*) _____ that teenagers (*love*)
                                          11
_____ computer games. She (*have*) _____ two teenage
               12   13
daughters, and they (*play*) _____ computer games all the time. Rosa (*smile*)
                                    14
_____ and (*relax*) _____ now. The train ride (*take,*
               15   16
usually) _____ longer than driving, but today it (*be*)
                              17
_____ a more enjoyable way for her to travel.
               18

▶ **Practice 24. Editing.** (Charts 1-1 → 1-6)
Correct the errors.

1. Don ~~does~~ not working now.
   is

2. Florida doesn't has mountains.

3. This train always is late.

4. Does Marta usually goes to bed early?

5. Mr. Chin always come to work on time.

6. Shhh! The concert starting now.

7. The refrigerator no work.

8. Is Catherine has a car?

9. Pam and Bob are getting married. They are loving each other.

10. Anne do not understand this subject. *(handwritten: doesn't)*

11. Jessica asks sometimes her parents for advice.

12. Does you do your laundry at the laundromat on the corner? *(handwritten: Do)*

13. When the color blue mix with the color yellow, the result is green.

14. Boris frys two eggs for breakfast every morning.

15. We are studing English.

▶ Practice 25. Present verbs: questions and short answers. (Chart 1-7)

Complete the questions with **Do**, **Does**, **Is**, or **Are**. Then complete both the affirmative and negative short answers.

1. A: _____Are_____ you leaving now?
   B: Yes, ___I am___. OR No, ___I'm not___.

2. A: ___Do___ your neighbors know that you are a police officer?
   B: Yes, ___they do___. OR No, ___they don't___.

3. A: ___Do___ you follow the same routine every morning?
   B: Yes, ___I do___. OR No, ___I don't___.

4. A: ___Does___ Dr. Jarvis know the name of her new assistant yet?
   B: Yes, ___she does___. OR No, ___she doesn't___.

5. A: ___Are___ Paul and Beth studying the problem?
   B: Yes, ___they are___. OR No, ___they are not___.

6. A: ___Do___ they understand the problem?
   B: Yes, ___they do___. OR No, ___they don't___.

7. A: ___Is___ Mike reading the paper and watching television at the same time?
   B: Yes, ___he is___. OR No, ___he isn't___.

8. A: _____ you listening to me?
   B: Yes, _____. OR No, ___I'm not___.

9. A: ___Does___ that building safe?
   B: Yes, ___it does___. OR No, ___it doesn't___.

10. A: _____ you and your co-workers get together outside of work?
    B: Yes, ___We do___. OR No, ___we don't___.

Complete the crossword puzzle. Use the clues to find the correct words.

Across

1. Mike _____ not have a job. He is unemployed.

2. Most birds _____.

4. Shhh! The movie is _____ now.

6. Textbooks are expensive. My textbook _____ more than my shoes.

Down

1. Sam doesn't _____ to work. He walks. He doesn't own a car.

2. Kim is a pilot. He _____ all over the world.

3. Every year, the university closes for the New Year holiday. Classes _____ again early in January.

5. The baby _____ not sleeping now.

Chapter 2
Past Time

▶ **Practice 1. Simple past: questions and negatives.** (Chart 2-1)
Write the question and negative forms of the sentences.

1. It started early. _____*Did it start early?*_____ _____*It didn't start early.*_____

2. Bob arrived late. _____ _____

3. Hal was here. _____ _____

4. Dad planted roses. _____ _____

5. Mom liked the game. _____ _____

6. Kim cooked dinner. _____ _____

7. Nat played tennis. _____ _____

8. They were late. _____ _____

9. Sam invited Ann. _____ _____

10. We did our work. _____ _____

▶ **Practice 2. Simple present and simple past.** (Chapter 1 and Chart 2-1)
Complete the chart with the correct form of the missing words.

Statement	Question	Negative
1. You work every day.	_____*Do you work*_____ every day?	You don't work every day.
2. You worked yesterday.	_____ yesterday?	_____ yesterday.
3. _____ every day.	_____ every day?	She doesn't work every day.
4. She worked yesterday.	_____ yesterday?	_____ yesterday.
5. _____ every day.	Do they work every day?	_____ every day.
6. They worked yesterday.	_____ yesterday?	_____ yesterday.
7. _____ every day.	_____ every day?	He doesn't work every day.
8. He worked yesterday.	_____ yesterday?	_____ yesterday.

▶ Practice 3. Past tense questions and answers. (Chart 2-1)

Circle the correct verb form in Sentence A. Then write the correct verb form in Sentence B. Add **not** as necessary.

Einstein

1. A: (*Is* / *Was* / *Did*) Einstein alive today?
   B: No, he ____isn't____.

2. A: (*Was* / *Were* / *Did*) he alive in the last century, the 20th century?
   B: Yes, he _____.

3. A: (*Was* / *Were* / *Did*) he live in the 20th century?
   B: Yes, he _____.

4. A: (*Was* / *Were* / *Did*) he a biologist?
   B: No, he _____.

5. A: (*Was* / *Is* / *Did*) he very intelligent?
   B: Yes, he _____.

6. A: (*Was* / *Were* / *Did*) he from Europe?
   B: Yes, _____.

7. A: (*Was* / *Is* / *Did*) he a university professor?
   B: Yes, he _____.

8. A: (*Are* / *Was* / *Did*) he teach?
   B: Yes, he _____.

9. A: (*Were* / *Is* / *Are*) he very famous?
   B: Yes, he _____.

10. A: (*Was* / *Is* / *Did*) people around the world know about him?
    B: Yes, they _____.

▶ Practice 4. Simple past: questions. (Charts 2-2 and 2-3)

Write past tense questions using the *italicized* words and **Did**, **Was**, or **Were**.

1. *he \ study*   ____Did he study____ yesterday?
2. *he \ sick*   ____Was he sick____ yesterday?
3. *she \ sad*   _____ yesterday?
4. *they \ eat*   _____ yesterday?
5. *they \ hungry*   _____ yesterday?
6. *you \ go*   _____ yesterday?
7. *she \ understand* _____ yesterday?
8. *he \ forget*   _____ yesterday?

▶ **Practice 5. Simple past and present: questions.** (Chapter 1, Charts 2-1 → 2-3)
Complete the questions with *Did, Was, Were,* or *Are.*

1. _____ you go to a party last night?

2. _____ it fun?

3. _____ it a birthday party?

4. _____ many of your friends there?

5. _____ you meet new people?

6. _____ you have a good time?

7. _____ you stay out late?

8. _____ you tired when you got home?

9. _____ your children asleep when you got home?

10. _____ you tired today?

▶ **Practice 6. Simple past: questions.** (Charts 2-1 → 2-3)
Make a question from the *italicized* words, and give a short answer. Each list has one or two extra words. Use a capital letter to start the question.

A driver's test

1. *did, pass, you, was*

   A: ____*Did you pass*____ your driver's test yesterday?

   B: Yes, ____*I did*____.

2. *were, did, you, be*

   A: _____ nervous?

   B: No, _____.

3. *practiced, you, did, practice*

   A: _____ a lot before the test?

   B: Yes, _____.

4. *did, was, the test, be*

   A: _____ difficult?

   B: No, _____.

5. *you, did, made, make*

   A: _____ any mistakes on the test?

   B: No, _____.

6. *was, did, the car*

   A: _____ easy to drive?

   B: Yes, _____.

7. *put, you, did, were*

A: _____ your new driver's license in your wallet right away?

B: Yes, _____!

8. *go, went, you, did*

A: _____ home right after the test?

B: No, _____.

▶ **Practice 7. Spelling of *-ing* and *-ed* forms.** (Chart 2-2)
Complete the chart. Refer to Chart 2-2 if necessary.

End of verb	Double the consonant?	Simple form	*-ing*	*-ed*
-e	No	live race	living	lived
Two Consonants		work start		
Two Vowels + One Consonant		shout wait		
One Vowel + One Consonant		ONE-SYLLABLE VERBS: pat shop		
		TWO-SYLLABLE VERBS: STRESS ON FIRST SYLLABLE listen happen		
		TWO-SYLLABLE VERBS: STRESS ON SECOND SYLLABLE occur refer		
-y		play reply study		
-ie		die tie		

▶ **Practice 8. Spelling of -ing forms.** (Chart 2-2)
Add *-ing* to the verbs and write them in the correct columns.

begin	✓hit	learn	smile	take
come	hop	listen	stay	win
cut	hope	rain	study	write

Double the consonant. (*stop* → *stopping*)	**Drop the -*e*.** (*live* → *living*)	**Just add -*ing*.** (*visit* → *visiting*)
hitting		

▶ **Practice 9. Spelling of -ing forms.** (Chart 2-2)
Complete each word with one *"t"* or two *"t"s* to spell the *-ing* verb form correctly. Then write the simple form of the verb for each sentence.

Simple Form

1. I'm wai _t_ ing for a phone call.   1. _____wait_____
2. I'm pe _tt_ ing my dog.   2. _____pet_____
3. I'm bi ____ing my nails because I'm nervous.   3. _____
4. I'm si ____ing in a comfortable chair.   4. _____
5. I'm wri ____ing in my book.   5. _____
6. I'm figh ____ing the urge to have some ice cream.   6. _____
7. I'm wai ____ing to see if I'm really hungry.   7. _____
8. I'm ge ____ing up from my chair now.   8. _____
9. I'm star ____ing to walk to the refrigerator.   9. _____
10. I'm permi ____ing myself to have some ice cream.   10. _____
11. I'm lif ____ing the spoon to my mouth.   11. _____
12. I'm ea ____ing the ice cream now.   12. _____
13. I'm tas ____ing it. It tastes good.   13. _____
14. I'm also cu ____ing a piece of cake.   14. _____
15. I'm mee ____ing my sister at the airport tomorrow.   15. _____
16. She's visi ____ing me for a few days. I'll save some 16. _____
    cake and ice cream for her.

► **Practice 10. Spelling of -ing and -ed forms.** (Chapter 1 and Chart 2-2)
Part I. Write the present progressive (*-ing*) form of each verb. If necessary, look at the chart in Practice 7.

The Boston Marathon

A TV sportscaster is reporting from the oldest annual marathon race in the world.

Good morning, ladies and gentlemen. Our coverage of the 2009 Boston Marathon (*begin*)

_____*is beginning*_____ right now, here on Channel 5. We (*broadcast*)
      1

_____ live from Boston. More than 20,000 men and women (*run*)
           2

_____ in this year's marathon. Citizens of 85 countries (*compete*)
           3

_____ in the 26-mile (42-km) course and (*race*)
           4

_____ through the city of Boston. There they go . . . the race (*start*)
           5

_____ now. Some of the runners (*get*) _____ off
           6   7

to a slow start and (*try*) _____ to save their energy, but others (*speed*)
                              8

_____ ahead. It (*rain, not*) _____ now, but
           9   10

it is cold, and some of the competitors (*worry*) _____ about the strong
                                                              11

east wind.

Part II. Complete the rest of the report. Write the simple past tense form of each verb. If necessary, look at the chart in Practice 7.

Here we are at the finish line at the end of the Boston Marathon. It was a great race!

As usual, spectators all along the course (*cheer*) _____*cheered*_____ for the runners. They
                                                            1

(*shout*) _____ words of encouragement to them and clearly (*enjoy*)
              2

_____ the famous event.
           3

What a great day for the men! Deriba Mergo from Ethiopia (*race*) _____
                                                                                    4

from start to finish in 2 hours, 8 minutes, and 42 seconds, and won in the men's division. He (*cross*)

_____ the finish line 50 seconds ahead of the next man.
           5

The women's race was slower this year than it was last year. Salina Kosgei of Kenya was the

winner. She (*finish*) _____ less than two seconds ahead of a runner from

Ethiopia. However, an unfortunate event (*occur*) _____ at the end of the race.

These two women (*crash*) _____ into each other, and the Ethiopian runner

(*need*) _____ medical attention.

More than 20,000 runners (*start*) _____ the race this year, and 98% of them

(*complete*) _____ it. Stay tuned for more news about all the exciting events that

(*happen*) _____ at the 2009 Boston Marathon.

▶ **Practice 11. Principal parts of a verb.** (Chart 2-3)
Complete the chart with the missing verb forms.

Simple Form	Simple Past	Past Participle	Present Participle
1. stop	*stopped*	stopped	stopping
2. pick		picked	picking
3.	arrived	arrived	arriving
4. cry	cried	cried	
5.	walked	walked	
6. go		gone	going
7. practice		practiced	practicing
8. refer	referred		referring
9. make		made	making
10. hop		hopped	hopping
11. hope		hoped	
12. put		put	putting
13. eat	ate	eaten	
14.	sang	sung	singing
15. listen		listened	

▶ **Practice 12. Spelling of irregular verbs.** (Chart 2-4)
Write the past tense of the given verbs.

Part I.

buy b _o_ _u_ _g_ _h_ t

bring br _ough_ t

fight f _ough_ t

think th _____ t

teach t _ough_ t

catch c _augh_ t

find f _ou_ d

Part II.

swim sw _am_

drink dr _ank_

sing s _ang_

ring r ____

Part III.

blow bl _ew_

draw dr _ew_

fly fl _ew_

grow gr _ew_

know kn _ew_

throw thr _ew_

Part IV.

break br _oke_

write wr _ote_

freeze fr _eze_

ride r _ode_

sell s _old_

steal st _ole_

Part V.

hit h __

hurt h ___ t

read r _ead_

shut sh _ut_

cost c _ost_

put p __ t

quit q _uit_

Part VI.

pay p _ai_ d

say s _ai_ d

▶ **Practice 13. Common irregular verbs.** (Chart 2-4)
Complete the passages with the past tense forms of the verbs in the list. Use each verb only once.
There is one extra verb in each list.

1. *be, fall, fly, spend*

Valentina Tereshkova _____ the first woman in space. In 1963, she

_____ in the spacecraft *Vostok 6* alone, with no other cosmonauts. She

_____ three days in space before she returned to earth.

2. *come, feel, lose, put, take*

Dr. Christiaan Barnard, who _____ from South Africa, performed the first

transplant of a heart from one human being to another. In 1967, he _____ out the

heart of a woman who died in an accident and _____ it into the chest of a man with

a diseased heart. The operation succeeded, but the man lived only a short time. He

_____ his life to complications from the surgery. Today, surgeons know much more

about this kind of surgery, and there are many successful heart transplants.

3. *begin, become, grow, know, sing, wear*

Michael Jackson was a world-famous singer and dancer. He

_____ his career at age six when he

_____ and danced with his brothers in a group called

the Jackson Five. After a few years, Michael _____ a

star. People all over the world _____ him and his songs.

He dressed in a unique way, and he often _____ one

white glove in his performances. Michael died in June, 2009, at the age of 50.

▶ **Practice 14. Expressing past time: simple past.** (Charts 2-1 and 2-4).
Change the sentences to past time. Use simple past verbs and *yesterday* or *last*.

PRESENT	PAST
every day	yesterday
every morning	yesterday morning
every afternoon	yesterday afternoon
every night	last night
every week	last week
every Monday, Tuesday, etc.	last Monday, Tuesday, etc.
every month	last month
every year	last year

1. I **walk** to my office **every morning**.

   I ____walked____ to my office ____yesterday____ morning.

2. I **talk** to my parents on the phone **every week**.

   I ____talked____ to my parents on the phone ____last____ week.

3. The post office **opens** at eight o'clock **every morning**.

   The post office _____ at eight o'clock _____

   morning.

4. Mrs. Hall **goes** to the fruit market **every Monday**.

   Mrs. Hall _____ to the fruit market _____ **Monday**.

5. The company managers **meet** at nine o'clock **every Friday morning**.

   The company managers _____ at nine o'clock _____

   Friday morning.

6. I **make** my own lunch and **take** it to work with me **every morning**.

   _____ **morning**, I _____ my own lunch and

   _____ it to work with me.

7. Mr. Clark **pays** his rent on time **every month**.

   Mr. Clark _____ his rent on time _____ **month**.

8. The baby **falls** asleep at three o'clock **every afternoon**.

yesterday **afternoon**, the baby _fell_ asleep at three o'clock.

9. The last bus from downtown **leaves** at ten o'clock **every night**.

The last bus from downtown _left_ at ten o'clock _____ **night**.

▶ **Practice 15. Present and past negatives.** (Chapter 1, Charts 2-1 and 2-4)
All of the sentences contain inaccurate information. Make true statements by

(1) making a negative statement and

(2) making an affirmative statement using accurate information.

1. a. George flew to school yesterday.

   b. No, he _____didn't fly_____ to school yesterday. He _____rode_____ his bike.

2. a. Lemons are sweet.

   b. No, lemons _____aren't_____ sweet. They _____are_____ sour.

3. a. You were a baby in the year 2000.

   b. No, I _____was not_____ a baby in 2000. I _____was____ _18_ years old in 2000.

4. a. Buddha came from China.

   b. No, Buddha _____didn't_ _come____ from China. Buddha _____came_____ from Nepal.

5. a. Coffee comes from cocoa beans.

   b. No, coffee _____doesn't_ _come____ from cocoa beans. It _____comes___ from coffee beans.

6. a. You slept outdoors last night.

   b. No, I _____didn't_ _sleep____ outdoors last night. I _____slept_____ indoors.

7. a. Ice is hot.

   b. No, ice _____isn't_____ hot. It _____is_____ cold.

8. a. Dinosaurs disappeared a hundred years ago.

   b. No, dinosaurs _____didn't_ _disappear____ a hundred years ago. They _____disappeared_____ millions of years ago.

9. a. Our bodies make Vitamin C from sunshine.

   b. No, our bodies _____don't_ _make____ Vitamin C from sunshine. They _____make_____ Vitamin D from sunshine.

▶ **Practice 16. Review: simple present, present progressive, and simple past forms.** (Chapter 1 and Charts 2-1 → 2-4)
Complete the chart with the correct forms of the verbs.

Every Day	Now	Yesterday
1. He **is** here every day.	He ___*is*___ here now.	He ___*was*___ here yesterday.
2. I ___*think*___ about you every day.	I **am thinking** about you now.	I ___*thought*___ about you yesterday.
3. We **play** tennis every day.	We _are playing_ tennis now.	We _played_ tennis yesterday.
4. I ___*drink*___ juice every day.	I'm _drinking_ juice now.	I **drank** juice yesterday.
5. He _teach_ every day.	He **is teaching** now.	He _taught_ yesterday.
6. She _swim_ every day.	She _is swimming_ now.	She **swam** yesterday.
7. You **sleep** late every day.	You _are sleeping_ now.	You _slept_ late yesterday.
8. He _read_ every day.	He **is reading** now.	He ___ yesterday.
9. They _try_ hard every day.	They _are trying_ hard now.	They **tried** hard yesterday.
10. We **eat** dinner every day.	We _are eating_ dinner now.	We _ate_ yesterday.

▶ **Practice 17. Past progressive.** (Chart 2-6)
Complete the sentences by using the past progressive of the given verbs. Use each verb only once.

| ✓hide | look | read | sing | sit | talk | watch |

1. Jack's wife arranged a surprise birthday party for him. When Jack arrived home, several people
   ____*were hiding*____ behind the couch or behind doors. All of the lights were out, and when
   Jack turned them on, everyone shouted "Surprise!"

2. The birds began to sing when the sun rose at 6:30. Dan woke up at 6:45. When Dan woke
   up, the birds _____.

3. I _____ a DVD last night when my best friend called.

4. While we _____ on the phone, the power went out.

5. The bus driver looked at all the passengers on her bus and noticed how quiet they were. Some
   people _____ newspapers or books. Most of the people
   _____ quietly in their seats and _____ out
   the windows of the bus.

26 CHAPTER 2

▶ **Practice 18. Simple past and past progressive.** (Chart 2-6)
Complete the sentences. Use the simple past for one clause and the past progressive for the other.

Activity in Progress	Nadia	George	Bill
play soccer	break her glasses	score a goal	hurt his foot
hike	find some money	see a bear	pick up a snake
dance	trip and fall	meet his future wife	get dizzy

1. While Nadia _____was playing_____ soccer, she _____broke_____ her glasses.
2. George _____scored_____ a goal while he _____was playing_____ soccer.
3. Bill _____ his foot while he _____ soccer.
4. While Nadia _____, she _____ some money.
5. George _____ a bear while he _____.
6. Bill _____ a snake while he _____.
7. Nadia _____ and _____ while she _____.
8. While George _____, he _____ his future wife.
9. While Bill _____, he _____ dizzy.

▶ **Practice 19. Simple past and past progressive.** (Chart 2-6)
Circle the correct forms of the verbs.

1. It began to rain while Amanda and I ((*were walking*) / *walked*) to school this morning.
2. While I (*was washing* / *washed*) the dishes last night, I (*was dropping* / *dropped*) a plate. The plate (*was breaking* / *broke*).
3. I (*was seeing* / *saw*) Ted at the student cafeteria at lunchtime yesterday. He (*was eating* / *ate*) a sandwich and (*was talking* / *talked*) with some friends. I (*was joining* / *joined*) them.
4. Robert didn't answer the phone when Sara called. He (*was singing* / *sang*) his favorite song in the shower and (*was not hearing* / *did not hear*) the phone ring.
5. A: There was a power outage in our part of town last night. (*Were your lights going out* / *Did your lights go out*) too?
   B: Yes, they did. It was terrible! I (*was taking* / *took*) a shower when the lights went out. My wife (*was finding* / *found*) a flashlight and rescued me from the bathroom. We couldn't cook dinner, so we (*were eating* / *ate*) sandwiches instead. I tried to read some reports by candlelight, but it was too dark, so I (*was going* / *went*) to bed and (*was sleeping* / *slept*).

► **Practice 20. Simple past and past progressive.** (Chart 2-6)
For each group, choose the correct completions from Column B.

Column A

1. When the professor walked into the classroom, __d__. Conversation filled the room.

2. When the professor walked to the front of the class, ____. Then they picked up their pens to take notes.

3. While the professor was giving his lecture, ____. They wanted to remember everything he said.

4. While the professor was speaking, ____. Everyone left the room immediately.

Column B

a. the fire alarm went off

b. the students took notes

c. the students stopped talking

d. students were talking to each other

5. When it was time to board Flight 177, ____.

6. When we finally got on the plane, ____.

7. While we were flying over the ocean at night, ____.

8. When we finally landed in the morning, ____.

e. the passengers stood up quickly and took their luggage down from the overhead racks.

f. many of the passengers tried to sleep in their small airplane seats.

g. we lined up at the gate and showed the airline staff our boarding passes.

h. we sat down quickly and fastened our seat belts.

► **Practice 21. Expressing past time: using time clauses.** (Chart 2-7)
Decide what happens first and what happens second. Number the clauses "1" and "2". Then combine the clauses and write a complete sentence.

               1   *2*

1. The fire alarm sounded. Everyone left the building.

    When _____*the fire alarm sounded, everyone left the building*_____.

2. They left the building. They stood outside in the rain.

    After _____, _____.

3. Everyone started to dance. The music began.

    As soon as _____, _____.

4. The music ended. They danced to all the songs.

_____ until _____ .

5. The fans in the stadium applauded and cheered. The soccer player scored a goal.

When _____ , _____

_____ .

6. Everyone left the stadium. The game was over.

_____ as soon as _____ .

7. I looked up her phone number. I called her.

Before _____ , _____ .

8. The phone rang 10 times. I hung up.

_____ after _____ .

▶ **Practice 22. Expressing past habit: *used to.*** (Chart 2-8)
Complete the sentences. Use *used to* and the given information.

1. When James was young, he hated school. Now he likes it.

James _____*used to hate school*_____ , but now he likes it.

2. Ann was a secretary for many years, but now she owns her own business.

Ann _____ , but now she owns her own business.

3. Before Adam got married, he played tennis five times a week.

Adam _____ five times a week.

4. When we raised our own chickens, we had fresh eggs every morning.

We _____ every morning when we raised our own

chickens.

5. When Ben was a child, he often crawled under his bed and put his hands over his ears when he

heard thunder.

Ben _____ and

_____ when he heard thunder.

6. When I lived in my home town, I went to the beach every weekend. Now I don't go to the

beach every weekend.

I _____ to the beach every weekend, but now I don't.

7. Joshua has a new job. He has to wear a suit every day. When he was a student, he always wore

jeans.

Joshua _____ jeans every day, but now he has to wear a suit.

8. In the past, Sara hated pets. But now she has two cats, and she likes them very much.

Sara _____ pets, but now she likes them a lot.

9. When I was young, I ate peanuts. Now I am allergic to them.

I _____ peanuts, but now I am allergic to them.

▶ **Practice 23. Review: past verbs.** (Chapter 2)

Part I. Read the passage* about Pluto. <u>Underline</u> all the verbs that refer to the present time. Circle all the verbs that refer to the past time.

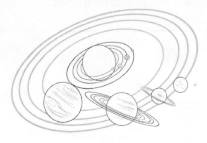

<u>Do</u> nine planets <u>orbit the sun?</u> Or do eight planets orbit the sun? Nine planets (used to orbit) the sun, but now only eight planets orbit the sun. How is that possible? Did one planet disappear?

A planet did not disappear. But in 2006, astronomers changed the classification of one of the planets, Pluto. Pluto is very small. The astronomers decided to call Pluto a *dwarf planet. Dwarf* means "smaller than usual."

Two years later, the astronomers reclassified Pluto again. This time they put Pluto into a different group with a new name: *plutoids.*

Before astronomers reclassified Pluto, nine planets orbited the sun. Now eight planets plus one plutoid orbit the sun.

Part II. Read the passage about Pluto again. Answer the questions according to the information in the passage. Circle "T" if the statement is true. Circle "F" if the statement is false.

1. Pluto orbits the sun.   T   F

2. The nine planets used to include Pluto.   T   F

3. Pluto disappeared from the sky in 2006.   T   F

4. Pluto received a new classification in 2006.   T   F

5. *Dwarf* refers to something that is very large.   T   F

6. In 2008, astronomers reclassified Pluto for the second time.   T   F

7. Nine planets and one plutoid orbit the sun now.   T   F

▶ **Practice 24. Editing.** (Chapter 2)
Correct the verb errors.

                 didn't visit
1. We ~~don't visited~~ my cousins last weekend.

2. They are walked to school yesterday.

3. I was understand all the teacher's questions yesterday.

4. Matt and I were talked on the phone when the lights went out.

5. When Flora hear the news, she didn't knew what to say.

6. David and Carol were went to Italy last month.

7. I didn't drove a car when I am a teenager.

8. Carmen no used to eat fish, but now she does.

---

*Possible new vocabulary:

     orbit = go in circles around something, revolve

     astronomer = a scientist who studies the stars and the planets

     classification = a defined class or group

     reclassified = past tense of *reclassify*: to put into a different classification or group

9. Ms. Pepper didn't died in the accident.

10. Were you seeing that red light? You didn't stopped!

11. I used to living in a big city when I was a child. Now I live in a small town.

12. Last night at about seven we were eaten a delicious pizza. Howard maked the pizza in his new oven.

13. Sally was breaking her right foot last year. After that, she hoped on her left foot for three weeks.

▶ **Practice 25. Review.** (Chapter 2)
Complete the sentences with the simple past or the past progressive form of the verbs in parentheses.

Late yesterday afternoon while I (*prepare*) _____was preparing_____ dinner and my son Billy (*play*)
1
_____ with his wagon, the doorbell (*ring*) _____. The water on
2   3
the stove (*boil*) _____, so I quickly (*turn*) _____ off the stove
4   5
and (*answer*) _____ the door. When I (*open*) _____ it, I (*saw*)
6   7
_____ a delivery man. He (*hold*) _____ a package and (*need*)
8   9
_____ me to sign for it. At that moment, Billy (*scream*) _____. He
10   11
cried, "Mommy, I (*fall*) _____ and (*hurt*) _____ my knee!" I (*slam*)
12   13
_____ the door shut and (*run*) _____ to Billy to help him. Then I
14   15
(*hear*) _____ the doorbell again. I remembered that the delivery man (*wait*)
16
_____ for me to sign for the package! I (*open*) _____ the door,
17   18
(*take*) _____ the package, (*thank*) _____ the delivery man, and (*sign*)
19   20
_____ the receipt.
21

▶ **Practice 26. Review.** (Chapter 2)
Choose the correct completion.

1. At 3:30 this afternoon, I _____ on the TV.
   a. turned   b. was turning   c. turning

2. After that, I _____ any more work.
   a. not do   b. didn't do   c. didn't

3. At 7:34 last night, we _____ dinner when the power went out.
   a. had   b. were having   c. have

4. We _____ to eat in the dark, so we lit some candles.
   a. didn't want   b. didn't wanted   c. weren't wanting

5. _____ to the meeting yesterday? What happened?
   a. Do you went   b. Did you went   c. Did you go

6. _____ Harvey told that funny joke, everyone laughed.
   a. As soon   b. Until   c. When

7. Kirk was texting on his cell phone and driving at the same time. He was not paying attention to the road _____ he was driving.
    a. after   b. while   c. until

8. _____ I heard about Kate's new baby, I phoned all her friends to tell them the good news right away.
    a. While   b. As soon as   c. Before

9. When Grandma was a child, she _____ three miles to school every day.
    a. was walking   b. used to walking   c. used to walk

10. It _____ when we left our office. The streets were all wet.
    a. rains   b. was raining   c. rain

11. After the teacher explained the grammar point clearly, all the students _____ it very well.
    a. understood   b. were understanding   c. used to understand

12. Jim _____ the keys on the table and left the room.
    a. put   b. putting   c. was putting

13. Alex _____ when I called her last night.
    a. was slept   b. sleeps   c. was sleeping

▶ **Practice 27. Word search puzzle.** (Chapter 2)
Circle the irregular past tense of these verbs in the puzzle: *bring, buy, go, grow, say, take*. The words may be horizontal, vertical, or diagonal. The first letter of each word is highlighted in gray.

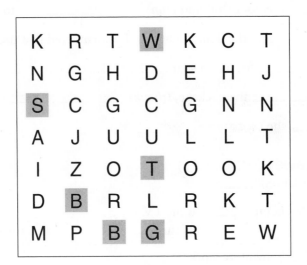

Chapter 3
Future Time

▶ **Practice 1. Expressing future time: *be going to* and *will*.** (Chart 3-1)
Check (✓) the sentences that refer to future time. <u>Underline</u> the future verb.

_____ 1. Nora is going to be an architect.

_____ 2. She's studying in Italy now.

_____ 3. She studied in England last year.

_____ 4. She will finish her classes next year.

_____ 5. She will design buildings.

_____ 6. She is looking for a job while she is in school.

_____ 7. She likes big cities.

_____ 8. She is going to live in a big city.

_____ 9. She does good work.

_____ 10. She'll be an excellent architect.

▶ **Practice 2. Forms with *be going to*.** (Charts 3-1 and 3-2)
Complete the sentences with the correct forms of *be going to*.

1. I (*leave*) _____ *am going to leave* _____ next Monday.

2. Mr. Rose (*leave*) _____ next Monday.

3. Mr. Liu (*not, leave*) _____ next Monday.

4. What about you? (*leave*) _____ you _____ next Monday?

5. Claire (*be*) _____ here next week.

6. Ole and Olga (*be*) _____ here next week.

7. I (*be, not*) _____ here next week.

8. What about Tom? (*be*) _____ he _____ here next week?

9. It (*rain*) _____ tomorrow.

10. It (*not, snow*) _____ tomorrow.

11. The sun (*not, shine*) _____ tomorrow.

12. What about next weekend? (*rain*) _____ it _____ next weekend?

▶ **Practice 3. *Be going to.*** (Charts 3-1 and 3-2)
Complete the sentence about each picture using the correct form of ***be going to*** and a verb from the list. You will not use all the verbs.

catch	eat	fall	wake up	jump

1. Mel

_____

in just one second.

2. Jane

_____

the ball.

3. Yoko

_____

into the water.

4. All the dishes

_____

on the floor.

▶ **Practice 4. *Will* and *be going to.*** (Charts 3-1 and 3-3)
Complete the chart with the correct forms of the verbs.

be going to

I ___*am going to*___ leave.

You _____ leave.

Mr. Rose _____ leave.

We _____ leave.

Our parents _____ leave.

The boys (not) _____ leave.

Ann (not) _____ leave.

I (not) _____ leave.

will

I ___*will*___ leave.

You _____ leave.

He _____ leave.

We _____ leave.

They _____ leave.

They (not) _____ leave.

She (not) _____ leave.

I (not) _____ leave.

▶ **Practice 5. Will.** (Chart 3-3)
Read the passage. Change all the verbs with *be going to* to *will*.

A 50th Wedding Anniversary Celebration

                      will
    The Smiths ~~are going to~~ celebrate their 50th wedding anniversary on December 1st of this year.

Their children are planning a party for them at a local hotel. Their family and friends are going to

join them for the celebration.

    Mr. and Mrs. Smith have three children and five grandchildren. The Smiths know that two of

their children are going to be at the party, but the third child, their youngest daughter, is far away in

Africa, where she is doing medical research. They believe she is not going to come home for the

party.

    The Smiths don't know it, but their youngest daughter is going to be at the party. She is

planning to surprise them. It is going to be a wonderful surprise for them! They are going to be

very happy to see her. The whole family is going to enjoy being together for this special occasion.

▶ **Practice 6. Questions with *will* and *be going to*.** (Charts 3-1 and 3-3)
Use the information in *italics* to complete the questions. Write the question forms for both *will*
and *be going to*.

1. Nick is thinking about *starting* an Internet company. His friends are wondering:

         Will Nick start _____ an Internet company?

         Is Nick going to start _____ an Internet company?

2. The teacher, Mr. Jones, is thinking about *giving* a test. His students are wondering:

    _____ a test?

    _____ a test?

3. Jacob is thinking about *quitting* his job. His co-workers are wondering:

    _____ his job?

    _____ his job?

4. Mr. and Mrs. Kono are thinking about *adopting* a child. Their friends are wondering:

    _____ a child?

    _____ a child?

5. The Johnsons are thinking about *moving*. Their friends are wondering:

    _____?

    _____?

6. Dr. Johnson is thinking about *retiring*. Her patients are wondering:

    _____?

    _____?

▶ **Practice 7. Forms with *will*.** (Charts 3-1 and 3-3)

Write the words in the list in the correct order to complete the sentence or question. Capitalize the first letter if necessary.

1. will / be / tomorrow

   Today is Tuesday. _____*Tomorrow will be*_____ Wednesday.

2. have / we / will

   We often have tests. _____ a test tomorrow?

3. have / will / we

   No, but _____ a test next week.

4. will / be / the test

   Our tests are sometimes difficult. _____ difficult?

5. not / be / will

   No. The test _____ difficult.

6. will / I / pass

   I'm nervous. _____ the test?

7. will / pass / you

   Yes. _____ the test.

8. pass / will / not

   Jack never studies. He _____ the test.

▶ **Practice 8. Present, past, and future.** (Chapters 1 → 3)

Complete the sentences with the given verbs. For a. use the simple present. For b. use the simple past. For c. use the future with *be going to*, and for d. use the future with *will*.

1. (*arrive*) a. Joe _____*arrives*_____ on time **every day**.

   b. Joe _____*arrived*_____ on time **yesterday**.

   c. Joe _____*is going to arrive*_____ on time **tomorrow**.

   d. Joe _____*will arrive*_____ on time **tomorrow**.

2. (*eat*) a. Ann _____ breakfast **every day**.

   b. Ann _____ breakfast **yesterday**.

   c. Ann _____ breakfast **tomorrow**.

   d. Ann _____ breakfast **tomorrow**.

3. (*arrive, not*) a. Mike _____ on time **every day**.

   b. Mike _____ on time **yesterday**.

   c. Mike _____ on time **tomorrow**.

   d. Mike _____ on time **tomorrow**.

4. (eat) a. _____ you _____ breakfast **every day?**

b. _____ you _____ breakfast **yesterday?**

c. _____ you _____ breakfast **tomorrow?**

d. _____ you _____ breakfast **tomorrow?**

5. (eat, not) a. I _____ breakfast **every day.**

b. I _____ breakfast **yesterday.**

c. I _____ breakfast **tomorrow.**

d. I _____ breakfast **tomorrow.**

▶ **Practice 9. Forms with *will* and contractions.** (Chart 3-3)
Complete each passage with contractions of *will* and the correct verbs from the list above the passage.

1. *begin, enjoy, teach*

Howard and I are going to take a painting class. I think we _____'ll enjoy_____ it very much.

It _____ next month. The teacher of the class is John Mack. He's very

good with beginners like us. He _____ us everything we need to know.

2. *be, call*

I can't talk on the phone right now, Tina. Our friends are coming for dinner, and

they _____ here in half an hour. I _____ you back

tomorrow.

3. *drive, ride, start*

Our daughter is four years old. She _____ school in the fall. Two other

children from our neighborhood are the same age. When school begins, they

_____ to school together in a carpool.* The parents will drive them on

different days. I _____ them on Mondays and Thursdays.

▶ **Practice 10. Forms with *will* and *be going to*.** (Charts 3-2 and 3-3)
Complete the conversations with *will* or *be going to*. Note: Pronouns are <u>not</u> contracted with
helping verbs in short answers. CORRECT: *Yes, I will.* INCORRECT: *Yes, I'll.*

1. A: (*you, help*) _____Will you / Are you going to help_____ me tomorrow?

B: Yes, _____I will / I am_____. OR No, _____I won't / I'm not_____.

2. A: (*Paul, lend*) _____ us some money?

B: Yes, _____. OR No, _____.

3. A: (*Jane, graduate*) _____ this spring?

B: Yes, _____. OR No, _____.

---

*carpool = a group of people who travel together to work, school, etc., in one car

4. A: (*her parents, be*) _____ at the ceremony?

   B: Yes, _____. or No, _____.

5. A: (*you, answer*) _____ your text message?

   B: Yes, _____. or No, _____.

6. A: (*Jill, text*) _____ you again tomorrow?

   B: Yes, _____. or No, _____.

▶ **Practice 11. *Will probably.*** (Chart 3-4)
Complete the sentences.

Part I. Use a pronoun + ***will*/*won't***. Use ***probably***.

1. I went to the library last night, and _____*I'll probably go*_____ there tonight too.

2. Ann didn't come to class today, and _____*she probably won't come*_____ to class tomorrow either.

3. Greg went to bed early last night, and _____ to bed early tonight too.

4. Jack didn't hand his homework in today, and _____ it in tomorrow either.

5. The students had a quiz today, and _____ one tomorrow too.

Part II. Use a pronoun + ***be going to*/*not be going to***. Use ***probably***.

6. I watched TV last night, and _____*I'm probably going to watch*_____ TV tonight too.

7. I wasn't at home last night, and _____ at home tonight either.

8. My friends didn't come over last night, and _____ over tonight either.

9. Alice didn't ride her bike to school today, and _____ it to school tomorrow either.

10. It's cold today, and _____ cold tomorrow too.

▶ **Practice 12. Certainty about the future.** (Chart 3-4)
How certain is the speaker? Check (✓) the correct box.

	100% Certain	About 90% Certain	About 50% Certain
1. You'll probably hear from our office tomorrow.		✓	
2. Al may not finish his work on time.			
3. Sue may call later.			
4. Carlos is probably going to buy a new car.			
5. Maybe Sanji is going to study architecture.			
6. You will find the key in my top drawer.			
7. Fay is going to drive to California.			
8. Roy is probably going to fail this class.			
9. Maybe Sam will be here later.			
10. The plane will probably arrive on time.			
11. The judge may not agree with you.			
12. I probably won't be here tomorrow.			

▶ **Practice 13. Certainty about the future.** (Chart 3-4)
Answer each question. Use the words in parentheses, and pay special attention to word order.

Joel and Rita's Wedding

1. A: Are Joel and Rita going to have a simple wedding? (*probably*)

   B: Yes. Joel and Rita _____are probably going to have_____ a simple wedding.

2. A: Are they going to invite a lot of people? (*probably not*)

   B: No. They _____ a lot of people.

3. A: Will they have the ceremony in Rita's garden? (*may*)

   Or will they have the ceremony at a place of worship? (*maybe*)

   B: They're not sure. They _____ the ceremony in Rita's

   garden. _____ they _____ it at a place of worship.

4. A: Is Rita going to rent her wedding dress? (*may*)

   B: She's trying to save money, so she's thinking about it. She _____ her

   wedding dress.

5. A: Will she decide that she wants her own wedding dress ? (*probably*)

   B: She _____ that she wants her own wedding dress.

6. A: Will Joel feel very relaxed on his wedding day? (*may not*)

    Will he be nervous? (*may*)

  B: Joel _____ very relaxed on his wedding day. He

    _____ a little nervous.

7. A: Are they going to go on a honeymoon? (*will*)

  B: Yes. They _____ on a honeymoon immediately after the wedding, but

    they haven't told anyone where they are going to go.

8. A: Will they go far away for their honeymoon? (*probably not*)

  B: They _____ far. They have only a few days before

    they need to be back at work.

▶ **Practice 14. *Be going to* vs. *will*.** (Chart 3-5)
Decide whether the sentence with ***will*** or be ***going to*** expresses a prediction, a prior plan, or a decision at the moment of speaking. Circle the correct letter.

1. The sun will rise tomorrow.
    a. prediction   b. prior plan   c. decision at the moment of speaking

2. The sun is going to rise tomorrow.
    a. prediction   b. prior plan   c. decision at the moment of speaking

3. Nobody answered the phone at Shelley's house. Well, I'll call again later this afternoon.
    a. prediction   b. prior plan   c. decision at the moment of speaking

4. We're going to see the new play. We bought tickets two months ago.
    a. prediction   b. prior plan   c. decision at the moment of speaking

5. Our team is going to win the game.
    a. prediction   b. prior plan   c. decision at the moment of speaking

6. Our team will win the game.
    a. prediction   b. prior plan   c. decision at the moment of speaking

7. You can't find your cell phone? Wait. I'll call your number.
    a. prediction   b. prior plan   c. decision at the moment of speaking

8. Uh-oh! The red light on my cell phone is flashing. This means that the battery is very low and that the phone is going to run out of power very soon.
    a. prediction   b. prior plan   c. decision at the moment of speaking

9. You're sick? Stay home. I'll get you anything you need.
    a. prediction   b. prior plan   c. decision at the moment of speaking

10. Jenny and I have a lunch date. We're going to meet at Gusto Café at noon.
    a. prediction   b. prior plan   c. decision at the moment of speaking

11. I'm sorry. I can't have dinner with you tonight. I'm going to help Harry with his science project. He's building a rocket!
    a. prediction   b. prior plan   c. decision at the moment of speaking

► **Practice 15. *Be going to* vs. *will*.** (Chart 3-5)

Part I. Complete each conversation with the correct form of ***be going to*** and a verb from the list. Use each verb only once.

> get   move   watch   ✓work

At the office
1. A: It's five o'clock. Are you leaving the office soon?
   B: No, I _'m going to work_ late tonight.

At home
2. A: It's almost 8:00. Don't you want to watch your favorite comedy on Channel 4?
   B: It's not on tonight. I _____ this movie instead.

At a party
3. A: Do you still live on Tenth Avenue?
   B: Yes, we do, but only for a few more days. We _____ on Saturday. We just bought a small house about ten miles north of the city.

Conversation between friends
4. A: I'm nervous about the flu epidemic.
   B: Me too. I _____ my flu shot this afternoon. I made an appointment with my doctor for it.

Part II. Complete each conversation with the correct form of ***will*** and a verb from the list. Use each verb only once. You may use contractions.

> ✓answer   ask   clean   pay

At the office
1. A: The phone's ringing.
   B: I _'ll answer_ it.

At a store
2. A: I'd like to return this jacket.
   B: We usually don't allow returns on sale items, but I _____ the manager.

At home
3. A: Oops. I just spilled my coffee.
   B: No problem. I _____ it up.

At a restaurant
4. A: Let's split the check.
   B: No, no. You paid last time. I _____ this time.

▶ **Practice 16. Be going to vs. will.** (Chart 3-5)
Complete the sentences with either **be going to** or **will**.* Use contractions.

1. SITUATION: Speaker B is planning to listen to the news at six.

    A: Why did you turn on the radio?

    B: I <u>'m going to</u> listen to the news at six.

2. SITUATION: Speaker B didn't have a plan to show the other person how to solve the math
    problem, but she is happy to do it.

    A: I can't figure out this math problem. Do you know how to do it?

    B: Yes. Give me your pencil. I _____ show you how to solve it.

3. SITUATION: Speaker B has made a plan. He is planning to lie down because he doesn't feel well.

    A: What's the matter?

    B: I don't feel well. I _____ lie down for a little while. If anyone calls,
    tell them I'll call them later.

    A: Okay. I hope you feel better.

4. SITUATION: Speaker B did not plan to take the other person home. He volunteers to do so only
    after the other person talks about missing his bus.

    A: Oh, no! I wasn't watching the time. I missed my bus.

    B: That's okay. I _____ give you a ride home.

    A: Hey, thanks!

5. SITUATION: Speaker B has already made her plans about what to wear. Then Speaker B
    volunteers to help.

    A: I can't figure out what to wear to the dance tonight. It's informal, isn't it?

    B: Yes. I _____ wear a pair of nice jeans.

    A: Maybe I should wear my jeans too. But I think they're dirty.

    B: I _____ wash them for you. I'm planning to do a load of laundry in a
    few minutes.

    A: Gee, thanks. That'll help me out a lot.

▶ **Practice 17. Be going to vs. will.** (Chart 3-5)
Circle the correct completion.

1. A: Anya is on the phone. She would like an appointment with you soon.
    B: Okay. Let's see. I have some time tomorrow. I (*am going to / will*) see her tomorrow.

2. A: How about joining us at the concert on Friday evening?
    B: We would love to, but we can't. We (*are going to / will*) fly to Florida on Friday.

---

*Usually **be going to** and **will** are interchangeable: you can use either one of them with little difference in meaning. Sometimes,
however, they are NOT interchangeable. In this exercise, only one of them is correct, not both. See Chart 3-5, p. 63, in the Student
Book.

3. A: We found this little kitten, Mom. Can we keep him?

   B: A new kitten? Well, I don't know . . .

   A: Please, Mom. He's so cute. And he needs a home.

   B: Well, okay. We (*are going to / will*) keep him.

   A: Yay, Mom!

4. A: We have two extra tickets for the Hot Stuff concert on Saturday night. Would you like to join us?

   B: Thanks, but we (*are going to / will*) attend that concert on Friday night. We already have tickets.

5. A: Why are you leaving the office so early?

   B: I (*am going to / will*) see my doctor. I've had a terrible pain in my side since yesterday.

6. A: Where are you going?

   B: I have an eye appointment. I (*am going to / will*) get new glasses.

7. A: Do you need help with those packages?

   B: Well . . .

   A: Don't worry. I (*am going to / will*) carry them for you.

▶ **Practice 18. Past and future time clauses.** (Charts 2-10 and 3-6)
Underline the time clauses.

1. Before Bill met Maggie, he was lonely.

2. He was an unhappy man until he met Maggie.

3. When he met Maggie, he fell in love.

4. He became a happy person after he met her.

5. After they dated for a year, he asked her to marry him.

6. As soon as Bill gets a better job, they will set a date for the wedding.

7. They will get married before they buy a house.

8. They will buy a house when they have enough money.

9. After they get married, they will live together happily.

10. They will live together happily until they die.

▶ **Practice 19. Future time clauses.** (Chart 3-6)
Combine the ideas of the two given sentences into one sentence by using a time clause. Use the word in parentheses to introduce the time clause.

1. *First:*   I'm going to finish my homework.
   Then: I'm going to go to bed.

   (*after*) _____After I finish_____ my homework, _____I'm going to go_____ to bed.

2. *First:*   I'll finish my homework.
   Then: I'm going to go to bed.

   (*until*) _____I'm not going to go_____ to bed _____until I finish_____ my homework.

3. *First:*   Ann will finish her homework.
   Then: She will watch TV tonight.*

   (*before*) _____ TV tonight, _____ her
   homework.

4. *First:*   Jim will get home tonight.
   Then: He's going to read the newspaper.

   (*after*) _____ the newspaper _____
   home tonight.

5. *First:*   I'll call John tomorrow.
   Then: I'll ask him to my party.

   (*when*) _____ John tomorrow, _____ him
   to my party.

6. *First:*   Mrs. Torres will stay at her office tonight.
   Then: She will finish her report.

   (*until*) _____ at her office tonight _____
   _____ her report.

7. *First:*   I will get home tonight.
   Then: I'm going to take a hot bath.

   (*as soon as*) _____ home tonight, _____ a
   hot bath.

▶ **Practice 20. *If*-clauses.** (Chart 3-6)
Complete each sentence by using an *if*-clause with the given ideas. Use a comma if necessary.**

1. Maybe it will rain tomorrow.

   _____*If it rains tomorrow,*_____ I'm going to go to a movie.

2. Maybe it will be hot tomorrow.

   _____ I'm going to go swimming.

3. Maybe Adam will have enough time.

   Adam will finish his essay tonight _____.

4. Maybe I won't get a check tomorrow.

   _____ I'll email my parents and ask for money.

5. Perhaps I'll get a raise soon.

   We will take a nice vacation trip next summer _____.

---

*The noun usually comes before the pronoun when you combine clauses:
*After **Ann** eats dinner, **she** is going to study.*
Ann *is going to study after* **she** *eats dinner.*

**Notice the punctuation in the example. A comma is used when the *if*-clause comes before the main clause. No comma is used
when the *if*-clause follows the main clause.

6. Maybe Gina won't study for her test.

_____ she'll get a bad grade.

7. Maybe I will have enough money.

I'm going to go to Hawaii for my vacation _____.

8. Maybe I won't study tonight.

_____ I probably won't pass the chemistry exam.

▶ **Practice 21. Future time clauses and *if*-clauses.** (Chart 3-6)
Circle the correct verbs. Pay attention to the words in **bold**.

Sam and I are going to leave on a road trip tomorrow. We'll pack our suitcases and put everything in the car **before** we (*go / will go*) to bed tonight. We'll leave tomorrow morning at dawn, **as soon as** the sun (*will come / comes*) up. We'll drive for a couple of hours on the interstate highway **while** we (*will talk / talk*) and (*listen / will listen*) to our favorite music. **When** we (*will see / see*) a nice rest area, we'll stop for coffee. **After** we (*walk / will walk*) around the rest area a little bit, we'll get back in the car and drive a little longer. We'll stay on that highway **until** we (*come / will come*) to Highway 44. Then we'll turn off and drive on scenic country roads. **If** Sam (*will get / gets*) tired, I'll drive. Then **when** I (*drive / will drive*), he'll probably take a little nap. We'll keep going **until** it (will *get / gets*) dark.

▶ **Practice 22. Future time clauses.** (Chart 3-6)
Choose the correct completion from Column B.

Facts:

• Water boils at 100 degrees Celsius (100° C) or 212 degrees Fahrenheit (212° F).
• Water freezes* at 0 degrees Celsius (0° C) or 32 degrees Fahrenheit (32° F).
• Spring follows winter.

Column A	Column B
1. The plants will die from the cold if _____.	a. the temperature reaches 212° F
2. If freezing weather from the north arrives tonight, _____.	b. spring comes
	c. spring will come
3. Water boils when _____.	d. it will melt**
4. When you put water in a pot and turn the stove on high, soon _____.	e. the temperature falls below 0° C
	f. the water will boil
5. The flowers will bloom when _____.	g. the temperature will fall below 0° C
6. After this long winter finally ends, _____.	
7. If you leave ice cream at room temperature, _____.	

---

*freeze = change from liquid to solid

**melt = change from solid to liquid

▶ **Practice 23. Future time clauses and *if*-clauses.** (Chart 3-6)
Combine the given ideas into one sentence by using the word in *italics* to make an adverb clause.
Omit the words in parentheses from your new sentence. <u>Underline</u> the adverb clause.

1. *when*   a. Sue is going to buy an apartment (then).

           b. Sue is going to have enough money (first).

           <u>   When Sue has enough money   </u>, she is going to buy an apartment. OR

           Sue is going to buy an apartment <u>   when she has enough money   </u>.

2. *before*   a. I'm going to clean up my apartment (first).

           b. My friends are going to come over (later).

           _____

           _____

3. *when*   a. The storm will be over (in an hour or two).

           b. I'm going to do some errands (then).

           _____

           _____

4. *if*   a. (Maybe) you won't learn how to use a computer.

         b. (As a result), you will have trouble finding a job.

         _____

         _____

5. *as soon as*   a. Joe is going to meet us at the coffee shop.

                  b. He is going to finish his report (soon).

                  _____

                  _____

6. *after*   a. Lesley will wash and dry the dishes.

           b. (Then) she will put them away.

           _____

           _____

7. *if*   a. They may not leave at seven.

         b. (As a result), they won't get to the theater on time.

          _____

          _____

▶ **Practice 24. Review: past and future.** (Chapter 2 and Charts 3-1 → 3-6)
Read Part I. Use the information in Part I to complete Part II with appropriate verb tenses. Use
will (not ***be going to***) for future time in Part II. Use the simple present for present time.

Part I.

    Yesterday morning was an ordinary morning. I got up at 6:30. I washed my face and brushed
my teeth. Then I put on my jeans and a sweater. I went to the kitchen and turned on the electric
coffee maker.

Then I walked down my driveway to get the morning newspaper. While I was walking to get the paper, I saw a deer. It was eating the flowers in my garden. After I watched the deer for a little while, I made some noise to make the deer run away before it destroyed my flowers.

As soon as I got back to the kitchen, I poured myself a cup of coffee and opened the morning paper. While I was reading the paper, my teenage daughter came downstairs. We talked about her plans for the day. We had breakfast together, and I made a lunch for her to take to school. After we said good-bye, I finished reading the paper.

Then I went to my office. It is in my home. My office has a desk, a computer, a radio, a fax machine, a copy machine, and a lot of bookshelves. I worked all morning. While I was working, the phone rang many times. I talked to many people. At 11:30, I went to the kitchen and made a sandwich for lunch. As I said, it was an ordinary morning.

Part II.

Tomorrow morning _____will be_____ an ordinary morning. I_____'ll get_____ up at 6:30.
                        1   2

I _____'ll wash_____ my face and _____brush_____ my teeth. Then I _____ probably
        3   4   5

_____ on my jeans and a sweater. I _____ to the kitchen and
        6   7

_____ the electric coffee maker.
        8

Then I _____ down my driveway to get the morning newspaper. If I
              9

_____ a deer in my garden, I _____ it for a while and then
        10   11

_____ some noise to chase it away before it _____ my flowers.
        12   13

As soon as I _____ back to the kitchen, I _____ myself a cup of
                    14   15

coffee and _____ the morning paper. While I'm reading the paper, my teenage
                  16

daughter _____ downstairs. We _____ about her plans for the day.
                17   18

We _____ breakfast together, and I _____ a lunch for her to take to
        19   20

school. After we _____ good-bye, I _____ reading the paper.
                        21   22

Then I _____ to my office. It _____ in my home. My office
              23   24

_____ a desk, a computer, a radio, a fax machine, a copy machine, and a lot of
        25

bookshelves. I _____ all morning. While I'm working, the phone
                      26

_____ many times. I _____ to many people. At 11:30, I
        27   28

_____ to the kitchen and _____ a sandwich for lunch. As I said, it
        29   30

_____ an ordinary morning.
        31

► **Practice 25. Using *be going to* and the present progressive to express future time.** (Chart 3-7)
Rewrite the sentences with *be going to* and the present progressive.

1. I'm planning to stay home tonight.

     _____I'm going to stay_____ home tonight.

     _____I'm staying_____ home tonight.

2. They're planning to travel across the country by train this summer.

     _____ across the country by train this summer.

     _____ across the country by train this summer.

3. We're planning to get married in June.

     _____ married in June.

     _____ married in June.

4. He's planning to start graduate school next year.

     _____ graduate school next year.

     _____ graduate school next year.

5. She's planning to go to New Zealand next month.

     _____ to New Zealand next month.

     _____ to New Zealand next month.

6. My neighbors are planning to build their dream home this spring.

     _____ their dream home this spring.

     _____ their dream home this spring.

► **Practice 26. Using the present progressive to express future time.** (Chart 3-7)
Complete the sentences with the present progressive. Use each verb in the list only once. Note the future time expressions in **bold**.

come	graduate	have	leave	meet	speak	take	✓travel

1. Kathy _____is traveling_____ to Caracas **next month** to attend a conference.

2. Carl _____ the office **early today**. He just made an appointment with the dentist for 3:00 P.M. He has a terrible toothache.

3. The president _____ on TV **at noon today**.

4. We _____ a party **tomorrow**. Would you like to come?

5. Amanda likes to take her two children with her on trips whenever she can, but she _____ not _____ them with her to El Paso, Texas, **next week**. It's strictly a business trip.

6. A: Your apartment is so neat! Are you expecting guests?
   B: Yes. My parents _____ **tomorrow** for a two-day visit.

7. A: Do you have any plans for lunch today?
   B: I _____ Shannon at the Shamrock Café **in an hour**. Want to join us?

8. A: Will you be at Ada and Alberto's tenth anniversary party **next Friday**?

    B: No, unfortunately. I also have a very important event on that day. I

    _____ from college, finally!

▶ **Practice 27. Using the present progressive to express future time.** (Chart 3-7)
Decide whether each sentence refers to a plan for the future or a prediction. Circle the correct letter.

1. A big storm is going to hit the coast tomorrow.
    a. a plan for the future   b. a prediction

2. We are going to leave for a safer location later today.
    a. a plan for the future   b. a prediction

3. Ralph is going to go to medical school after he graduates from college.
    a. a plan for the future   b. a prediction

4. Ralph is smart and serious. I am sure he is going to be an excellent doctor.
    a. a plan for the future   b. a prediction

5. This car is going to run out of gas very soon! The indicator is on empty.
    a. a plan for the future   b. a prediction

6. We're going to stop to buy gas at the next gas station.
    a. a plan for the future   b. a prediction

7. This little seed is going to be a large tree one day.
    a. a plan for the future   b. a prediction

8. We are going to plant vegetables in our garden tomorrow.
    a. a plan for the future   b. a prediction

▶ **Practice 28. Using the present progressive to express future time.** (Chart 3-7)
Check (✓) the correct sentence. Both sentences may be correct.

1. ___ a. It is going to snow tomorrow.
    ___ b. It is snowing tomorrow.

2. ___ a. I'm going to attend a conference in April.
    ___ b. I'm attending a conference in April.

3. ___ a. Irv is going to come for dinner tomorrow night.
    ___ b. Irv is coming for dinner tomorrow night.

4. ___ a. A new bookstore is going to open next month.
    ___ b. A new bookstore is opening next month.

5. ___ a. This old building is going to fall down pretty soon.
    ___ b. This old building is falling down pretty soon.

6. ___ a. Jackie and I are going to take her uncle out to dinner tonight.
    ___ b. Jackie and I are taking her uncle out to dinner tonight.

7. ___ a. You're going to feel better after you take that medicine.
    ___ b. You're feeling better after you take that medicine.

8. ___ a. The plane is going to leave on time.
   ___ b. The plane is leaving on time.

9. ___ a. Take an umbrella. If you don't, you're going to get wet.
   ___ b. Take an umbrella. If you don't, you're getting wet.

10. ___ a. I ordered a new computer. It's going to arrive next week.
    ___ b. I ordered a new computer. It's arriving next week.

▶ **Practice 29. Using the simple present to express future time.** (Chart 3-8)
Complete each sentence with one of the verbs in the list. Use the simple present to express future time.

arrive	close	end	get in	open
begin	depart	finish	leave	start

1. A: What time _____*does*_____ class _____*begin / start*_____ tomorrow morning?

    B: It _____*begins / starts*_____ at eight o'clock sharp.

2. A: The coffee shop _____ at seven o'clock tomorrow morning. I'll meet you

    there at 7:15.

    B: Okay. I'll be there.

3. A: What time are you going to go to the airport tonight?

    B: Tom's plane _____ around 7:15, but I think I'll go a little early in case it

    gets in ahead of schedule.

4. A: What's the hurry?

    B: I've got to take a shower, change clothes, and get to the stadium fast. The game

    _____ in forty-five minutes, and I don't want to miss the beginning.

5. A: What time _____ the dry cleaners _____ this evening? If I

    don't get there in time, I'll have nothing to wear to the party tonight.

    B: It _____ at 6:00. I can pick up your dry cleaning for you.

    A: Hey, thanks! That'll really help!

6. A: What time should we go to the theater tomorrow night?

    B: The doors _____ at 6:00 P.M., but we don't need to be there that early.

    The show _____ at 8:00. If we _____ at the theater by 7:15,

    we'll be there in plenty of time. The show _____ around 10:30, so we can

    be back home by a little after 11:00.

7. A: I've enjoyed my visit with you, but tomorrow I have to go back home.

    B: What time _____ your flight _____ tomorrow?

    A: It _____ at 12:34 P.M. I want to be at the airport an hour early, so we

    should leave here around 10:30, if that's okay with you.

B: Sure. What time _____ your flight _____ in Mexico City?

A: It's about a three-hour flight. I'll get in around 4:30 Mexico City time.

▶ **Practice 30. Using *be about to*.** (Chart 3-9)
Write the letter in Column B that correctly answers the question in Column A.

What does it usually mean if . . .

Column A

1. the sky is very gray and cloudy? _____
2. Jack is leaving his house with his keys in his hand? _____
3. the teacher is picking up a piece of chalk? _____
4. it is 6:59 A.M. and your alarm clock is set for 7:00 A.M.? _____
5. it is 7:58 P.M. and the president is going to give a speech at 8:00 P.M.? _____
6. Tim is holding a fork in his hand and looking at a plate of warm pasta? _____
7. Bob is standing up inside a canoe? _____
8. the plane is slowly coming toward the runway and its wheels are down? _____

Column B

a. It means that he is about to write on the blackboard.
b. It means that he is about to speak.
c. It means that he is about to eat.
d. It means that it is about to rain.
e. It means that it is about to land.
f. It means that he is about to get into his car.
g. It means that he is about to fall out.
h. It means that it is about to ring.

▶ **Practice 31. Parallel verbs.** (Chart 3-10)
Complete the sentences with the correct form of the verbs in parentheses.

1. My classmates are going to meet at Danny's and (*study*) _____*study*_____ together tonight.
2. Tomorrow the sun will rise at 6:34 and (*set*) _____ at 8:59.
3. Last night, I was listening to music and (*do*) _____ my homework when Kim stopped by.
4. Next weekend, Nick is going to meet his friends downtown and (*go*) _____ to a soccer game.
5. My pen slipped out of my hand and (*fall*) _____ to the floor.
6. Alex is at his computer. He (*write*) _____ emails and (*wait*) _____ for responses.
7. Every morning without exception, Mrs. Carter (*take*) _____ her dog for a walk and (*buy*) _____ a newspaper at Charlie's newsstand.
8. Before I (*go*) _____ to your boss and (*tell*) _____ her about your mistake, I want to give you an opportunity to explain it to her yourself.

9. Next month, I (take) _____ my vacation and (forget) _____ about everything that is connected to my job.

10. Kathy thinks I was the cause of her problems, but I wasn't. Someday she (discover) _____ the truth and (apologize) _____ to me.

▶ **Practice 32. Editing.** (Chapter 3)
Correct the errors.

1. My friends will to join us after work.

2. Maybe the party ends soon.

3. On Friday, our school close early so teachers can go to a workshop.

4. It's raining tomorrow.

5. Our company is going to sells computer equipment to schools.

6. Give Grandpa a hug. He's about to leaving.

7. Mr. Scott is going to retire and moving to a warmer climate.

8. If your soccer team will win the championship tomorrow, we'll have a big celebration for you.

9. I bought this cloth because I will make some curtains for my bedroom.

10. I moving to London when I will finish my education here.

11. Are you going go to the meeting?

12. I opened the door and walk to the front of the room.

13. When will you going to move into your new apartment?

14. Maybe I celebrate my 30th birthday with my friends at a restaurant.

▶ **Practice 33. Verb tense review.** (Chapters 1 → 3)
Complete the sentences with the correct form of the verb in parentheses.

Part I.

Right now it's almost midnight. I'm still at my computer. I (work) _____am working_____ late
1
tonight because I (need) _____ to finish this report before tomorrow. Before I
2
(go) _____ to bed tonight, I (finish) _____ the report and
3 4
(write) _____ a couple of emails too.
5

Part II.

I (stay) _____ up very late last night too. While I (read) _____ a
6 7
book, I (hear) _____ a noise outside. When I (go) _____ outside to
8 9
find out about the noise, I (see, not) _____ anything in the dark. But when I
10
(go) _____ outside early this morning, I (find) _____ garbage all
11 12
over my lawn. A bear from the woods probably (make) _____ the mess.
13

Part III.

Jack (*watch*) _____ a football game on TV right now. He
(14)
(*watch, always*) _____ football on Sunday afternoons. As soon as the
(15)
game (*be*) _____ over, he (*mow*) _____ the grass in the back yard.
(16)   (17)

Part IV.

It's cold today. Right now I (*make*) _____ potato soup . It (*cook*)
(18)
_____ on the stove. I remember potato soup from my childhood days. When
(19)
we (*be*) _____ children, my mother (*make, used to*) _____ potato soup for
(20)   (21)
us when the weather (*get*) _____ cold.
(22)

Part V.

We (*go*) _____ to New York next week. When we (*be*) _____ in New
(23)   (24)
York next week, we (*see*) _____ a couple of plays on Broadway. Last week we
(25)
(*buy*) _____ tickets online for two plays. We (*buy, always*)
(26)
_____ the tickets online before we (*leave*) _____ on a trip. We
(27)   (28)
(*stay, usually*) _____ at a small hotel near the theater district.
(29)
But, when we (*be*) _____ in New York next week, we (*stay, not*)
(30)
_____ at that hotel. When we (*try*) _____ to make reservations
(31)   (32)
last week, the hotel (*be*) _____ full. We (*stay, may*) _____ with friends
(33)   (34)
in the city, or maybe we (*stay*) _____ with our cousins in the suburbs.
(35)

Part VI.

Mark is obsessed with video games. He (*play*) _____ video games morning, noon,
(36)
and night. Sometimes he (*skip*) _____ class to play them. Right now he (*do, not*)
(37)
_____ very well in school. If he (*study, not*) _____ harder
(38)   (39)

and (*go*) _____ to class every day, he (*flunk*) _____ out of
40   41
school.

Part VII.

I had a dream last night. In the dream, I (*see*) _____ the man who stole the radio from my
42
car last Friday. I (*run*) _____ after him, (*catch*) _____ him, and (*knock*)
43   44
_____ him down. A passerby (*call*) _____ the police on her cell
45   46
phone. I sat on the man while I (*wait*) _____ for them to come. After the police (*get*)
47
_____ there and (*understand*) _____ the situation, they (*put*)
48   49
_____ handcuffs on him and (*take*) _____ him to jail. Then the dream
50   51
(*end*) _____ and I (*wake*) _____ up.
52   53

▶ **Practice 34. Crossword puzzle.**
Complete the puzzle. Use the clues to find the correct words.

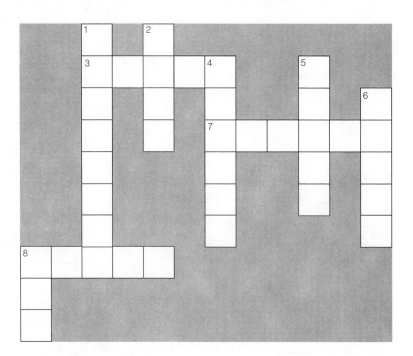

Across

  3. We won't go to the beach if it _____.

  7. We'll call you as soon as we _____ at the airport.

  8. _____ I will pass this course. I just don't know!

Down

  1. Carl _____ won't get the job. He really doesn't have the right skills for it.

  2. If Ted needs a ride, tell him that I _____ pick him up at 6:30.

  4. Maria is going to have a cup of coffee before she _____ work.

  5. The schools are _____ to be closed on Monday because it's a holiday.

  6. Please turn off your cell phones. The concert is about to _____.

  8. Helen _____ come to the movie with us. She's not sure.

Chapter 4
Present Perfect and Past Perfect

▶ **Practice 1. Past participles.** (Chart 4-1)
Circle the past participle in each group.

1. finish (finished) finishing
2. stopped stopping stops
3. puts put putting
4. knew knowing known
5. be been were
6. wanting wanted wants
7. saying said say
8. having have had
9. gone go went
10. took taken taking

▶ **Practice 2. Review: irregular verbs.** (Charts 2-4, 2-5, and 4-1)
Write each verb in the correct group.

bring	feed	keep	quit	sink	teach
buy	fight	let	✓ring	sit	think
catch	find	meet	set	stand	upset
cut	have	pay	shut	stick	weep
drink	✓hurt	put	sing	swim	✓win

Group I. Simple form, simple past, and past participle are the same.

Simple Form	Simple Past	Past Participle	Simple Form	Simple Past	Past Participle
hurt	hurt	hurt			

Group II. The vowel changes: i → a → u.

Simple Form	Simple Past	Past Participle
ring	rang	rung

Group III. Simple past and past participle are the same.

Simple Form	Simple Past	Past Participle
win	won	won

▶ **Practice 3. Present perfect with *since* and *for.*** (Chart 4-2)
Complete the sentence with the present perfect form of the verb in the first sentence.

1. Mr. Woods **teaches** chemistry at Central High School. He _____ there for 17 years.

2. Marvin **sells** cars. He began selling cars in 2000. Marvin _____ cars since 2000.

3. John **loves** Mary. He _____ her since they were teenagers.

4. I **have** a pain in my side. I _____ this pain for about two weeks.

5. You **know** my cousin Rita, don't you? You _____ her since you were in college, right?

6. Clara and Tom are going to **play** tennis on Saturday morning. They _____ tennis together on Saturday mornings for years.

7. I am going to **get up** early again tomorrow so that I can do my exercises. I _____ up early for the past month, and I have exercised every day.

8. My cousins **go** to their house in the mountains every summer. They

    _____ to their summer home ever since I can remember.

9. Alaska and Hawaii **are** the newest states of the United States. They became states in 1950.

    They _____ states for more than 50 years.

10. Brazil **is** an independent country. Brazil _____ an independent

    country since 1822.

▶ **Practice 4. Present perfect with *since* and *for*.** (Chart 4-2)
Complete the sentences with *since* or *for*.

1. David has worked for the power company ____*since*____ 1999.

2. His brother has worked for the power company ____*for*____ five years.

3. I have known Peter Gowan _____ September.

4. I've known his sister _____ three months.

5. Jonas has been in a wheelchair _____ a year.

6. He's had a bad back _____ he was in a car accident.

7. My vision has improved _____ I got new reading glasses.

8. I've had a toothache _____ yesterday morning.

9. The shoe store on the corner has been there _____ 1920.

10. It has been there _____ almost a hundred years.

▶ **Practice 5. Present perfect with *since* and *for*.** (Chart 4-2)
Rewrite the sentences using *since* or *for*.

1. I was in this class a month ago, and I am in this class now.
   I have been in this class for a month.

2. I knew my teacher in September, and I know her now.

3. Sam wanted a dog two years ago, and he wants one now.

4. Sara needed a new car last year, and she still needs one.

5. Our professor was sick a week ago, and she is still sick.

6. My parents live in Canada. They moved there in December.

7. I know Mrs. Brown. I met her in 1999.

8. Tom works at a fast-food restaurant. He got the job three weeks ago.

▶ **Practice 6. Negative, question, and short-answer forms.** (Chart 4-3)
Complete the conversations with the given verbs and any words in parentheses. Use the present perfect.

1. *eat*   A: (*you, ever*) _____*Have you ever eaten*_____ pepperoni pizza?

   B: Yes, I ____*have*____. I ____*have eaten*____ pepperoni pizza many

   times. OR

   No, I ____*haven't*____. I (*never*) ____*have never eaten*____

   pepperoni pizza.

2. *talk*   A: (*you, ever*) _____ to a famous person?

           B: Yes, I _____. I _____ to a lot of famous people.

              OR

              No, I _____. I (*never*) _____ to a famous person.

3. *rent*   A: (*Erica, ever*) _____ a car?

           B: Yes, she _____. She _____ a car many times.

              OR

              No, she _____. She (*never*) _____ a car.

4. *see*   A: (*you, ever*) _____ a shooting star?

          B: Yes, I _____. I _____ a lot of shooting stars.

             OR

             No, I _____. I (*never*) _____ a shooting star.

5. *catch*   A: (*Joe, ever*) _____ a big fish?

            B: Yes, he _____. He _____ lots of big fish. OR

              No, he _____. He (*never*) _____ a big fish.

6. *have*   A: (*you, ever*) _____ a bad sunburn?

            B: Yes, I _____. I _____ a bad sunburn several times. OR

              No, I _____. I (*never*) _____ a bad sunburn.

7. *meet*   A: (*I, ever*) _____ you before?

            B: Yes, you _____. You _____ me before. OR

              No, you _____. You (*never*) _____ me before.

8. *be*   A: (*the boys, ever*) _____ to a baseball game before?

          B: Yes, they _____. They _____ to a few baseball games. OR

              No, they _____. They (*never*) _____ to a baseball game.

▶ **Practice 7. Negative, question, and short-answer forms.** (Charts 4-3 and 4-4)
Complete the questions and statements with the given verbs and any words in parentheses.

A TV Interview with a Famous Actress

BRYAN: Welcome to our show, Ms. Starr.

LARA: Thank you. I'm glad to be here. By the way, please call me Lara.

BRYAN: Okay, Lara. Well, first, how long (*be*) _____*have you been*_____ in movies?
                                                             1

LARA: For many years — since I was a teenager.

BRYAN: Really? How many movies (*make, you*) _____ so far?
                                                                  2

LARA: I've made about twenty movies.

BRYAN: (*enjoy, you, always*) _____ your work,
                                                            3

           ever since you began in your teens?

LARA: Yes, I _____. I have always loved my work.
                        4

BRYAN: Lara, you travel a lot in your work, right?

LARA: Oh, yes. I travel very often.

BRYAN: Where (*travel, you*) _____ to so far?
                                          5

LARA: I (*be*) _____ to Europe, Africa, and Asia for my work.
                    6

BRYAN: Do you miss your friends and family when you are away? Have you ever wanted a more

normal life?

LARA: Well, I miss my friends and family, but I (*never, want*)

_____ a regular life. I've always been very happy in
              7

my work.

BRYAN: (*think, you, ever*) _____ about getting married?
                                                  8

LARA: Well, no, I _____. Maybe that's because I (*not, meet*)
                        9

_____ any really nice guys recently. Maybe I will meet
            10

someone nice, and maybe I won't. Either way, it's okay with me.

▶ **Practice 8. Present perfect with unspecified time.** (Chart 4-4)
Choose the correct completions. Both answers may be correct.

1. The year hasn't ended _____. There is still time to pay your taxes before December 30th.
   a. already   b. yet

2. Winter arrived early this year. It has snowed twice _____, and summer isn't even over!
   a. already   b. yet

3. Have you finished your homework _____?
   a. already   b. yet

4. Kate has _____ returned from a year in Tokyo.
   a. already   b. yet

5. I'm not quite ready to leave. I haven't finished packing my suitcase _____.
   a. already   b. yet

6. Have you seen the new Indian movie _____?
   a. already   b. yet

7. Malcolm doesn't need to take another science course. He has
   _____ taken the required number of science classes.
   a. already   b. yet

8. Since he retired, our neighbor Mr. Evans has _____ gained about
   30 pounds. That's because he just sits in front of the TV all day.
   He has become a real couch potato!*
   a. already   b. yet

---

couch potato = an informal phrase to describe someone who spends a lot of time sitting or lying down and watching television

► **Practice 9. Present perfect with unspecified time.** (Chart 4-4)
Complete the sentences with the words in the list. There is one extra word in each list.

1. *has, school, started, not, yet, already*

   Our daughter is only two years old, so she _____ *has not started school yet.* _____

   She is too young.

2. *has, learned, already, yet, the alphabet*

   Our daughter is only two years old, but she _____

   _____. Isn't she smart?

3. *already, corrected, has, yet, our tests*

   Our teacher works very quickly. She _____

   _____. She corrected them all in one hour!

4. *returned, the tests, not, has, already, yet*

   Our teacher corrected the tests last night, but she left them at home. She _____

   _____. I guess that she will return

   them tomorrow.

5. *not, already, yet, dinner, cooked, has*

   Anita _____ because she came home

   late from her job.

6. *cooked, already, yet, has, dinner*

   Anita _____. She got home early and she wants

   to go to bed early.

► **Practice 10. Present perfect with unspecified time.** (Chart 4-4)
Complete each sentence with a verb from the list. Include any words that are in parentheses. Use
the present perfect form of the verb. Use a negative form if appropriate.

change	invite	✓meet	retire	spend
give	live	pick	see	travel

Neighbors in My Apartment Building

A few months ago, I moved to a new apartment. I (*all my neighbors / yet*)

_____ *haven't met all my neighbors yet* _____, but I have met some of them. They are
$\quad$ 1

interesting people.

My neighbor in 3G is a private pilot. Last week he returned from the South Pole, and before that

he was in Africa. He _____ all over the world.
$\qquad\qquad$ 2

My neighbor in 4F is a doctor, but she looks like a punk rocker*. She (*already*)

_____ the color of her hair four or five times since I moved in.
₃

Now it's purple.

The young man across the hall has a lot of parties. He (*already*)

_____ several parties since I moved in, but he (*not*)
₄

_____ me to any of them.
₅

My next-door neighbors are musicians. They (*just*) _____ from
₆

the City Symphony Orchestra. They were with the orchestra for more than 20 years. Now they are

looking forward to traveling and spending more time with their family.

The neighbors on the other side are mysterious. I saw them only once, but I (*not*)

_____ them for a while. Nobody has. They (*not*)
₇

_____ up their newspapers for a week. There are six or seven newspapers
₈

on the floor in front of their door.

A young woman in the building is my new best friend. She _____ here
₉

for about a year. She owns a small advertising business. We (*already*) _____

_____ many fun evenings together.
₁₀

▶ **Practice 11. Review: irregular verbs.** (Charts 2-4, 2-5, and 4-4)
Complete the sentences with the correct verb from the list. Use the present perfect tense.

| begin | drink | meet | ✓put |
| buy | find | pay | win |

1. I _____*have*_____ just _____*put*_____ the dinner in the oven. It will be ready in twenty

    minutes.

2. Stuart is very thirsty from playing tennis in the hot sun. He _____ three

    glasses of water already, and he is asking for more.

3. Hurry, Sal. The program _____ already _____. We can clean up

    the kitchen later.

4. Our basketball team _____ every game so far this season. What a great team!

5. I _____ the president twice. He said, "It's good to meet you. Thank you for

    your support."

6. Two police officers _____ just _____ the missing boy, and they

    are taking him home to his family.

---

punk rocker = someone who likes loud punk music and wears things that are typical of it, such as torn clothes, metal chains, and
colored hair.

7. This bill is a mistake. I _____ already _____ this bill.

8. The new electric car is a big success. Thousands of people _____

one, and many more customers are waiting to buy one.

▶ **Practice 12. Simple past vs. present perfect.** (Chart 4-5)
Write "F" if the activity or situation is finished and "C" if it continues to the present.

1. _C_ My grandfather has worked since he was in high school.

2. _F_ My grandmother worked for 20 years.

3. _F_ I finished my work two hours ago.

4. _F_ I have already finished my work, so I'm leaving the office.

5. ____ My father has been sick since yesterday.

6. ____ Jane was sick last Monday.

7. ____ Tom has already left. He's not here.

8. ____ Tom left five minutes ago.

9. ____ I have known Max Shell since we were children.

10. ____ The baby has had a fever since midnight. I think I'll call the doctor.

11. ____ The baby had a fever all night, but he's better now.

12. ____ I had the flu last year.

13. ____ Sue has had the flu since last Friday.

14. ____ Claude has slept outside under the stars several times this summer.

▶ **Practice 13. Present perfect and simple past with time words.** (Charts 4-1 → 4-5)
Choose (✓) all the phrases that correctly complete the sentences.

1. The Petersons took a trip _____.

____ a. two weeks ago

____ b. since yesterday

____ c. yesterday

____ d. last year

____ e. several months ago

____ f. since last month

____ g. the day before yesterday

____ h. in March

____ i. since winter began

2. The Petersons have been out of town _____.

____ a. the day before yesterday

____ b. one month ago

____ c. since Friday

____ d. last week

____ e. since winter began

____ f. since last week

____ g. in April last year

____ h. several weeks ago

____ i. for several weeks

▶ **Practice 14. Simple past vs. present perfect.** (Chart 4-5)
Complete the sentences with the letter of the correct verbs in the list.

a. paid	g. have paid
b. sent	h. have sent
c. met	i. have met
d. took	j. have taken
e. watched	k. have watched
f. withdrew	l. have withdrawn

1. I _c_ many new people at the conference last week. I _i_ a lot of new people since I started going to conferences ten years ago.

2. I ____ a lot of good movies on TV in my lifetime. I ____ an excellent new movie last night.

3. I ____ my rent this morning. I ____ my rent on time for twenty years.

4. I ____ lots of difficult tests since I started college. I ____ a very difficult test yesterday in my World History class.

5. I ____ more than a thousand dollars from my bank account so far this month. Yesterday I ____ three hundred dollars.

6. I ____ several emails to my friends last night. I ____ thousands of emails to my friends in my lifetime.

▶ **Practice 15. Simple past vs. present perfect.** (Chart 4-5)
Complete the sentences with the correct verb in parentheses. Notice the time expressions.

The Okay Candy Company

(1) The Okay Candy Company is 100 years old this year. The Foxworthy family (*started / has started*) this business in 1910. In the beginning, the company (*was / has been*) small and (*had / has had*) about 20 employees. Now the company (*became / has become*) much larger, and it has more than 200 employees. It (*was / has been*) a very successful company for many years because of good management.

(2) The current president, Oscar M. Foxworthy, (*led / has led*) the company for the last eleven years. The company (*made / has made*) a profit every year since he first (*took / has taken*) over the company. Last year, for example, the company's profits (*went / have gone*) up 4%, and this year profits (*went / have gone*) up 4.2% since January. The year (*didn't end / hasn't ended*) yet, and people are optimistic about the future of the company.

► **Practice 16. Present perfect progressive.** (Chart 4-6)
Complete the sentences with the correct form of the present perfect progressive verb and the appropriate time phrase.

1. I am waiting for the downtown bus. I arrived at the bus stop twenty minutes ago.

   I _____*have been waiting*_____ for the bus for _____*twenty minutes*_____.

2. Sandy is watching TV. She turned on the TV two hours ago.

   She _____ TV for _____.

3. Ivo is working at the hospital. He began working at 7:00 this morning, and he hasn't stopped. It is now 10 P.M.

   Ivo _____ at the hospital since _____.

4. Kim is driving. He got in his car six hours ago, and he hasn't stopped.

   Kim _____ for _____.

5. Ruth is writing a novel. She began it three years ago, and she hasn't finished it yet.

   Ruth _____ the novel for _____.

6. Jim and Dan are arguing. They began their argument when Jim brought home a stray cat.

   Jim and Dan _____ since _____

   _____.

7. It began to rain two days ago. It is still raining.

   It _____ for _____.

8. Jenny is losing weight. She began her diet on her birthday.

   She _____ weight since _____.

► **Practice 17. Present perfect progressive vs. present perfect.** (Charts 4-6 and 4-7)
Read the passage about Max. Then answer the questions that follow. Circle "T" if the statement is true, and "F" if the statement is false.

   Max has written four books. Three of his books did not sell well. The fourth, however, — called *A Tiger's Life* — has been very successful. In fact, right now a production company in Hollywood is making a movie of *A Tiger's Life*. Max is taking a break from writing and is a consultant for the movie. He hasn't written anything new for about a year because he has been working on the movie.

1. Max is writing a book now.	T	F
2. All four of his books have been successful.	T	F
3. *A Tiger's Life* has been a success.	T	F
4. A production company has already made a movie of *A Tiger's Life*.	T	F
5. Max began working on the movie about a year ago.	T	F
6. Max has finished working on the movie.	T	F

► **Practice 18. Present progressive, present perfect progressive and the present perfect.** (Charts 4-6 and 4-7)
Choose the correct verb.

1. Where have you been? The boss _____ for you for over an hour!
   a. is looking   b.) has been looking

2. I'm exhausted! I _____ for the last eight hours without a break.
   a. am working   b. have been working

3. Shhh! Susan _____ now. Let's not make any noise. We don't want to wake her up.
   a. is sleeping   b. has been sleeping

4. Annie, go upstairs and wake your brother up. He _____ for over ten hours. He has chores to do.
   a. is sleeping   b. has been sleeping

5. Erin has never gone camping. She _____ in a tent.
   a. has never slept   b. has never been sleeping

6. This is a great shirt! I _____ it at least a dozen times, and it still looks like new.
   a. have washed   b. have been washing

7. Are you still washing the dishes? You _____ dishes for thirty minutes. How long can it take to wash dishes?
   a. have washed   b. have been washing

8. We _____ to the Steak House restaurant many times. The food is excellent.
   a. have gone   b. have been going

▶ **Practice 19. Present perfect progressive vs. present perfect.** (Charts 4-6 and 4-7)
Complete the passage with either the present perfect or present perfect progressive form of the verbs from the lists. More than one verb form may be correct.

Global Warming

> get   know

The earth _____ warmer for many years, as most people realize.
                         1
And the temperatures will continue to increase. People in the Arctic regions

_____ this for a long time: In those regions, the winters are shorter than they
         2
used to be and the ice in the ocean has become thinner.

> become   collect   rise   study

Scientists _____ the climate in the Arctic for many
                         3
years, and they will continue to study it. These scientists _____ a lot
                                                                         4
of information about climate change. For example, air temperatures in the Arctic are getting

warmer. They _____ 5° Celsius since 1910. Another result is that the Arctic
                         5
sea ice is melting. It _____ 40 percent thinner since 1970.
                         6

▶ **Practice 20. Verb tense review.** (Chapters 1–3, and Chart 4-1 → 4-7)
Complete the sentences with the words in parentheses.

Looking for a Job

BEN: I (*need*) _____need_____ to find a job. Where (*be*) _____ a good place for a
                   1   2
      student to work?

ANN: (*you, work, ever*) _____ at a restaurant?
                               3

BEN: Yes. I (*work*) _____ at several restaurants. I (*have*) _____ a
                        4   5
      job as a dishwasher last fall.

ANN: Where?

BEN: At The Bistro, a little café on First Street.

ANN: How long (*you, work*) _____ there?
                             6

BEN: For two months.

ANN: I (*work*) _____ in a lot of restaurants, but I (*have, never*)
                 7
      _____ a dishwashing job. How (*you, like*)
              8
      _____ your job as a dishwasher?
              9

BEN: I (*like, not*) _____ it very much. It (*be*) _____ hard
                      10   11
      work for low pay.

ANN: Where (*you, work*) _____ right now?
                               12

BEN: I (*have, not*) _____ a job right now. I (*have, not*)
                   13
      _____ a job since I (*quit*) _____ the dishwashing one.
          14   15

ANN: (*you, look*) _____ for a part-time or a full-time job now?
                        16

BEN: A part-time job, maybe twenty hours a week.

ANN: I (*go*) _____ to Al's Place tomorrow to see about a job. The
                17
      restaurant (*look*) _____ for help. Why don't you come along
                        18
      with me?

BEN: Thanks. I (do) _____ that. I (look, never)
            19
_____ for a job at Al's Place before. Maybe the pay (be)
            20
_____ better than at The Bistro.
            21

ANN: I (know, not) _____. We (find) _____ out when
            22   23

we (go) _____ there tomorrow.
            24

▶ **Practice 21. Past perfect.** (Chart 4-8)
For each item, write "1" before the action that happened first. Write "2" before the action that happened second.

1. Larry called Jane last night, but she had gone out for the evening.

   _2_ Larry called Jane.

   _1_ Jane went out.

2. I opened the door because someone had knocked on it. But no one was there.

   ____ I opened the door.

   ____ Someone knocked on the door.

3. My sister was happy because her boyfriend had called.

   ____ Her boyfriend called.

   ____ My sister was happy.

4. Our dog stood excitedly at the front door. He had seen me as I was putting on my coat to go out for a walk.

   ____ He saw me putting on my coat.

   ____ Our dog stood at the front door.

5. Ken had heard my joke a hundred times before. But he laughed anyway.

   ____ Ken laughed at my joke.

   ____ Ken heard the joke many times.

6. Don opened his car door with a wire hanger. He had lost his keys.

   ____ Don lost his keys.

   ____ Don opened his car door with a wire hanger.

▶ **Practice 22. Past perfect.** (Chart 4-8)
Read the passage and underline the past perfect verbs and the modifying adverbs **always** and **never**. Then complete the sentences that follow the passage. Use the past perfect in your completions.

A New Life for Alan

(1) Alan Green got married for the first time at age 49. His new life is very different because he has had to change many old habits. For example, before his marriage, he had always watched TV during dinner, but his wife likes to talk at dinnertime, so now the TV is off.

(2) Until his marriage, Alan had always read the front page of the newspaper first, but his wife likes to read the front page first too, so now Alan reads the sports page first.

(3) Until he got married, he had never let anyone else choose the radio station in the car. He had always listened to exactly what he wanted to listen to. But his wife likes to choose what's on the radio when she's in the car with him.

(4) When he was a bachelor, Alan had always left his dirty socks on the floor. Now he picks them up and puts them in the laundry basket.

(5) Before he was married, he'd never put the cap back on the toothpaste. He left it off. His wife prefers to have the cap back on. She also squeezes from the bottom of the tube, and Alan doesn't. Alan can't remember to put the cap back on, so now they have separate toothpaste tubes.

(6) Alan had never shared the TV remote control with anyone before he got married. He still likes to have control of the TV remote, but he doesn't say anything when his wife uses it.

Complete these sentences.

1. Until Alan got married, he _____had always watched_____ TV during dinner.

2. Before his marriage, he _____ the front page of the newspaper first.

3. Before he got married, he _____ other people choose the station on his car radio.

4. Until he began married life, he _____ his dirty socks on the floor.

5. Before his marriage, he _____ the toothpaste cap back on.

6. Until he had a wife who also liked to use the TV remote control, he

_____ the remote with anyone.

▶ **Practice 23. Review of time expressions.** (Chapter 4)
Choose the correct completions.

1. Sacha is sleeping _____.	a. since the world began
2. I have called Martin _____ this evening, but he hasn't answered the phone.	b. for twenty-one years
	c. at this moment
3. I'll call Martin one more time _____.	d. yet
4. Where's Hal? I hope he hasn't gone home _____.	e. after the 11:00 P.M. news
5. My family has lived in this house _____.	f. five times
6. How many people have lived on earth _____?	

▶ **Practice 24. Verb tense review.** (Chapters 1–4)
Choose the correct verbs.

1. A: ((Did you enjoy) / Have you enjoyed) the concert last night?
   B: Oh, yes. I (have enjoyed / enjoyed) it very much.

2. A: (Did you see / Have you seen) John yesterday?
   B: Yes, I did. It (was / has been) good to see him again. I (haven't seen / hadn't seen) him in a long time.

3. A: Hi, Jim! It's good to see you again. I (haven't seen / didn't see) you in weeks.
   B: Hi, Sue! It (was / is) good to see you again, too. I (haven't seen / don't see) you since the end of last semester. How's everything going?

4. A: (Did you get / Have you gotten) to class on time yesterday morning?
   B: No. When I (get / got) there, class (has already begun / had already begun).

5. A: I called Ana, but I couldn't talk to her.

   B: Why not?

   A: She (*had already gone / has already gone*) to bed, and her sister didn't want to wake her up for a phone call.

6. A: You're a wonderful artist. I love your paintings of the valley.

   B: Thank you. I (*have painted / was painting*) the same valley many times because it has such interesting light at different times of the day.

7. A: How many pictures of the valley (*have you painted / are you painting*) so far?

   B: Oh, more than twenty.

8. A: I see that you (*have been painting / were painting*) when I (*walked / have walked*) in.

   B: Yes. I (*have painted / have been painting*) since early this morning.

▶ **Practice 25. Editing.** (Chapters 1 → 4)
Correct the errors.

　　　　　　　　　　have been
1. Where were you? I ~~am~~ waiting for you for an hour.

2. Anna have been a soccer fan since a long time.

3. Since I have been a child, I have liked to solve puzzles.

4. Have you ever want to travel around the world?

5. The family is at the hospital since they hear about the accident.

6. My sister is only 30 years old, but her hair has began to turn gray.

7. Jake has been working as a volunteer at the children's hospital since several years.

8. Steve has worn his black suit only once since he has bought it.

9. My cousin is studying for medical school exams since last month.

10. I don't know the results of my medical tests already. I'll find out soon.

11. The phone has already stopped ringing when Michelle entered her apartment.

Circle the irregular past participles of these verbs in the puzzle: *become, break, find, go, know, see, take, understand.* Use the clues below the puzzle to help you. The words may be horizontal, vertical, or diagonal. The first letter of each word is highlighted in gray.

U	N	F	P	N	T	A	K	E	N
L	N	W	Q	L	K	L	Y	D	T
F	N	D	O	M	R	Q	D	N	F
D	E	R	E	N	T	C	L	O	H
M	K	H	M	R	K	M	U	T	B
X	O	C	N	M	S	N	Y	E	K
G	R	S	K	T	D	T	N	F	M
J	B	E	R	N	J	O	O	R	W
Y	D	E	P	L	G	M	M	O	L
Q	T	N	E	M	O	C	E	B	D

1. Traffic in this city has _____ very bad recently.

2. I have _____ this bus every morning since I started my new job.

3. How long have you _____ Ali's family?

4. This is a terrible washing machine. It has _____ again.

5. I love that movie. I have _____ it seven times.

6. Is Beth still here? Or has she _____ home already?

7. Hal lost his keys. He hasn't _____ them yet.

8. I am not good at math. I have never _____ those complicated math problems.

Chapter 5
Asking Questions

▶ **Practice 1. Short answers for yes/no questions.** (Chart 5-1)
Read the interview and circle the correct completions.

Job Interview

1. ANA LOPEZ: Hello! I'm looking for the biochemistry department. There's no number on the door. Is this the right place?

   PROFESSOR HIATT: Yes, it _____.
   a. does   b. has   c. is

2. PROF: And you must be the student who called for an interview! Are you Ana Lopez?

   ANA: Yes, I _____.
   a. do   b. am   c. have

3. PROF: I'm Professor Hiatt. It's nice to meet you. Welcome to the biochemistry department.

   ANA: Thank you. I'm very glad to meet you.

   PROF: Well, first of all, we want an assistant who really likes to work on research projects in the lab. Do you like that kind of work?

   ANA: Yes, I _____. I like it very much.
   a. do   b. am   c. have

4. PROF: Good. Have you had a lot of experience in a biochemistry lab?

   ANA: Yes, I _____. I worked as the student assistant in high school. And I also worked at a small chemical company for two summers.
   a. do   b. am   c. have

   PROF: Did you work on any research projects at that company?

   ANA: Yes, I _____. I assisted two chemists in medical research.
   a. did   b. have   c. do

5. PROF: Now, are you taking a lot of classes this semester?

   ANA: Yes, I _____. I'm taking biology, statistics, and two chemistry courses.
   a. do   b. am   c. will

6. PROF: Those are difficult classes. Will you have time to study and work here in the lab too?

   ANA: Yes, I _____.
   a. do   b. will   c. have

Make questions using the information in B's response.

		helping verb	subject	main verb	rest of sentence
1.	SIMPLE	A: _Do_	_you_	_like_	_coffee?_
	PRESENT	B: Yes, I like coffee.			

		helping verb	subject	main verb	rest of sentence
2.	SIMPLE	A: _____	_____	_____	_____
	PRESENT	B: Yes, Tom likes coffee.			

		helping verb	subject	main verb	rest of sentence
3.	PRESENT	A: _____	_____	_____	_____
	PROGRESSIVE	B: Yes, Pietro is watching TV.			

		helping verb	subject	main verb	rest of sentence
4.	PRESENT	A: _____	_____	_____	_____
	PROGRESSIVE	B: Yes, I'm having lunch with Raja.			

		helping verb	subject	main verb	rest of sentence
5.	SIMPLE	A: _____	_____	_____	_____
	PAST	B: Yes, Rafael walked to school.			

		helping verb	subject	main verb	rest of sentence
6.	PAST	A: _____	_____	_____	_____
	PROGRESSIVE	B: Yes, Clarita was taking a nap.			

		helping verb	subject	main verb	rest of sentence
7.	SIMPLE	A: _____	_____	_____	_____
	FUTURE	B: Yes, Ted will come to the meeting.			

		form of *be*	subject	rest of sentence
8.	MAIN VERB: *BE*	A: _____	_____	_____
	SIMPLE			
	PRESENT	B: Yes, Ingrid is a good artist.		

		form of *be*	subject	rest of sentence
9.	MAIN VERB: *BE*	A: _____	_____	_____
	SIMPLE PAST	B: Yes, I was at the wedding.		

► **Practice 3. Yes/no questions and short answers.** (Chart 5-1)
Choose the correct completions.

1. A: (*Is / Does*) this your new laptop?
   B: Yes, it (*is / does*).

2. A: It's so small. (*Is / Does*) it difficult to see text on that tiny screen?
   B: No, it (*isn't / doesn't*).

3. A: (*Is / Does*) it run on a battery?
   B: Yes, it (*has / does*).

4. A: (*Do / Are*) you carry it with you all day?
   B: Yes, I (*am / do*).

5. A: (*Have / Do*) you had it for a long time?
   B: No, I (*haven't / don't*).

6. A: (*Was / Did*) it cost a lot?
   B: No, it (*wasn't / didn't*).

7. A: (*Are / Do*) you going to take it on your trip to Africa?
   B: Yes, I (*am / do*).

8. A: (*Are / Will*) you send emails from Africa ?
   B: Yes, I (*am / will*).

► **Practice 4. Yes/no questions and short answers.** (Chart 5-1)
Complete the conversations. Use the correct forms of **be**, **do**, **have**, or **will**.

1. A: I need a map. _____*Do*_____ you have one?
   B: No, I _____*don't*_____.

2. A: _____*Are*_____ the Andes Mountains in North America?
   B: No, they _____*aren't*_____.

3. A: _____ Africa the largest continent?
   B: No, it _____. Asia is.

4. A: _____ rivers flow toward the oceans?
   B: Yes, they _____.

5. A: _____ penguins live in the Arctic?
   B: No, they _____. They live in Antarctica.

6. A: _____ a penguin swim under water?
   B: Yes, it _____.

7. A: _____ the Nile the longest river in the world?
   B: Yes, it _____.

8. A: _____ it snow in Hawaii?
   B: No, it _____. It's too warm there for snow.

9. A: _____ 2029 be a leap year?

B: No, it _____. A leap year is a year that you can divide by 4, like 2012, 2016, and 2020.

▶ **Practice 5. Yes/no questions.** (Chart 5-1)
The chart describes the exam schedule of four students. Complete the conversations using the information in the chart.

	Last week	This week	Next week
Jane		math	computer science
George	Spanish		business
Anna		biology	chemistry
John	history		

1. A: _____Does Jane_____ have an exam this week?

   B: Yes, _____she does._____ (Jane has an exam this week.)

2. A: _____ have an exam this week?

   B: No, _____. (George doesn't have an exam this week.)

3. A: _____ have exams this week?

   B: Yes, _____. (Jane and Anna have exams this week.)

4. A: _____ have an exam last week?

   B: No, _____. (Jane didn't have an exam last week.)

5. A: _____ have an exam last week?

   B: Yes, _____. (George had an exam last week.)

6. A: _____ have exams last week?

   B: No, _____. (Jane and Anna didn't have exams last week.)

7. A: _____ have exams last week?

   B: Yes, _____. (George and John had exams last week.)

8. A: _____ have an exam next week?

   B: Yes, _____. (Jane will have an exam next week.)

9. A: _____ have an exam next week?

   B: Yes, _____. (George and Anna will have exams next week.)

10. A: _____ have an exam next week?

    B: No, _____. (John will not have an exam next week.)

▶ **Practice 6. Forming information questions.** (Chart 5-2)
Choose the correct completion.

1. Phil works **someplace**.

   Where (*works Phil* / *does Phil work*) ?

2. He works **sometimes**.

   When (*does Phil work* / *works Phil*) ?

3. Marta is making **something**.

   What (*Marta is making* / *is Marta making*) ?

4. She said **something**.

   What (*did she say* / *she said*) ?

5. Jean and Don visited **someone**.

   Who (*Jean and Don did visit* / *did Jean and Don visit*) ?

6. They visited her **for a reason**.

   Why (*did they visit her* / *they visited her*) ?

▶ **Practice 7. Yes/no and information questions.** (Charts 5-1 and 5-2)
Complete the sentences with words from the list.

| Does | Is | When | Where |

1. _____ Marvin work in a restaurant?
2. _____ does Marvin work? Downtown?
3. _____ Marvin working today?
4. _____ does Marvin have a day off? On Saturday?

| Are | Will | When | Where |

5. _____ Mike and Kate get married next year?
6. _____ will Mike and Kate get married? Soon?
7. _____ they going to have a honeymoon?
8. _____ are they going to go on their honeymoon? Hawaii?

| Did | Is | When | Where |

9. _____ Iris in class now?
10. _____ is Iris?
11. _____ she come to class yesterday?
12. _____ will Iris come back to class?

► **Practice 8. Yes/no and information questions.** (Charts 5-1 and 5-2)
Make questions using the information in B's response. Write Ø if no word is needed.

	(question word)	helping verb	subject	main verb	rest of sentence
1. A:	Ø	Did	you	hear	the news yesterday?

B: Yes, I did. (I heard the news yesterday.)

	(question word)	helping verb	subject	main verb	rest of sentence
2. A:	When	did	you	hear	the news?

B: Yesterday. (I heard the news yesterday.)

	(question word)	helping verb	subject	main verb	rest of sentence
3. A:	Ø				

B: Yes, he is. (Eric is traveling in South America.)

	(question word)	helping verb	subject	main verb	rest of sentence
4. A:					Ø

B: In South America. (Eric is traveling in South America.)

	(question word)	helping verb	subject	main verb	rest of sentence
5. A:					

B: Yes, it will. (The class will end in December.)

	(question word)	helping verb	subject	main verb	rest of sentence
6. A:					

B: In December. (The class will end in December.)

	(question word)	helping verb	subject	main verb	rest of sentence
7. A:					

B: Yes, she did. (The teacher helped a student.)

	(question word)	helping verb	subject	main verb	rest of sentence
8. A:					

B: Mei Lei. (The teacher helped Mei Lei.)

	(question word)	helping verb	subject	main verb	rest of sentence
9. A:					

B: Yes, he will. (The chef will cook his special chicken dinner tonight.)

	(question word)	helping verb	subject	main verb	rest of sentence
10. A:					

B: His special chicken dinner. (The chef will cook his special chicken dinner tonight.)

► **Practice 9. Yes/no and information questions.** (Charts 5-1 and 5-2)
Read the passage. Then write questions using the given words, and circle the correct answers.
Capitalize the first word of the question.

Apples

Apple trees first grew in central Asia thousands of years ago. Today apples grow in cooler climates all over the world. Each spring, apple trees produce pink flowers. In the summer and fall, the trees produce apples. Inside each apple there are tiny brown seeds. If you plant these seeds, some of them will become new apple trees.

1. *did, originate, apple trees, where*

    _____Where did apple trees originate_____?
    a. Yes, they did.   b. In central Asia.

2. *do, where, grow, apple trees*

    _____?
    a. Yes, they do.   b. In cooler climates everywhere.

3. *they, do, grow*

    _____ in hot climates?
    a. No, they don't.   b. In central Asia.

4. *do, apples, the trees, produce*

    _____ in the summer and fall?
    a. Yes, they do.   b. Apples.

5. *produce, do, they, when*

    _____ pink flowers?
    a. Yes, they do.   b. In the spring.

6. *what, find, you, do*

    _____ inside each apple?
    a. Yes, you do.   b. Seeds.

7. *some of the seeds, become, will*

    _____ new apple trees?
    a. Yes, they will.   b. New apple seeds.

► **Practice 10.** *Where, When, What time, Why, How come, What . . . for.*
(Chart 5-3)
For each question, write the correct completion from Column B.

Column A	Column B
1. _____ do oranges come from? Florida.	a. What
2. _____ is the sky blue? Because the sun reflects the light in a certain way.	b. What time
3. _____ did the 21st century begin? In the year 2000.	c. When d. Where
4. _____ is the flight going to arrive? At 5:30.	e. Why
5. _____ you left early? I went to the dentist.	f. How come
6. _____ did you go to the dentist for? I had a bad toothache.	

► **Practice 11.** *Why, How come, and What for.* (Chart 5-3)
Rewrite the sentences beginning with the given words.

1. What are you going downtown for?
   a. How come _____?
   b. Why _____?

2. Why did Paul leave early?
   a. What _____?
   b. How come _____?

3. How come your clothes are on the floor?
   a. Why _____?
   b What _____?

4. What does Mira need more money for?
   a. How come _____?
   b. Why _____?

► **Practice 12.** *Where, Why, When, and What time.* (Chart 5-3)
Make information questions. Use *where*, *why*, *when*, or *what time*. Use the information in
parentheses in your question.

1. A: _____ to see the principal?
   B: Because I need his signature on this application. (I'm waiting to see the principal because I
      need his signature on this application.)

2. A: _____ her new job?
   B: Next Monday morning. (Rachel starts her new job next Monday morning.)

3. A: _____ the business meeting?

   B: Because I fell asleep after dinner and didn't wake up until 9:00. (I missed the meeting because I fell asleep after dinner and didn't wake up until 9:00.)

4. A: _____ for home?

   B: Next Saturday. (I'm leaving for home next Saturday.)

5. A: _____ to finish this project?

   B: Next month. (I expect to finish this project next month.)

6. A: _____ today?

   B: At the cafeteria. (I ate lunch at the cafeteria today.)

7. A: _____ lunch?

   B: At 12:15. (I ate lunch at 12:15.)

8. A: _____ at the cafeteria?

   B: Because the food is good. (I eat lunch at the cafeteria because the food is good.)

9. A: _____?

   B: From Osaka to Tokyo. (The bullet train goes from Osaka to Tokyo.)

10. A: _____

    from New York to Los Angeles ?

    B: One day in the future, I think! (They will build a bullet train from New York to Los Angeles one day in the future.)

11. A: _____ English?

    B: In Germany. (I studied English in Germany.)

12. A: _____ English in Germany?

    B: Because I had a scholarship to study in Germany. (I studied English in Germany because I had a scholarship to study in Germany.)

▶ **Practice 13. Who, Who(m), and What.** (Chart 5-4)
Write "S" over the boldface word if it is the subject of the verb. Write "O" over the word if it is the object of the verb. Then make questions with *who*, *who(m)*, and *what*.

       S

1. **Someone** is talking.

   _____ Who is talking _____ ?

       O

2. We hear **someone**.

   _____ Who(m) do we hear _____ ?

3. You know **someone** in my class.

   _____ in my class?

4. **Someone** was on TV last night.

   _____ last night?

5. **Something** is happening in that building.

   _____ in that building?

6. Jason knows **something**.

_____?

7. Gilda called **someone**.

_____?

8. **Someone** answered the phone.

_____?

9. You said **something**.

_____?

10. **Something** is important.

_____?

▶ **Practice 14. Who, Who(m), and What.** (Chart 5-4)
Complete the questions with *who*, *who(m)*, or *what*.
Part I. Looking for the subject.

At an Office Meeting

1. _____ happened at the meeting?

2. _____ was there?

3. _____ spoke about the reorganization of the company?

4. _____ is going on in the finance department?

5. _____ is going to be the next chief financial officer?

6. _____ is the problem with the air-conditioning system?

Part II. Looking for the object.

Planning a Dinner Party

1. _____ are you inviting to dinner?

2. _____ has already responded?

3. _____ are you going to serve, meat or fish?

4. _____ do you need to buy for the dinner?

5. _____ are you going to make for dessert?

6. _____ do you need me to do?

▶ **Practice 15. Who, Who(m), and What.** (Chart 5-4)
Make questions with *who*, *who(m)*, and *what*.

	QUESTION	ANSWER
1.	_Who knows Julio?_	**Someone** knows Julio.
2.	_Who(m) does Julio know?_	Julio knows **someone**.
3.	_____	**Someone** will help us.
4.	_____	I will ask **someone**.
5.	_____	Eric is talking to **someone** on the phone.
6.	_____	**Someone** is knocking on the door.

7. _____ **Something** surprised them.

8. _____ Jack said **something**.

9. _____ Sue talked about **something**.

10. _____ Rosa talked about **someone**.

▶ **Practice 16. Who, Who(m), and What.** (Chart 5-4)
Make questions using the information in parentheses.

1. A: _____*Who taught*_____ you to play chess?
   B: My mother. (My mother taught me to play chess.)

2. A: _____?
   B: A bank robbery. (Robert saw a bank robbery.)

3. A: _____ a good look at the bank robber?
   B: Robert did. (Robert got a good look at the bank robber.)

4. A: _____?
   B: A toy for my brother's children. (I'm making a toy for my brother's children.)

5. A: _____ to?
   B: Joe. (That cell phone belongs to Joe.)

6. A: _____ on the front window of your car?
   B: A parking ticket. (A parking ticket is on the front window of my car.)

▶ **Practice 17. Asking for the meaning of a word.** (Chart 5-4)
Ask for the meaning of the words in *italics*. Complete the conversations in your own words.

1. A: Jenny is going to study *abroad* next year.
   B: What _____*does "abroad" mean*_____?
      It means _____*in a foreign country*_____.

2. A: The kitten is hiding *underneath* the blanket.
   B: _____?
   A: It means _____.

3. A: The weather this winter has been *mild*.
   B: _____?
   A: It means _____.

4. A: Todd thinks I'm *cool*.
   B: _____?
   A: It means _____.

5. A: My boss says that I'm *industrious*.
   B: _____?
   A: It means _____.

Make questions using ***what*** and a form of ***do***. Use the information in parentheses. Use the same verb tense that is <u>underlined</u> in parentheses.

1. A: _____<u>*What is Alex doing*</u>_____ now?
   B: Watching a movie on TV. (Alex <u>is watching</u> a movie on TV.)

2. A: _____ last weekend?
   B: Nothing. We just stayed home. (We did nothing last weekend. We just <u>stayed</u> home.)

3. A: _____?
   B: They explore space. (Astronauts <u>explore</u> space.)

4. A: _____ next Saturday morning?
   B: Play tennis at Waterfall Park.
      (I'<u>m going to play</u> tennis at Waterfall Park next Saturday morning.)

5. A: _____ when she heard the good news?
   B: She cried with happiness. (Sara <u>cried</u> with happiness when she heard the good news.)

6. A: _____ after she graduates?
   B: I think she plans to look for a job in hotel management. (Emily <u>is going to look</u> for a job in hotel management after she graduates.)

7. A: _____ after school today?
   B: Let's go to the mall, okay? (I <u>want</u> to go to the mall after school today.)

8. A: _____ for a living?
   B: He's an airplane mechanic. (Nick <u>repairs</u> airplanes for a living.)

▶ **Practice 19. Using *which* and *what*.** (Chart 5-6)
Choose the correct word in each sentence.

1. A: Ali broke his hand playing basketball.
   B: That's terrible. (*Which* / *What*) hand did he break, the right or left?

2. A: I heard the president's speech last night. Did you?
   B: No, I didn't. (*Which* / *What*) did he say about the economy?

3. A: This book is excellent. It's the best book I have ever read.
   B: Really? (*Which* / *What*) is it about?

4. A: Look at those two pandas! They are so cute.
   B: They are. (*Which* / *What*) one is the mother and (*which* / *what*) one is the daughter?

5. A: We have an invitation to the art show on Friday night.
   B: I'd like to go. But I've never been to an art show before. (*Which* / *What*) do people wear to art shows?

6. A: Alec lives on this street, right?
   B: This is the street, but (*which* / *what*) house is it? Do you have the exact address?

7. A: I don't have the address.
   B: Let's call him. (*Which* / *What*) is his phone number?

8. A: Hey, Bernie! I'm surprised to see you here.

   B: Hey, Marty! (*Which* / *What*) are you doing these days?

   A: Me? Not much. But my son just got an offer from the Broilers to play professional soccer on their team.

   B: That's great! Uh . . . (*which* / *what*) son is that? Is it Jeff?

   A: No. Jeff's in medical school. I'm talking about Alan, my youngest.

▶ **Practice 20. Using *which* and *what kind of.*** (Chart 5-6)
Make questions with ***what kind of*** and one of the nouns in the list for each question.

books	clothes	Italian food	✓music
car	government	job	person

1. A: _____What kind of music_____ do you like?

   B: Rock 'n roll.

2. A: _____ do you usually wear?

   B: Jeans and a T-shirt.

3. A: _____ do you like best?

   B: Pizza with double cheese, onions, peppers, and garlic.

4. A: _____ do you like to read?

   B: Romance novels.

5. A: _____ are you going to buy?

   B: A hybrid. One that uses a battery and gas.

6. A: _____ does your country have?

   B: It's a democratic republic.

7. A: _____ would you like to have?

   B: I'd like to have one that pays well, is interesting, and allows me to travel a lot.

8. A: _____ would you like to marry?

   B: Someone who is kind-hearted, loving, funny, serious, and steady.

▶ **Practice 21. *Who* vs. *Whose.*** (Chart 5-7)
Complete the questions with ***who*** or ***whose***.

1. A: _____Who_____ is driving to the game tonight?

   B: Heidi is.

2. A: _____Whose_____ car are we taking to the game?

   B: Heidi's.

3. A: This notebook is mine. _____ is that? Is it yours?

   B: No, it's Sara's.

4. A: There's Ms. Adams. _____ is standing next to her?

   B: Mr. Wilson.

5. A: _____ was the first woman doctor in the United States?

   B: Elizabeth Blackwell. She became a doctor in 1849.

6. A: _____ forgot to put the ice cream back in the freezer?

   B: I don't know. It wasn't me!

7. A: _____ suitcase did you borrow for your trip?

   B: Andy's.

▶ **Practice 22. *Who* vs. *Whose*.** (Chart 5-7)
Make questions with ***who*** or ***whose***.

1. A: _____*Whose house is that?*_____

   B: Pat's. (That's Pat's house.)

2. A: _____*Who's living in that house?*_____

   B: Pat. (Pat is living in that house.)

3. A: _____

   B: Pedro's. (I borrowed Pedro's umbrella.)

4. A: _____

   B: Linda's. (I used Linda's book.)

5. A: _____

   B: Nick's. (Nick's book is on the table.)

6. A: _____

   B: Nick. (Nick is on the phone.)

7. A: _____

   B: Sue Smith. (That's Sue Smith.) She's a student in my class.

8. A: _____

   B: Sue's. (That's Sue's.) This one is mine.

▶ **Practice 23. Using *How*.** (Chart 5-8)
Complete the sentences with appropriate words from the list.

busy	fresh	safe	soon
expensive	✓hot	serious	well

1. A: How ____*hot*____ does it get in Chicago in the summer?

   B: Very ____*hot*____. It can get over 100°.*

2. A: How _____ will dinner be ready? I'm really hungry.

   B: In just a few more minutes.

3. A: Look at that beautiful painting! Let's get it.

   B: How _____ is it?

   A: Oh, my gosh! Never mind. We can't afford it.

4. A: How _____ are you today, Ted? Do you have time to read over this report?

   B: Well, I am really _____, but I'll make time to read it.

---

*100°F = 37.8°C

5. A: How _____ is Toshi about becoming an astronomer?

   B: He's very _____ about it. He already knows more about the stars and planets than his high school teachers.

6. A: How _____ is a car with an airbag?

   B: Statistics say that cars with airbags are very safe.

7. A: Tomatoes for sale! Do you want to buy some tomatoes?

   B: Hmmm. They look pretty good. How _____ are they?

   A: They are really _____. I picked them myself from the field just this morning.

8. A: Do you know Jack Young?

   B: Yes.

   A: Oh? How _____ do you know him?

   B: Very _____. He's one of my closest friends. Why?

   A: He's applied for a job at my store.

▶ **Practice 24. Using *How often*.** (Chart 5-9)
Complete the questions using *how often* or *how many times*.

1. A: (*How often / How many times*) are the summer Olympic Games held?

   B: The summer games are held every four years.

2. A: (*How often / How many times*) have the Olympic Games been held in Australia? One or two?

   B: Two, I think. In 1956 and in 2000.

3. A: (*How often / How many times*) did Michael Phelps compete in the Olympics?

   B: I'm not sure. Maybe three or four.

4. A: (*How often / How many times*) do you take vitamin C?

   B: I take it every day. I think it prevents colds.

5. A: (*How often / How many times*) do you get a cold?

   B: Rarely. I rarely get a cold.

6. A: (*How often / How many times*) a year do you visit your doctor?

   B: Sometimes none! I never see my doctor unless I'm sick.

▶ **Practice 25. Using *How far, It + take,* and *How long*.** (Charts 5-10 and 5-11).
Read each paragraph and write questions. Include the word in parentheses in your question. Use the correct tenses, according to the paragraph.

1. The Nile River is the longest river in the world. It is about 6,677 kilometers, or 4,150 miles, long. It flows from Burundi in eastern Africa to the Mediterranean Sea in northeast Egypt. A slow ship takes several days to make the trip.

   A: (*far*) _____ from the beginning, or source, of the Nile River to the end of the Nile River?

   B: It's a long way.

A: (*miles*) _____ from the source of the

Nile River to the end of the Nile River?

B: About 4,150.

A: (*long*) _____ a slow ship to make the trip?

B: Several days.

2. Mount Everest is 8,850 meters, or 29,035 feet high — the highest mountain in the world. It is in the central Himalaya Mountains, on the border of Tibet and Nepal. Edmund Hillary and his group climbed to the top of the mountain in 1953. It took them seven weeks to get to the top but only three days to come down.

A: (*high*) _____?

B: It's very high. It's more than 29,000 feet high.

A: (*meters*) _____?

B: It's 8,850.

A: (*long*) _____ Edmund Hillary and his

group to climb Mount Everest?

B: Seven weeks.

A: (*days*) _____ them to come down

from the top of the mountain?

B: Three.

3. The Trans-Siberian Railway is the longest railway in the world. It goes from Moscow to Vladivostok on the Sea of Japan, a distance of 9,311 kilometers, or 5,786 miles. The trip takes seven days.

A: (*long*) _____ the Trans-Siberian Railway?

B: Very long. Over 9,100 kilometers.

A: (*miles*) _____ the Trans-Siberian Railway?

B: It's 5,786.

A: (*days*) _____ to go from Moscow

to Vladivostok on the Trans-Siberian Railway?

B: Seven.

▶ **Practice 26. Using *How often, How far,* and *How long*.** (Charts 5-9 → 5-11)
Complete the questions with *far*, *long*, or *often*.

1. A: How ___far___ is it to the nearest police station?
   B: Four blocks.

2. A: How _____ does it take you to get to work?
   B: Forty-five minutes.

3. A: How _____ do you see your family?
   B: Once a week.

4. A: How _____ is it to your office from home?
   B: About twenty miles.

5. A: How _____ is it from here to the airport?
   B: Ten kilometers.

6. A: How _____ does it take to get to the airport?
   B: Fifteen minutes.

7. A: How _____ above sea level is Denver, Colorado?
   B: One mile. That's why it's called the Mile High City.

8. A: How _____ does it take to fly from Chicago to Denver?
   B: About three hours.

9. A: How _____ does the bus come?
   B: Every two hours.

10. A: How _____ is it from here to the bus stop?
    B: About two blocks.

11. A: How _____ does the ride downtown take?
    B: About twenty minutes.

12. A: How _____ do you take the bus?
    B: Every day.

▶ **Practice 27. More questions with *How.*** (Chart 5-13)
Make simple present tense questions with *how* and *you* as the subject. Use the verbs in the list only once.

feel	like	pronounce	say	spell

1. A: _____?
   B: I spell my name R-I-C-H-A-R-D.

2. A: _____ your eggs?
   B: I like them scrambled, not too hard.

3. A: _____ *I love you* in French?
   B: *Je t'aime.* That's how you say it.

4. A: _____ *Mississippi*?
   B: This is how you pronounce it: say *missus* – like *Mrs.,* and then say *sip* like *sip a drink with a straw,* and then *E* like the letter *E.*

5. A: _____ about losing your job?
   B: Pretty bad, as you would expect.

▶ **Practice 28. Using *How about* and *What about.*** (Chart 5-13)
Write the letter of the appropriate response for each conversation.

1. A: We aren't taking a vacation this summer. What about you?
   B: _____. Jim can't leave his job right now.

   a. We're staying home too.
   b. No, we didn't.
   c. Oh? Where are you going this year?

2. A: I really don't like our history professor. How about you?

   B: _____.

       a. I don't feel well today.
       b. What's the matter with her? I like her a lot.
       c. Yes, I will.

3. A: I'm voting for the new, young candidate. How about you?

   B: Not me. _____.

       a. Where are you going?
       b. I think I will.
       c. I like the older guy, the one with experience.

4. A: I like sailing and being on the water. I like it a lot. How about you?

   B: _____.

       a. I love it.
       b. Yes, I have.
       c. Yes, I did.

5. A: You don't eat meat, sir? What about fish? We have an excellent salmon tonight.

   B: _____.

       a. No, thank you. I don't take sugar with my coffee.
       b. Okay, I'll have that.
       c. Yes, I am.

6. A: I thought the concert was the best concert I had ever been to. How about you?

   B: _____.

       a. The book was excellent.
       b. I like music.
       c. Me too.

▶ **Practice 29. Review of questions.** (Charts 5-1 → 5-14)
Make questions using the given words.

1. *be, dry, the clothes, will*

   A: When _____*will the clothes be dry*_____?
   B: In about an hour.

2. *did, do, you*

   A: What _____ on Saturday afternoon?
   B: I went to a baseball game.

3. *book, download, did, you*

   A: Which _____?
   B: A novel by Jorge Amado.

4. *did, it, long, take*

   A: How _____ to clean your apartment
   before your parents visited?
   B: Four hours.

5. *bread, do, like, you*

   A: What kind of _____?

   B: I don't like bread. I never eat it.

6. *are, calling, me, you*

   A: Why _____ so late at night?

   B: Sorry! I hit the wrong number on my phone and dialed you by mistake.

7. *are, meeting, you*

   A: Who _____ at the restaurant?

   B: Maria and her sister.

8. *is, you, taking*

   A. Who _____ to the airport?

   B: Eric.

9. *are, leaving, you*

   A: How come _____ so early?

   B: I'm really very tired.

▶ **Practice 30. Review of questions.** (Charts 5-1 → 5-14)
Complete the conversations by writing questions for the given answers. Use the information in parentheses to form the questions.

A Tennis Game

1. A: _____*What is Jack doing*_____ now?

   B: He's playing tennis. (Jack is playing tennis.)

2. A: _____ with?

   B: Anna. (He is playing tennis with Anna.)

3. A: _____?

   B: Serving the ball. (Anna is serving the ball.)

4. A: _____ in the air?

   B: A tennis ball. (She is throwing a tennis ball in the air.)

5. A: _____?

   B: Rackets. (Anna and Jack are holding rackets.)

6. A: _____ between them?

   B: A net. (A net is between them.)

7. A: _____?

   B: On a tennis court. (They are on a tennis court.)

8. A: _____?

   B: For an hour and a half. (They have been playing for an hour and a half.)

9. A: _____ right now?

   B: Jack. (Jack is winning right now.)

10. A: _____ the last game?

    B: Anna. (Anna won the last game.)

▶ **Practice 31. Tag questions.** (Chart 5-15)
Complete the tag questions with the correct verbs.

1. Simple present
   a. You work at the university, _____*don't*_____ you?
   b. Claire teaches at Midwood High School, _____ she?
   c. Bob and Mike sell real estate, _____ they?
   d. Kevin has a van, _____ he?
   e. You're in Professor Rossiter's class, _____ you?
   f. Your mother likes green tea, _____ she?
   g. Jill and Andrew don't have any children yet, _____ they?
   h. Bryan isn't a lawyer, _____ he?
   i. I'm not wrong, _____ I?

2. Simple past
   a. Jennifer went to Mexico, _____ she?
   b. You spoke to Paul about this, _____ you?
   c. That was a good idea, _____ it?
   d. The police officer didn't give you a ticket, _____ he?
   e. John and Mary had a fight, _____ they?

3. Present progressive, *be going to,* and past progressive
   a. You're coming tomorrow, _____ you?
   b. Jim isn't working at the bank, _____ he?
   c. It's probably going to snow tomorrow, _____ it?
   d. Susie was sleeping in class, _____ she?
   e. The printer was working, _____ it?
   f. They weren't leaving, _____ they?

4. Present perfect
   a. The weather has been nice this spring, _____ it?
   b. We've had a lot of work this semester, _____ we?
   c. You haven't told the truth, _____ you?
   d. Shirley has gone home already, _____ she?
   e. Natalie hasn't left yet, _____ she?
   f. I have never met you before, _____ I?

▶ **Practice 32. Tag questions.** (Chart 5-15)
Add tag questions. Write the <u>expected</u> responses.

1. A: You've already seen that movie, _____*haven't you*_____?
   B: _____*Yes, I have*_____.

2. A: John hasn't called, _____?
   B: _____.

3. A: You talked to Mike last night, _____?
   B: _____.

4. A: You usually bring your lunch to school, _____?
   B: _____.

5. A: Rita and Philip have been married for five years, _____?
   B: _____.

6. A: Kathy has already finished her work, _____?
   B: _____.

7. A: This isn't a hard exercise, _____?
   B: _____.

8. A: Tony Wah lives in Los Angeles, _____?
   B: _____.

9. A: Tomorrow isn't a holiday, _____?
   B: _____.

10. A: This isn't your book, _____?
    B: _____.

11. A: Jack and Elizabeth were in class yesterday, _____?
    B: _____.

12. A: Maria won't be here for dinner tonight, _____?
    B: _____.

▶ **Practice 33. Editing.** (Chapter 5)
Correct the errors.

Who
1. ~~Whom~~ saw the car accident?

2. How about ask Julie and Tim to come for dinner Friday night?

3. What time class begins today?

4. Where people go to get a driver's license in this city?

5. How long it takes to get to the beach from here?

6. She is working late tonight, doesn't she?

7. Who's glasses are those?

8. How much tall your father?

9. Who you talked to about registration for next term?

10. How come are you here so early today?

▶ **Practice 34. Review: questions.** (Chapter 5)

Make questions using the information in parentheses.

1. A: _____*When are you going to buy*_____ a new bicycle?
   B: Next week. (I'm going to buy a new bicycle next week.)

2. A: _____*How are you going to pay*_____ for it?
   B: With my credit card. (I'm going to pay for it with my credit card.)

3. A: _____ your old bike?
   B: Ten years. (I have had my old bike for ten years.)

4. A: _____ your bike?
   B: Four or five times a week. (I ride my bike four or five times a week.)

5. A: _____ to work?
   B: I usually ride my bike. (I usually get to work by riding my bike.)

6. A: _____ your bike to work today?
   B: No. Today I got a ride. (I didn't ride my bike to work today.)

7. A: Oh. _____ you a ride?
   B: Paul did. (Paul gave me a ride.)

8. A: _____ your bike over the weekend?
   B: Yes, I did. (I rode my bike over the weekend.)

9. A: _____ over the weekend?
   B: Twenty-five miles. (I rode my bike twenty-five miles over the weekend.)

10. A: _____ a comfortable seat?
    B: Yes, it does. (My bike has a comfortable seat.)

11. A: _____?
    B: A ten-speed bike. (I have a ten-speed bike.)

12. A: _____ his new bike?
    B: Two weeks ago. (Jason got his new bike two weeks ago.)

13. A: _____ Jason's new bike?
    B: Billy. (Billy broke Jason's new bike.)

14. A: _____?
    B: He ran it into a brick wall. (He broke it by running it into a brick wall.)

15. A: _____?

    B: No, he didn't. (Billy didn't get hurt.)

16. A: _____?

    B: No, it didn't. Only one wheel fell off. (The bike didn't have a lot of damage.)

17. A: _____?

    B: The front wheel. (The front wheel fell off, not the back wheel.)

18. A: _____?

    B: No, he hasn't. (Jason hasn't fixed the bike yet.)

▶ **Practice 35. Crossword puzzle.** (Chapter 5)
Complete the crossword puzzle. Use the clues to find the correct words.

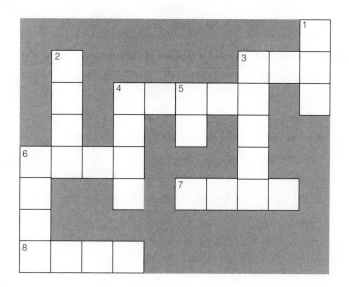

Across

3. I need someone to translate this letter from Chinese. _____ speaks Chinese?

4. _____ hand do you write with, your right or your left?

6. _____ you at home last night? I called, but no one answered.

7. _____ Florida have any mountains?

8. I need to buy some flour. What _____ do the stores open?

Down

1. _____ far is the main road from here?

2. How long does it _____ to go downtown on the bus?

3. _____ are you going now? To your yoga lesson?

4. _____ are you going to return? This afternoon or tonight?

5. _____ Rome the capital of Italy?

6. _____ happened over there? I see several police cars.

Chapter 6
Nouns and Pronouns

▶ **Practice 1. Forms of nouns.** (Chart 6-1)
Read the paragraph. Circle each singular noun. Underline each plural noun.

Sharks

A (shark) is a fish. Sharks live in oceans all over the world. Some types are very large. The largest shark is the size of a bus. It has 3,000 teeth, in five rows in its mouth. When one tooth falls out, a new tooth grows in quickly. Many sharks are dangerous, and people try to avoid them.

▶ **Practice 2. Forms of nouns.** (Chart 6-1)
Write the plural form of the noun under each heading.

apple	child	lamp	river
bed	city	man	shelf
carrot	country	mouse	table
cat	fox	ocean	tomato
cherry	lake	peach	tiger

Living things that breathe	Furniture	Places on a map	Fruits and vegetables

▶ Practice 3. Forms of nouns. (Chart 6-1)
Write the correct singular or plural form of the given words.

1. one house   two ___*houses*___
2. a ___*door*___   two doors
3. one box   a lot of _____
4. one _____   three shelves
5. a copy   two _____
6. a family   several _____
7. a _____   two women
8. one child   three _____
9. one fish   several _____
10. a _____   a lot of flies
11. a dish   two _____
12. a glass   many _____
13. one _____   two dollars
14. one euro   ten _____
15. a _____   several roofs
16. one life   many _____
17. a radio   a few _____

▶ Practice 4. Forms of nouns. (Chart 6-1)
Underline each noun. Write the correct plural if necessary. Do not change any other words.

1. Airplane*s* have wing*s*.

2. Some baby are born with a few tooth.

3. Child like to play on swing.

4. A child is playing on our swing now.

5. I eat a lot of potato, bean, pea, and tomato.

6. I had a sandwich for lunch.

7. Some animal live in zoo.

8. Human have two foot.

9. The government of my country is a democracy.

10. Government collect tax.

► **Practice 5. Subjects, verbs, and objects.** (Chart 6-3)
Write "S" over the subject and "V" over the verb. If there is an object, write "O" over it.

       S   V   O
1. Caroline dropped a dish.

2. The dish fell.

3. The noise woke her baby.

4. The baby cried.

5. Caroline rocked her baby.

6. The phone rang.

7. A man came to the door.

8. The dog barked loudly.

9. Caroline answered the door.

► **Practice 6. Subjects, verbs, and objects.** (Chart 6-3)
Write the words in the lists in the correct order. Capitalize the first word in each sentence.
Write a **Ø** if there is no object.

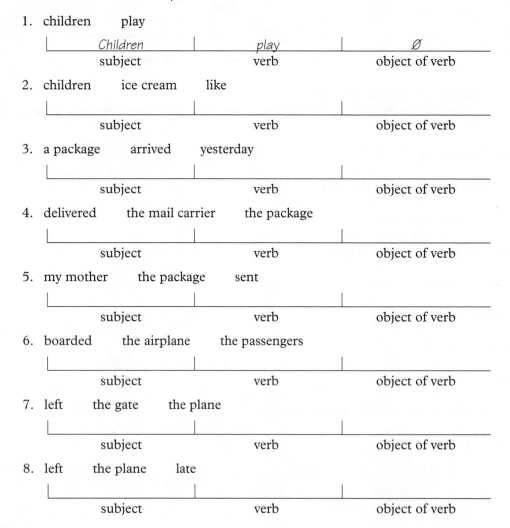

1. children   play

Children	*play*	*Ø*
subject	verb	object of verb

2. children   ice cream   like

subject	verb	object of verb

3. a package   arrived   yesterday

subject	verb	object of verb

4. delivered   the mail carrier   the package

subject	verb	object of verb

5. my mother   the package   sent

subject	verb	object of verb

6. boarded   the airplane   the passengers

subject	verb	object of verb

7. left   the gate   the plane

subject	verb	object of verb

8. left   the plane   late

subject	verb	object of verb

► **Practice 7. Subjects, verbs, and objects.** (Chart 6-3)
Decide whether the word in **bold** is a noun or a verb. Write "N" for noun and "V" for verb above the word.

                                N

1. Andy hurt his **hand**.

                             V

2. Students **hand** in homework assignments to their teachers.

3. Ed has a loud **laugh**.

4. People always **laugh** at the comedian's jokes.

5. I usually **wash** my car on Saturday.

6. Maria put a big **wash** in the washing machine.

7. The Northeast got a lot of **snow** last night.

8. It's going to **snow** tomorrow.

9. The **text** is too small for me to read.

10. I **text** several friends every day.

11. Please **sign** your name on the dotted line.

12. The **sign** says *No left turn*.

► **Practice 8. Objects of prepositions.** (Chart 6-4)
Describe the picture. Complete the sentences with the correct prepositions.

1. The bird is (*in* / *on*) the cage.

2. The bird is standing (*in* / *on*) the bar.

3. The cage is (*in* / *on*) the table.

4. The cat is (*beside* / *under*) the table.

5. The light is (*above* / *below*) the cat and the bird.

6. The bird and the cat are (*above* / *below*) the light.

7. The plant is (*behind* / *below*) the cage.

8. The cat is (*on* / *at*) the door of the cage.

9. The cat wants to go (*into* / *out*) the cage.

10. Maybe the bird will fly (*at* / *out*) of the cage.

► **Practice 9. Objects of prepositions.** (Chart 6-4)
Choose the correct completion from Column B.

Column A

1. The earth revolves ____.
2. The new office building is ____.
3. If you want an education, go ____.
4. A submarine travels ____.
5. If you are sick, stay ____.
6. The plane flew ____.

Column B

a. over the mountain
b. in bed
c. below the surface of the water
d. to college
e. between Fifth Avenue and Sixth Avenue
f. around the sun

Submarine

► **Practice 10. Prepositions.** (Chart 6-4)
Complete the sentences with the correct words from the lists.

in	into	near	of	on	to

1. A mosquito flew _____*in / into*_____ the room from the patio. It didn't bother me because I had
   put insect repellent _____ my face and arms.
2. My checkbook is _____ the top drawer _____ my desk.
3. My home is not _____ my office. It takes me more than an hour to drive
   _____ my office every morning. That's a long drive.

above	below	from	of	on	through

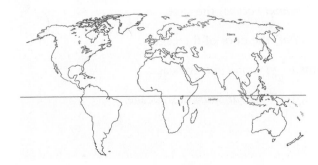

4. The equator is an imaginary line that divides the earth in half. The Northern Hemisphere is
   _____ the equator, and the Southern Hemisphere is _____ the equator.

5. Europe is north _____ the equator.

6. Ecuador is a country in South America. It is called Ecuador—the Spanish word for equator—because the equator runs _____ the middle of it. When you look at a map, you see that Ecuador is _____ the equator.

7. Antarctica is very far south. It's far _____ the equator.

▶ **Practice 11. Objects of prepositions.** (Chart 6-4)

Part I. Read the passage. Circle the prepositions and <u>underline</u> the nouns that are objects of the prepositions.

A Hurricane in Jamaica

(1) We had a hurricane (in) <u>Jamaica</u>. Dark clouds appeared in the sky. Big waves rolled over the beaches. A strong wind blew through the trees. The rain fell hard on our roof. The water came under the door and into the house.

(2) After the storm, we walked around the neighborhood. Across the street, a tree was on the ground. Another tree was leaning against the house. Some electrical wires were hanging near the house too.

(3) The sun, which had been behind the clouds, finally appeared again. We were happy and grateful because we were standing beneath the hot Jamaican sun again.

Part II. Each statement is incorrect. Make true statements by correcting the prepositional phrases.

1. Dark clouds appeared through the trees.

   _____Dark clouds appeared in the sky._____

2. The water came in through the open window.

   _____

3. After the storm, the people walked outside the neighborhood.

   _____

4. The tree had fallen down on my house.

   _____

5. The sun had been in the clouds.

   _____

6. The neighbors felt happy and grateful when they were standing in the rain.

   _____

► **Practice 12. Prepositions of time.** (Chart 6-5)
Complete the sentences with *in*, *at*, or *on*.

The Jacksons got married . . .

1. _____*In*_____ the summer.
2. _____ June.
3. _____ June 17th.
4. _____ Saturday.
5. _____ 12:00 P.M.
6. _____ noon.
7. _____ 2007.
8. _____ Saturday afternoon.

Their baby was born . . .

9. _____ midnight.
10. _____ 12:00 A.M.
11. _____ the morning.
12. _____ April 12th.
13. _____ 2009.
14. _____ April.
15. _____ Wednesday.

► **Practice 13. Prepositions of time.** (Chart 6-5)
Complete the sentences with *in*, *at*, or *on*.

1. Jan is a nurse on the night shift. She works in the hospital _____ night. She sleeps _____ the morning. She does her errands _____ the afternoon. She works _____ weekends. She has her days off _____ Wednesdays and Thursdays.

2. Melissa is a new doctor at the hospital. She began work there _____ July 1st. _____ the present time, she is working in cardiology.* She is going to attend a lecture on cardiology _____ noon tomorrow. She is going to take an exam for cardiologists** _____ the summer. _____ the future, she wants to be a cardiologist.

► **Practice 14. Word order: place and time.** (Chart 6-6)
Complete the sentences. Use all the words in the list and the correct word order.

1. *to the airport, tomorrow morning*

   I'll take you _____.

2. *last month, a new job*

   Harry got _____.

3. *in January, in the mountains, skis*

   Our family always _____.

4. *at the coffee shop, in the morning, has breakfast*

   Gladys usually _____.

5. *last Sunday, jogged, in the park*

   We _____.

6. *bought, in the suburbs, last year, a house*

   The Green family _____.

---

*cardiology = the medical study of the heart

**cardiologist = a doctor who treats heart diseases

▶ **Practice 15. Word order: place and time.** (Chart 6-6)
Complete each sentence by putting the phrases in the correct order.

1. The police officer stopped __1__ the driver.

   __2__ at a busy intersection.

   __3__ at midnight.

2. My friends rented ____ on the lake.

   ____ last summer.

   ____ a sailboat.

3. The children caught ____ in the river.

   ____ several fish.

   ____ last weekend.

4. We ate ____ at noon.

   ____ our lunch.

   ____ in the park.

5. I bought ____ a magazine.

   ____ at the corner newsstand.

   ____ after work yesterday.

▶ **Practice 16. Subject-verb agreement.** (Chart 6-7)
Complete the sentences with *is* or *are*.

1. These DVDs __are__ from the library.

2. The DVDs from the library _____ past due.

3. Everyone _____ here.

4. Everybody _____ on time for class.

5. All the teachers _____ here.

6. Every teacher at this school _____ patient.

7. Some people _____ wise.

8. There _____ a good movie at the Sunset Theater this weekend.

9. There _____ some good movies in town over the weekend.

10. The rules of this game _____ easy.

11. This information about taxes _____ helpful.

▶ **Practice 17. Subject-verb agreement.** (Chart 6-7)
Choose the correct verb.

1. Bees (*make* / *makes*) honey.

2. Tomatoes (*needs* / *need*) lots of sunshine to grow.

3. (*Do* / *Does*) the people in your neighborhood help each other?

4. There (*is* / *are*) some people already in line for the movie.

5. The vegetables in the bowl on the table (*is* / *are*) fresh.

6. Everybody always (*comes* / *come*) to class on time.

7. Everyone in the class (*is* / *are*) paying attention.

8. The students in the class always (*pay* / *pays*) attention.

9. The dishes on the counter (*is* / *are*) dirty.

10. Every person (*needs* / *need*) to bring identification.

11. The people next door (*goes* / *go*) hiking every weekend in the summer.

12. My father and mother (*works* / *work*) for the same company.

13. The pictures on the wall (*is* / *are*) of my father's family.

▶ **Practice 18. Adjectives.** (Chart 6-8)
Underline each adjective. Draw an arrow to the noun it describes.

1. Paul has a loud voice.

2. Sugar is sweet.

3. The students took an easy test.

4. Air is free.

5. We ate some delicious food at a Mexican restaurant.

6. The child was sick.

7. The sick child got into his warm bed and sipped hot tea with honey and lemon in it.

▶ **Practice 19. Adjectives.** (Chart 6-8)
Complete each phrase with an adjective that has the opposite meaning.

1. new cars _____old_____ cars

2. a young man an _____ man

3. a good day a _____ day

4. hard exercises _____ exercises

5. a soft pillow a _____ pillow

6. a _____ street a wide street

7. _____ plates dirty plates

8. _____ cups full cups

9. dangerous cities _____ cities

10. a dark color a _____ color

11. a heavy box a _____ box

12. a _____ place a private place

13. my left foot my _____ foot

14. the wrong answer the _____ answer

15. a _____ walk a short walk

Use the information in *italics* to complete the sentences. Each completion should have a noun that is used as an adjective in front of another noun.

1. *Numbers on pages* are _____*page numbers*_____.

2. *Money that is made of paper* is _____.

3. *Buildings that have apartments* are _____.

4. *Gardens with roses* are _____.

5. *Chains for keys* are _____.

6. *Governments in cities* are _____.

7. *Walls made of bricks* are _____.

8. *Cartons that hold eggs* are _____.

9. *Views of mountains* are _____.

10. *Lights that control traffic* are _____.

11. *Pies that are made with apples* are _____.

12. *Bridges made from steel* are _____.

▶ **Practice 21. Using nouns as adjectives.** (Chart 6-9)
Choose the correct completion.

1. A: What kind of tree is that?
   B: It's a _____. It produces peaches in the summer.
   a. peaches tree   b. peach tree   c. tree peaches

2. A: So, you grew up on a farm. What kind of farm?
   B: A _____. We had chickens on the farm.
   a. farm chickens   b. chickens farm   c. chicken farm

3. A: We have a special dessert tonight. It's a cake made with carrots from the chef's own garden.
   B: Sounds good! I'll have the _____.
   a. carrot cake   b. carrots cake   c. cake carrots

4. A: What is a good present to get for your son? He likes to play games on the computer, right?
   B: Right. He loves _____.
   a. computers games   b. computer games   c. game computers

5. A: Are you going to travel in Canada by train?
   B: Yes, we are. We like _____.
   a. trip trains   b. train trips   c. trains trips

6. A: Look at that unusual building. Is it a new hotel?
   B: No. It's _____. A lot of big companies have their offices there.
   a. an office building   b. an offices building   c. a building office

▶ **Practice 22. Adjectives.** (Charts 6-8 and 6-9)

Part I. Read the passage. It is adapted from a blog by astronaut Sandra Magnus. It was written from space in 2008.

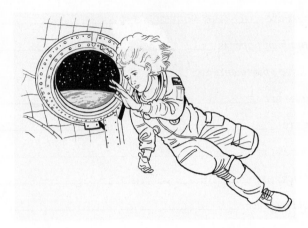

The night sky below is not completely dark. The cloud cover over the earth reflects the city lights. There are lights above us too—white lights, red lights, and orange lights. They are all around us in space. They are everywhere. They sparkle.* You are swimming in a sea of beautiful lights. These bright lights in space are stars. You know that these shining stars are large, like our sun, and you know that they are very far from us. But from here, each star seems so tiny. You feel that space is enormous.**

Part II. Answer the questions according to the information in the passage. Circle "T" if the statement is true. Circle "F" if the statement is false.

1. Astronauts can see the earth's night sky from space.	T	F
2. The writer sees lights of different colors.	T	F
3. These lights are stars.	T	F
4. Each star looks small, but it is not really small.	T	F
5. The writer feels that space is tiny.	T	F

▶ **Practice 23. Review: nouns.** (Charts 6-1 → 6-9)

These sentences have mistakes in the use of nouns. Find each noun. Decide if the noun should be plural and add the correct plural form as necessary. Do not change any other words in the sentences.

1. The mountain ^s^ in Chile are beautiful.

2. Cat hunt mouse.

3. Mosquito are small insect.

4. Everyone has eyelash.

---

*sparkle = shine in bright flashes

**enormous = very big in size or in amount

5. Do you listen to any podcasts when you take plane trip?

6. Forest sometimes have fire. Forest fire endanger wild animal.

7. Sharp kitchen knife can be dangerous.

8. I couldn't get concert tickets for Friday. The ticket were all sold out.

9. There are approximately 250,000 different kind of flower in the world.

10. I applied to several foreign university because I want to study in a different country.

11. Ted lives with three other university student.

12. In the past one hundred year, our daily life have changed in many way. We no longer need to use oil lamp or candle in our house, raise our own chicken, or build daily fire for cooking.

▶ **Practice 24. Personal pronouns: subjects and objects.** (Chart 6-10)
<u>Underline</u> the personal pronouns. Then write each pronoun and the noun it refers to.

1. Dr. Gupta is a math professor. Students like her very much. She makes them laugh. They enjoy Dr. Gupta's classes because they are fun.

    a. _____her_____ → _____Dr. Gupta_____

    b. _____ → _____

    c. _____ → _____

    d. _____ → _____

    e. _____ → _____

2. Dr. Reynolds is a dentist. Not many patients like him. He is not patient or gentle with them, but he is the only dentist in town, so many people go to him.

    a. _____ → _____

    b. _____ → _____

    c. _____ → _____

    d. _____ → _____

    e. _____ → _____

3. Beth says: "My hometown is a wonderful place. It's a small town. I know all the people there, and they know me. They are friendly. If you visit, they will welcome you."

    a. _____ → _____

    b. _____ → _____

    c. _____ → _____

    d. _____ → _____

    e. _____ → _____

    f. _____ → _____

    g. _____ → _____

    h. _____ → _____

▶ **Practice 25. Personal pronouns: subjects and objects.** (Chart 6-10)
Decide if the <u>underlined</u> word is a subject or object prounoun. Write "S" for subject and "O" for object above the underlined word.

1. Jackie just texted <u>me</u>. *O*

2. <u>She</u>'s going to be late. *S*

3. Jia and Ning are arriving tomorrow. <u>They</u>'ll be here around noon.

4. Their parents will be happy to see <u>them</u>.

5. The doctor canceled the appointment. <u>He</u> has had an emergency.

6. If you need to speak to the doctor, call <u>him</u> tomorrow morning.

7. Bob and <u>I</u> had dinner last night.

8. <u>We</u> went to a restaurant on the lake.

9. George invited <u>us</u> to his wedding.

10. <u>It</u>'s going to be in June.

11. Your mother called and left a message. Call <u>her</u> right away.

12. Please answer <u>me</u> as soon as possible.

13. <u>You</u> live in the dorms, right?

14. See <u>you</u> tomorrow!

▶ **Practice 26. Personal pronouns: subjects and objects.** (Chart 6-10)
Check (✓) all the pronouns that can complete each sentence.

1. Mark called _____ last night.

   ☐ he   ☐ her
   ☐ I   ☐ him
   ☐ me   ☐ she
   ☐ them   ☐ they
   ☐ us   ☐ we
   ☐ you

2. _____ called Mark last night.

   ☐ He   ☐ Her
   ☐ Him   ☐ I
   ☐ Me   ☐ She
   ☐ Them   ☐ They
   ☐ Us   ☐ We
   ☐ You

3. Sharon saw _____ on the plane.

   ☐ he and I   ☐ her and I
   ☐ him and me   ☐ him and I
   ☐ you and me   ☐ you and I
   ☐ she and I   ☐ she and me
   ☐ her and me   ☐ them and I
   ☐ they and me   ☐ them and us

4. _____ saw Sharon on the plane.

   ☐ He and I   ☐ Her and I
   ☐ Him and me   ☐ Him and I
   ☐ You and me   ☐ You and I
   ☐ She and I   ☐ She and me
   ☐ Her and me   ☐ Them and I
   ☐ They and me   ☐ They and us

Choose the correct pronoun.

1. Will you take (*I / me*) to the airport?

2. Will you take Jennifer and (*I / me*) to the airport?

3. Jennifer and (*I / me*) will be ready at 7:00 A.M.

4. Did you see Marta? *(She / Her)* was waiting in your office to talk to you.

5. I saw Ann a few minutes ago. I passed Sara, and (*she / her*) was talking to (*she / her*) in the hallway.

6. Nick used to work in his father's store, but his father and (*he / him*) had a serious disagreement. I think his father fired (*he / him*).

7. Prof. Molina called (*we / us*). He wants to see (*we / us*) in his office tomorrow morning.

8. Take these documents and destroy (*they / them*). (*They / Them*) contain personal and financial information.

▶ **Practice 28. Possessive nouns.** (Chart 6-11)
Choose the correct spelling of each possessive noun.

1. I have one cousin. My _____ name is Paul.
   a. cousin's   b. cousins'

2. I have two cousins. My _____ names are Paul and Kevin.
   a. cousin's   b. cousins'

3. I have three sons. My _____ names are Ryan, Jim, and Scott.
   a. son's   b. sons'

4. I have a son. My _____ name is Ryan.
   a. son's   b. sons'

5. I have a puppy. My _____ name is Rover.
   a. puppy's   b. puppies'

6. I have two puppies. My _____ names are Rover and Rex.
   a. puppie's   b. puppies'

7. I have one child. My _____ name is Anna.
   a. child's   b. childs'

8. I have two children. My _____ names are Anna and Keith.
   a. children's   b. childrens'

9. The winner of the dance contest was the judges' choice but not the _____ choice.
   a. people's   b. peoples'

10. Excuse me. Where is the _____ restroom?
    a. men's   b. mens'

► **Practice 29. Possessive nouns.** (Chart 6-11)
Write the possessive form of the *italicized* noun in the second sentence.

1. The book belongs to my *friend*. It's my _____<u>friend's</u>_____ book.

2. These books belong to my *friends*. They are my _____<u>friends'</u>_____ books.

3. The car belongs to my *parents*. It's my _____ car.

4. The car belongs to my *mother*. It's my _____ car.

5. This phone belongs to *Carl*. It's _____ phone.

6. The keys belong to *Carl*. They're _____ keys.

7. The toys belong to the *baby*. They are the _____ toys.

8. The toy belongs to the *baby*. It's the _____ toy.

9. The toys belong to the *babies*. They are the _____ toys.

10. This jacket belongs to *Ann*. It's _____ jacket.

11. The shoes belong to *Bob*. They are _____ shoes.

12. The shirt belongs to *James*. It's _____ shirt.

► **Practice 30. Possessive nouns.** (Chart 6-11)
Write the correct possessive form if necessary.

         Dan's
1. I met ~~Dan~~ sister yesterday.

2. I met Dan and his sister yesterday. (No change.)

3. I know Jack roommates.

4. I know Jack well. He's a good friend of mine.

5. I have one roommate. My roommate desk is always messy.

6. You have two roommates. Your roommates desks are always neat.

7. Jo Ann and Betty are sisters.

8. Jo Ann is Betty sister. My sister name is Sonya.

9. My name is Richard. I have two sisters. My sisters names are Jo Ann and Betty.

10. I read a book about the changes in women roles and men roles in modern society.

► **Practice 31. Possessive pronouns vs. possessive adjectives.** (Chart 6-12)
Complete the sentences with possessive pronouns or possessive adjectives that refer to the words in *italics*.

1. A: Can I look at your grammar book?
   B: Why? *You* have _____<u>your</u>_____ own* book. *You* have _____<u>yours</u>_____, and I have mine.

_____

*__Own__ frequently follows a possessive adjective: e.g., *my own, your own, their own.* The word __own__ emphasizes that nobody else possesses the exact same thing(s); ownership belongs **only** to me *(my own book)*, to you *(your own book)*, to them *(their own books),* to us *(our own books),* etc.

2. A: Kim wants to look at your grammar book.

    B: Why? *She* has _____ own book. *She* has _____, and I have mine.

3. A: Jake wants to look at your grammar book.

    B: Why? *He* has _____ own book. *He* has _____, and I have mine.

4. A: Jake and I want to look at your grammar book.

    B: Why? *You* have _____ own books. *You* have _____, and I have mine.

5. A: Jake and Kim want to look at our grammar books.

    B: Why? *They* have _____ own books. *We* have _____ own books. *They*

    have _____, and *we* have _____.

▶ **Practice 32. Possessive pronouns vs. possessive adjectives.** (Chart 6-12)
Choose the correct word.

1. *Mrs. Lee* asked (*her / hers*) kids to clean up the kitchen.

2. I don't need to borrow your bicycle. *My sister* lent me (*her / hers*).

3. *Ted and I* are roommates. (*Our / Ours*) apartment is small.

4. *Brian and Louie* have a bigger apartment. In fact, (*their / theirs*) is huge.

5. *You* can find (*your / yours*) keys in the top drawer of the desk.

6. The keys in the drawer belong to you. *I* have (*my / mine*) in (*my / mine*) pocket. *You* should
   look in the drawer for (*your / yours*).

7. *Tom and Paul* talked about (*their / theirs*) experiences in the wilderness areas of Canada.
   I've had a lot of interesting experiences in the wilderness, but nothing to compare with
   (*their / theirs*).

8. *I* know Eric well. He is a good friend of (*my / mine*). *You* know him too, don't you? Isn't he a
   friend of (*you / yours*) too?

▶ **Practice 33. Reflexive pronouns.** (Chart 6-13)
Complete the sentences with reflexive pronouns that refer to the words in *italics*.

1. *I* enjoyed _____*myself*_____ at Disney World.

2. *We* all enjoyed _____ there.

3. *Uncle Joe* enjoyed _____.

4. *Aunt Elsa* enjoyed _____.

5. *Jessica and Paul* enjoyed _____.

6. Hi, Emily! Did *you* enjoy _____?

7. Hi, Emily and Dan! Did *you* enjoy _____?

8. In its advertising, *Disney World* calls _____ "the happiest place in the
   world."

▶ **Practice 34. Reflexive pronouns.** (Chart 6-13)
Complete each sentence with an appropriate expression from the list. Be sure to use the correct reflexive pronoun.

be proud of	✓cut	help	take care of	teach
blame	enjoy	introduce	talk to	work for

1. Ouch! I just _____cut myself_____ with a knife.

2. You got a scholarship to State College? Congratulations, Anna! You must _____
_____ .

3. John often _____ . People think there is more than one person
in the room, but there isn't. It's only John.

4. When I was young, I _____ to ride a bicycle. Then I taught the
other children in the neighborhood.

5. Sheri _____ for the accident, but it wasn't her fault. The other
car didn't stop at the stop sign and crashed into hers.

6. Eat, eat! There's lots more pizza in the oven. Please, all of you, _____
_____ to more pizza.

7. Adam seldom gets sick because he eats healthy food and exercises regularly. He _____
_____ .

8. They went to a party last night. Let's ask them if they _____ .

9. My father never worked for anyone. He always owned his own company. He
_____ throughout his entire adult life.

10. At the beginning of each term, my students _____ to the whole class.

▶ **Practice 35. Review: pronouns and possessive adjectives.** (Charts 6-10 → 6-13)
Choose the correct pronouns.

1. Alan invited (*I* /*me*) to go to dinner with (*he* /*him*).

2. Sam and you should be proud of (*yourself* / *yourselves*). The two of you did a good job.

3. The room was almost empty. The only furniture was one table. The table stood by (*it* / *itself*)
in one corner.

4. The bird returned to (*its* / *it's*★) nest to feed (*its* / *it's*) baby bird.

5. Nick has his tennis racket, and Ann has (*her* / *hers* / *her's*★).

6. Where's Eric? I have some good news for Joe and (*he* / *him* / *his* / *himself*).

7. Don't listen to Greg. You need to think for (*yourself* / *yourselves*), Jane. It's
(*you* / *your* / *your's*★) life.

8. We all have (*us* / *our* / *ours*) own ideas about how to live (*our* / *ours* / *our's*★) lives.

★REMINDER: Apostrophes are NOT used with possessive pronouns. Note that *its* = possessive adjective; *it's* = *it is*. Also note that *her's, your's,* and *our's* are NOT POSSIBLE in grammatically correct English.

9. You have your beliefs, and we have (*our / ours*).

10. People usually enjoy (*themselves / theirselves**) at family gatherings.

11. History repeats (*himself / herself / itself*).

12. David didn't need my help. He finished the work by (*him / himself / hisself*).

▶ **Practice 36. Review: pronouns and possessive adjectives.** (Charts 6-10 → 6-13)
Complete each passage with words from the list. You may use a word more than once. Capitalize words as necessary.

he	him	himself	his

(1) Tom is wearing a bandage on _____*his*_____ arm. _____*He*_____ hurt _____*himself*_____

　　　　　　　　　　　　　　　　1　　　　　　　　　2　　　　　　　　　　3
    while _____ was repairing the roof. I'll help _____ with the
    　　　　　　　　4　　　　　　　　　　　　　　　　　　　　　　　5
    roof later.

her	I	mine	she
hers	it	our	we

(2) I have a sister. _____ name is Katherine, but we call _____
    　　　　　　　　　　　　1　　　　　　　　　　　　　　　　　　　　　　　　　2
    Kate. _____ and I share a room. _____ room is pretty small.
    　　　　　　　3　　　　　　　　　　　　　　　　　　　　4
    _____ have only one desk. _____ has five drawers. Kate puts
    　　　5　　　　　　　　　　　　　　　　　　6
    _____ things in the two drawers on the right. I keep _____ in
    　　　7　　　　　　　　　　　　　　　　　　　　　　　　　　　8
    the two drawers on the left. Kate doesn't open my two drawers, and I don't open
    _____. She and _____ share the middle drawer.
    　　9　　　　　　　　　　　　　10

he	his	their	them	they
her	my	theirs	themselves	

(3) Mr. Ramirez is the manager of our office. _____ has a corner office with
    　　　　　　　　　　　　　　　　　　　　　　　　　　1
    _____ name on the door. Ms. Lake is _____ assistant.
    　　2　　　　　　　　　　　　　　　　　　　　　　　3
    _____ office is next to Mr. Ramirez's office. _____ often work
    　　4　　　　　　　　　　　　　　　　　　　　　　　　　　　5
    together on projects by _____, but I work with _____
    　　　　　　　　　　　　6　　　　　　　　　　　　　　　　7
    sometimes. They never come to _____ office to meet. I always go to
    　　　　　　　　　　　　　　　　8
    _____. I take an elevator to get to _____ offices, or I walk up a
    　　9　　　　　　　　　　　　　　　　　　　　10
    long flight of stairs.

_____

*NOTE: *Themself* and *theirselves* are not really words—they are NOT POSSIBLE in grammatically correct English. Only ***themselves*** is the correct reflexive pronoun form.

► **Practice 37. Singular forms of *other: another* vs. *the other*.** (Chart 6-14)
Write *another* or *the other* under each picture.

1. four boxes: _____one_____   _____another_____   _____another_____   _____the other_____

2. three circles: _____one_____   _____   _____

3. five flowers: _____one_____   _____   _____   _____   _____

4. two cups: _____one_____   _____

5. six spoons: _____one_____   _____   _____   _____   _____   _____

► **Practice 38. Singular forms of *other: another* vs. *the other*.** (Chart 6-14)
Complete the sentences with *another* or *the other*.

1. There are two girls in Picture A. One is Ann. _____ is Sara.

PICTURE A — ANN   SARA
PICTURE B — ALEX   MIKE   DAVID

2. There are three boys in Picture B. One is Alex. _____ one is Mike.

3. In Picture B, Alex and Mike are smiling. _____ boy looks sad.

4. There are three boys in Picture B. All three have common first names. One is named Alex.

a. _____ is named David.

b. The name of _____ one is Mike.

5. There are many common English names for boys. Alex is one.

a. Mike is _____ .

b. David is _____ .

c. John is _____ common name.

d. Joe is _____ .

e. What is _____ common English name for a boy?

▶ **Practice 39. Plural forms of *other*: *other(s)* vs. *the other(s)*.** (Chart 6-15)
Complete the sentences with *the other*, *the others*, *other*, or *others*.

1. There are four common nicknames for "Robert." One is "Bob." Another is "Bobby."
_____*The others*_____ are "Robbie" and "Rob."

2. There are five English vowels. One is "a." Another is "e." _____ are "i,"
"o," and "u."

3. There are many consonants in English. The letters "b" and "c" are consonants.
_____ are "d," "f," and "g."

4. Some people are tall, and _____ are short. Some people are neither tall
nor short.

5. Some people are tall, and _____ people are short.

6. Some animals are huge. _____ are tiny.

7. Some animals are huge. _____ animals are tiny.

8. Of the twenty students in the class, eighteen passed the exam. _____
failed.

9. Out of the twenty students in the class, only two failed the exam. _____
students passed.

▶ **Practice 40. Summary: forms of *other*.** (Charts 6-14 → 6-16)
Choose the correct completion.

1. Gold is one kind of metal. Silver is ____ .
   a. another   b. the other   c. the others   d. others   e. other

2. Summer is one season. Spring is ____ .
   a. another   b. the other   c. the others   d. others   e. other

3. There are four seasons. Summer is one. ____ are winter, fall, and spring.
   a. Another   b. The other   c. The others   d. Others   e. Other

4. What's your favorite season? Some people like spring the best. ____ think fall is the nicest
   season.
   a. Another   b. The other   c. The others   d. Others   e. Other

5. This cat's eyes are different colors. One eye is gray, and ____ is green.
   a. another   b. the other   c. the others   d. others   e. other

6. There are two reasons not to buy that piece of furniture. One is that it's expensive. _____ is that it's not well made.
    a. Another   b. The other   c. The others   d. Others   e. Other

7. Alex failed his English exam, but his teacher is going to give him _____ chance to pass it.
    a. another   b. the other   c. the others   d. others   e. other

8. Some people drink tea in the morning. _____ have coffee. I prefer fruit juice.
    a. Another   b. The other   c. The others   d. Others   e. Other

9. There are five digits in the number 20,000. One digit is a 2. _____ digits are all zeroes.
    a. Another   b. The other   c. The others   d. Others   e. Other

▶ **Practice 41. Review.** (Chapter 6)
Choose the correct completion.

1. The people at the market (*is / are*) friendly.

2. How many (*potato / potatoes*) should I cook for dinner tonight?

3. I wanted to be alone, so I worked (*myself / by myself*).

4. The twins were born (*in / on*) December 25th (*on / at*) midnight.

5. On the small island, there are seven (*vacation / vacations*) houses.

6. The bus driver waited for (*we / us*) at the bus stop.

7. Can you tell a good book by (*its / it's*) title?

8. This is (*our / ours*) dessert, and that is (*your / yours*).

9. Jack has so much confidence. He really believes in (*him / himself*).

10. These bananas are okay, but (*the other / the others*) were better.

▶ **Practice 42. Editing.** (Chapter 6)
Correct the errors.

1. Look at those beautifuls mountains!

2. The children played on Saturday afternoon at the park a game.

3. There are two horse, several sheeps, and a cow in the farmers field.

4. The owner of the store is busy in the moment.

5. The teacher met her's students at the park after school.

6. Everyone want peace in the world.

7. I grew up in a city very large.

8. This apple tastes sour. There are more, so let's try the other one.

9. Some tree lose their leaf in the winter.

10. I am going to wear my shirt blue to the party.

11. People may hurt theirselves if they use this machine.

12. Our neighbors invited my friend and I to visit they.

13. My husband boss works for twelve hour every days.

14. The students couldn't find they're books.

15. I always read magazines articles while I'm in the waiting room at my dentists office.

▶ **Practice 43. Word search puzzle.**
Circle the plural forms of the these words in the puzzle: *man, woman, child, tooth, fly, foot, fox, wolf, monkey.* The words may be horizontal, vertical, or diagonal. The first letter of each word is highlighted in gray.

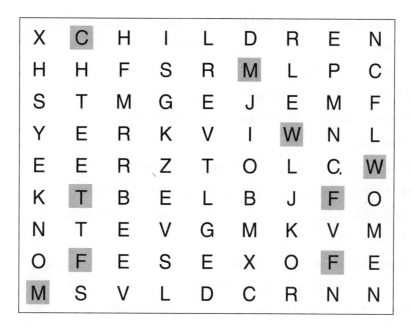

Chapter 7
Modal Auxiliaries

▶ **Practice 1. The form of modal auxiliaries.** (Chart 7-1)
Add the word **to** where necessary. Write **Ø** if **to** is not necessary.

1. Mr. Alvarez spilled ketchup on his shirt. He must ____Ø____ change clothes before dinner.

2. Mr. Alvarez has ____to____ change his shirt before dinner.

3. Tom and I might _____ play soccer after work tomorrow.

4. Would you _____ speak more slowly, please?

5. The students have _____ take a test next Friday.

6. Everyone should _____ wash their hands before meals.

7. Everyone ought _____ cover their mouth when they cough.*

8. May I please _____ have the salt and pepper? Thanks.

9. You'd better not _____ come to the meeting late. The boss will _____ be angry if you're late.

10. I've been going to bed after midnight. The next day, I can't _____ stay awake in class. I've got _____ go to bed earlier from now on.

11. With that cough, you had better _____ see a doctor soon. I think you may have _____ pneumonia.**

▶ **Practice 2. Expressing ability.** (Chart 7-2)
Complete each sentence with the correct word in parentheses. Note the words in **boldface**.

1. (*giraffe, zebra*)   A ____zebra____ **can't stretch** its neck to reach the tops of trees.

2. (*bee, cat*)   A single _____ **can kill** a thousand mice in a year.

3. (*Rabbits, Elephants*)   _____ **can break** small trees under their huge feet.

4. (*Monkeys, Chickens*)   _____ **can climb** trees easily.

5. (*ducks, camels*)   Did you know that _____ **can survive** 17 days without any water at all?

6. (*cow, bull*)   One _____ **can produce** as much as 8,500 lbs. (3,860 kgs) of milk in a year.

7. (*horse, cat*)   A person **can sit** on a _____ without hurting it.

---

*cough = a sudden push of air out of your throat with a shout sound.

**pneumonia = a serious illness that affects your lungs and makes it difficult for you to breathe.

8. (*donkey, snake*)   A _____ **can carry** heavy loads on its back.

9. (*squirrel, polar bear*)   A _____ **can stay** high up in the trees for weeks and jump from branch to branch.

10. (*people, ants*)   Most _____ **can lift** objects that are ten times heavier than their own bodies.

▶ **Practice 3. Expressing possibility and permission.** (Chart 7-3)
Decide if the meaning of the modal verb is *possibility* or *permission*.

		Meaning	
1.	Both of my grandparents are retired. They like to travel. They **may travel** overseas next summer.	(possibility)	permission
2.	They **may take** their two grandchildren with them.	possibility	permission
3.	A: Yes, Tommy, you **may play** outdoors until dinner. B: Okay, Mom.	possibility	permission
4.	A: What's wrong with the dog's foot? B: He **may have** an infection.	possibility	permission
5.	The dog has an infected foot. He **might need** to go to the vet.	possibility	permission
6.	A: I'm sorry, sir, but passengers **can't walk** around the plane when the "Fasten seat belt sign" is on. B: Oh, okay. I'm sorry.	possibility	permission
7.	It **may be** hot and humid all weekend.	possibility	permission
8.	If you finish the test early, you **may** leave.	possibility	permission
9.	I **might not stay** up to watch the end of the game on TV. I'm very sleepy.	possibility	permission
10.	A: Excuse me. **Can I ask** you a personal question? B: Hmmm . . . I don't know about that. I really don't like personal questions.	possibility	permission

▶ **Practice 4. Expressing possibility.** (Chart 7-3)
Rewrite each sentence using the word in parentheses.

1. Maybe I will take a nap. (*might*) _____ *I might take a nap.* _____

2. She might be sick. (*maybe*) _____ *Maybe she is sick.* _____

3. There may be time later. (*maybe*) _____

4. Maybe our team will win. (*may*) _____

5. You may be right. (*might*) _____

6. Maybe we'll hear soon. (*may*) _____

7. It might rain. (*may*) _____

8. Maybe it will snow. (*might*) _____

9. She might come tomorrow. (*maybe*) _____

10. She might be at home right now. (*maybe*) _____

► **Practice 5. Expressing ability and possibility.** (Charts 7-2 and 7-3)
Choose the correct completion.

1. A: Are you running in the big race tomorrow, Alan?
    B: No, I'm not. I _____ run. I broke my foot on Saturday
       and now it's in a cast.
       a. can   c. may
       b. can't   d. may not

2. A: Where's Tracy? I've been looking for her all morning.
    B: I haven't seen her. She _____ be sick.
       a. can   c. might
       b. can't   d. might not

3. A: I heard that Jessica has gotten a scholarship to Duke University!
    B: It's not definite yet, but she _____ get one. The admissions office says that it's possible and
       they will let us know next month.
       a. can   c. might
       b. can't   d. might not

4. A: Larry has been in New York for a couple of months. Is he going to stay there or return
       home?
    B: It depends. If he _____ find a job there soon, he'll stay. If not, he'll come home.
       a. can   c. may
       b. can't   d. may not

5. A: Is Jodie a doctor now?
    B: Not yet, but almost. She finished medical school last month, but she hasn't taken her
       exams yet. She _____ be a doctor until she passes them.
       a. can   c. might
       b. can't   d. might not

6. A: When are you going to sell your old car?
    B: As soon as I _____ find someone to buy it!
       a. can   c. may
       b. can't   d. may not

► **Practice 6. Meanings of *could*.** (Charts 7-2 and 7-4)
Choose the expression that has the same meaning as the *italicized* verb.

1. A: How long will it take you to paint two small rooms?
    B: I'm not sure. If the job is not complicated, I *could finish* by Thursday.
       a. was able to finish   b. might finish

2. I think I'll take my umbrella. It *could rain* today.
    a. was able to rain   b. might rain

3. My niece *could read* by the time she was four years old.
    a. was able to read   b. might read

4. You *could see* that the little boy was unhappy because of the sad expression in his eyes.
    a. were able to see   b. might see

5. Sally is in excellent condition. I think she *could win* the 10-kilometer race on Saturday.
    a. was able to win   b. might win

6. John *couldn't drive* for a month because of a broken ankle, but now it's healed.
   a. wasn't able to drive   b. might not drive

7. Jane *could arrive* before dinner, but I don't really expect her until nine or later.
   a. was able to arrive   b. might arrive

8. Simon was in an accident, but he *couldn't remember* how he had hurt himself.
   a. wasn't able to remember   b. might not remember

▶ **Practice 7. Polite questions: *May I, Could I, Can I.*** (Chart 7-5)
Complete the conversations. Write the letter of the question that matches each answer.

> a. Can I borrow the book when you finish it?
> b. Could I pick you up at 6:30 instead of 6:00?
> c. Could we watch the comedy instead of the war movie?
> d. May I ask you a question?
> e. May I have some more potatoes, please?
> f. May I help you?

1. A: _____
   B: Yes. They're delicious, aren't they?

2. A: _____
   B: Yes. What would you like to know?

3. A: _____
   B: Thanks. I want to buy this.

4. A: _____
   B: That's a little late.

5. A: _____
   B: Sure. I'm in the mood for something funny.

6. A: _____
   B: Yes. I'll probably finish it tonight.

▶ **Practice 8. Polite questions.** (Charts 7-5 and 7-6)
Complete each part of the conversation with the correct word from the list. More than one word may be correct.

(1) *may, would*

A: Hello, Tracy Johnson's office. _____ I help you?
                                              1

B: Yes, please. I'd like to speak to Ms. Johnson.

A: I'm sorry. She's in a meeting. _____ you leave your name and number? I'll
                                              2
ask her to call you back.

B: Yes. It's 555-7981.

A: _____ I ask what this is about?
          3

B: Well, I have some good news for her. _____ you please tell her that?
                                                          4

(2) *will, could*

A: Of course.

B: And _____ you please tell her that this is important?
5

A: All right, I certainly will. _____ I ask you just one more thing?
6

B: Yes?

A: _____ you please leave me your name? You forgot to tell me that.
7

▶ **Practice 9. Polite questions.** (Charts 7-5 and 7-6)
Check (✓) all the modal auxiliaries that correctly complete each question.

1. It's cold in here. ___ you please close the door?
   ___ May   ✓ Could   ✓ Can   ✓ Would

2. Oh, I forgot my wallet. ___ I borrow ten dollars from you until tomorrow?
   ___ Could   ___ May   ___ Will   ___ Can

3. I can't lift this box by myself. ___ you help me carry it?
   ___ Would   ___ Could   ___ May   ___ Will

4. Hello. ___ I help you find something in the store?
   ___ Can   ___ Would   ___ May   ___ Could

5. The store closes in ten minutes. ___ you please bring all your purchases to the counter?
   ___ Will   ___ May   ___ Can   ___ Could

▶ **Practice 10. Expressing advice.** (Chart 7-7)
Complete the sentences. Use *should* or *shouldn't* and the expressions in the list.

always be on time for an appointment	drive the speed limit
attend all classes	give too much homework
be cruel to animals	quit
✓ drive a long distance	throw trash out of your car window

1. If you are tired, you _____ *shouldn't drive a long distance* _____.

2. Cigarette smoking is dangerous to your health. You _____.

3. A good driver _____.

4. A teacher _____.

5. A student _____.

6. Animals have feelings. You _____.

7. It is important to be punctual. You _____.

_____.

8. Littering is against the law. You _____
_____.

▶ **Practice 11. Expressing advice.** (Chart 7-7)
Write the letter of the word or phrase that correctly completes each sentence.

a. ask her again	f. read the instructions first
b. eat it	g. stick to my diet
c. find a new girl friend	h. study
d. go to the game	i. wash it in cold water
e. keep pushing all the buttons	j. wash it in hot water

1. A: Should I wash this sweater in hot water to get the spot out?

    B: No. You shouldn't _____. The sweater will shrink if you wash it in hot water. You
    should _____.

2. A: This is my new TV remote,* but I can't figure out how to use it.

    B: You shouldn't _____. You should _____.

3. A: You like this chocolate cake, don't you?

    B: I love it, but I shouldn't _____. I'm trying to lose weight. I should _____.

4. A: Are you going to study for the exam tonight?

    B: I should _____, but I'm not going to. I'm going to the basketball game.

    A: How come?

    B: Well, I shouldn't _____, but I really want to see it. Our team might win the
    championship tonight!

5. A: I have asked Linda to marry me five times. She always says "No." What should I do?
    Should I ask her again?

    B: No, of course not! You shouldn't _____. You should _____.

---

*remote = remote control

► **Practice 12. Expressing advice.** (Charts 7-7 and 7-8)
Choose the correct completion.

1. Danny doesn't feel well. He _____ see a doctor.
   (a.) should   b. ought   c. had

2. Danny doesn't feel well. He _____ better see a doctor.
   a. should   b. ought   c. had

3. Danny doesn't feel well. He _____ to see a doctor.
   a. should   b. ought   c. had

4. It's very warm in here. We _____ open some windows.
   a. should   b. ought   c. had

5. It's really cold in here. We _____ to close some windows.
   a. should   b. ought   c. had

6. There's a police car behind us. You _____ better slow down!
   a. should   b. ought   c. had

7. People who use public parks _____ clean up after themselves.
   a. should   b. ought   c. had

8. I have no money left in my bank account. I _____ better stop charging things on my credit card.
   a. should   b. ought   c. had

9. It's going to be a formal dinner and dance. You _____ to change clothes.
   a. should   b. ought   c. had

10. This library book is overdue. I _____ better return it today.
    a. should   b. ought   c. had

► **Practice 13. Expressing necessity.** (Chart 7-9)
Read the passage. Complete each sentence with a word from the list.

have	has	had	must

Applying to College

I'm applying to colleges now. I would like to go to Stellar University, but they probably won't accept me. First, students _____ to have excellent grades to go there, and my grades
₁
are only average. Second, a student _____ be in the top 10 percent of the class, and
₂
I am not. I am in the top 30 percent. Third, everybody _____ to take a difficult
₃
examination and do well on it. I am not good at examinations. I _____ to take
₄
many examinations when I was younger, and I didn't do well on any of them.

On the other hand, I think they will accept me at People's University. First, at this school, a student doesn't _____ to have excellent grades, just good ones. Second, there is no

5

entrance examination. Instead, you just _____ to write a couple of good essays, and

6

I am good at writing. I _____ to write a lot of compositions last year, and I always

7

did well.

You _____ got to be realistic when you choose your university. I think I am very

8

realistic and I expect People's University will be a good fit for me.

▶ **Practice 14. Necessity: *must, have to, have got to.*** (Chart 7-9)
Choose the correct verb.

1. Last week, John (*had to / must*) interview five people for the new management position.

2. Professor Drake (*had got to / had to*) cancel several lectures when she became ill.

3. Why did you (*have to / had to*) leave work early?

4. I (*must / had to*) take my daughter to the airport yesterday.

5. Where did John (*have to / had to*) go for medical help yesterday?

6. We (*had to / had got to*) contact a lawyer last week about a problem with our neighbors.

7. I (*have got to / had to*) leave now. I (*have to / had to*) pick up my kids. They're waiting at school.

8. You (*had to / must*) have a pencil with an eraser for the exam. Do not bring a pen.

▶ **Practice 15. Necessity: *must, have to, have got to.*** (Chart 7-9)
Write the past tense of the verbs in *italics*.

1. I *have to study* for my medical school exams.

   PAST: I _____had to study_____ for my medical school exams.

2. We *have to turn off* our water because of a leak.

   PAST: We _____ our water because of a leak.

3. *Do* you *have to work* over the holidays?

   PAST: _____ you _____ over the holidays?

4. Jerry *has got to see* the dentist twice this week.

   PAST: Jerry _____ the dentist twice last month.

5. Who *has got to be* in early for work this week?

   PAST: Who _____ in early for work last week?

6. The bank *must close* early today.

   PAST: The bank _____ early yesterday.

► **Practice 16. Expressing necessity.** (Chart 7-9)
Check (✓) the sentence that best completes each conversation.

1. A: Ma'am, show me your driver's license, please.
   B: Of course, officer. But what did I do? Why did you pull me over?
   A: ☐ You didn't stop at the red light. You have to stop at red lights.
      ☐ You've got to be on time for work.
      ☐ You have to fill out this form.

2. A: Son, what happened? You didn't call to say that you were going to be late.
   B: I'm sorry. I forgot.
   A: ☐ You must get better grades.
      ☐ You have to clean up your room.
      ☐ You've got to be more responsible.

3. A: Nice shoes. But they're big for you!
   B: Well, I ordered them from an Internet site, but they sent the wrong ones instead.
   A: ☐ You must wear better shoes.
      ☐ You've got to walk a lot.
      ☐ You have to send them back and get the right ones.

4. A: May I help you?
   B: Yes. I'm here to apply for the assistant teacher's job.
   A: ☐ Okay. Everyone has to apply for a job.
      ☐ Okay. Everyone must fill out an application. Here it is.
      ☐ Okay. Everyone has got to pay attention.

5. A: Ms. Honeywell, Jimmy will be better in a few days.
   B: Should he take any medicine, doctor?
   A: ☐ No. He has got to play football tomorrow.
      ☐ No. He has to take this medicine three times a day.
      ☐ No. He just has to stay in bed for a couple of days and drink plenty of water.

► **Practice 17. Expressing lack of necessity and prohibition.** (Chart 7-10)
Complete the sentences with **don't have to** or **must/must not**.

1. To fly from one country to another, you _____*must*_____ have a plane ticket and a passport.

2. To fly from one city to another in the same country, it's necessary to have a plane ticket, but you _____ have a passport.

3. Billy, you are allergic to bees. There are a lot of bees in the flowers. You _____ play near them.

4. You _____ order fish in this seafood restaurant. You can have chicken or beef if you prefer.

5. Because you are feeling better, you _____ take this medicine.

6. Susie, you _____ take this medicine. It's for adults, not children. It will make you sick.

7. If you see a sign that says "No Left Turn," you _____ turn left there.

8. When your phone rings, you _____ answer it. The caller can leave a message.

9. When you are in a theater, you _____ use your cell phone. You have to turn it off.

10. It's warm all the time in Hawaii, so you _____ wear heavy sweaters and jackets there.

11. The wedding is very formal. Everyone has to wear formal clothes. You _____ wear jeans or sandals.

▶ **Practice 18. Expressing necessity, lack of necessity, and prohibition.**
(Charts 7-9 and 7-10)
Write the phrases in the correct columns.

---

cook every meal themselves
drive without a license
eat and drink in order to live
✓fall asleep while driving
pay taxes

say "sir" or "madam" to others
stay in their homes in the evening
stop when they see a police car's lights behind them
take other people's belongings

People have to / must . . . (necessary)	People must not . . . (Don't!)	People don't have to . . . (not necessary)
	fall asleep while driving	

► **Practice 19. Logical conclusions.** (Chart 7-11)
Write the letter of the sentence in Column B that correctly describes the sentence in Column A.

Five Cousins at the Dinner Table

Column A

1. Isabel has eaten two potatoes and now she is asking for another one. _____

2. Rose is sitting at the table, but she isn't eating anything. She had a dish of ice cream just before dinner. _____

3. Emlly is telling everyone about her trip to Costa Rica. She is leaving next week. _____

4. Jill just tasted some fish and made a funny face. _____

5. Natalie has fallen asleep at the dinner table! _____

Column B

a. She must not like it.

b. She must be very tired.

c. She must like them.

d. She must not be hungry.

e. She must be excited about it.

► **Practice 20. Logical conclusion or necessity.** (Charts 7-9 and 7-11)
Write "1" if *must* expresses a logical conclusion. Write "2" if *must* expresses necessity.

1 = logical conclusion
2 = necessity

1. _____2_____ You *must have* a passport to travel abroad.
2. _____1_____ You *must like* to read. You have such a large library.
3. _____ You *must take off* your shoes before entering this room.
4. _____ The dessert *must be* good. It's almost gone.
5. _____ You *must try* this dessert. It's wonderful.
6. _____ Children *must stay* seated during the flight.
7. _____ You *must pay* in advance if you want a front-row seat for the performance.
8. _____ Ellen *must* really *like* being at the beach. She goes there every vacation.

► **Practice 21. Tag questions with modal auxiliaries.** (Chart 7-12)
Complete the tag questions with the correct modal auxiliary.

1. You won't tell anyone, _____ you?

2. George can help us, _____ he?

3. Mr. Cheng would like to come with us, _____ he?

4. You would rather stay home, _____ you?

5. Sally can't speak French, _____ she?

6. You don't have to work next weekend, _____ you?

7. Teachers shouldn't give too much homework, _____ they?

8. I'll see you tomorrow, _____ I?

9. You couldn't hear me, _____ you?

10. We should cross the street here, _____ we?

11. Ms. Scott has to take a driving course, _____ she?

12. If Grandma is expecting us at 6:00, we should leave here at 4:00, _____ we?

▶ **Practice 22. Giving instructions: imperative sentences.** (Chart 7-13)
Pretend that someone says the following sentences to you. Which verbs give instructions?
<u>Underline</u> the imperative verbs.

1. I'll be right back. <u>Wait</u> here.

2. <u>Don't wait</u> for Rebecca. She's not going to come.

3. Read pages 39 to 55 before class tomorrow.

4. What are you doing? Don't put those magazines in the trash. I haven't read them yet.

5. Come in and have a seat. I'll be right with you.

▶ **Practice 23. Polite questions and imperatives.** (Charts 7-5, 7-6, and 7-13)
Number the sentences in each group in order of politeness. "1" is the ***most polite***.

1. __1__ Could you open the door?

   __3__ Open the door.

   __2__ Can you open the door?

2. ____ Get the phone, please.

   ____ Would you please get the phone?

   ____ Get the phone.

   ____ Can you get the phone?

3. ____ Hand me the calculator.

   ____ Will you hand me the calculator, please?

   ____ Would you hand me the calculator, please?

   ____ Please hand me the calculator.

► **PRACTICE 24. Let's and Why don't.** (Chart 7-14)
Complete the conversation with verbs from the lists.

Six Neighborhood Friends

Six neighborhood friends have grown up together. They are very close. They meet for breakfast on Sundays and then try to do something active together during the day. Here's a conversation they had on one recent Sunday.

Part I.   *fly, listen, sail, walk*

JOHNNY: There's a strong wind today. Let's _____ our kites on the beach today.
                                                        1

BOBBY: No, the wind is perfect for sailing. Let's _____ on the lake today. We could
                                                             2

rent two boats for a few hours.

GRACE: Why don't we _____ over to the park? It's a beautiful day, and we could have a
                               3

great time. There's a country music festival there today.

DORA: Yes, let's go to the park and _____ to country music.
                                            4

Part II.   *go, see, shop*

ALICE: I don't like country music very much. I'd rather go to the mall. Let's _____
                                                                                  5

shopping. They're having a big holiday sale today.

TIMMY: Shopping is boring. I'll tell you what. Alice, why don't you _____ and the rest
                                                                         6

of us will do something else.

ALICE: Hmmm. Grace, do you want to drive over to the mall with me?

GRACE: No, I'd rather do something as a group. Okay, guys—let's _____. What can
                                                                      7

the rest of us enjoy as a group?

Part III.   *do, have, plan, tell*

JOHNNY: I think we should go to the country music festival together. They have a lot of great

musicians. After that, let's _____ pizza at my house. We can order it from the
                                  8

Pizza Pan.

BOBBY: Okay. Let's _____ that today—go to the festival and end up at Johnny's. Then
                          9

let's _____ a sailing day next week. Johnny, why don't you _____
          10   11

your parents we're having a pizza dinner and invite them to join us too?

Complete the sentences with *prefer*, *like(s)*, or *would rather*.

1. I _____*prefer*_____ cold weather to hot weather.

2. A: What's your favorite fruit?
   B: I _____*like*_____ strawberries better than any other fruit.

3. Mary _____*would rather*_____ save money than enjoy herself.

4. A: Why isn't your brother going with us to the movie?
   B: He _____ stay home and read than go out on a Saturday night.

5. A: Does Peter _____ football to baseball?
   B: No. I think he _____ baseball better than football.
   A: Then why didn't he go to the game yesterday?
   B: Because he _____ watch sports on TV than go to a ball park.

6. A: Do you want to go out to the Japanese restaurant for dinner?
   B: That would be okay, but in truth I _____ Chinese food to Japanese food.
   A: Really? I _____ Japanese food better than Chinese food. What shall we do?
   B: Let's go to the Italian restaurant.

▶ **Practice 26. Stating preferences.** (Chart 7-15)
Use the words in parentheses to make a new sentence with the same meaning.

1. Alex would rather swim than jog. (*prefer*)
   _____*Alex prefers swimming to jogging.*_____

2. My son would rather eat fish than beef. (*would rather*)
   _____

3. Kim likes salad better than dessert. (*prefer*)
   _____

4. In general, Nicole would rather have coffee than tea. (*like*)
   _____

5. Bill prefers teaching history to working as a business executive. (*would rather*)
   _____

6. When considering a pet, Sam prefers dogs to cats. (*like*)
   _____

7. On a long trip, Susie would rather drive than ride in the back seat. (*prefer*)
   _____

8. I like studying in a noisy room better than studying in a quiet room. (*would rather*)
   _____

9. Alex likes soccer better than baseball. (*would rather*)
   _____

The words in **bold** are modal auxiliaries. Read the passage, and then answer the question.

Doing Chores

Everyone in my family **has to** do chores around the house. A chore is a special job that one
person **must** perform. The chore **could** be to wash the dinner dishes, for example, or it **might** be
to sweep the porch. My parents give chores to my brother Joe and me, and we **have to** do these
chores every day.

Sometimes if one of us is busy and **can't** do a chore, the other one **may** take care of it. For
example, last Friday it was Joe's turn to wash the dishes after dinner. But he said he **couldn't** wash
them at that time because he had to hurry to school for a basketball game. Joe asked me, "**Will** you
do the dishes for me, please? I promise to do them for you tomorrow when it's your turn.
I've got to be on time for the game at school." I agreed to do Joe's chore and washed the dishes
after dinner.

But the next night, Joe "forgot" that we had traded days. When I reminded him to wash the
dishes, he said, "Who, me? It's not my turn."

In the future, we **should** put our agreements in writing. That **ought to** solve any problems if
anyone says, "It's not my turn."

What is the meaning of these modal auxiliaries from the passage? Circle the word or words closest
in meaning to the modal.

Modal Auxiliary			Meaning	
(1) Everyone **has to** do . . .	(must)	should	is able to	might
(2) . . . one person **must** perform . . .	has to	should	is able to	might
(3) The chore **could** be to wash . . .	must	should	is able to	might

(4) . . . it **might** be to sweep . . .	*must*	*should*	*is able to*	*could*
(5) . . . we **have to** do these chores . . .	*must*	*should*	*are able to*	*might*
(6) . . . and **can't** do a chore . . .	*must not*	*shouldn't*	*isn't able to*	*might not*
(7) . . . the other one **may** . . .	*must*	*should*	*is able to*	*might*
(8) But he said he **couldn't** . . .	*must not*	*shouldn't*	*wasn't able to*	*may not*
(9) **Will** you do the dishes . . .	*Must you*	*Should you*	*Are you able to*	*Would you*
(10) I**'ve got to** be on time . . .	*must*	*should*	*am able to*	*may*
(11) . . . we **should** put our . . .	*must*	*ought to*	*are able to*	*may*
(12) That **ought to** solve . . .	*must*	*should*	*is able to*	*may*

▶ **Practice 28. Editing.** (Chapter 7)
Correct the errors.

1. Before I left on my trip last month, I ~~must~~ *had to* get a passport.

2. Could you to bring us more coffee, please?

3. Ben can driving, but he prefers take the bus.

4. A few of our classmates can't to come to the school picnic.

5. May you take our picture, please?

6. Come in, come in! It's so cold outside. You must to be freezing!

7. Jim would rather has Fridays off in the summer than a long vacation.

8. I must reading several long books for my literature class.

9. Take your warm clothes with you. It will maybe snow.

10. It's such a gorgeous day. Why we don't go to a park or the beach?

▶ **Practice 29. Crossword puzzle.** (Chapter 7)
Complete the puzzle with modal auxiliaries. Use the clues to find the correct words.

Across

2. If you want to be a lawyer, you _____ to graduate from law school.

3. I _____ go with you. I don't know yet. If I finish my homework, I'll go with you.

5. _____ don't you join us for lunch today?

6. I'd _____ go fishing than go sailing.

7. You haven't eaten all day. You _____ be very hungry!

8. When I was a child, I _____ jump high into the air. Now I can't.

Down

1. Uh oh! You had _____ slow down! I see a police officer on his motorcycle over there.

3. _____ I come in? I'd like to talk to you.

4. I _____ study tonight, but I'm not going to. I'm going to watch a good movie on TV.

Chapter **8**
Connecting Ideas

▶ **Practice 1. Connecting ideas with *and*.** (Chart 8-1)
Underline the words that are connected with ***and***. Label these words as nouns, verbs, or adjectives.

                  noun + noun   +   noun
1. My kitchen has a new <u>sink</u>, <u>refrigerator</u>, and <u>oven</u>.

           adjective + adjective
2. Danny is a <u>bright</u> and <u>happy</u> child.

      verb   +   verb
3. I picked up the telephone and dialed Steve's number.

4. I have a computer, a printer, and a scanner in my home office.

5. The cook washed the vegetables and put them in boiling water.

6. My feet were cold and wet.

7. Anita is responsible, considerate, and trustworthy.

8. The three largest land animals are the elephant, the rhinoceros, and the hippopotamus.

9. A hippopotamus rests in water during the day and feeds on land at night.

► **Practice 2. Punctuating sentences.** (Chart 8-1)
Each of these sentences contains two independent clauses. Find the subject "S" and verb "V" of each clause. Add a comma or a period. Capitalize as necessary.

       S   V   S   V
1. Birds fly, and fish swim.

       S   V   S   V
             F
2. Birds fly. fish swim.

3. Dogs bark lions roar.

4. Dogs bark and lions roar.

5. A week has seven days a year has 365 days.

6. A week has seven days and a year has 365 days.

7. Ahmed raised his hand and the teacher pointed at him.

8. Ahmed raised his hand the teacher pointed at him.

► **Practice 3. Punctuating items connected with *and*.** (Chart 8-1)
Add commas where necessary.

1. I opened the door and walked into the room. (No change.)

2. I opened the door, walked into the room, and sat down at my desk.

3. Their flag is green and black.

4. Their flag is green black and yellow.

5. Tom ate a sandwich and drank a glass of juice.

6. Tom made a sandwich poured a glass of juice and sat down to eat his lunch.

7. Ms. Parker is intelligent friendly and kind.

8. Mr. Parker is grouchy and unhappy.

9. Did you bring copies of the annual report for Sue Dan Joe and Mary?

10. I always read the newspaper online and listen to the news on the radio in the morning.

11. Can you watch television listen to the radio and read the newspaper at the same time?

► **Practice 4. Punctuating sentences.** (Chart 8-1)
Write "C" if the punctuation is correct and "I" for incorrect. Make the necessary corrections.

1. _____ Amy jogged along the road I rode my bicycle.

2. _____ Amy stopped after 20 minutes. I continued on for an hour.

3. _____ Trained dogs can lie down and perform other tricks on command.

4. _____ My mother trained our dog to get the newspaper, my father trained it to bark at strangers.

5. _____ The river rose, it flooded the towns in the valley.

6. _____ The river and streams rose. They flooded the towns and farms in the valley.

7. _____ Astrology is the study of the stars, planets and their effect on our lives.

8. _____ Sharon reads her horoscope every day. She believes her life is shaped by the positions of the stars and planets.

9. _____ Sharon's children don't believe in astrology, they dismiss the information she gives them.

▶ **Practice 5. Connecting ideas with *and*.** (Chart 8-1)

Part I. Read the passage.

Very Old Twins

Kin Narita and Gin Kanie were twin sisters from Japan. They were born in 1892. Their family name was Yano. Their first names are names of valuable metals: silver and gold. Kin means silver and Gin means gold.

They were 99 years old when the mayor of Nagoya, their hometown, visited them. He visited them on a national holiday—Respect for the Aged Day. In Japan, many people live a long time and receive a lot of respect when they are old. The mayor congratulated the twins on their long and healthy lives.

After the mayor's visit, the twins became famous and popular. They appeared on television game shows and in advertisements. People liked their wide smiles and their lively interest in the world. They laughed and smiled a lot. They said they stayed healthy because they had a simple lifestyle, walked everywhere, and enjoyed people, especially each other.

Kin had 11 children, and Gin had five children. They had many grandchildren and great-grandchildren. Kin died in January, 2000, at the age of 107, and Gin died in February, 2001, at the age of 108.

Part II. Each statement is incorrect. Make true statements. Write the correct punctuation.

1. The twins' first names mean health and happiness.

   _____*The twins' first names mean silver and gold.*_____

2. In Japan, many people don't live a long time, and they don't receive respect when they are old.

   _____

   _____

3. The twins were young and sick.

   _____

4. The twins rarely laughed and smiled.

   _____

5. The twins never had a simple lifestyle and always drove everywhere.

   _____

6. They didn't enjoy people and they didn't enjoy each other.

   _____

7. Kin and Gin didn't have any children or grandchildren.

   _____

8. When they died Kin and Gin were together.

   _____

► **Practice 6. Using *and, but,* and *or.*** (Chart 8-2)
Add commas where necessary.

1. I talked to Amy for a long time, but she didn't listen.

2. I talked to Martin for a long time and asked him many questions. (No change.)

3. Please call Jane or Ted.

4. Please call Jane and Ted.

5. Please call Jane Ted or Anna.

6. Please call Jane Ted and Anna.

7. Did you call Kim or Luis?

8. I didn't call Leo Sarah or Hugo.

9. I waved at my friend but she didn't see me.

10. I waved at my friend and she waved back.

► **Practice 7. Connecting ideas with *so.*** (Chart 8-3)
Complete each sentence with a correct phrase from the list.

a. everybody laughed	e. she doesn't walk yet
b. I hung up	f. she walks and runs everywhere
c. I left a message	g. the grass got brown and dry
d. nobody laughed	h. the grass was green and bright

1. The joke was very funny, so _____.

2. The joke wasn't funny, so _____.

3. It didn't rain all summer, so _____.

4. It rained a lot this summer, so _____.

5. Our baby is only three months old, so _____.

6. Our baby is two years old, so _____.

7. The phone rang ten times, and nobody answered, so _____.

8. The phone rang three times, and a machine answered, so _____.

► **Practice 8. Using *and, but, or,* and *so.*** (Charts 8-1 → 8-3)
Choose the correct completion.

1. I was tired, _____ I went to bed.
   a. but   b. or   c. so

2. I sat down on the couch _____ opened the newspaper.
   a. but   b. and   c. so

3. The students were on time, _____ the teacher was late.
   a. but   b. or   c. so

4. I would like one pet. I'd like to have a bird _____ a cat.
   a. but   b. and   c. or

5. Our children are happy _____ healthy.
   a. but   b. and   c. or

6. I wanted a cup of tea, _____ I boiled some water.
   a. but   b. and   c. so

7. The phone rang, _____ I didn't answer it.
   a. but   b. and   c. so

8. You can have an apple _____ an orange. Choose one.
   a. but   b. and   c. or

▶ **Practice 9. Using *and, but, or,* and *so.*** (Charts 8-1 → 8-3)
Write "C" if the punctuation is correct and "I" for incorrect. Make the necessary corrections.

1. _____ I washed and dried the dishes.

2. _____ I washed the dishes, and my son dried them.

3. _____ Victor offered me an apple or a peach.

4. _____ I bought some apples peaches and bananas.

5. _____ I was hungry so I ate an apple.

6. _____ Carlos was hungry and ate two apples.

7. _____ My sister is generous and kind-hearted.

8. _____ My daughter is affectionate shy independent and smart.

▶ **Practice 10. Using *and, but, or,* and *so.*** (Charts 8-1 → 8-3)
Add periods, commas, and capital letters as necessary. Don't change any of the words or the order of the words.

1. James has a cold. *H*͏e needs to rest and drink plenty of fluids, so he should go to bed and drink water fruit juices or soda pop he needs to sleep a lot so he shouldn't drink fluids with caffeine, such as tea or coffee.

2. The normal pulse for an adult is between 60 and 80 beats per minute but exercise nervousness excitement and a fever will all make a pulse beat faster the normal pulse for a child is around 80 to 90.

3. Edward Fox was a park ranger for 35 years during that time, he was hit by lightning eight times the lightning never killed him but it severely burned his skin and damaged his hearing.

▶ **Practice 11. Using *and, but, or,* and *so.*** (Chart 8-1 → 8-3)
Add commas where necessary. Some sentences need no commas.

An English School for Gina

Gina wants a job as an air traffic controller. Every air traffic controller worldwide uses English so it is important for her to become fluent in the language. She has decided to take some intensive English courses at a private language institute but she isn't sure which one to attend. There are many schools available and they offer many different kinds of classes. She has also heard of air traffic control schools that include English as part of their coursework but she needs to have a fairly high level of English to attend. She has to decide soon or the classes will be full. She's planning to visit her top three choices this summer and decide on the best one for her.

► **Practice 12. Using auxiliary verbs after *but*.** (Chart 8-4)
Complete each sentence with the correct auxiliary verb.

1. Dan didn't study for the test, but Amy _____*did*_____.

2. Alice doesn't come to class every day, but Julie _____.

3. Jack went to the movie last night, but I _____.

4. I don't live in the dorm, but Rob and Jim _____.

5. My roommate was at home last night, but I _____.

6. Mr. Wong isn't here today, but Miss Choki _____.

7. Susan won't be at the meeting tonight, but I _____.

8. Susan isn't going to go to the meeting tonight, but I _____.

9. I'll be there, but she _____.

10. I haven't finished my work yet, but Erica _____.

11. My son enjoys monster movies, but I _____.

12. I enjoy romantic comedies, but my son _____.

► **Practice 13. Using auxiliary verbs after *and*.** (Chart 8-5)
Complete each sentence with the correct auxiliary verb.

1. Rob lives in the dorm, and Jim _____ too.

2. I don't live in the dorm, and Carol _____ either.

3. Ted isn't here today, and Linda _____ either.

4. The teacher is listening to the CD, and the students _____ too.

5. I'll be there, and Mike _____ too.

6. I can speak French, and my wife _____ too.

7. Jane would like a cup of coffee, and I _____ too.

8. I like rock music, and my roommate _____ too.

9. Paul can't speak Spanish, and Larry _____ either.

10. I am exhausted from the long trip, and my mother _____ too.

11. I have a dimple in my chin, and my brother _____ too.

12. I visited the museum yesterday, and my friend _____ too.

► **Practice 14. Using *and* + *too, so, either, neither*.** (Chart 8-5)
Complete the sentences by using the word in *italics* and an appropriate auxiliary.

1. *Tom*   Jack has a mustache, and so _____*does Tom*_____.

   Jack has a mustache, and _____*Tom does*_____ too.

2. *Brian*   Alex doesn't have a mustache, and neither _____.

   Alex doesn't have a mustache, and _____ either.

3. *I*   Mary was at home last night, and so _____.

   Mary was at home last night, and _____ too.

4. *Jean*   I went to a movie last night, and so _____.

   I went to a movie last night, and _____ too.

5. *Jason* I didn't study last night, and neither _____.

I didn't study last night, and _____ either.

6. *Rick* Jim can't speak Arabic, and neither _____.

Jim can't speak Arabic, and _____ either.

7. *Laura* I like to go to science-fiction movies, and so _____.

I like to go to science-fiction movies, and _____ too.

8. *Alice* I don't like horror movies, and neither _____.

I don't like horror movies, and _____ either.

▶ **Practice 15. Using *too, so, either,* or *neither* after *and.*** (Chart 8-5)

Part I. Complete the sentences with an auxiliary + *too* or *either*.

1. I can't sew, and my roommate _____*can't either*_____.

2. I don't like salty food, and my wife _____.

3. Yesterday, Rosa Gomez came to class late and Mr. Nazari _____.

4. Andy knew the answer to the question, and Tina _____.

5. I couldn't understand the substitute teacher, and Yoko _____.

6. I'd rather stay home this evening, and my husband _____.

Part II. Complete the sentences with an auxiliary + *so* or *neither*.

7. Pasta is a famous Italian dish, and _____*so is*_____ pizza.

8. I didn't go to the bank, and _____ my husband.

9. I'm not a native speaker of English, and _____ Mr. Chu.

10. I've never seen a monkey in the wild, and _____ my children.

11. When we heard the hurricane warning, I nailed boards over my windows, and

_____ all of my neighbors.

12. My brother and I are taking the same chemistry course. It is difficult, but I like it and

_____ he.

▶ **Practice 16. Auxiliary verbs after *but* and *and.*** (Charts 8-4 and 8-5)
A woman is talking about her housemate, Hanna. Choose the correct completion from Column B.

Column A	Column B
1. I like cooking, and _*h*_.	a. do too
2. I don't like housework, and Hanna ____.	b. does too
3. I like gardening, and she ____.	c. doesn't either
4. I don't like snakes in our garden, and ____.	d. don't either
5. She likes to go jogging after work, and ____.	e. neither do I
6. She doesn't like to play golf, and I ____.	f. neither does she
7. She likes to watch old movies, and I ____.	g. so do I
8. She doesn't like to sleep late on weekends, and ____	h. so does Hanna

► **Practice 17. Adverb clauses with *because*.** (Chart 8-6)
Add periods, commas, and capital letters as necessary.

1. Because his coffee was cold, Jack didn't finish it. ~~h~~*H*e left it on the table and walked away.

2. I opened the window because the room was hot a nice breeze came in.

3. Because the weather was bad we canceled our trip into the city we stayed home and watched TV.

4. Debbie loves gymnastics because she hopes to be on an Olympic team she practices hard every day.

5. Francisco is very good in math because several colleges want him to attend they are offering him full scholarships.

► **Practice 18. Adverb clauses with *because*.** (Chart 8-6)
Read each pair of phrases and circle the one that gives the reason (explains "why"). Then check the correct sentence.

1. (lose weight,) go on a diet
   __✓__ Eric went on a diet because he wanted to lose weight.
   _____ Because Eric went on a diet, he wanted to lose weight.

2. didn't have money, couldn't buy food
   _____ The family couldn't buy food because they didn't have money.
   _____ Because the family couldn't buy food, they didn't have money.

3. be very busy, have several children
   _____ Because our neighbors are very busy, they have several children.
   _____ Our neighbors are very busy because they have several children.

4. go to bed, be tired
   _____ I am tired because I am going to bed.
   _____ Because I am tired, I am going to bed.

5. be in great shape, exercise every day
   _____ Because Susan exercises every day, she is in great shape.
   _____ Susan exercises every day because she is in great shape.

6. have a high fever, go to the doctor
   _____ Because Jennifer has a high fever, she is going to the doctor.
   _____ Jennifer has a high fever because she is going to the doctor.

► **Practice 19. Adverb clauses with *so* or *because*.** (Charts 8-3 and 8-6)
Complete the sentences with *so* or *because*. Add commas where appropriate. Capitalize as necessary.

1. a. He was hungry __, so__ he ate a sandwich.
   b. ____Because____ he was hungry, he ate a sandwich.
   c. He ate a sandwich _____ he was hungry.

2. a. _____ my sister was tired she went to bed.

   b. My sister went to bed _____ she was tired.

   c. My sister was tired _____ she went to bed.

3. a. Schoolchildren can usually identify Italy easily on a world map _____ it is shaped like a boot.

   b. _____ Italy has the distinctive shape of a boot schoolchildren can usually identify it easily.

   c. Italy has the distinctive shape of a boot _____ schoolchildren can usually identify it easily on a map.

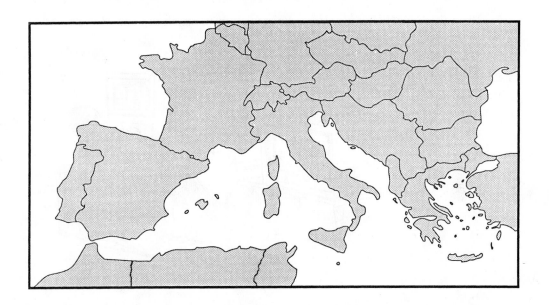

▶ **Practice 20. Adverb clauses with *even though* and *although*.** (Chart 8-7)
Complete each sentence with the correct form of the verb in *italics*. Some verbs will be negative.

1. Even though I (*like*) _____*like*_____ fish, I don't eat it much.

2. Even though I (*like*) _____*don't like*_____ vegetables, I eat them every day.

3. Although my hairdresser (*be*) _____ expensive, I go to her once a week.

4. Even though the basketball game was over, the fans (*stay*) _____ in their seats cheering.

5. Although my clothes were wet from the rain, I (*change*) _____ them.

6. Even though Po studied for weeks, he (*pass*) _____ his exams.

7. Even though the soup was salty, everyone (*eat*) _____ it.

8. Although the roads (*be*) _____ icy, no one got in an accident.

► **Practice 21. Using *because* and *even though*.** (Charts 8-6 and 8-7)
Choose the correct completion.

1. Even though I was hungry, I _____ a lot at dinner.
   a. ate   b. didn't eat

2. Because I was hungry, I _____ a lot at dinner.
   a. ate   b. didn't eat

3. Because I was cold, I _____ my coat.
   a. put on   b. didn't put on

4. Even though I was cold, I _____ my coat.
   a. put on   b. didn't put on

5. Even though Mike _____ sleepy, he stayed up to watch the end of the game on TV.
   a. was   b. wasn't

6. Because Linda _____ sleepy, she went to bed.
   a. was   b. wasn't

7. Because Kate ran too slowly, she _____ the race.
   a. won   b. didn't win

8. Even though Jessica ran fast, she _____ the race.
   a. won   b. didn't win

► **Practice 22. Adverb clauses with *because* and *even though*.**
(Charts 8-6 and 8-7)
Complete the sentences with *even though* or *because*.

1. Yuko went to a dentist _____*because*_____ she had a toothache.

2. Colette didn't go to a dentist _____ she had a toothache.

3. Jennifer went to a dentist _____ she didn't have a toothache. She just
   wanted a checkup.

4. Louie didn't iron his shirt _____ it was wrinkled.

5. Eric ironed his shirt _____ it was wrinkled.

6. _____ Dan is fairly tall, he can't reach the ceiling.

7. _____ Matt is very tall, he can reach the ceiling.

8. _____ Tim is shorter than Matt, he can't reach the ceiling.

9. _____ Nick isn't tall, he can reach the ceiling by standing on a chair.

DAN   MATT   TIM   NICK

▶ **Practice 23. Adverb clauses with *because* and *although*.** (Charts 8-6 and 8-7)
Complete the passage with *because* or *although*.

Pill Bottles with Child-Proof Caps

It's difficult to open some pill bottles _____ they have child-proof caps. In
                                                    1
recent years, pill manufacturers have been making this type of bottle _____
                                                                              2
they don't want children to open the bottles and eat the pills. The pills inside the bottle are often

attractive, and _____ they look like candy, they are not candy.
                        3

Last week there was a story on the news about a lucky baby. The baby found an open bottle of

aspirin tablets. _____ the pills looked just like candy, he started to eat them.
                        4

When his mother walked into the room, she saw her baby and the open bottle.

_____ she was frightened, she acted calmly. She immediately took the baby to
                5
the emergency room at the nearby hospital. There the doctors realized that

_____ the baby had eaten pills for adults, he needed only minor treatment.
                6
The mother saved her baby _____ she had acted quickly.
                                              7

▶ **Practice 24. Using *even though/although* and *because*.** (Charts 8-6 and 8-7)
Choose the best completion.

1. I gave him the money because __c__.
   a. I didn't want to
   b. he had a lot of money
   c. I owed it to him

2. Although _____, the hungry man ate every bit of it.
   a. the bread was old and stale
   b. the cheese tasted good to him
   c. an apple is both nutritious and delicious

3. The nurse didn't bring Mr. Hill a glass of water even though _____.
   a. she was very busy
   b. she forgot
   c. he asked her three times

4. When she heard the loud crash, Marge ran outside in the snow although _____.
   a. her mother ran out with her
   b. she wasn't wearing any shoes
   c. she ran as fast as she could

5. Even though his shoes were wet and muddy, Brian _____.
   a. took them off at the front door
   b. walked right into the house and across the carpet
   c. wore wool socks

6. Alex boarded the bus in front of his hotel. He was on his way to the art museum. Because he
_____, he asked the bus driver to tell him where to get off.
   a. was late for work and didn't want his boss to get mad
   b. was carrying a heavy suitcase
   c. was a tourist and didn't know the city streets very well

7. Although _____, Eric got on the plane.
   a. he is married
   b. he is afraid of flying
   c. the flight attendant welcomed him aboard

8. When I attended my first business conference out of town, I felt very uncomfortable during
the social events because _____.
   a. we were all having a good time
   b. I didn't know anyone there
   c. I am very knowledgeable in my field

9. Everyone listened carefully to what the speaker was saying even though _____.
   a. they had printed copies of the speech in their hands
   b. she spoke loudly and clearly
   c. the speech was very interesting

10. Talil works in the city, but once a month he visits his mother, who lives in the country. He has
to rent a car for these trips because _____.
   a. it is expensive
   b. he doesn't have a driver's license
   c. he doesn't own a car

▶ **Practice 25. Editing.** (Chapter 8)
Correct the errors.

1. I don't drink coffee, and my roommate ~~isn't~~ *doesn't* either.

2. The flight was overbooked, I had to fly on another airline.

3. Many people use computers for email the Internet and word processing.

4. Even my father works two jobs, he always has time to play soccer or baseball on weekends with

   his family.

5. I saw a bad accident and my sister too.

6. Oscar always pays his bills on time but his brother wasn't.

7. Because my mother is afraid of heights, I took her up to the observation deck at the top of the

   building.

8. Janey doesn't like to get up early and either Joe.

9. My mother and my father. They immigrated to this country 30 years ago.

10. Even though Maya is very intelligent, her parents want to put her in an advanced program at

    school.

► **Practice 26. Word search puzzle.** (Chapter 8)
Circle the connecting words from Chapter 8 in the puzzle. The words may be horizontal, vertical, or diagonal. The first letter of each word is highlighted in gray.

T	B	M	R	L	R	B	A
O	M	P	E	E	U	B	L
A	O	M	H	T	J	E	T
W	N	T	T	K	T	C	H
R	I	D	I	P	K	A	O
E	J	T	E	F	B	U	U
M	R	O	N	T	W	S	G
T	B	V	S	O	J	E	H

Chapter 9
Comparisons

▶ **Practice 1. As . . . as.** (Chart 9-1)
Make comparisons using *as . . . as*.

1. Rita is very busy. Jason is very busy.

   → Rita is ____(just) as busy as Jason (is)____.

2. Rita is not very busy at all. Jason is very, very busy.

   → Rita isn't ____(nearly) as busy as Jason (is)____.

3. I was tired. Susan was very tired.

   → I wasn't _____.

4. Adam wasn't tired at all. Susan was very tired.

   → Adam wasn't _____.

5. Anne is lazy. Her sister Amanda is equally lazy.

   → Anne is _____.

6. Their brother Alan is extremely lazy.

   → Anne and Amanda are lazy, but they are not _____.

▶ **Practice 2. As . . . as.** (Chart 9-1)
Make comparisons using *as . . . as* and the adjective in parentheses. Use *not* as necessary.

1. Adults have more strength than children. (*strong*)

   → Children ____aren't as strong as____ adults.

2. Tom and Jerry are the same height. (*tall*)

   → Tom _____ Jerry.

3. Dr. Green has a little money. Dr. Brown has a lot of money. (*wealthy*)

   → Dr. Green _____ Dr. Brown.

4. City air is often polluted. Country air is often fresh and clear. (*polluted*)

   → Country air _____ city air.

5. Paula studies a little bit. Jack studies a lot. (*studious*)

   → Paula _____ Jack.

6. Math courses are easy for me, but language courses aren't. (*difficult*)

   → Math courses _____ language courses for me.

▶ **Practice 3. As . . . as.** (Chart 9-1)
Part I. Complete the sentences with one of the following:

- just as . . . as
- almost as . . . as / not quite as . . . as
- not nearly as . . . as

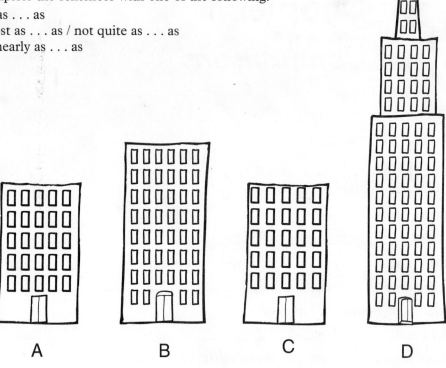

A   B   C   D

1. Building B is _____*not nearly as*_____ high as Building D.

2. Building A is _____ high as Building B.

3. Building C is _____ high as Building D.

4. Building A is _____ high as Building C.

Part II. Compare the arrival times. Meeting time: 9:00 A.M.

       Arrival times

       David 9:01 A.M.

       Julia 9:14 A.M.

       Laura 9:15 A.M.

       Paul 9:15 A.M.

       James 9:25 A.M.

5. Paul was _____*just as*_____ late as Laura.

6. David was _____ late as James.

7. Julia was _____ late as Laura and Paul.

8. Julia was _____ late as James.

Part III. Compare world temperatures.

Bangkok	92°F / 33°C
Cairo	85°F / 30°C
Madrid	90°F / 32°C
Moscow	68°F / 20°C
Tokyo	85°F / 30°C

9. Tokyo is _____ hot as Cairo.

10. Moscow is _____ hot as Bangkok.

11. Madrid is _____ hot as Bangkok.

Part IV. Compare world temperatures today and yesterday.

	Yesterday	*Today*
Bangkok	95°F / 35°C	92°F / 33°C
Cairo	95°F / 35°C	85°F / 30°C
Madrid	90°F / 32°C	90°F / 32°C
Moscow	70°F / 21°C	68°F / 20°C
Tokyo	81°F / 27°C	85°F / 30°C

12. Cairo was _____ hot as Bangkok yesterday.

13. It's _____ warm in Moscow today as yesterday.

14. Madrid is _____ hot today as yesterday.

15. It was _____ hot in Tokyo yesterday as in Bangkok.

16. It's _____ hot in Bangkok today as yesterday.

▶ **Practice 4. As . . . as.** (Chart 9-1)
Part I. Complete each expression with the correct phrase.

as a bat	as a mouse	as a pillow
as a bird	as a picture	✓as snow
as a bone	as pie	as a wink
as ice		

bat

1. very white: as white ___*as snow*___.

2. very cold: as cold _____.

3. very pretty: as pretty _____.

4. can't see anything: as blind _____.

5. very dry: as dry _____.

6. very soft: as soft _____.

7. very quick: as quick _____.

8. very quiet: as quiet _____.

9. very free: as free _____.

10. very easy: as easy _____.

wink

pie

Part II. Complete the sentences with the given adjectives and the phrases from Part I.

blind	dry	free	quick	soft
✓cold	easy	pretty	quiet	white

11. Brrrr! Come inside. Your hands are freezing. They are as ____*cold as ice*____ .

12. I'm just running down to the corner store. I'll be back in a few minutes. I'll be as

    _____ .

13. I can't see anything without my glasses on. I'm as _____ .

14. What laundry detergent do you use? Your white shirts were covered with dirt, and now they're

    so clean and bright. They're as _____ .

15. Shhh! Don't wake up Janet. She's sleeping on the couch. Be as _____ .

16. Your little girl looks darling in that pink dress and hat. She looks as _____

    _____ .

17. Don't worry. You'll pass the swimming test. It's not hard at all. It'll be as

    _____ for you.

18. Charles looks so relaxed since he quit his job. He has no responsibilities for now. He must feel

    as _____ .

19. I have back problems and need to sleep on a bed that has a very firm mattress. My husband

    can sleep on anything, even something that is as _____ .

20. It hasn't rained in weeks. The grass is brown, and the flowers are dead. The ground is as

    _____ .

▶ **Practice 5. Comparative and superlative forms.** (Charts 9-2 and 9-3)
Write the comparative and superlative forms of the given words.

		COMPARATIVE		SUPERLATIVE	
1.	strong	____*stronger*____ than	____*the strongest*____ of all.
2.	important	____*more important*____ than	____*the most important*____ of all.
3.	soft	_____ than	_____ of all.
4.	lazy	_____ than	_____ of all.
5.	wonderful	_____ than	_____ of all.
6.	calm	_____ than	_____ of all.
7.	tame	_____ than	_____ of all.
8.	dim	_____ than	_____ of all.
9.	convenient	_____ than	_____ of all.
10.	clever	_____ than	_____ of all.
11.	good	_____ than	_____ of all.
12.	bad	_____ than	_____ of all.
13.	far	_____ than	_____ of all.

14. slow _____ than _____ of all.

15. slowly _____ than _____ of all.

▶ **Practice 6. Comparative forms.** (Charts 9-2 and 9-3)
Complete each sentence with the correct comparative form of the word in parentheses.

1. My mother is a few years (*old*) _____ my father.

2. An airplane is (*expensive*) _____ a car.

3. Which is (*large*) _____: Greenland or Iceland?

4. Red or cayenne pepper tastes (*hot*) _____ black pepper.

5. A typewriter is (*slow*) _____ a computer.

6. White chocolate is (*creamy*) _____ dark chocolate because it has more fat.

7. Is smoking (*bad*) _____ alcohol for your health?

8. A jaguar is (*fast*) _____ a lion.

9. Which is (*important*) _____: happiness or wealth?

10. For long-distance trips, flying is (*quick*) _____ driving or taking a train.

11. Which is (*heavy*) _____: a kilo of cotton or a kilo of rocks?★

12. Driving in a car equipped with a seat belt and an airbag is (*safe*) _____ driving in a car with just a seat belt.

13. Calculus is (*difficult*) _____ arithmetic.

▶ **Practice 7. Comparatives.** (Charts 9-2 and 9-3)
Complete the sentences with the correct comparative form of the words from the list.

cheap	dry	foggy	high	sunny
cold	expensive	healthy	international	

1. Locations near the equator are hot. Locations near the North Pole and the South Pole are cold. For example, Siberia is much _____ Cuba. The average temperature in Cuba is a lot _____ than the average temperature in Siberia.

2. Some places in northern Europe are often foggy. London is famous for its fog. It's much _____ in London, for example, than it is in southern Europe. The island of Majorca, in southern Spain, is very sunny. It's a lot _____ in Majorca than it is in London.

★This is a trick question.
Answer: They weigh the same.

3. Some people with illnesses have to move to places where there is dry air. For example, my
   uncle had to move to Arizona because the air there is a lot _____
   than it is in Chicago, where he lived. The air in Arizona was good for him, and he became a lot
   _____ there.

4. New York is an international city. My hometown is just a small town. New York is much
   _____ than my hometown. It's expensive to live in New York. It's far
   _____ to live in New York than it is to live in my hometown. It's
   much _____ to live in my hometown than it is to live in New York.

▶ **Practice 8. Comparatives.** (Charts 9-2 and 9-3)
The given sentences contain words from Column A. Column B has words with the opposite
meaning. Complete the sentences with the correct comparative form of the words in Column B.

Column A	Column B
careless	careful
uncomfortable	comfortable
lazy	energetic
stingy	generous
noisy, noisily	quiet, quietly
quiet, quietly	noisy, noisily
poor	rich
ugly	✓pretty

1. The James family painted their house. It was an ugly brown, but now it's a bright yellow. The
   house is much _____*prettier*_____ than it was before.

2. Jenny, that was very careless! You have to learn to be _____ with
   your things.

3. I love this cool weather. I don't feel lazy anymore. I feel _____ than
   I felt in the hot weather.

4. I felt very uncomfortable in the hot weather. I feel much _____
   in this cool weather.

5. My parents are not stingy at all, but Frank's parents are stingy. My parents are
   _____ than Frank's parents.

6. Frank's parents are not poor. They are _____ than my parents.

7. In a library, some students are noisy, but most work _____. I can do
   a lot of work in a _____ place.

8. Our dog is big and noisy, but our new, little kitten is very soft and _____.
   Our dog is _____ than our cat. He walks
   _____ than our cat, he eats _____, and
   even sleeps _____. He snores!

► **Practice 9. Comparatives and superlatives.** (Charts 9-2 and 9-3)
Complete the sentences with *better*, *the best*, *worse*, or *the worst*.

1. I just finished a terrible book. It's _____the worst_____ book I've ever read.

2. The weather was bad yesterday, but it's terrible today. The weather is _____worse_____ today than it was yesterday.

3. This cake is really good. It's _____ cake I've ever eaten.

4. My grades this term are great. They're much _____ than last term.

5. Being separated from my family in time of war is one of _____ experiences I can imagine.

6. I broke my nose in a football game yesterday. Today it's very painful. For some reason, the pain is _____ today than it was yesterday.

7. The fire spread and burned down an entire city block. It was _____ fire we've ever had in our town.

8. I think my cold is almost over. I feel a lot _____ than I did yesterday. I can finally breathe again.

► **Practice 10. *Farther* and *Further*.** (Chart 9-3)
Choose the correct answer(s).

1. The planet Earth is _____ from the sun than the planet Mercury is.
   a. farther   b. further

2. I have no _____ need of this equipment. I'm going to sell it.
   a. farther   b. further

3. I'm tired. I walked _____ than I wanted to.
   a. farther   b. further

4. I'll be available by phone if you have any _____ questions.
   a. farther   b. further

5. A: Tell us more.
   B: Sorry, I have no _____ comment.
      a. farther   b. further

6. A: I heard that you and Tom are engaged to be married.
   B: Nothing could be _____ from the truth!
      a. farther   b. further

► **Practice 11. Adjectives vs. adverbs in the comparative.** (Chart 9-3)
Write the correct comparative form of the adjective or adverb in each sentence. If the word is an adjective, circle ADJ If it is an adverb, circle ADV.

1. *slow*   I like to drive fast, but my brother William doesn't. As a rule, he drives
   slowly   _____more slowly_____ than I do.   ADJ (ADV)

2. *slow*
   slowly
   Alex is a _____slower_____ driver than I am. (ADJ) ADV

3. *serious*
   seriously
   Some workers are _____ about their jobs than others.   ADJ   ADV

4. *serious*
   seriously
   Some workers approach their jobs _____ than others.   ADJ   ADV

5. *polite*
   politely
   Why is it that my children behave _____ at other people's houses than at home?   ADJ   ADV

6. *polite*
   politely
   Why are they _____ at Mrs. Miranda's house than at home?   ADJ   ADV

7. *careful*
   carefully
   I'm a cautious person when I express my opinions, but my sister will say anything to anyone. I'm much _____ when I speak to others than my sister is.   ADJ   ADV

8. *careful*
   carefully
   I always speak _____ in public than my sister does.   ADJ   ADV

9. *clear*
   clearly
   I can't understand Mark's father very well when he talks, but I can understand Mark. He speaks much _____ than his father.
   ADJ   ADV

10. *clear*
    clearly
    Mark is a much _____ speaker than his father.   ADJ   ADV

▶ **Practice 12. Completing comparisons with pronouns.** (Chart 9-4)
Complete the sentences with a pronoun and the correct auxiliary verb. Use both formal and informal completions.

1. Bob arrived at ten. I arrived at eleven.

   He arrived earlier than _____I did_____ / _____me_____.

2. Linda is a good painter. Steven is better.

   He is a better painter than _____she is_____ / _____her_____.

3. I won the race. Anna came in second.

   I ran faster than _____ / _____.

4. My parents were nervous about my motorcycle ride. I was just a little nervous.

   They were a lot more nervous than _____ / _____.

5. My aunt will stay with us for two weeks. My uncle has to return home to his job after a couple of days.

   She will be here with us a lot longer than _____ / _____.

6. I've been here for two years. Sam has been here for two months.

   I've been here a lot longer than _____ / _____.

7. I have a brother. His name is David. He's really tall. I'm just medium height.

   He's taller than _____ / _____.

8. My brother is sixteen. I'm seventeen.

   I'm older than _____ / _____.

9. My sister is really pretty. I've never thought I was pretty.

   She's a lot prettier than _____ / _____.

10. I'm quite smart, though. My sister isn't interested in school.

   I'm smarter than _____ / _____.

▶ **Practice 13. Very vs. a lot / much / far.** (Chart 9-5)
Circle the correct answer. More than one answer may be correct.

1. This watch is not ____ expensive.
   a. very   b. a lot   c. much   d. far

2. That watch is ____ more expensive than this one.
   a. very   b. a lot   c. much   d. far

3. My nephew is ____ polite.
   a. very   b. a lot   c. much   d. far

4. My nephew is ____ more polite than my niece.
   a. very   b. a lot   c. much   d. far

5. Ted is ____ taller than his brother.
   a. very   b. a lot   c. much   d. far

6. Ted is ____ tall.
   a. very   b. a lot   c. much   d. far

7. I think astronomy is ____ more interesting than geology.
   a. very   b. a lot   c. much   d. far

8. I think astronomy is ____ interesting.
   a. very   b. a lot   c. much   d. far

9. It took me a lot longer to get over my cold than it took you to get over your cold. My cold was
   ____ worse than yours.
   a. very   b. a lot   c. much   d. far

▶ **Practice 14. Not as . . . as and less . . . than.** (Chart 9-6)
The passage contains nine phrases with **not as . . . (as)**. <u>Underline</u> these phrases, and if possible, change them to sentences with the same meaning using **less . . . (than)**.

A Move to a New Town

(1) Lia has been unhappy ever since she and her family moved to Southland, a suburb of a big city. She was very happy with her life in the city, where she had lived since she was born. She liked her friends, her school, and her neighborhood there.

(2) In her new school, the students are <u>not as friendly as</u> her old schoolmates. The classes are not as interesting as the ones in her old school, and she is a little bored. The classes are not as difficult, and she feels that she isn't learning much.

(3) She doesn't like her new neighborhood. It is not as convenient as her old neighborhood. In the city, all the stores were near her home. In the suburbs, the stores are not as close to her home as they were in the city. In the city, she didn't have to travel far to shop or go to a movie. Lia also misses the cultural events of the city. The cultural life in Southland is not as exciting as it is in the city, where she often went to concerts, plays, and interesting lectures.

(4) Lia is not as comfortable with her life now as she used to be. But, she is not as unhappy as she was at first. She is working on changing her attitude. She is hoping that with time, she will find that life in Southland is not as bad as she thought.

9-A Unclear Comparisons

UNCLEAR (a) Ann likes her dog better than her husband.	Sometimes it is necessary to complete the idea following **than** in order to make a comparison clear.
CLEAR (b) Ann likes her dog better than her husband does. (c) Ann likes her dog better than she does her husband.	In (b): *does* means "likes the dog." In (c): *does* means "likes."

▶ **Practice 15. Unclear comparisons.** (Chart 9-A)
Read the given sentence. Then choose all the sentences that are true.

1. Jana likes tennis more than her husband.
   - (a.) Jana likes tennis.
   - (b.) Jana might not like her husband.
   - (c.) Jana's husband doesn't like tennis as much as Jana does.

2. Jana likes tennis more than her husband does.
   - a. Jana likes tennis.
   - b. Jana might not like her husband.
   - c. Jana's husband doesn't like tennis as much as Jana does.

3. Franco helped me more than Debra.
   - a. Franco didn't help Debra very much.
   - b. Debra didn't help me very much.
   - c. Franco was helpful to me.

4. Franco helped me more than Debra did.
    a. Franco didn't help Debra very much.
    b. Debra didn't help me very much.
    c. Franco was helpful to me.

5. I pay my plumber more than my dentist.
    a. My plumber is more expensive than my dentist.
    b. My dentist doesn't pay the plumber as much as I do.
    c. I pay only my plumber, not my dentist.

6. I pay my plumber more than I pay my dentist.
    a. My plumber is more expensive than my dentist.
    b. My dentist doesn't pay the plumber as much as I do.
    c. I pay only my plumber, not my dentist.

▶ **Practice 16. Unclear comparisons.** (Chart 9-A)
Check (✓) the sentences that have unclear comparisons. Make the necessary corrections.

1. __✓__ Sam enjoys football more than his best friend *does*.

2. _____ Andy writes better financial reports than his boss.

3. _____ The coach helped Anna more than Nancy.

4. _____ Sara likes tennis more than her husband.

5. _____ Cathy leaves more generous tips at restaurants than her husband.

6. _____ Kelly eats more organic food than his roommate.

7. _____ Charles knows Judy better than Kevin.

▶ **Practice 17. Using *more* with nouns.** (Chart 9-7)
Complete each sentence with a word from the list. Use *more* to make the comparison.

books	enjoyment	readers
cell phones	news	things

1. There are _____ in the public library than there are in my home. I have a few hundred, but the library has thousands.

2. A lot of people download books onto their computers or other devices. I prefer to hold a book, though. I get _____ from holding a real book than I do from reading one on a computer.

3. People read _____ on their computers than they do in newspapers

4. In fact, several big newspapers have closed down. The newspapers used to have many _____ than they do now.

5. In many countries, there are a lot _____ than land lines. Phones in homes are less common than mobile phones.

6. A cell phone can do _____ than a land line can. For example, it can take pictures, keep a calendar, and even connect to the Internet.

▶ **Practice 18. Using *more* with nouns and adjectives.** (Charts 9-3 and 9-8)

Part I. Adjectives
Complete the sentences with the correct comparative form (***morel-er***).

> difficult   loud   pleasant

1. A warm, sunny day is _____ than a cold windy day.

2. Karen doesn't need a microphone when she speaks to the audience. She's the only person I know whose voice is _____ than mine.

3. My course in microbiology is much _____ than my biology course was.

Part II. Adverbs
Use the adverb forms of these adjectives.

> careful   clear   fast

4. Your new phone is excellent, Joe. I can hear you much _____ on this phone than on your old one.

5. Aunt Anna has been driving _____ since she had her accident on the highway. In fact, she drives very slowly now, and she is quite nervous.

6. You can cook food in a microwave oven much _____ than you can cook it in a regular oven. It takes only seven minutes to bake a potato, for example.

Part III. Nouns
Use the plural form of these nouns if necessary.

> car   friend   homework   money   problem   snow

7. University students study hard. They have a lot _____ than high school students.

8. There is far _____ in winter in Alaska than there is in Texas.

9. I'm lonely. I wish I had _____ to spend time with.

10. Sam's car is ten years old. He has _____ with it than he did when it was new.

11. Traffic in this city has become a big problem. There are many _____ on the road now than there were five years ago.

12. The economy is improving in this area. Small businesses made _____ this year than they did last year.

► **Practice 19. Repeating a comparative.** (Chart 9-8)
Complete the sentences with words from the list. Repeat the comparative.

| bad | big | expensive | friendly | ✓good | long | mad | noisy | warm |

1. His health is improving. He's getting _____*better and better*_____.
2. The Davidsons just had their sixth child. Their family is getting

   _____.

3. People are worried about the environment. The ice at the North and South poles is melting because the earth is getting _____.

4. This neighborhood used to be quiet, but since a new mall opened nearby, it is getting

   _____.

5. I was really angry! I got _____ until my brother touched my arm and told me to calm down.

6. We were so glad we had arrived early at the ticket office. As we waited for it to open, the line got _____.

7. Textbooks are costly. They are getting _____ every year.

8. When Maya first came into our class, she was very shy. She didn't talk to anyone. But little by little, she has relaxed, and now she is getting _____.

9. The weather is getting _____. The airport has canceled most flights because of the snowstorm.

► **Practice 20. Double comparatives.** (Chart 9-9)
Complete the sentences with double comparatives.

1. I exercise every day. Exercise makes me strong. The _____*more*_____ I exercise, the _____*stronger*_____ I get.

2. If butter is soft, it is easy to spread on bread. The _____ the butter is, the _____ it is to spread on bread.

3. I'm trying to make my life simpler. It makes me feel more relaxed.
   The _____ I make my life, the _____ I feel.

4. I spend a long time each day looking at a computer screen. My eyes get very tired.
   The _____ I look at a computer screen, the

   _____ my eyes get.

5. When the wind blows hard, it whistles through the trees.
   The _____ the wind blows, the _____ it

   whistles through the trees.

► **Practice 21. Double comparatives.** (Chart 9-9)
Complete the sentences with double comparatives, using the ideas in parentheses.

1. (*She talked. She got excited.*)

   I met a woman at a party last night. She told us many stories about her exciting job as a
   wildlife photographer. The _____, _____.

2. (*He talked. I got hungry.*)

   I also met a man who is a chef. He talked about some of the great meals he makes. I got
   hungry just listening to him. The _____, _____.

3. (*You understand more. You are old.*)

   There are many advantages to being young, but the _____,

   _____.

4. (*Bill talked very fast. I became confused.*)

   Bill was trying to explain some complicated physics problems to help me prepare for an exam.
   He kept talking faster and faster. The _____,

   _____.

5. (*The fans clapped and cheered. The basketball team made more shots.*)

   The fans in the arena were excited and noisy, and it seemed to make their team play better.
   The _____,

   _____.

► **Practice 22. Using superlatives.** (Chart 9-10)
Complete the sentences with the given ideas and the superlative form.

bad flood	far planet	intelligent animals
big organ	good policy	popular sport
common word	high level	tall mountain

1. Mount McKinley in Alaska is the _____ in North America.
2. The skin is _____ in the human body. It covers the largest area.
3. *The* is _____ in the English language.
4. Neptune is _____ from the sun.
5. _____ in the world is football.
6. Bottle-nosed dolphins are _____ that live in the water.

$E = MC^2$

7. Last spring, the towns on the river experienced _____ of this century. The water rose to _____ that it ever had in the towns' history.

8. A famous proverb, and a rule for living, is "Honesty is _____." It means that you should always be honest.

▶ **Practice 23. Using superlatives.** (Chart 9-10)
Part I. Complete the sentences with superlatives and the appropriate word: *in*, *of*, or *ever*.

1. Economics is (*difficult*) ____the most difficult____ course I have ____ever____ taken.

2. For me, English is (*easy*) _____ course I have _____ taken.

3. A lot of students take a course called *The History of Rap Music* because it is one of (*interesting*) _____ courses _____ the college.

4. The professor who teaches it is excellent. He is one of (*good*) _____ professors _____ all the professors in the college.

5. My friends say that my grandmother is (*wise*) _____ person they have _____ met.

6. My wife won our town's annual marathon race twice. She was (*fast*) _____ runner _____ all.

7. My three children all have artistic talent, but Jimmy is (*artistic*) _____ _____ all.

8. My cousin Carolina has won a scholarship to Harvard University to study mathematics. She is one of (*brilliant*) _____ mathematics students _____ the whole country.

9. One of (*successful*) _____ business people _____ our town is Mitchell Brown, the owner of our only independent bookstore.

10. He established the store ten years ago, and now it is (*busy*) _____ bookstore _____ our area.

11. Mitchell is not only a successful businessperson, but he is one of (*generous*) _____ people that our town has _____ known. He has given a lot of time and money to local charities.

12. Mitchell believes that contributing to the quality of life in his community is (*important*) _____ thing that he can do _____ life.

Part II. Make comparisons using **the least** with the word in parentheses, and **in**, **of**, or **ever**.

13. Ed is not lazy, but he is certainly (*ambitious*) ____the least ambitious of____ all the people I have worked with.

14. That painting didn't cost much. It is (*expensive*) _____ work of art we have _____ bought.

15. Antarctica is (*populated*) _____ continent _____ the world.

16. Kim is never tense or nervous. She is (*anxious*) _____ person that I have _____ known. She is always calm.

▶ **Practice 24. As . . . as, more / -er, and most / -est.** (Charts 9-1 → 9-10)

Part I. Compare the cost of the items in parentheses. Use the given expressions.

1. (*a pencil vs.* * *a phone*)

   _____A pencil_____ is less expensive than _____a phone_____.

2. (*a paper clip vs. a diamond ring*)

   _____ is much more expensive than _____.

3. (*a cup of coffee vs. a bag of coffee beans*)

   _____ is not as expensive as _____.

4. (*radios vs. MP3 players vs. big screen TVs*)

   _____ and _____ are both less expensive

   than _____.

5. (*a compact car vs. a house*)

   _____ is not nearly as expensive as _____.

6. (*footballs vs. soccer balls vs. table-tennis balls vs. basketballs*)

   _____, _____, and

   _____ are all more expensive than _____.

Part II. Compare the waterfalls by using the given expressions.

7. _____Angel Falls_____ is much higher _____than Niagara Falls**_____.

8. _____ is almost as high _____.

9. _____ is the highest _____.

10. _____ is not nearly as high _____.

11. _____ is not quite as high _____.

Waterfalls of the World

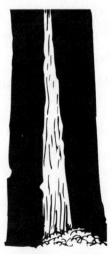

Niagara Falls	Giessbach Falls	Cuquenán Falls	Angel Falls
United States and Canada	Switzerland	Venezuela	Venezuela
53 meters	604 meters	610 meters	807 meters

---

*vs. is an abbreviation for *versus*, which means "as opposed to, as compared to."

**A singular verb is used after Angel Falls because it is the name of a place. Angel Falls is in Venezuela. Similarly, the United States takes a singular verb because it is the name of a place: *The United States is a big country.*

Part III. Compare the weight of the items in parentheses. Use the given expressions.

12. (*air, iron*) _____Air_____ is lighter _____than iron_____ .

13. (*iron, wood*) _____ is heavier _____ .

14. (*water, iron, wood, air*) Of the four elements, _____ is the heaviest

    _____ .

15. (*water, air*) _____ is not as heavy _____ .

16. (*water, iron, wood, air*) Of the four elements, _____ is the lightest

    _____ .

17. (*water, air*) _____ is not nearly as light _____ .

18. (*water, iron, wood*) _____ and _____ are both heavier

    _____ .

▶ **Practice 25. Using *never* with comparatives.** (Chart 9-10)
Choose the sentence that is closest in meaning to the given sentence.

1. I've never taken a harder test in this class.
   a. The test was hard.
   b. The test wasn't hard.

2. I've never taken a hard test in this class.
   a. The tests in this class are hard.
   b. The tests in this class aren't hard.

3. Professor Jones has never given a difficult test.
   a. His tests are difficult.
   b. His tests aren't difficult.

4. Professor Smith has never given a more difficult test.
   a. The test was difficult.
   b. The test wasn't difficult.

5. There have never been worse economic conditions in Leadville.
   a. Leadville has bad economic conditions.
   b. Leadville doesn't have bad economic conditions.

6. There have never been bad economic conditions in Leadville.
   a. Leadville has bad economic conditions.
   b. Leadville doesn't have bad economic conditions.

7. We've never stayed in a more comfortable hotel room.
   a. The room was comfortable.
   b. The room wasn't comfortable.

8. We've never stayed in a comfortable room at that hotel.
   a. The rooms are comfortable.
   b. The rooms aren't comfortable.

▶ **Practice 26. Using *ever* and *never* in comparisons.** (Charts 9-3 and 9-10)
Complete the sentences with the comparative and superlative forms of the words in *italics*.

1. Pierre told a really *funny* story. It is _____the funniest_____ story I've ever heard (in my life). I've never heard a _____funnier_____ story (than that one).

2. John felt very *sad* when he saw the child begging for money. In fact, he has never felt _____ (than he did then). That is _____ he has ever felt (in his life).

3. Jan just finished a really *good* book. She thinks it was _____ book she has ever read. She says that she has never read a _____ book.

4. The villagers fought the rising flood all through the night. They were *exhausted* the next morning. They have never had a _____ experience. That was _____ experience they have ever had.

5. When her daughter was born, Rachel felt extremely *happy*. In fact, she has never felt _____ (than she did then). That was _____ she has ever felt (in her life).

6. Oscar told a very *entertaining* story after dinner. In fact, he has never told a _____ _____ story. It is one of _____ stories I have ever heard in my life.

7. Mari studied very *hard* for her college entrance exams. In fact, she has never studied _____. That was _____ she has ever studied in her life.

8. The weather is really *hot* today! In fact, so far this year the weather has never been _____. This is _____ weather we've had so far this year.

▶ **Practice 27. Review of comparatives and superlatives.** (Charts 9-1 → 9-10)
Choose the correct completion.

1. I feel _____ in a plane than I do in a car.
   a. safe   b. more safer   c. safer

2. Mountain climbing takes _____ than walking on a level path.
   a. the more strength   b. the most strength   c. more strength

3. The _____ distance between two points is a straight line.
   a. shorter   b. more shorter   c. shortest

4. My grandfather feels _____ speaking his native language than he does speaking English.
   a. more comfortable   b. the more comfortable   c. the most comfortable

5. My friend has studied many languages. He thinks Japanese is _____ of all the languages he has studied.
   a. the more difficult   b. the most difficult   c. very difficult

6. I think learning a second language is _____ than learning chemistry or mathematics.
   a. more difficult   b. very difficult   c. the most difficult

7. One of ____ natural disasters in the world was the tsunami that happened in Asia in 2004.
   a. the worse   b. the worst   c. the most worse

8. In the United States, Florida produces ____ oranges of any state.
   a. more   b. the more   c. the most

9. It produces even ____ oranges than California does.
   a. more   b. the more   c. the most

10. Of all the countries in the world, Brazil produces ____ crop of oranges.
   a. the bigger   b. the more bigger   c. the biggest

▶ **Practice 28. Review of comparatives and superlatives.** (Charts 9-1 → 9-10)
Complete the sentences. Use any appropriate form of the words in parentheses and add any other necessary words.

1. Sometimes I feel like all of my friends are (*intelligent*) ____*more intelligent than*____ I am, and yet, sometimes they tell me that they think I am (*smart*) ____*the smartest*____ person ____*in*____ the class.

2. One of (*popular*) _____ holidays _____ Japan is New Year's.

3. A mouse is (*small*) _____ a rat.

4. Europe is first in agricultural production of potatoes. (*potatoes*) _____ are grown in Europe _____ on any other continent.

5. Mercury is (*close*) _____ planet to the sun. It moves around the sun (*fast*) _____ any other planet in the solar system.

6. In terms of area, (*large*) _____ state _____ the United States is Alaska, but it has one of (*small*) _____ populations _____ all the states.

7. I need more facts. I can't make my decision until I get (*information*) _____ _____.

8. Rebecca is a wonderful person. I don't think I've ever met a (*kind*) _____ and (*generous*) _____ person.

9. You can trust Rebecca. You will never meet a (*honest*) _____ person _____ she is.

10. I'm leaving. This is (*bad*) _____ movie I've ever seen! I won't sit through another second of it.

11. One of (*safe*) _____ places to be during a lightning storm is inside a car.

12. Small birds have a much (*fast*) _____ heartbeat _____ large birds.

13. Are your feet exactly the same size? Almost everyone's left foot is (*big*) _____ their right foot.★

★Grammar note: In formal English, a singular pronoun is used to refer to *everyone*:
   *Almost **everyone's** left foot is bigger than **his or her** right foot.*
In everyday informal usage, a plural pronoun is frequently used:
   *Almost **everyone's** left foot is bigger than **their** right foot.*

► **Practice 29. *Like, alike.*** (Chart 9-11)
Complete the sentences with *like* or *alike*.

1. My mother and my father rarely argue because they think _____*alike*_____.

2. The Browns designed their summer cabin to look _____*like*_____ the inside of a boat.

3. Joe and John are twins, but they don't look _____.

4. They dress _____ because they have the same taste in clothes.

5. This lamp doesn't look _____ the one I ordered.

6. Mike is 30, but he acts _____ a child.

7. Professor Miller's lectures are all _____: repetitive and boring.

8. This coffee doesn't taste _____ the coffee we sampled at the store.

9. The clouds in the east look _____ rain clouds.

10. My grandmother and mother sound _____ on the phone.

► **Practice 30. *The same, similar, different.*** (Chart 9-11)
Complete the sentences with *the same*, *similar*, or *different* and the correct preposition: *as, to,* or *from*.

1. My coat is not like yours. It's _____*different from*_____ yours.

2. Our apartment is a lot like my cousin's apartment. It's _____ hers.

3. The news report on Channel 4 at 7:00 P.M. was exactly _____ the report we heard on Channel 6 at 6:00 P.M.

4. Is the North Pole really _____ the South Pole? I thought they were exactly alike.

5. Your jacket is just like mine. It's exactly _____ mine.

6. I enjoyed reading your letters from China. My experiences in Beijing were a lot like yours. They were _____ yours in many ways.

7. The movie on our flight to London was _____ the movie on our flight to Paris. The name of the movie was *Forever Lost*.

8. Except for some minor differences in grammar, spelling, and vocabulary, American English is _____ British English. It's one language.

9. The English spoken in the United States is only slightly _____ the English spoken in Britain, Canada, and Australia. The most noticeable difference is the accent.

10. Lemons are _____ limes. They both taste sour.

11. My sisters are twins, but they are very _____ each other. They don't even look alike.

▶ **Practice 31. *Like, alike, similar, different.*** (Chart 9-11)
Part I. Compare the figures using the given words.

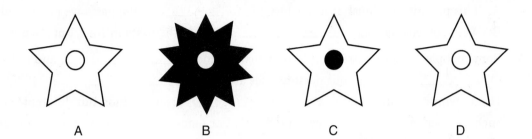

A　　　　　B　　　　　C　　　　　D

1. like _____*A is like D*_____ .

2. alike _____ .

3. similar (to) _____ and _____ .

4. different (from) _____ , _____ , and _____ .

Part II. Compare the figures. Use ***the same (as)***, ***similar (to)***, or ***different (from)***.

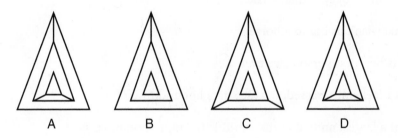

A　　　　　B　　　　　C　　　　　D

5. All of the triangles are _____ each other.

6. A and D are _____ each other.

7. A and C are _____ .

8. A isn't _____ C.

9. B and C are _____ D.

▶ **Practice 32. *The same, similar, different, like, alike.*** (Chart 9-11)
Complete the sentences with ***the same, similar, different, like***, or ***alike***.

1. Dana swims _____*like*_____ a fish. She never wants to come out of the water.

2. The lake doesn't have a ripple on it. It looks _____ glass.

3. There are six girls in our family, but none of us look _____ . Our brothers also look different.

4. A: Some people can tell we're sisters. Do you think we look _____ ?

   B: Somewhat. The color of your hair is not _____ , but your eyes are exactly _____ color. You also have _____ oval face.

5. A: Excuse me. I believe you have my umbrella.

    B: Oh, you're right. It looks almost exactly _____ mine, doesn't it?

6. A: This pasta is delicious! It tastes just _____ the pasta we had in Italy.

    B: Well, not exactly. It's _____ to the pasta in Italy, but it's not as good.

7. Some people think my sister and I are twins. We look _____ and talk _____, but our personalities are quite _____.

8. Homonyms are words that have _____ pronunciation but different spelling, such as "pair" and "pear" or "sea" and "see." For many people, "been" and "bean" are homonyms and have _____ pronunciation. For other people, however, "been" and "bean" are words with _____ pronunciations. These people pronounce "been" like "bin" or "ben."

▶ **Practice 33. Editing.** (Chapter 9)
Correct the errors.

                      than
1. My brother is older ~~from~~ me.

2. A sea is more deeper than a lake.

3. A donkey isn't as big to a horse.

4. Ellen is happiest person I've ever met.

5. When I feel embarrassed, my face gets hot and more hot.

6. One of a largest animal in the world is the hippopotamus.

7. The traffic on the highway is more bad from than it used to be.

8. Jack is the same old from Jerry.

9. Peas are similar from beans, but they have several differences.

10. Last winter was pretty mild. This winter is cold and rainy. It's much rain than last winter.

11. Mrs. Peters, the substitute teacher, is very friendly than the regular instructor.

12. Although alligators and crocodiles are similar, alligators are less big than crocodiles.

13. Mohammed and Tarek come from different countries, but they became friends easily because they speak a same language, Arabic.

Complete the crossword puzzle. Use the clues to find the correct words.

Across

2. My husband is a good cook, but my mother is the _____ cook in the world.

6. A turtle walks more _____ than a rabbit.

8. The weather is really bad this summer. It rains all the time, and the heat is terrible. It's the _____ summer we've ever had.

9. Arithmetic is _____ than advanced calculus.

10. I have a bad cold. I went to work, but that was a mistake. I had to go home early. I feel even _____ than I did this morning.

Down

1. Kim speaks English much _____ than he did last year.

3. We are taking the _____ plane tomorrow morning. It leaves at 6:00 A.M.

4. The _____ swimmer won first prize.

5. Many people think that Paris is the _____ beautiful city in the world.

7. There are _____ letters in the word *happy* than in the word *sad*.

Chapter 10
The Passive

▶ **Practice 1. Active vs. passive.** (Charts 10-1 and 10-2)
Circle *active* if the given sentence is active; circle *passive* if it is passive. <u>Underline</u> the verb.

1. (active) passive   Farmers <u>grow</u> rice.
2. active   (passive) Rice <u>is grown</u> by farmers.
3. active   passive   Sara wrote the letter.
4. active   passive   The letter was written by Sara.
5. active   passive   The teacher explained the lesson.
6. active   passive   The lesson was explained by the teacher.
7. active   passive   Bridges are designed by engineers.
8. active   passive   Engineers design bridges.
9. active   passive   Workers are fixing the highway.
10. active   passive   The highway is being fixed by workers.

▶ **Practice 2. Active vs. passive.** (Charts 10-1 and 10-2)
Change the active verbs in *italics* to passive.

1. Mr. Case *delivers* our mail every day.   Our mail _____*is delivered*_____
   by Mr. Case every day.

2. Mr. Case *is delivering* our mail   Our mail _____
   right now.   by Mr. Case right now.

3. Mr. Case *has delivered* our mail   Our mail _____
   for ten years.   by Mr. Case for ten years.

4. Mr. Case *delivered* our mail early   Our mail _____
   today.   by Mr. Case early today.

5. Mr. Case *was delivering* our mail   Our mail _____
   when a loud explosion occurred.   by Mr. Case when a loud explosion occurred.

6. Mr. Case *is going to deliver* our mail   Our mail _____
   late today.   by Mr. Case late today.

7. Mr. Case *will deliver* the mail early   Our mail _____
   on Saturday.   by Mr. Case early on Saturday.

► **Practice 3. Forms of the passive.** (Charts 10-1 and 10-2)
Choose the correct completion from the list for each sentence.

Present

a. are flown
b. are led
c. is grown
d. is followed

1. Coffee __c__ in hot climates.
2. Planes _____ by pilots.
3. Armies _____ by generals.
4. The month of May _____ by the month of June.

Past

e. was bitten
f. was discovered
g. were shot
h. were made

5. I _____ by a mosquito.
6. The bears _____ by hunters.
7. These cookies _____ by my grandmother.
8. Penicillin _____ by Alexander Fleming, a Scottish scientist.

Future

i. are going to be elected
j. is going to be sent
k. will be taken
l. will be won

9. The wedding photos _____ by a professional photographer.
10. A new president and vice-president _____ by the people.
11. The gold medal _____ by the fastest runner.
12. This package _____ by overnight mail. You'll receive it tomorrow.

Present perfect

m. has been bought
n. has been written
o. have been arrested
p. have been invited

13. I _____ by the governor to attend a special conference.
14. A book about our town _____ by my sociology professor.
15. The house next to ours _____ by an airline pilot.
16. Two men _____ by the police for robbing the bank last month.

Progressive

q. are being taught
r. is being chased
s. was being served
t. were being carried

17. Look at that. That little dog _____ by that big cat!
18. The children _____ French by a native French speaker.
19. Dinner _____ at the restaurant when the lights suddenly went out.
20. We saw scenes of the fire on TV. People _____ from the burning building by fire fighters. Fortunately, no one died in the fire.

► **Practice 4. Review of past participles.** (Charts 2-3 and 2-4)
Write the past participles of the verbs. The list contains both regular and irregular verbs.

1. bring _____ *brought* _____
2. build _____
3. buy _____
4. carry _____
5. do _____
6. eat _____
7. find _____
8. give _____
9. go _____
10. grow _____
11. hit _____
12. hurt _____
13. leave _____
14. lose _____

15. make _____
16. plan _____
17. play _____
18. pull _____
19. read _____
20. save _____
21. send _____
22. speak _____
23. spend _____
24. take _____
25. teach _____
26. visit _____
27. wear _____
28. write _____

► **Practice 5. Passive form.** (Charts 10-1 and 10-2)
Complete the sentences with the given form of **be** and the past participle of any appropriate verbs in the list in Practice 4.

1. *is*   Arabic _____ by more than 800 million people.

2. *are*   Books _____ by authors.

3. *are*   Books _____ by readers.

4. *was*   A new school _____ in our town last year.

5. *were*   The two lost children _____ at the ice cream shop.

6. *has been*   There's no more pizza. All the pizza _____ by the kids.

7. *is going to be*   Niagara Falls _____ by thousands of tourists this year.

8. *will be*   The championship football game _____ in Milan next week.

9. *are going to be*   Our pictures _____ by a professional photographer at the wedding.

10. *have been*   Oranges _____ by farmers in Jordan since ancient times.

11. *are being*   Jeans _____ by everyone these days: young people, old people, men, and women.

12. *was being*   Yesterday I saw something unusual on the highway. A house

_____ by a truck.

▶ **Practice 6. Tense forms of the passive.** (Charts 10-1 and 10-2)
Complete the sentences with the passive form of the given verbs.

Part I. Use the <u>simple present</u>.

✓collect	grow	understand
eat	pay	write

1. Taxes _____ <u>are collected</u> _____ by the government.
2. Books _____ by authors.
3. Rice _____ by farmers in Korea.
4. Small fish _____ by big fish.
5. I _____ for my work by my boss.
6. The meaning of a smile _____ by everyone.

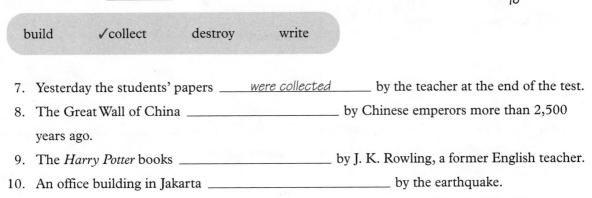

Part II. Use the <u>simple past</u>.

build	✓collect	destroy	write

7. Yesterday the students' papers _____ <u>were collected</u> _____ by the teacher at the end of the test.
8. The Great Wall of China _____ by Chinese emperors more than 2,500 years ago.
9. The *Harry Potter* books _____ by J. K. Rowling, a former English teacher.
10. An office building in Jakarta _____ by the earthquake.

Part III. Use the <u>present perfect</u>.

> | read | speak | ✓visit | wear |
> |------|-------|--------|------|

11. The pyramids in Egypt _____<u>have been visited</u>_____ by millions of tourists.

12. Spanish _____ by people in Latin America for nearly 600 years.

13. *War and Peace* is a famous book. It _____ by millions of people.

14. Perfume _____ by both men and women since ancient times.

Part IV. Use <u>future</u> (**will**).

> | ✓discover | save | visit |
> |-----------|------|-------|

15. New information about the universe _____<u>will be discovered</u>_____ by scientists during this century.

16. Hawaii _____ by thousands of tourists this year.

17. Pandas _____ from extinction by the Chinese government and organizations like the World Wildlife Federation.

Part V. Use <u>future</u> (a form of **be going to**).

> | choose | ✓hurt | offer |
> |--------|-------|-------|

18. Your friend _____<u>is going to be hurt</u>_____ by your unkind remark when she hears about it.

19. New computer courses _____ by the university next year.

20. The winner of the essay contest _____ by the English teachers of our school.

Part VI. Use **am** / **is** / **are** / **was** / **were** + **being**.

> | ✓announce | cover | follow | treat | wash |
> |-----------|-------|--------|-------|------|

21. The scholarship winner _____<u>is being announced</u>_____ by the college president right now.

22. There's a big storm in the mountains right now. The roads _____ by ice and snow, and driving conditions are becoming dangerous.

23. I _____ by a headache specialist for my headaches. I see him every month.

24. In the spy movie we saw last night, the suspect _____ by the detective, but he moved faster than the detective and disappeared into the city.

25. Yesterday, while I was at work, a man suddenly appeared outside my office window. It took a few seconds for me to realize that the windows _____ by window washers.

▶ **Practice 7. Passive vs. active meaning.** (Charts 10-1 and 10-2)
Circle the letter of the sentence that has the same meaning as the given sentence.

1. My grandmother makes her own bread. Have a slice.
   a. This bread is made by my grandmother.
   b. Someone makes my grandmother's bread.

2. Bob was taken to the hospital by car.
   a. Bob drove to the hospital.
   b. Someone drove Bob to the hospital.

3. Suzanne has just been asked to her first dance.
   a. Suzanne has asked someone to the dance.
   b. Someone has asked Suzanne to the dance.

4. You will be informed of the test results.
   a. Someone will inform you of the test results.
   b. You will inform someone of the test results.

5. A sign: "You are not allowed to enter."
   a. You do not allow people to enter.
   b. Someone says you cannot enter.

6. The child was saved after five minutes in the water.
   a. Someone saved the child.
   b. The child saved herself.

7. An announcement on the phone: "For security purposes, this telephone conversation is being recorded."
   a. You are recording the phone conversation.
   b. Someone else is recording the telephone conversation.

▶ **Practice 8. Forms of passive questions.** (Charts 10-1 and 10-2)
Change the questions from active to passive.

1. Did many people see the game?

   _____Was the game seen by many people?_____

2. Will the news shock Pat?

   _____

3. Is the restaurant serving lunch now?

   _____

4. Does everyone understand the rules?

   _____

5. Is the professor going to explain the solution?

   _____

6. Has the university accepted you?

_____

7. Have both the seller and the buyer signed the contract?

_____

8. Did the police find the thief?

_____

▶ **Practice 9. Passive to active.** (Charts 10-1 and 10-2)
Rewrite the paragraph in the active voice. Keep the same tense.

   Taxes are collected by governments. The tax money is used by the governments. Many services are provided by the tax money. These services are used by us regularly. For example: Roads are built and repaired by local workers. Police forces are trained by experts. The fire department is operated by the city. Teachers are paid by the county. Professional licenses are issued by the state. The postal system is run by the country. Armies are maintained by countries. Health care is managed by many governments.

   Governments _____collect taxes_____. Governments _____.
                           1   2
   The tax money _____. We _____
                               3   4
   regularly. For example: Local workers _____. Experts
                                                        5
   _____. The city _____.
                     6   7
   The county _____. The state _____.
                         8   9
   The country _____. Countries _____.
                          10   11
   Many governments _____.
                              12

▶ **Practice 10. Passive to active.** (Charts 5-2, 10-1, and 10-2)
Change the passive sentences to active. Keep the same tense of each sentence. Some of the sentences are questions.

1. A new film from India, *Falling Rocks*, will be shown by the City Film Society.

   _____The City Film Society will show a new film from India, Falling Rocks._____

2. The film has been reviewed by movie critics.

   _____

3. The movie was given good ratings by audiences.

   _____

4. Was the movie written by a famous writer?

   _____

5. The main female part is played by a new actress.

   _____

6. Is a murder committed by someone in the movie?

   _____

7. Is the main character killed by a spy?

_____

8. Will the movie be seen by many people?

_____

9. Is an award going to be won by the movie?

_____

▶ **Practice 11. Transitive vs. intransitive.** (Chart 10-3)
Circle transitive if the verb takes an object; circle intransitive if it does not. <u>Underline</u> the object of the verb.

1. (transitive)	intransitive	Alex wrote <u>a letter</u>.
2. transitive	(intransitive)	Alex waited for Amy. *(There is no object of the verb.)*
3. transitive	intransitive	Rita lives in Mexico.
4. transitive	intransitive	Sam walked to his office.
5. transitive	intransitive	Kate caught the ball.
6. transitive	intransitive	My plane arrived at six-thirty.
7. transitive	intransitive	Emily is crying.
8. transitive	intransitive	Our cat broke the vase.
9. transitive	intransitive	Someone returned the book to the library.
10. transitive	intransitive	A meteor appeared in the sky last night.

▶ **Practice 12. Active and passive.** (Charts 10-1 → 10-3)
<u>Underline</u> the object of the verb if the sentence has one. Then change the sentence to the passive if possible.

Active

1. It was raining hard last night.

2. Around midnight, loud sounds awakened <u>me</u>.

3. Lightning struck a tree.

4. The tree fell down.

5. The tree hit my neighbor's car.

6. The impact activated the car alarm.

7. The car alarm sounded very loud.

8. The tree damaged the roof of the car.

9. Fortunately, no one was inside the car.

10. The damage is going to upset my neighbor.

Passive

1. _No change_ .

2. _I was awakened by loud sounds around midnight_ .

3. _____.

4. _____.

5. _____.

6. _____.

7. _____.

8. _____.

9. _____.

10. _____.

► **Practice 13. Review: identifying passives with transitive and intransitive verbs.**
(Charts 10-1 → 10-3)
Check (✓) the sentences that are passive.

1. _____ I came by plane.

2. _✓_ I was invited to the party by Alex.

3. _____ Many people died during the earthquake.

4. _____ Many people were killed by collapsing buildings.

5. _____ The earthquake has killed many people.

6. _____ The game will be won by the home team.

7. _____ The home team will win the game.

8. _____ Gina's baby cried for more than an hour.

9. _____ Most of the fresh fruit at the market was bought by customers.

10. _____ Some customers bought boxes full of fresh fruit.

11. _____ Accidents always occur at that intersection.

► **Practice 14. The *by*-phrase.** (Chart 10-4)
Underline the passive verbs. Answer the questions. If you don't know the exact person or people who performed the action, write *unknown*.

1. Soft duck feathers <u>are used</u> to make pillows.

    Who uses duck feathers to make pillows? _____unknown_____

2. The mail <u>was opened</u> by Shelley.

    Who opened the mail? _____Shelley_____

3. Eric Wong's new book will be translated into many languages.

    Who will translate Eric Wong's new book? _____

4. Rebecca's bike was stolen yesterday from in front of the library.

    Who stole Rebecca's bike? _____

5. The Warren's house was designed by a famous architect.

    Who designed the Warren's house? _____

6. Malawi is a small country in southeastern Africa. A new highway is going to be built in Malawi next year.

    Who is going to build the new highway? _____

7. There are no more empty apartments in our building. The apartment next to ours has been rented by a young family with two small children.

    Who rented the apartment next to ours? _____

8. The apartment directly above ours was empty for two months, but now it has also been rented.

    Who rented the apartment directly above ours? _____

▶ **Practice 15. Active to passive.** (Charts 10-1 → 10-4)
Change the active sentences to passive. Use the *by*-phrase only if necessary.

1. Someone has canceled the soccer game.

    <u>The soccer game has been canceled.</u>

2. The president has canceled the meeting.

    <u>The meeting has been canceled by the president.</u>

3. Someone serves ethnic dishes at that restaurant.

    _____

4. Something confused me in class yesterday.

    _____

5. The teacher's directions confused me.

    _____

6. No one has washed the dishes yet.

    _____

7. Someone should wash them soon.

    _____

8. Did someone wash this sweater in hot water?

    _____

9. Luis invited me to the party.

    _____

10. Has anyone invited you to the party?

    _____

▶ **Practice 16. Review: active vs. passive.** (Charts 10-1 → 10-4)
Make sentences with the given words. Use the present tense. Some are passive and some are not.
Do not change the word order.

1. Sometimes keys \ hide \ under cars

    <u>Sometimes keys are hidden under cars.</u>

2. Cats \ hide \ under cars

    <u>Cats hide under cars.</u>

3. Students \ teach \ by teachers

    _____

4. Students \ study \ a lot

    _____

5. Cereal \ often eat \ at breakfast

    _____

6. Cats \ eat \ cat food

    _____

7. Mice \ eat \ by cats

_____

8. Songs \ sing \ to children \ by their mothers

_____

9. Thai food \ cook \ in Thai restaurants

_____

10. Chefs \ cook \ in restaurants

_____

▶ **Practice 17. Meaning of passive verbs.** (Charts 10-1 → 10-4)
Choose the sentence that has the same meaning as the given sentence.

1. A mouse is being chased.
   a. A mouse is trying to catch something.
   (b.) Something is trying to catch a mouse.

2. The mouse was caught.
   a. The mouse caught something.
   b. Something caught the mouse.

3. The soldiers are being trained.
   a. Someone is training the soldiers.
   b. The soldiers are training someone.

4. The earthquake victims are being helped by the medics.
   a. The medics are receiving help.
   b. The victims are receiving help.

5. Some pets are taught to do tricks.
   a. Some pets teach themselves to do tricks.
   b. Someone teaches the pets to do tricks.

6. The children were trying to find their parents after the school play.
   a. The children were looking for their parents.
   b. The parents were looking for their children.

7. The airline passengers were being asked to wait while the plane was cleaned.
   a. The passengers made a request.
   b. Someone asked the passengers to wait.

8. The flight attendants were instructed to be seated.
   a. Someone told the flight attendants to be seated.
   b. The flight attendants told people to be seated.

▶ **Practice 18. Review: active vs. passive.** (Charts 10-1 → 10-4)
Write "C" if the sentence is correct and "I" if incorrect. Make any necessary corrections.

1. __I__ It ~~was~~ happened many years ago.

2. __C__ Wheat is grown in Canada.

3. _____ I was go to school yesterday.

4. _____ Two firefighters injure while they were fighting the fire.

5. _____ Sara was accidentally broken the window.

6. _____ Kara was eating a snack when the phone rang.

7. _____ Timmy was eaten when the phone rang.

8. _____ I am agree with you.

9. _____ The little boy was fallen down while he was running in the park.

10. _____ The swimmer was died from a shark attack.

11. _____ The swimmer was killed by a shark.

12. _____ I was slept for nine hours last night.

▶ **Practice 19. Passive modals.** (Chart 10-5)
Complete the sentences by changing the active modals to passive modals.

1. This book (*have to return*) _____has to be returned_____ to the library today.

2. That book (*should return*) _____ tomorrow.

3. This letter (*must send*) _____ today.

4. This package (*could send*) _____ tomorrow.

5. That package (*should send*) _____ by overnight mail.

6. That box (*can put away*) _____ now.

7. These boxes (*may throw away*) _____ soon.

8. Those boxes (*might pick up*) _____ this afternoon.

9. This room (*will clean up*) _____ soon.

▶ **Practice 20. Passive modals.** (Chart 10-5)
Change the answers from active to passive. Include the *by*-phrase only if it contains important information.

1. *What happens when an animal is sick?*
   a. A veterinarian should treat the animal.

      _____The animal should be treated by a veterinarian._____

   b. Someone will give the animal medicine.

      _____The animal will be given medicine._____

2. *Can I send this letter now?*
   a. No, someone has to change the last paragraph.

      _____

   b. No, Mr. Hayes must sign it.

      _____

3. *What's going to happen to that big old house on Maple Street?*
   a. A famous hockey star might buy it.

   _____

   b. Someone may convert it into apartments.

   _____

4. *There's a mistake on my credit card bill.*
   a. You should call the credit card company immediately.

   _____

   b. The company ought to fix the mistake right away.

   _____

5. *There's a new book about everyday heroes.*
   a. Everyone should read it.

   _____

   b. They will make a movie of the book.

   _____

6. *This dress is too long for me.*
   a. Someone should shorten it.

   _____

   b. Someone has to do it soon.

   _____

▶ **Practice 21. Summary: active vs. passive.** (Charts 10-1 → 10-5)
Choose the correct verbs.

Telling Time

(1) Sundials (*used* / (*were used*)) in ancient times to tell time. Clocks
first (*appeared* / *were appeared*) during the 13th century. The first watches
(*made* / *were made*) in Europe six hundred years ago. These watches
(*worn* / *were worn*) around a person's neck. In the 1600s, men (*began* / *were begun*)
to put the watches inside their pockets. These watches (*called* / *were called*) pocket
watches. The watches (*became* / *were become*) popular and (*were remained* / *remained*)
popular until World War I. During that war, watches (*put* / *were put*)
on bands, and soldiers (*wore* / *were worn*) the bands around their
wrists. It was more practical to look quickly at a watch on the wrist than to pull a watch out of a
pocket. Since then, millions of wrist watches (*have been manufactured* / *have manufactured*).

(2) However, not as many watches (*are being sold* / *sold*) now as previously. That's because the
time (*is displayed* / *displayed*) by clocks on computers and cell phones. Since computers and cell
phones are everywhere, watches (*aren't needed* / *don't need*) as much as they were. Many young
adults (*have never worn* / *have never been worn*) watches. Some people think that the need for
watches (*may disappear* / *may be disappeared*) completely and that in the future, a wrist watch
(*will be considered* / *will consider*) an antique item, like the pocket watch.

▶ **Practice 22. Using past participles as adjectives.** (Chart 10-6)
Complete the sentences with the correct prepositions.

Part I. Jack is . . .

1. married ____*to*____ Katie.

2. excited _____ vacation.

3. exhausted _____ work.

4. frightened _____ heights.

5. disappointed _____ his new car.

6. tired _____ rain.

7. pleased _____ his new boss.

8. involved _____ charity work.

9. worried _____ his elderly parents.

10. acquainted _____ a famous movie star.

Part II. Jack's friend is . . .

11. interested _____ sports.

12. done _____ final exams.

13. terrified _____ spiders.

14. related _____ a famous movie star.

15. opposed _____ private gun ownership.

16. pleased _____ his part-time job.

17. divorced _____ his wife.

Part III. Jack's house is . . .

18. made _____ wood.

19. located _____ the suburbs.

20. crowded _____ antique furniture.

21. prepared _____ emergencies.

▶ **Practice 23. Using past participles as adjectives.** (Chart 10-6)
Correct the errors.

                  excited about
1. The little girl is ~~excite in~~ her birthday party.

2. Mr. and Mrs. Rose devoted each other.

3. Could you please help me? I need directions. I lost.

4. The students are boring in their chemistry project.

5. The paper bags at this store is composed in recycled products.

6. Your friend needs a doctor. He hurt.

7. How well are you prepare the driver's license test?

8. Mary has been engaging with Paul for five years. Will they ever get married?

▶ **Practice 24. -ed vs. -ing.** (Chart 10-7)
Complete the sentences with the appropriate **-ed** or **-ing** form of the words in parentheses.

Ben is reading a book. He really likes it. He can't put it down. He has to keep reading.

1. The book is really _____*interesting*_____. (*interest*)

2. Ben is really _____. (*interest*)

3. The story is _____. (*excite*)

4. Ben is _____ about the story. (*excite*)

5. Ben is _____ by the characters in the book. (*fascinate*)

6. The people in the story are _____. (*fascinate*)

7. Ben didn't finish the last book he started because it was _____ and
_____. (*bore, confuse*)

8. Ben doesn't like to read books when he is _____ and
_____. (*bore, confuse*)

9. What is the most _____ book you've read lately? (*interest*)

10. I just finished a _____ mystery story that had a very
_____ ending. (*fascinate, surprise*)

▶ **Practice 25. -ed vs. -ing.** (Chart 10-7)
Choose the correct adjective.

1. The students are (*interesting / interested*) in learning more about Kung Fu.

2. Ms. Green doesn't explain things well. She's (*confusing / confused*). The students are
(*confusing / confused*).

3. Have you heard the news about Jamie and Hal? They are going trekking in Nepal. They are
really (*exciting / excited*) about it. It's really an (*exciting / excited*) thing to do.

4. There was a (*surprising / surprised*) event in the news yesterday: the governor had resigned
suddenly. Everyone was (*surprising / surprised*).

5. It's (*embarrassing* / *embarrassed*) to forget someone's name. Yesterday I couldn't remember the name of my boss's wife, and I felt very (*embarrassed* / *embarrassing*).

6. Mr. Ball fascinates me. He has lived in 13 countries and he speaks five languages. I think he is a (*fascinating* / *fascinated*) person. Whenever I am with him, I listen to everything he says. I am (*fascinating* / *fascinated*) by Mr. Ball.

7. Victor and his wife Sylvia are different. Sylvia is a vegetarian, but Victor isn't. Victor doesn't like Sylvia's cooking. He thinks that the salads she prepares are not (*satisfying* / *satisfied*). He thinks a (*satisfying* / *satisfied*) meal should have plenty of meat.

8. The story of Steven Hawking's life has been (*inspiring* / *inspired*) to many people. Despite terrible handicaps, Steven Hawking became known as a brilliant scientist. I am (*inspiring* / *inspired*) by him.

▶ **Practice 26. -ed vs. -ing.** (Chart 10-7)
Choose the correct adjective.

1. The street signs in our city are (*confused* / (*confusing*)).

2. The drivers are (*frustrated* / *frustrating*).

3. The professor's lecture on anatomy was (*confused* / *confusing*) for the students.

4. Sophie was very (*embarrassed* / *embarrassing*) by all the attention she got for her high test scores.

5. Sophie said it was (*embarrassed* / *embarrassing*) to have so many people congratulate her.

6. I am really (*interested* / *interesting*) in eighteenth-century art.

7. Eighteenth-century art is really (*interested* / *interesting*).

8. What an (*exhausted* / *exhausting*) day! I am so (*tired* / *tiring*) from picking strawberries.

9. Some of the new horror movies are (*frightened* / *frightening*) because they are so realistic.

10. If young children see a horror movie, they often become (*frightened* / *frightening*).

▶ **Practice 27. -ed vs. -ing.** (Chart 10-7)
Write "I" next to the incorrect sentence in each group.

1. a. _____ Science fascinates me.
   b. _____ Science is fascinating to me.
   c. ___*I*___ Science is fascinated to me.

2. a. _____ The baby is exciting about her new toy.
   b. _____ The baby is excited about her new toy.
   c. _____ The new toy is exciting to the baby.

3. a. _____ The book is really interesting.
   b. _____ The book is really interested.
   c. _____ The book interests me.

4. a. _____ I am exhausting from working in the fields.
   b. _____ I am exhausted from working in the fields.
   c. _____ Working in the fields exhausts me.
   d. _____ Working in the fields is exhausting.

5. a. _____ Your grandmother is amazing to me.

   b. _____ Your grandmother amazes me.

   c. _____ Your grandmother is amazed to me.

   d. _____ I am amazed by your grandmother.

▶ **Practice 28. *Get* + adjective and past participle.** (Chart 10-8)
Choose the correct completion from Column B.

Column A	**Column B**
1. We couldn't go on our vacation to Hawaii because we got ____ with the flu.	a. dressed
2. Jerry couldn't find our house. He got ____ on the way.	b. late
	c. lost
3. Susie is five years old now. She can get ____ by herself.	d. arrested
4. When's dinner going to be ready? I'm getting very ____ .	e. wet
5. We'll be late for the concert if we don't hurry. It's getting ____.	f. rich
6. I want to make a lot of money. Do you know a good way to get ____ quick?	g. sick
7. Jake's in jail now. Yesterday he got ____ for stealing a car.	h. hungry
8. Last Saturday we were enjoying our picnic when it suddenly started to rain. We all got ____.	

▶ **Practice 29. *Get* + adjective and past participle.** (Chart 10-8)
Complete the sentences with an appropriate form of *get*.

1. Hurry up! _____*Get*_____ busy. There's no time to waste.

2. Tom and Sue _____*got*_____ married last month.

3. Let's stop working for a while. I _____*am getting*_____ tired.

4. I _____ interested in biology when I was in high school, so I decided to major in it in college.

5. When I was in the hospital, I got a card from my aunt and uncle. It said, "_____ well soon."

6. Karen has a new GPS in her car. It tells her exactly how to go everywhere, street by street. She used to _____ lost all the time, but she doesn't anymore.

7. A: What happened to you just now?

   B: I don't know. Suddenly I _____ dizzy, but I'm okay now.

8. I always _____ nervous when I have to give a speech.

9. A: Where's Bud? He was supposed to be home two hours ago. He always calls when he's late. I _____ worried. Maybe we should call the police.

   B: Relax. He'll be home soon.

10. A: I'm going on a diet.

 B: Oh?

 A: See? This shirt is too tight. I _____ fat.

▶ **Practice 30. Be used/accustomed to.** (Charts 2-8 and 10-9)
Choose the correct completion. More than one answer may be correct.

1. Frank has lived alone for 20 years. He ____ alone.
 a. used to live   (b.) is used to living   (c.) is accustomed to living

2. I ____ with my family, but now I live alone.
 a. used to live   b. am used to living   c. am accustomed to living

3. Rita rides her bike to work every day. She ____ her bike to work.
 a. used to ride   b. is used to riding   c. is accustomed to riding

4. Thomas rode his bike to work for many years, but now he takes the bus. Tom ____ his bike to work.
 a. used to ride   b. is used to riding   c. is accustomed to riding

5. Carl ____ to work, but now he takes a train.
 a. used to drive   b. is used to driving   c. is accustomed to driving

6. Carl drives 50 miles to work every day. He ____ 50 miles a day.
 a. used to drive   b. is used to driving   c. is accustomed to driving

7. Ari ____ dinner at 9:00 P.M. He has dinner at that time every night. That's too late for me.
 a. used to eat   b. is used to eating   c. is accustomed to eating

8. Maria ____ dinner at 9:00 P.M., but now she eats at 6:00 P.M. with her roommates.
 a. used to eat   b. is used to eating   c. is accustomed to eating

▶ **Practice 31. Used to vs. be used to.** (Chart 10-10)
Add an appropriate form of *be* if necessary. If no form of *be* is needed, write **Ø**.

1. People ___Ø___ used to take trains to travel long distances, but today, most people take airplanes.

2. Polly Hudson often has to travel for her job. She ___is___ used to traveling by plane.

3. You and I are from different cultures. You _____ used to having fish for breakfast. I _____ used to having cheese and bread for breakfast.

4. When I lived at home, I _____ used to have big breakfasts. Now I am living in an apartment on my own, and I don't eat breakfast anymore.

5. Jeremy wakes up at 5:00 every morning for work. After a year of doing this, he _____ used to getting up early, even on weekends.

6. Our neighbor, Dr. Jenkins, retired last year. He _____ used to get up early to go to work at the hospital, but now he gets up whenever he wants.

7. Before email, people _____ used to write letters. Letters are less common nowadays.

8. My grandfather doesn't use the computer much. He _____ used to talking on the phone. When he wants to communicate with us, he phones us.

9. Minna Lee has been our senator for several years. She has never lost an election. She
_____ used to winning elections.

10. Sam Sibley _____ used to be our senator. He was our senator for 26 years until he died at
age 87.

▶ **Practice 32. *Used to* vs. *be used to*.** (Chart 10-10)
Complete the sentences with *used to* or *be used to* and the correct form of the verb in
parentheses.

1. Kate grew up on a farm. She (*get*) _____*used to get*_____ up at dawn and go to bed as
soon as the sun went down. Now she works in the city at an advertising agency and has
different sleeping hours.

2. Hiroki's workweek is seven days long. He (*work*) _____ on
Saturdays and Sundays.

3. Luis spends weekends with his family now. He (*play*) _____ soccer on a
team before he was married, but now he enjoys staying home with his young children.

4. Sally (*be*) _____ a nurse. But six years ago, she applied to medical school
and was accepted. Now she is a doctor.

5. Joan has taught kindergarten for eight years. She is very patient with small children. She
(*work*) _____ with them.

6. Bebo really likes hot and spicy food. He always orders it in a restaurant. He (*eat*)
_____ hot and spicy food, and he never orders anything
else.

▶ **Practice 33. *Be supposed to*.** (Chart 10-11)
Make sentences with a similar meaning by using a form of *be supposed to*.

1. Someone expected me to return this book to the library yesterday, but I didn't.
_____*I was supposed to return this book to the library.*_____

2. Our professor expects us to read Chapter 9 before class tomorrow.

_____

3. Someone expected me to go to a party last night, but I stayed home.

_____

4. The teacher expects us to do Exercise 10 for homework.

_____

5. The weather bureau has predicted rain for tomorrow.

_____

6. The directions on the pill bottle say, "Take one pill every six hours."

_____

7. My mother expects me to dust the furniture and vacuum the carpet.

_____

▶ Practice 34. Editing. (Chapter 10)

Correct the errors.

             were
1. The moving boxes ∧ packed by Pierre.

2. My uncle was died in the war.

3. Miami located in Florida.

4. I was very worry about my son.

5. Mr. Rivera interested in finding a new career.

6. Did you tell everyone the shocked news?

7. After ten years, I finally used to this wet and rainy climate.

8. The newspaper suppose to come every morning before eight.

9. The Millers have been marry with each other for 60 years.

10. I am use to drink coffee with cream, but now I drink it black*.

11. What was happen at the party last night?

12. Several people almost get kill when the fireworks exploded over them.

13. A new parking garage being build for our office.

14. I have been living in England for several years, so I accustom driving on the left side of the road.

---

*black = without cream.

Change this sentence to the passive:

The fisherman caught six large fish.

There will be eight words in the new passive sentence. Find the words in the puzzle and circle them. The words may be horizontal, vertical, or diagonal. The first letter of each word is highlighted in gray.

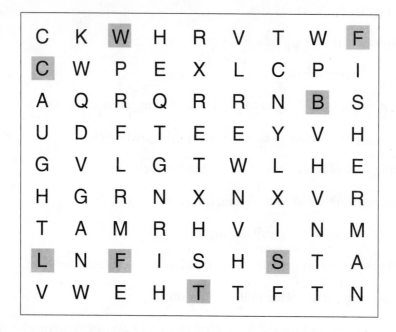

Chapter 11
Count/Noncount Nouns and Articles

▶ **Practice 1. *A* vs. *an*: singular count nouns.** (Chart 11-1)
Write **a** or **an**.

1. ___a___ game
2. ___an___ office
3. ___a___ car
4. ___an___ egg
5. ___a___ man
6. ___a___ university ?
7. ___an___ umbrella
8. ___a___ house
9. ___an___ island
10. ___a___ ocean
11. ___an___ hour

12. ___a___ horse
13. ___a___ star
14. ___an___ eye
15. ___a___ new game
16. ___an___ large office
17. ___a___ old car
18. ___an___ used car ?
19. ___an___ honest man
20. ___a___ large university
21. ___a___ small house
22. ___an___ empty house

▶ **Practice 2. Count and noncount nouns.** (Chart 11-2)
Circle the correct answer.

1. Sal is sitting in (*chair* / *a chair*).
2. There are four (*chair* / *chairs*) at the table.
3. There are some (*chair* / *chairs*) near the wall.
4. One (*chair* / *chairs*) is broken.
5. I like the (*furniture* / *furnitures*) in this room.
6. (*Some* / *A*) furniture in this room came from Italy.
7. (*Furniture* / *A furniture*) can be expensive.
8. Tomorrow we are going to buy (*one* / *some*) furniture.
9. Sal needs a new (*desk* / *desks*).
10. He looked at some (*desk* / *desks*) last week, but they weren't the right size.

▶ **Practice 3. Noncount nouns.** (Chart 11-3)
Write the words in their correct categories.

✓apples	bracelets✓	letters ✓	rings ✓
bananas ✓	chairs ✓	necklaces ✓	sofas ✓
beds ✓	checks ✓	oranges ✓	strawberries ✓
✓bills	earrings ✓	packages ✓	tables ✓

Mail	Fruit	Jewelry	Furniture
bills	apples	bracelets	beds
checks	bananas	earrings	chairs
letters	oranges	necklaces	sofas
packages	Strawberries	Rings	tables

▶ **Practice 4. More noncount nouns.** (Chart 11-4)
Complete the sentences with words from the list.

fun	gold	help	light	thunder	water

1. Sally drank some ____water____.
2. It's too dark in here. We need some ____light____.
3. Listen! Is that ____thunder____?
4. These rings are made of ____gold____.
5. I need some ____help____. Can you please carry this package for me?
6. It was a great party. Everybody had ____fun____.

▶ **Practice 5. Count and noncount nouns.** (Charts 11-1 → 11-4)
Fill in the blanks with *-s/-es* or Ø if nothing should be added.

1. Would you please pass the salt __Ø__ and pepper __Ø__?
2. It's very cold here and there's been a lot of snow __Ø__. You'll need to bring your warm
   boot __S__ and a heavy jacket. And don't forget wool sock __S__.
3. Dad made some cookie __S__ for the children to have with their milk __Ø__.

4. I wasn't hungry for lunch. I just had some soup _Ø_ and some bread _Ø_ and butter _Ø_.

5. Pat slipped on the ice _Ø_ and broke two bone _s_ in his foot.

6. There has been rain _Ø_ all week. I'd like to see some sunshine _Ø_ soon.

7. Teachers need patience _Ø_ with their students. The teachers are <u>satisfied</u> when the students make progress _Ø_.

▶ **Practice 6. Count and noncount nouns.** (Charts 11-2 and 11-4)
Which of the words can follow *one* and which can follow *some?* Write the correct form for each noun. If the noun does not have a singular form, write Ø.

	one	**some**
1. word	_word_	_words_
2. vocabulary	_Ø_	_vocabulary_
3. slang	_____	_____
4. homework	_____	_____
5. assignment	_____	_____
6. dress	_____	_____
7. clothing	_____	_____
8. family	_____	_____
9. knowledge	_____	_____
10. information	_____	_____
11. fact	_____	_____
12. luck	_____	_____

▶ **Practice 7. Count and noncount nouns.** (Charts 11-1 → 11-4)
Complete the sentences with *a/an* or *Ø*.

1. Tom lived in _a_ big city for many years. However, three years ago he left the city. It had _Ø_ pollution and ____ smog, and he couldn't breathe well. Now he lives in ____ small town in the mountains. He breathes ____ clean air and drinks ____ fresh water. He knows that it was ____ good idea to leave the city because his health is better.

2. Cornell University is named for Ezra Cornell. Ezra Cornell was a philanthropist* who lived in Ithaca, New York. He loved the area and wanted to improve it. People there didn't have ____ library, and so he built one for them. Then, he wanted to build ____ university where people could gain ____ knowledge in ____ practical subjects, such as farming, as well as in ____ history, ____ literature, and ____ science. Cornell owned ____ large farm in the area, and in an act of generosity, he donated it as the site for the new university. Cornell University opened in 1865, and today it is known as ____ excellent university — one of the best universities in the world.

---

*philanthropist = a rich person who gives a lot of money to help poor people or good causes.

► **Practice 8. Count and noncount nouns.** (Charts 11-2 → 11-4)
Complete the sentences with words from the list. Use the plural form as necessary.

apple tree	grass	machine	rice
bracelet	jewel	machinery	ring
✓bread	jewelry	mountain	scenery
corn	lake	pea	tool
equipment			

1. I went to the grocery store and bought some _____ *bread,* _____

   _____

2. I stood on a hill in the countryside and saw some _____

   _____

3. I went to a jewelry store and saw some _____

   _____

4. At the auto repair shop, I saw some _____

   _____

► **Practice 9. Count and noncount nouns.** (Charts 11-2 → 11-5)
Complete the sentences with *one*, *much*, or *many*.

Do you have . . .

1. _____ *one* _____ chair?   9. _____ child?

2. _____ *much* _____ furniture?   10. _____ money?

3. _____ *many* _____ vegetables?   11. _____ facts?

4. _____ fruit?   12. _____ information?

5. _____ water?   13. _____ stuff?

6. _____ sand?   14. _____ thing?

7. _____ clothing?   15. _____ things?

8. _____ clothes?   16. _____ problems?

► **Practice 10. *Many* vs. *much*.** (Chart 11-5)
Complete the sentences with the correct words from the list. Use the plural form of the noun where necessary.

1. *apple, coffee, fruit, sugar, vegetable*

   a. I didn't buy many _____ *apples* _____ or _____.

   b. I didn't buy much _____ *coffee* _____, _____, or _____.

2. *English, answer, person, slang, thing*

   a. Mr. Wade doesn't know many _____, _____ and _____.

   b. Mr. Wade doesn't know much _____ or _____.

3. *homework, idea, information, suggestion, work*

   a. Does Sue have many _____ or _____?

   b. Does Sue have much _____, _____ or _____?

4. *crime, garbage, police officer, traffic, violence*

    a. Does this city have many _____.

    b. Does this city have much _____, _____, _____, or _____.

▶ **Practice 11. *How many* and *how much*.** (Chart 11-5)
Complete the questions with *many* or *much*. Add final *-s/-es* if necessary to make a noun plural. (Some of the count nouns have irregular plural forms.) If a verb is needed, circle the correct one in the parentheses. If final *-s/-es* is not necessary, write **Ø**.

1. How _____*many*_____ letter _*s*_ (is / (are)) there in the English alphabet?*

2. How _____*much*_____ mail _*Ø*_ did you get yesterday?

3. How _____*many*_____ man _*men*_ (has / (have)) a full beard at least once in their life?

4. How _____ English **literature** _____ have you studied?

5. How _____ English **word** _____ do you know?

6. How _____ **gasoline** _____ does it take to fill the tank in your car?

7. (*British:* How _____ **petrol** _____ does it take to fill the tank?)

8. How _____ **grandchild** _____ does Mrs. Cunningham have?

9. How _____ **fun** _____ did you have at the amusement park?

10. How _____ **island** _____ (*is / are*) there in Indonesia?**

11. How _____ **people** _____ will there be by the year 2050?***

12. How _____ **zero** _____ (*is / are*) there in a billion?****

▶ **Practice 12. Review: count and noncount nouns.** (Charts 11-1 → 11-5)
Choose all the words that can be used with each given noun.

1. flower	(a)	an	some	much	many
2. flowers	a	an	(some)	much	(many)
3. coin	a	an	some	much	many
4. money	a	an	some	much	many
5. coins	a	an	some	much	many
6. salt	a	an	some	much	many
7. error	a	an	some	much	many
8. mistake	a	an	some	much	many
9. honest mistake	a	an	some	much	many
10. mistakes	a	an	some	much	many
11. dream	a	an	some	much	many
12. interesting dream	a	an	some	much	many
13. questions	a	an	some	much	many

---

*There are twenty-six (26) letters, in the English alphabet.

**More than thirteen thousand seven hundred (13,700).

***Estimated at more than thirteen billion (13,000,000,000).

****Nine (9)

14. soap	a	an	some	much	many
15. bar of soap	a	an	some	much	many
16. beauty	a	an	some	much	many
17. cup of tea	a	an	some	much	many
18. unsafe place	a	an	some	much	many
19. fruit	a	an	some	much	many
20. pieces of fruit	a	an	some	much	many

▶ **Practice 13. A few vs. a little.** (Chart 11-5)
Complete the sentences with *a few* or *a little*. Add a final *-s/-es/-ies* to the noun if necessary. Otherwise, write Ø.

1. Everyone needs _____*a little*_____ **help** __Ø__ sometimes.

2. The children's native language is Spanish, but they speak _____ **English** _____.

3. We bought _____ **orange** _____ to make fresh orange juice.

4. I like _____ **sugar** _____ in my coffee.

5. I'm going to give you _____ **advice** _____.

6. I need _____ **suggestion** _____.

7. He asked _____ **question** _____.

8. We talked to _____ **people** _____ on the plane.

9. Please give me _____ more **minute** _____.

10. I have _____ **work** _____ to do over the weekend.

11. Pedro already knew _____ English **grammar** _____ before he took this English course.

12. I've been making _____ **progress** _____ in the last couple of weeks.

▶ **Practice 14. Count and noncount nouns: summary.** (Chart 11-5)
Draw a line through the expressions of quantity that <u>cannot</u> be used to complete the sentences.

1. I get ____ mail every day.

   a. a lot of

   b. some

   c. a little

   d. ~~a few~~

   e. too much

   f. too many

   g. several

   h. three

2. I get ____ letters every day.

   a. a lot of

   b. some

   c. a little

   d. a few

   e. too much

   f. too many

   g. several

   h. three

3. I ate _____ fruit.
   a. some
   b. a little
   c. a few
   d. too many
   e. too much

4. I ate _____ apples.
   a. several
   b. many
   c. too much
   d. some
   e. a lot of

5. There is _____ traffic in the street.
   a. several
   b. some
   c. too many
   d. a little
   e. a lot of
   f. a few
   g. too much
   h. five

6. There are _____ cars in the street.
   a. several
   b. some
   c. too many
   d. a little
   e. a lot of
   f. a few
   g. too much
   h. five

▶ **Practice 15. Count and noncount nouns.** (Charts 6-2 and 11-1 → 11-6)
Add -*s* where necessary.

Plants

(1) Scientist _____ divide living things into two groups: animal _____ and plant _____. Animals move around from one place _____ to another, but plants don't. Plants stay in one place.

(2) Many plants, such as flower _____, grass, and tree _____, grow on land. Some plants grow only in desert _____ and some grow only in ocean _____. There are a few plants that grow on the tops of mountain _____ and even in the polar regions.

(3) Plants that people grow for food are called crops. Rice _____ is a crop _____ that grows in many parts of the world _____. Other common crops include potatoes, wheat, and corn. All crop _____ depend on nature. Bad weather _____, such as too much or too little rain, can destroy wheat or corn field _____.

(4) Plant _____ are also important to our health _____. We get a lot of medicines from plants. In addition, plants clean the air _____. Many tree _____ and other plants remove bad gasses from the atmosphere and release oxygen into the air. The more plants we have on earth _____, the healthier the air _____ is.

► **Practice 16. Nouns that can be count or noncount.** (Chart 11-6)
Complete the sentences with the correct word from Column B.

Column A

1. We have been to Italy several ____.

2. I don't like beef, but I do like ____.

3. On the table there were plates, forks, knives, and ____.

4. Drivers should turn on their ____ before it gets dark.

5. Please open the curtains. There's not enough ____ in this room.

6. Rosa is 40. She has a few gray ____.

7. A fish bowl is made of ____.

8. My grandparents have a small farm with about 50 ____.

9. Al is getting bald. He is losing his ____.

10. I couldn't finish the exam. There wasn't enough ____.

Column B

a. chicken

b. glass

c. hair

d. time

e. times

f. chickens

g. glasses

h. hairs

i. lights

j. light

► **Practice 17. Units of measure with noncount nouns.** (Chart 11-7)
What units of measure are usually used with the following nouns? More than one unit of measure can be used with some of the nouns.

bag	bottle	box	can / tin*	jar

1. a ____jar____ of pickles.

2. a _____ of aspirin.

3. a _____ of laundry detergent

4. a _____ of instant coffee

5. a _____ of sardines

6. a _____ of sugar

7. a _____ of peanut butter

8. a _____ of soy sauce

9. a _____ of uncooked noodles

10. a _____ of beans

► **Practice 18. Units of measure with noncount nouns.** (Chart 11-7)
Complete the sentences with words from the list. Use the plural form if necessary. Some sentences have more than one possible completion.

bottle	✓cup	glass	loaf	pound
carton	gallon	kilo	piece	sheet

1. I drank a _____cup_____ of coffee.

2. I bought two ____pounds/kilos____ of flour.

---

a can = a tin in British English

3. I drank a _____ of orange juice.

4. I put ten _____ of gas in my car.

5. I bought a _____ of milk at the supermarket.

6. I need a _____ of chalk.

7. I used two _____ of bread to make a sandwich.

8. There is a _____ of fruit on the table.

9. There are 200 _____ of lined paper in my notebook.

10. I bought one _____ of bread at the store.

11. Let me give you a _____ of advice.

12. I just learned an interesting _____ of information.

▶ **Practice 19. _Much_ vs. _many_.** (Charts 11-5 → 11-7)
Complete the questions with **much** or **many** and the appropriate noun.

Going on a Trip

1. A: Are you all packed for your trip to Tahiti? How _____ _many suitcases_ _____ are you taking with you?
   B: Three. (I'm taking three suitcases.)

2. A: How _____ _much sunscreen_ _____ are you taking?
   B: A lot. (I'm taking a lot of sunscreen.)

3. A: How _____ are you taking?
   B: Two pairs. (I'm taking two pairs of sandals.)

4. A: How _____ did you pack?
   B: One tube. (I packed one tube of toothpaste.)

5. A: How _____ will you and Sandy have?
   B: I'm not sure. Maybe 20 kilos. (We may have 20 kilos of luggage.)

6. A: How _____ will you pay in overweight baggage charges?
   B: A lot. (We will pay of lot of money for overweight baggage.)

7. A: How _____ will you be away?
   B: Twelve. (We'll be away for twelve days.)

▶ **Practice 20. _A/an_ vs. _some_.** (Chart 11-8)
Complete the sentences with **a/an** or **some**.

1. I wrote ___ _a_ ___ **letter**.

2. I got ___ _some_ ___ **mail**.

3. We bought _____ **equipment** for our camping trip.

4. You need _____ **tool** to cut wood.

5. I wore _____ old **clothing**.

6. I wore _____ old **shirt**.

7. Jim asked me for _____ **advice**.

8. I gave Jim _____ **suggestion**.

9. I gave Jim _____ **suggestions**.

10. I read _____ interesting **story** in the paper.

11. The paper has _____ interesting **news** today.

12. I know _____ **song** from India.

13. I know _____ Indian **music**.

14. I learned _____ new **word**.

15. I learned _____ new **slang**.

▶ **Practice 21. *A/an* vs. *some*.** (Chart 11-8)
Complete the sentences with *a/an* or *some*.

1. A: What did you do this morning?
   B: I woke up early. I ate a big breakfast. I had ____*a*____ glass of fresh orange juice,
   _____ eggs, _____ piece of toast with _____ butter, and _____ delicious
   coffee.

2. A: What did you do this afternoon?
   B: I went to the store. I bought _____ sugar, _____ flour, and _____ milk to
   make dessert for my grandma's birthday tonight. We'll have it with _____ vanilla ice
   cream.

3. A: What did you do last weekend?
   B: We went bird watching. We saw _____ beautiful birds and we heard _____ bird
   songs. We heard _____ bird that was singing _____ song very loudly. Soon
   another bird was singing. Then many birds began to sing at the same time. They made
   _____ lovely music.

▶ **Practice 22. *A/an* vs. *the*: singular count nouns.** (Chart 11-8)
Complete the sentences with *a/an* or *the*.

1. A: ____*A*____ dog makes a good pet.
   B: I agree.

2. A: Did you feed ____*the*____ dog?
   B: Yes, I did.

3. My dorm room has _____ desk, _____ bed, _____ chest of drawers, and two
   chairs.

4. A: Jessica, where's the stapler?
   B: On _____ desk. If it's not there, look in _____ top drawer.

5. A: Sara, put your bike in _____ garage before dark.
   B: Okay, Dad.

6. Our house has _____ garage. We keep our car and our bikes there.

7. Almost every sentence has _____ subject and _____ verb.

8. Look at this sentence: *Luca lives in Miami.* What is _____ subject, and what is _____
   verb?

9. A: I can't see you at four. I'll be in _____ meeting then. How about four-thirty?
   B: Fine.

10. A: What time does _____ meeting start Tuesday?
    B: Eight o'clock.

11. Max's car ran out of gas. He didn't have cell phone reception, so he had to walk _____ long distance to find _____ telephone and call his brother for help.

12. _____ distance from _____ sun to _____ earth is 93,000,000 miles.

13. A: Where do you live?
    B: We live on _____ quiet street in the suburbs.

14. A: Is this _____ street where Jamie lives?
    B: Yes, it is.

▶ **Practice 23. Using *the* for second mention.** (Charts 11-6 → 11-8)
Complete the sentences with *a/an*, *some*, or *the*. Note: Use *the* when a noun is mentioned for the second time.

1. I had _____ soup and _____ sandwich for lunch. _____ soup was too salty, but _____ sandwich was pretty good.

2. Yesterday I bought _____ clothes. I bought _____ suit, _____ shirt, and _____ tie. _____ suit is gray and comes with a vest. _____ shirt is pale blue, and _____ tie has black and gray stripes.

3. A: I saw _____ accident yesterday.
   B: Oh? Where?
   A: On Grand Avenue. _____ man in _____ Volkswagen drove through a stop sign and hit _____ bus.
   B: Was anyone hurt in _____ accident?
   A: I don't think so. _____ man who was driving _____ Volkswagen got out of his car and seemed to be okay. His car was only slightly damaged. No one on _____ bus was hurt.

4. Yesterday I saw _____ man and _____ woman. They were having _____ argument. _____ man was yelling at _____ woman, and _____ woman was shouting at _____ man. I don't know what _____ argument was about.

▶ **Practice 24. Using *the* for second mention.** (Charts 11-6 → 11-8)
Complete the sentences with *a/an, some*, or *the*.

One day last month while I was driving through the countryside, I saw __*a*__ man and
                                                                        1
_____ truck next to _____ covered bridge. _____ bridge crossed _____ small
   2   3   4   5
river. I stopped and asked _____ man, "What's the matter? Can I help?"
                              6

"Well," said _____ man, "My truck is about a half-inch* too tall. Or maybe _____ top
                  7   8
of _____ bridge is a half-inch too short. Either way, my truck won't fit under _____
       9   10
bridge."

"Hmmm. There must be _____ solution to this problem," I said.
                            11

"I don't know. I guess I'll have to turn around and take another route," he replied.

After a few moments of thought, I said, "I have _____ solution!"
                                                      12

"What is it?" asked the man.

"Let a little air out of your tires. Then _____ truck won't be too tall, and you can cross
                                              13

_____ bridge over _____ river."
   14   15

"Hey, that's _____ great idea. Let's try it!" So _____ man let a little air out of
                  16   17

_____ tires and was able to cross _____ river and go on his way.
   18   19

▶ **Practice 25. Summary: *a/an* vs. *the* vs. Ø.** (Chart 11-8)
Complete the sentences with ***a/an, the***, or **Ø**. Add capital letters as necessary.

1. It is _____ scientific fact: _____ steam rises when _____ water boils.

2. _____ gas is expensive nowadays.

3. _____ gas I got yesterday cost more than I've ever paid.

4. _____ sun is _____ star. We need _____ sun for _____ heat, _____
   light, and _____ energy.

5. A: Do you see _____ man who is standing next to Janet?
   B: Yes. Who is he?

   A: He's _____ president of this university.

6. A one-dollar bill has a picture of _____ president of the United States. It's a picture of
   George Washington. He was _____ first president of the country.

---

*One-half inch = 1.27 centimeters

7. _____ pizza originated in Italy. It is a pie with _____ cheese, _____ tomatoes, and other things on top.

8. A: Hey, Nick. Pass _____ pizza. I want another piece.
   B: There are only two pieces left. You take _____ big piece, and I'll take _____ small one.

9. I had _____ interesting experience yesterday. _____ man in _____ blue suit came into my office and handed me _____ bouquet of _____ flowers. I had never seen _____ man before in my life, but I thanked him for _____ flowers. Then he walked out _____ door.

▶ **Practice 26. Using *the* or Ø with names.** (Chart 11-9)
Complete the sentences with ***the*** or **Ø**.

1. Although Ingrid has been in Orly Airport several times, she has never visited ____Ø____ Paris.
2. ____Ø____ Dr. James was the youngest person at her university to get a Ph.D.
3. _____ Mount Rainier in Washington state is in _____ Cascade Mountain Range.
4. _____ Nile is the longest river in _____ Africa.
5. Is _____ Toronto or _____ Montreal the largest city in Canada?
6. During her tour of Africa, Helen climbed _____ Mount Kilimanjaro and visited several national parks in _____ Kenya.
7. _____ New Zealand is made up of two islands: North Island and South Island.
8. _____ Himalayas extend through several countries, including Pakistan, _____ India, and _____ Nepal.
9. _____ President Davis was surprised to be elected to a fourth term.
10. _____ Ho Chi Minh City in _____ Vietnam was formerly called _____ Saigon.
11. _____ Andes Mountains in South America extend for 5000 miles.
12. _____ Dominician Republic and _____ Haiti share an island called Hispaniola. _____ Atlantic Ocean is at the north, and _____ Caribbean Sea is at the south.

► **Practice 27. Using _the_ or Ø with names.** (Chart 11-9)
Answer the questions. Choose from the list below. Use _the_ if necessary. (Not all names on the list will be used.)

Africa	Europe	Mont Blanc	Saudi Arabia
Alps	Gobi Desert	Mount Vesuvius	Shanghai
Amazon River	Indian Ocean	Netherlands	South America
Beijing	Lagos	Nepal	Taipei
Black Sea	Lake Baikal	Nile River	Thames River
✓Dead Sea	Lake Tanganyika	North America	United Arab Emirates
Elbe River	Lake Titicaca	Sahara Desert	Urals

Geography Trivia

Question   **Answer**

1. What is the lowest point on earth? _____ _the Dead Sea_ _____

2. What is the second-longest river in the world? _____

3. What is the most populated city in China? _____

4. What is the largest desert in the world? _____

5. What river runs through London? _____

6. On what continent is the Volga River? _____

7. What mountains border France and Italy? _____

8. What lake is in east central Africa? _____

9. On what continent is Mexico? _____

10. What is the third-largest ocean in the world? _____

11. What country is also known as Holland? _____

12. What is the third-largest continent in the world? _____

13. What country is located in the Himalayas? _____

14. What mountains are part of the boundary between
    Europe and Asia? _____

15. What is the capital of Nigeria? _____

16. What country consists of seven kingdoms? _____

► **Practice 28. Capitalization.** (Chart 11-10)
Add capital letters where necessary.

1. I'm taking ƀiology 101 this semester.
   _B

2. I'm taking history, biology, english, and calculus this semester.

3. Some lab classes meet on saturday.

4. My roommate likes vietnamese food, and i like thai food.

5. Shelia works for the xerox corporation. it is a very large corporation.

6. Pedro is from latin america. He speaks spanish.

7. My favorite park is central park in new york.

8. Do you know my uncle?

9. I like uncle joe and aunt sara.

10. susan w. miller is a professor.

11. I am in prof. miller's class.

12. In january, it's winter in canada and summer in argentina.

13. I would like to visit los angeles.

14. It's the largest city in california.

▶ **Practice 29. Editing.** (Chapter 11)
Correct the errors.

1. The mail carrier brought only one ~~mail~~ *letter* today.

2. Mr. Dale gave his class long history assignment for the weekend.

3. Tariq speaks several language, including Arabic and German.

4. I usually have glass water with my lunch.

5. A helpful police officer gave us an information about the city.

6. This recipe calls for two cup of nut.

7. Much vegetable are believed to have cancer-fighting ingredients.

8. Only applicants with the necessary experiences should apply for the computer position.

9. When Vicki likes a movie, she sees it several time.

10. A popular children's story is *Snow White and the Seven Dwarfs*.

11. Is it possible to stop all violences in the world?

12. Some of the homeworks for my English class was easy, but many of the assignment were unclear.

13. Diane has been to Rome several time recently. She always has wonderful time.

14. Many parents need advices about raising children.

15. A person doesn't need many equipment to play baseball: just ball and a bat.

Complete the puzzle. Use the clues to find the correct words. All the words are from Chapter 11.

Across

1. There isn't much _____ from the earthquake area. All the communication lines are down, and we can't get any news.

8. Our teacher gave us some good _____ to find helpful websites.

9. Please hurry. We don't have much _____.

10. There are too _____ cars on the road.

Down

2. I wanted to buy some candy, so my grandfather gave me a _____ dollars.

3. The doctor gave me some good _____: Exercise regularly.

4. I have seen this movie four _____.

5. My grandmother handed me a _____ money — about 10 dollars.

6. You don't need _____ equipment to play tennis: just a tennis racket and some tennis balls.

7. I was afraid to hear the truth, but now I am glad you told me everything. I appreciate your _____.

Chapter 12
Adjective Clauses

▶ **Practice 1. Using *who* and *that* in adjective clauses to describe people.**
(Charts 12-1 and 12-2)
<u>Underline</u> the adjective clause in the long sentence. Then change the long sentence into two short sentences.*

1. *Long sentence:*   I thanked the man <u>*who helped me move the refrigerator*</u>.

   Short sentence 1: _____<u>I thanked</u>_____ the man.

   Short sentence 2: _____<u>He helped</u>_____ me move the refrigerator.

2. *Long sentence:*   A woman who was wearing a gray suit asked me for directions.

   Short sentence 1: _____ me for directions.

   Short sentence 2: _____ a gray suit.

3. *Long sentence:*   I saw a man that was wearing a blue coat.

   Short sentence 1: _____ a man.

   Short sentence 2: _____ a blue coat.

4. *Long sentence:*   The parents hugged the boy who had pulled his brother from the icy river.

   Short sentence 1: _____ the boy.

   Short sentence 2: _____ his brother from the icy river.

5. *Long sentence:*   The girl that broke the vase apologized to Mrs. Cook.

   Short sentence 1: _____ to Mrs. Cook.

   Short sentence 2: _____ the vase.

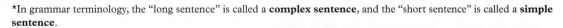

*In grammar terminology, the "long sentence" is called a **complex sentence**, and the "short sentence" is called a **simple sentence**.

- A complex sentence has an independent clause and one or more dependent clauses. For example:
  I thanked the man who helped me. = a complex sentence consisting of one independent clause (*I thanked the man*) and one dependent clause (*who helped me*)
- A simple sentence has only an independent clause. For example:
  I thanked the man. = a simple sentence consisting of one independent clause
  He helped me. = a simple sentence consisting of one independent clause

► **Practice 2. Using *who* and *that* in adjective clauses to describe people.**
(Chart 12-2)
<u>Underline</u> each adjective clause. Then write "S" above its subject, and "V" above its verb.

                          S   V

1. The people <u>who live next to me</u> are nice.

2. My neighbors who live across the street have a new baby.

3. A family that is from India just moved to our street.

4. Our neighborhood is a good place for people who have children.

5. A professor who teaches at the university just moved to our street.

6. One of my neighbors has a disabled child who is training to play basketball in the Special Olympics.

► **Practice 3. Using *who* and *that* in adjective clauses to describe people.**
(Chart 12-2)
Combine the two short sentences into one long sentence using "short sentence 2" as an adjective clause. Write two sentences: the first with ***who*** and the second with ***that***.

1. *Short sentence 1:*   The woman was polite.

    Short sentence 2:   She answered the phone.

    Long sentence 1:   The woman   _____*who answered the phone*_____   was polite.

    Long sentence 2:   The woman   _____*that answered the phone*_____   was polite.

2. *Short sentence 1:*   The man is also a singer.

    Short sentence 2:   The man played the guitar.

    Long sentence 1:   The man _____ is also a singer.

    Long sentence 2:   The man _____ is also a singer.

3. *Short sentence 1:*   I read about the soccer player.

    Short sentence 2:   He was injured yesterday.

    Long sentence 1:   I read about the soccer player _____ yesterday.

    Long sentence 2:   I read about the soccer player _____ yesterday.

4. *Short sentence 1:*   I know a man.

   Short sentence 2:   He has sailed around the world.

   Long sentence 1:   I know a man _____ around the world.

   Long sentence 2:   I know a man _____ around the world.

▶ **Practice 4. Using *who* and *that* in adjective clauses to describe people.**
(Chart 12-2)

Complete the sentences using either ***who*** or ***that***.

1. A hair cutter is a person _____<u>who / that cuts hair</u>_____ .

2. A pizza maker is a person _____ .

3. A tennis player is a person _____ .

4. An English teacher is a person _____ .

5. A horse trainer is a person _____ .

6. A meat eater is a person _____ .

7. Tea drinkers are people _____ .

8. Firefighters are people _____ .

▶ **Practice 5. Using *who*, *whom*, *that*, and Ø in adjective clauses.** (Chart 12-3)

Change the two short sentences into one long sentence as indicated. <u>Underline</u> the adjective clause.

1. *Short sentence 1:*   The woman was polite.
   Short sentence 2:   Jack met her.

   *Long sentence with **that**:*   The woman _____<u>that Jack met</u>_____ was polite.

2. *Short sentence 1:*   The woman was very tall.
   Short sentence 2:   Jack saw her.

   Long sentence with Ø: The woman _____ was very tall.

3. *Short sentence 1:*   The woman is a professor.
   Short sentence 2:   Jack knows her.

   *Long sentence with **that**:*   The woman _____ is a professor.

4. *Short sentence 1:*   The student was grateful.
   Short sentence 2:   The teacher helped the student.

   *Long sentence with **that**:*   The student _____ was grateful.

5. *Short sentence 1:*   The student was happy about the exam.
   Short sentence 2:   I helped the student.

   Long sentence with Ø: The student _____ was happy
   about the exam.

6. *Short sentence 1:*   The student won a scholarship.
   Short sentence 2:   I just met the student.

   *Long sentence with **who**:*   The student _____ won a
   scholarship.

7. *Short sentence 1:*   The student is the class president.
   Short sentence 2:   You see the student over there.

   Long sentence with **whom:**   The student _____ is the class president.

▶ **Practice 6. Using *who* and *that* in adjective clauses.** (Charts 12-2 and 12-3)
Write "S" if *who* or *that* is the subject of the adjective clause. Write "O" if *who* or *that* is the object of the adjective clause. Cross out the words *who* or *that* where possible.

1. __*S*__ The students **who** go to this school are friendly.
2. __*O*__ The people ~~that~~ I saw in the park were practicing yoga.
3. _____ I saw several people **who** were practicing yoga.
4. _____ I know the woman **that** my uncle hired.
5. _____ I like the woman **that** manages my uncle's store.
6. _____ Do you like the mechanic **that** fixed your car?
7. _____ Mr. Polanski is a mechanic **who** you can trust.
8. _____ What's the name of the woman **who** Hank invited to the dance?
9. _____ Do you know the man **who**'s dancing with Katrina?
10. _____ The singer **that** we just heard comes from Mexico.
11. _____ The singer **who** just performed comes from Mexico.

▶ **Practice 7. Using *who*, *whom*, *that*, and Ø in adjective clauses.** (Chart 12-3)
Circle all the correct completions.

1. A man _____ works on a submarine.
   a. I know
   b. whom I know
   c. who I know
   d. that I know

2. I know a man _____ on a submarine.
   a. works
   b. he works
   c. who works
   d. that works

3. My mother is a woman _____ tremendously.
   a. I admire
   b. whom I admire
   c. who I admire
   d. that I admire

4. My mother is a woman _____
   a. is always optimistic
   b. she is always optimistic
   c. who is always optimistic
   d. that is always optimistic

5. I'm pleased with the person _____.
   a. he is going to be our next mayor
   b. who is going to be our next mayor
   c. whom is going to be our next mayor
   d. that is going to be our next mayor

6. I'm pleased with the person _____.
   a. the people elected
   b. that the people elected
   c. who the people elected
   d. the people elected him

► **Practice 8. Using *that*, *who*, *whom* and Ø in adjective clauses.** (Chart 12-3)
In the box, write every possible pronoun that can be used to connect the adjective clause to the main clause: *who*, *that*, or *whom*. Also, write Ø if the pronoun can be omitted.

1. The woman

who
that

   sat next to me on the plane was very friendly.

2. The woman

that
Ø
who
whom

   I met on the plane was very friendly.

3. Two people

   I didn't know walked into the classroom.

4. The people

   walked into the classroom were strangers.

5. My cousin's wife is the woman

   is talking to Mr. Horn.

6. I like the woman

   my brother and I met on the bus.

► **Practice 9. *Who* vs. *which*.** (Charts 12-2 → 12-4)
Choose the correct completion.

1. The magazine _____ I read on the plane was interesting.
   a. who   (b.) which

2. The artist _____ drew my picture is very good.
   a. who   b. which

3. I really enjoyed the experiences _____ I had on my trip to Nigeria.
   a. who   b. which

4. Most of the games _____ we played as children no longer entertain us.
   a. who   b. which

5. All of the people _____ I called yesterday can come to the meeting on Monday.
   a. who   b. which

6. The teacher _____ was ill canceled her math class.
   a. who   b. which

7. The flight _____ I took to Singapore was on time.
    a. who   b. which

8. I read an article _____ discussed the current political crisis.
    a. who   b. which

▶ **Practice 10. *That* and *which*.** (Chart 12-4)
Write "S" if *that* or *which* is the subject of the adjective clause. Write "O" if *that* or *which* is the object of the adjective clause. Cross out the words *that* or *which* where possible.

1. _O_ The medicine **which** the doctor prescribed for me was very expensive.

2. _S_ The medicine **which** is on the shelf is no longer good.

3. ____ The computer **that** I bought recently has already crashed several times.

4. ____ The car **which** my husband drives is very reliable.

5. ____ The house **which** sits on top of the hill has won several architecture awards.

6. ____ The restaurant **that** offered low-cost dinners to senior citizens has recently closed.

7. ____ The trees **that** shade our house are over 300 years old.

8. ____ The trees **that** we planted last year have doubled in size.

▶ **Practice 11. Using *that*, *which*, and Ø in adjective clauses.** (Chart 12-4)
Write the pronouns *which* or *that* that can be used to connect the adjective clause to the main clause. Also write Ø if the pronoun can be omitted.

1. I really enjoyed the movie | that / which / Ø | we saw last night.

2. Tim liked the movie | ____ | was playing at the Fox Theater.

3. The plane | ____ | I took to Korea was two hours late because of bad weather.

4. The books | ____ | Jane ordered came in the mail today.

5. Jane was glad to get the books | ____ | came in the mail today.

► **Practice 12. Adjective clauses.** (Charts 12-3 and 12-4)
Complete the sentences with adjective clauses using words from the lists. There is one extra word in each list.

1. *them, I, visited*

   I enjoy the relatives _____ I visited _____ in Mexico City last year.

2. *I, that, drank, it*

   The coffee _____ was cold and weak.

3. *wearing, was, I, them*

   The tennis shoes _____ in the garden got wet and muddy.

4. *that, him, I've, known, and, loved*

   My cousin Ahmed is a person _____ since he was born.

5. *her, I, married, who*

   I have a great deal of respect for the wonderful woman _____ 11 years ago.

6. *have, had, him, we, that*

   The dog _____ for several years is very gentle with young children.

7. *which, it, we, bought*

   The car _____ last year has turned out to be a lemon.*

► **Practice 13. Pronoun usage in adjective clauses.** (Charts 12 → 12-4)
Choose <u>all</u> the correct answers.

1. I liked the teacher _____ I had for chemistry in high school.
   (a.) who   (b.) whom   c. which   (d.) that   (e.) Ø

2. I liked chemistry because the teacher _____ taught the class was excellent.
   a. who   b. whom   c. which   d. that   e. Ø

3. The researchers in the Amazon River basin found many plants _____ were previously unknown.
   a. who   b. whom   c. which   d. that   e. Ø

4. The plants _____ the researchers found were carefully taken to a laboratory.
   a. who   b. whom   c. which   d. that   e. Ø

5. Mr. Rice made sandwiches for the children _____ were hungry.
   a. who   b. whom   c. which   d. that   e. Ø

6. The children enjoyed the sandwiches _____ Mr. Rice made for them.
   a. who   b. whom   c. which   d. that   e. Ø

7. Have you read any books by the author _____ the teacher mentioned in class?
   a. who   b. whom   c. which   d. that   e. Ø

---

*lemon = something, especially a car, that doesn't work properly and needs a lot of repairs.

8. A book _____ I read last year has become a best-seller.

    a. who   b. whom   c. which   d. that   e. Ø

9. The fans _____ were sitting in the stadium jumped up and cheered when their team scored a point.

    a. who   b. whom   c. which   d. that   e. Ø

10. The fans jumped up and cheered when their team scored the point _____ won the game.

    a. who   b. whom   c. which   d. that   e. Ø

▶ **Practice 14. Singular and plural verbs in adjective clauses.** (Chart 12-5)
Choose the correct form of the verb in *italics*. <u>Underline</u> the noun that determines whether the verb in the adjective clause is singular or plural.

1. The <u>students</u> who (*is* / (*are*)) in my class come from many countries.

2. The people who (*is* / *are*) standing in line to get into the theater have been here for a couple of hours.

3. Water is a chemical compound that (*consists* / *consist*) of oxygen and hydrogen.

4. There are two students in my class who (*speaks* / *speak*) Portuguese.

5. I met some people who (*knows* / *know*) my brother.

6. The student who (*is* / *are*) talking to the teacher is from Peru.

7. Do you know the people that (*lives* / *live*) in that house?

8. A carpenter is a person who (*makes* / *make*) things out of wood.

9. Sculptors are artists who (*make* / *makes*) things from clay or other materials.

► **Practice 15. Prepositions in adjective clauses.** (Chart 12-6 and Appendix 2)
Complete the sentences with adjective clauses. Add prepositions as necessary.

1. We went to a movie. The movie was good.

   a. The movie that _____*we went to*_____ was good.

   b. The movie Ø _____*we went to*_____ was good.

2. I enjoyed meeting the people yesterday. You introduced me to them.

   a. I enjoyed meeting the people that _____ yesterday.

   b. I enjoyed meeting the people who _____ yesterday.

3. English grammar is a subject. I am quite familiar with English grammar.

   a. English grammar is a subject Ø _____.

   b. English grammar is a subject with _____.

4. Ms. Perez can help you. You should talk with her.

   a. Ms. Perez is the person Ø _____.

   b. Ms. Perez is the person with _____.

5. The train is usually late. We are waiting for it.

   a. The train that _____ is usually late.

   b. The train Ø _____ is usually late.

6. The job requires several years of experience. I'm interested in the job.

   a. The job that _____ requires several years of experience.

   b. The job which _____ requires several years of experience.

► **Practice 16. Prepositions in adjective clauses.** (Chart 12-6)
Give all the possible patterns for the adjective clause: *that, which, who, whom,* or *Ø*. Add the necessary prepositions.

1. a. The bus ___*that*___ we were waiting ___*for*___ was an hour late.

   b. The bus ___*which*___ we were waiting ___*for*___ was an hour late.

   c. The bus ___*Ø*___ we were waiting ___*for*___ was an hour late.

   d. The bus for ___*which*___ we were waiting ___*Ø*___ was an hour late.

2. a. The music _____ I listened _____ was pleasant.

   b. The music _____ I listened _____ was pleasant.

   c. The music _____ I listened _____ was pleasant.

   d. The music to _____ I listened _____ was pleasant.

3. a. Psychology is a subject _____ I am very interested _____.

   b. Psychology is a subject _____ I am very interested _____.

   c. Psychology is a subject _____ I am very interested _____.

   d. Psychology is a subject in _____ I am very interested _____.

4. a. The man _____ Maria was arguing _____ was very angry.

   b. The man _____ Maria was arguing _____ was very angry.

   c. The man _____ Maria was arguing _____ was very angry.

   d. The man _____ Maria was arguing _____ was very angry.

   e. The man with _____ Maria was arguing _____ was very angry.

▶ **Practice 17. Prepositions in adjective clauses.** (Chart 12-6 and Appendix 2)
Write the appropriate prepositions or Ø. Draw brackets around the adjective clause.

1. I enjoyed the CD [we listened ___to___ at Sara's apartment.]

2. I paid the shopkeeper for the glass cup [I accidentally broke ___Ø___.]

3. The bus we were waiting _____ was only three minutes late.

4. Mrs. Chan is someone I always enjoy talking _____ about politics.

5. I showed my roommate a text message I got from a co-worker _____.

6. One of the subjects I've been interested _____ for a long time is astronomy.

7. The people I talked _____ at the reception were interesting.

8. One of the places I want to visit _____ next year is Mexico City.

9. The website I was looking _____ had useful reviews of new computers.

10. The book I wanted _____ wasn't available at the library.

11. English grammar is one of the subjects _____ which I enjoy studying the most.

12. The friend I waved _____ didn't wave back. Maybe he just didn't see me.

▶ **Practice 18. Adjective clauses with *whose*.** (Chart 12-7)
<u>Underline</u> the adjective clause in each long sentence. Then change the long sentence into two short sentences.

1. *Long sentence:* I know a man <u>whose daughter is a test-pilot</u>.

   Short sentence 1: _____I know a man._____

   Short sentence 2: _____His daughter is a test-pilot._____

2. *Long sentence:* The woman whose husband is out of work found a job at Mel's Diner.

   Short sentence 1: _____

   Short sentence 2: _____

3. *Long sentence:* The man whose wallet I found gave me a reward.

   Short sentence 1: _____

   Short sentence 2: _____

► **Practice 19. Adjective clauses with *whose*.** (Chart 12-7)
Follow these steps:

1. Underline the possessive word.
2. Draw an arrow to the noun it refers to.
3. Replace the possessive word with *whose*.
4. Combine the two sentences into one.

1. The firefighters are very brave. Their department has won many awards.

      *The firefighters **whose** deparment has won many awards are very brave.*

2. I talked to the boy. His kite was caught in a tree.

      _____

3. The family is staying in a motel. Their house burned down.

      _____

4. I watched a little girl. Her dog was chasing a ball in the park.

      _____

5. The reporter won an award. Her articles explained global warming.

      _____

6. I know a man. His daughter entered college at the age of 14.

      _____

7. We observed a language teacher. Her teaching methods included role-playing.

      _____

8. The teachers are very popular. Their methods include role-playing.

      _____

► **Practice 20. Meaning of adjective clauses.** (Charts 12-1 → 12-7)
Check all the sentences that are true.

1. The policeman who gave Henry a ticket seemed very nervous.
    a. _✓_ Henry received a ticket.
    b. ____ Henry seemed nervous.
    c. _✓_ The policeman seemed nervous.

2. A co-worker of mine whose wife is a pilot is afraid of flying.
    a. ____ My co-worker is a pilot.
    b. ____ My co-worker's wife is afraid of flying.
    c. ____ The pilot is a woman.

3. The man that delivers office supplies to our company bought a Ferrari.
    a. ____ Our company bought a Ferrari.
    b. ____ A man delivers office supplies.
    c. ____ A delivery man bought a Ferrari.

4. The doctor who took care of my father had a heart attack recently.
    a. ____ My father had a heart attack.
    b. ____ The doctor treated a heart attack patient.
    c. ____ The doctor had a heart attack.

5. The forest fire which destroyed two homes in Woodville burned for two weeks.
   a. _____ The forest fire burned for two weeks.
   b. _____ Two homes burned for two weeks.
   c. _____ The forest fire destroyed Woodville.

6. The salesman who sold my friend a used car was arrested for changing the mileage on cars.
   a. _____ My friend bought a car.
   b. _____ My friend was arrested.
   c. _____ The salesman changed the mileage on cars.

▶ **Practice 21. Adjective clauses.** (Charts 12-1 → 12-7)
Write all the possible completions: *who*, *that*, *which*, *whose*, *whom*, or **Ø**.

1. What do you say to people _____*who / that*_____ ask you personal questions that you don't want to answer?

2. People _____ live in New York City are called New Yorkers.

3. Tina likes the present _____ I gave her for her birthday.

4. George Washington is the president _____ picture is on a one-dollar bill.

5. Have you seen the movie _____ is playing at the Majestic Theater?

6. Do you know the woman _____ Michael is engaged to?

7. That's Tom Jenkins. He's the boy _____ parents live in Switzerland.

8. A thermometer is an instrument _____ measures temperature.

9. A high-strung person is someone _____ is always nervous.

10. The man _____ I told you about is standing over there.

11. In my country, any person _____ is 18 years old or older can vote. I turned 18 last year. The person _____ I voted for in the national election lost. I hope the next candidate for _____ I vote has better luck.

▶ **Practice 22. Reading.** (Chapter 12)
Read each paragraph. Then choose the correct completion for each sentence that follows.

Sticky Notes

Maybe you have a sticky note in this book. Sticky notes are those small, colored papers that you can stick in books, on your own papers, on walls, and in other places. You may know them as Post-it® Notes, which was their original name. These notes are common today, but they were not a product that was planned. Like many other products, the sticky note was invented by accident.

1. This passage is about ____.
   a. paper that you can stick to something
   b. paper that you use to write letters

2. The sticky notes were a product ____.
   a. that was developed through research
   b. that was the result of an accident

In 1970, a man whose name was Spencer Silver was working at 3M, a chemical company. The company was trying to find a strong, new glue that could hold things together. Silver created a new glue, but the glue was not strong. In fact, it was very weak. The objects he tried to stick together with the glue soon fell apart. The company didn't use the glue that Silver had created, but Silver kept it in his desk.

3. Spencer Silver invented a glue _____.
    a. that held things together
    b. that was very weak

4. The company _____.
    a. used Silver's product
    b. didn't find uses for the glue

Four years later, another 3M scientist, Arthur Fry, was singing in a choir. The bookmarks that he used to mark the songs in his songbook kept falling out. Fry wanted something that worked better and he remembered Silver's invention: the glue that was too weak.

5. Arthur Fry wanted _____.
    a. bookmarks that stuck to pages
    b. a new book of songs

6. He thought of the invention _____.
    a. that Spencer had made
    b. that 3M was using

Fry put a small amount of Silver's glue on top of his bookmarks. Success! The bookmarks on which he had placed the glue stayed on the pages. Even better, they also came off easily without damaging the pages. Fry and Silver then worked together and developed the glue which was eventually used on the Post-it ® Notes. That glue is on the back of each sticky note.

7. Fry put some glue _____.
    a. on top of the bookmarks
    b. on top of the book

8. The result was a kind of paper _____.
    a. that stuck very tightly
    b. that stuck, but could also be pulled off easily.

▶ **Practice 23. Editing.** (Chapter 12)
Correct the errors.

                    looks
1. A movie that ~~look~~ interesting opens tomorrow.

2. My family lived in a house which it was built in 1900.

3. There's the man that we saw him on TV.

4. I don't know people who their lives are carefree.

5. It is important to help people who has no money.

6. At the airport, I was waiting for friends which I hadn't seen them for a long time.

7. The woman live next door likes to relax by doing crossword puzzles every evening.

8. My teacher has two cats who their names are Ping and Pong.

9. I enjoyed the songs which we sang them.

10. The person to that you should speak is Gary Green.

► **Practice 24. Word search puzzle.** (Chapter 12)
Circle the five words in the puzzle. The words are the pronouns that begin adjective clauses.

The words may be horizontal, vertical, or diagonal. Note: *who* appears as a separate word in addition to appearing inside one of other words.

T	P	Y	G	E	T
W	H	O	M	S	W
T	T	T	O	O	H
Z	H	H	K	H	I
T	W	A	V	W	C
P	F	H	T	N	H

Chapter 13
Gerunds and Infinitives

▶ **Practice 1. Verb + gerund.** (Chart 13-1)
Complete the sentences with the correct form of the verbs in parentheses.

1. Joan often talks about (*move*) _____moving_____ overseas.

2. The Browns sometimes discuss (*live*) _____ in a smaller town.

3. Christine enjoys (*take*) _____ care of her young niece.

4. Nathan keeps (*buy*) _____ lottery tickets, but he never wins.

5. My manager considered (*give*) _____ pay raises but decided not to.

6. I always put off (*do*) _____ my math homework.

7. The students finished (*review*) _____ for the test at 3:00 A.M.

8. Ann talked about (*find*) _____ a new roommate.

9. Dana quit (*drive*) _____ after she had a serious car accident.

10. My dentist thinks about (*retire*) _____, but he enjoys his work too much.

11. Last week, Joan and David postponed (*get married*) _____ for the second time.

12. Do you mind (*work*) _____ an extra shift tonight?

▶ **Practice 2. *Go* + gerund.** (Chart 13-2)
Complete each sentence with a form of ***go*** and a word from the list.

camp	fish	sail	sightsee	skydive
✓dance	hike	shop	ski	swim

1. I love to dance. Last night, my husband and I danced for hours.
   Last night, my husband and I _____went dancing_____.

2. Later this afternoon, Ted is going to take a long walk in the woods.
   Ted _____ later today.

3. Yesterday, Alice visited many stores and bought some clothes and makeup.
   Yesterday, Alice _____.

4. On a hot day, I like to go to the beach and jump in the water.
   On a hot day, I like to _____.

5. My grandfather takes his fishing pole to a pond every Sunday.
   My grandfather _____ every Sunday.

6. When I visit a new city, I like to look around at the sights.

When I visit a new city, I like to _____.

7. I love to put up a small tent by a stream, make a fire, and listen to the sounds of the forest during the night.

I love to _____.

8. I want to take the sailboat out on the water this afternoon.

I want to _____ this afternoon.

9. Once a year, we take our skis to our favorite mountain resort and enjoy an exciting weekend.

Once a year, we _____ at our favorite mountain resort.

10. Last year on my birthday, my friends and I went up in an airplane, put on parachutes, and jumped out of the plane at a very high altitude.

Last year on my birthday, my friends and I

_____ .

▶ **Practice 3. Identifying gerunds and infinitives.** (Charts 13-1 and 13-3)
Underline the gerunds and infinitives in the sentences. Circle GER for gerunds. Circle INF for infinitives.

1. Ann promised <u>to wait</u> for me.	GER	(INF)
2. I kept <u>walking</u> even though I was tired.	(GER)	INF
3. Alex offered to help me.	GER	INF
4. Karen finished cleaning up the kitchen and went to bed.	GER	INF
5. We decided to order a pizza.	GER	INF
6. David discussed quitting his job several times.	GER	INF
7. The police officers planned to work overtime during the conference.	GER	INF
8. Kevin would like to grow organic vegetables in his garden.	GER	INF

▶ **Practice 4. Verb + gerund or infinitive.** (Charts 13-1 → 13-3)
Choose the correct completion.

1. I would like (*inviting* / (*to invite*)) you and some of my other friends for dinner sometime.

2. I enjoyed (*being* / *to be*) with my family at the lake last summer.

3. My parents can't afford (*paying* / *to pay*) all of my college expenses.

4. Theresa, would you mind (*mailing* / *to mail*) this letter on your way home?

5. Do you expect (*passing* / *to pass*) this course? If so, you'd better work harder.

6. Mr. Reed refused (*considering* / *to consider*) my proposal. He had already made up his mind.

7. I wish he would consider (*accepting* / *to accept*) my proposal. I know I can do the job.

8. I don't think I'll ever finish (*reading* / *to read*) this report. It just goes on and on.

9. I would enjoy (*visiting* / *to visit*) you in Cairo while you're studying there.

10. I'm really sorry. I didn't mean (*hurting* / *to hurt*) your feelings.

11. Why do you keep (*asking* / *to ask*) me the same question over and over again?

12. I've decided (*looking* / *to look*) for another job. I'll never be happy here.

13. You need (*trying* / *to try*) harder if you want to get a promotion.

14. Why do you pretend (*enjoying* / *to enjoy*) Leon's company? I know you don't like him.

15. Let's get together tonight. I want to talk about (*opening* / *to open*) a new business.

16. I have a secret. Do you promise (*keeping* / *to keep*) it to yourself?

17. The president plans (*giving* / *to give*) everyone a bonus at the end of the year.

18. I have a good job, and I hope (*supporting* / *to support*) myself all through school.

19. I can't wait (*finishing* / *to finish*) work today. I'm starting my vacation tonight.

▶ **Practice 5. Verb + gerund or infinitive.** (Charts 13-1 → 13-4)
Choose the correct answer. Both answers may be correct.

1. I want _____ the comedy special on TV tonight.
   a. seeing   (b.) to see

2. I'm a people-watcher. I like _____ people in public places.
   (a.) watching   (b.) to watch

3. I've already begun _____ ideas for my new novel.
   a. collecting   b. to collect

4. A group of Chinese scientists plan _____ their discovery at the conference next spring.
   a. presenting   b. to present

5. Whenever I wash my car, it starts _____.
   a. raining   b. to rain

6. Angela and I continued _____ for several hours.
   a. talking   b. to talk

7. I love _____ on the beach during a storm.
   a. walking   b. to walk

8. I would love _____ a walk today.
   a. taking   b. to take

9. Are you sure you don't mind _____ Johnny for me while I go to the store?
   a. watching   b. to watch

10. Annie hates _____ in the rain.
    a. driving   b. to drive

11. My roommate can't stand _____ to really loud rock music.
    a. listening   b. to listen

12. I don't like _____ in front of other people.
    a. singing   b. to sing

13. Would you like _____ to the concert with us?
    a. going   b. to go

14. Charlie likes to go _____ when the weather is very windy.
    a. sailing   b. to sail

15. Most children can't wait _____ their presents on their birthday.
    a. opening   b. to open

▶ **Practice 6. Verb + gerund or infinitive.** (Charts 13-1, 13-3, and 13-4)
Complete the passages with the infinitive or gerund form of the words in parentheses.

1. Cindy wants (*go*) _____*to go*_____ to graduate school next year. However, she can't afford (*pay*) _____ all the tuition, so she needs (*get*) _____ a scholarship. She intends (*apply*) _____ for a scholarship which is given to students who have done outstanding work in biology. She is optimistic, and she expects (*receive*) _____ it.

2. Carla and Marco are planning (*take*) _____ a vacation. Carla would love (*go*) _____ to a tropical beach, but Marco doesn't like hot weather. He prefers cold weather and would like (*go*) _____ skiing in the mountains. Although Carla prefers hot weather, she doesn't mind (*be*) _____ in cold weather. They will probably decide (*go*) _____ to the mountains this year, and Marco will enjoy (*ski*) _____. Next year, they'll go to the tropics and go (*swim*) _____ and (*sail*) _____ in the warm ocean.

3. Tom Fan was considering (*get*) _____ another job. The job that he has is a good one, but it doesn't have opportunities to advance. Tom decided (*tell*) _____ his boss, Sharon, that he was thinking about (*leave*) _____ the company because he needed (*have*) _____ more opportunities to advance. Sharon offered (*create*) _____ a new position for Tom, one with more responsibility. Tom happily accepted the offer and agreed (*take*) _____ the new job as regional sales manager of a large area.

▶ **Practice 7. Gerunds and infinitives.** (Charts 13-1, 13-3, and 13-4)
Complete the sentences with the gerund or infinitive form of the verb. Some verbs may take both.

Part I. Use ***work***.

1. I agreed _____*to work*_____.
2. I put off _____*working*_____.
3. I would love _____.
4. I thought about _____.
5. I promised _____.
6. I began _____.
7. I decided _____.
8. I offered _____.
9. I quit _____.
10. I refused _____.
11. I hoped _____.
12. I finished _____.

Part II. Use ***leave***.

13. She expected _____.

14. She wanted _____.

15. She considered _____.

16. She talked about _____.

17. She postponed _____.

18. She put off _____.

19. She refused _____.

20. She needed _____.

21. She thought about _____.

22. She hoped _____.

Part III. Use ***know***.

23. They seemed _____.

24. They expected _____.

25. They would like _____.

26. They don't mind _____.

27. They would love _____.

28. They want _____.

29. They can't stand _____.

30. They needed _____.

31. They appeared _____.

32. They hated _____.

▶ **Practice 8. Preposition + gerund.** (Chart 13-5)
Complete the sentences with the correct preposition. <u>Underline</u> the gerund.

Part I. Liz . . .

1. is afraid _____*of*_____ <u>flying</u>.

2. apologized _____ hurting her friend's feelings.

3. believes _____ helping others.

4. is good _____ listening to her friends' concerns.

5. is tired _____ working weekends.

6. is nervous _____ walking home from work late at night.

7. dreams _____ owning a farm with horses, cows, and sheep.

8. talks _____ buying a farm in the country.

Part II. Leonard . . .

9. is responsible _____ closing the restaurant where he works at night.

10. thanked his father _____ lending him some money.

11. plans _____ becoming an accountant.

12. forgave his roommate _____ taking his car without asking.

13. insists _____ eating only fresh fruits and vegetables.

14. is looking forward _____ finishing school.

15. stopped his best friend _____ making a bad decision.

16. is worried _____ not having enough time for family and friends.

▶ **Practice 9. Preposition + gerund.** (Chart 13-5 and Appendix 2)
Complete the sentences. Use prepositions and gerunds.

1. Bill interrupted me. He apologized ___for___ that.

   Bill apologized ___for interrupting___ me.

2. I like to learn about other countries and cultures. I'm interested _____ that.

   I'm interested _____ about other countries and cultures.

3. I helped Ann. She thanked me _____ that.

   Ann thanked me _____ her.

4. Nadia wanted to walk to work. She insisted _____ that.

   We offered Nadia a ride, but she insisted _____ to work.

5. Nick lost my car keys. I forgave him _____ that.

   I forgave Nick _____ my car keys when he borrowed my car.

6. Sara wants to go out to eat just because she feels _____ it.

   She feels _____ out to eat.

7. I'm not a good artist. I try to draw faces, but I'm not very good _____ it.

   I'm not good _____ faces.

8. Mr. and Mrs. Reed have been saving some money for their retirement. They believe

   _____ that.

   Mr. and Mrs. Reed believe _____ money for their retirement.

9. I may forget the words I'm supposed to say in my graduation speech. I'm worried _____

   that. I'm worried _____ the words in my speech.

10. The children are going to go to Disneyland. They're excited _____ that.

    The children are excited _____ to Disneyland.

11. Their parents are going to Disneyland too. They are looking forward _____ that.

    Their parents are looking forward _____ there too.

12. Max doesn't like to stay in hotels because he is scared of heights. He is afraid _____ that.

    Max is afraid _____ in hotels.

▶ **Practice 10. Review.** (Charts 13-1 → 13-5)
Choose the correct completions for each group.

Part I. Completions with **ask**.

a. about asking for more money	d. to ask you about a grammar rule
b. about asking the Petersons	e. to ask for a few days off
c. asking "why"	f. to ask for directions

1. A: You look tired, Yoko. Can you stay home from work for a few days?
   B: Yes. I intend __e__.

2. A: Sid, we're lost! Why don't you ask someone where the highway is?
   B: You know that I hate ____.

3. A: You're going to talk to the boss about getting a raise, aren't you?
   B: I don't know. I'm really nervous ____

4. A: Who do you want to invite to our holiday party?
   B: I'm thinking _____.

5. A: Your little girl has a lot of questions, doesn't she?
   B: Yes, she's very curious. She keeps _____ over and over again.

6. A: Yes, do you have a question about the exercise?
   B: Yes, I do. I'd like _____.
   A: Which one?

Part II. Completions with *fix*.

g. about fixing it	j. to fix everything herself
h. at fixing things	k. to fix it myself
i. for fixing it	l. to fix it tomorrow

7. A: Are you going to fix your mother's car?
   B: No, she doesn't need help. She prefers _____.

8. A: Are you going to call the technician to fix your computer?
   B: No, I intend _____ right now.

9. A: Is the plumber coming to fix your faucet?
   B: No. My husband promised _____.

10. A: This sidewalk has been broken for a long time! When is the city going to fix it?
    B: They've been talking _____ for months, but they never do.

11. A: Oh, I'm so sorry! I didn't mean to break your chair.
    B: Don't worry about it. Jerry will fix it. He's excellent _____.

12. A: My car has a real problem. It's very hard to steer.
    B: Did you know that the company is responsible _____? All the cars have been recalled, and the company has to fix them for free.

▶ **Practice 11. Review.** (Charts 13-1 → 13-5)
Choose the correct completion in each pair. More than one answer may be possible.

(1) I am a procrastinator. A procrastinator is a person who puts off (*(doing)* / *to do*) something that she hates (*doing* / *to do*) until a later time. Unfortunately, although the person may intend (*doing* / *to do*) the task soon, it may not be done for a long time.

(2) Here's an example. I received a beautiful silk sweater from my Aunt Sarah. I meant (*write* / *to write*) to her immediately to thank her, but I postponed (*doing* / *to do*) so. I kept (*thinking* / *to think*), "I'll write tomorrow." After a month, I hadn't written to her, and I was too embarrassed to call her. Finally I wrote this:

Dear Aunt Sarah,

(3) I apologize (*for being* / *to be*) so late with this note. I want (*to thank* / *thanking*) you for (*sending* / *to send*) me the lovely blue silk sweater. I will certainly enjoy (*wearing* / *to wear*) it to parties and special events. In fact, I'm planning (*wearing* / *to wear*) it to your birthday dinner next week.

(4) I really look forward (*to seeing* / *to see*) you then. Please forgive me (*for taking* / *to take*) so long to say thank you.

Complete the sentences with the appropriate gerund or infinitive of the word in *italics*. Some sentences also require a preposition.

1. Matthew wants to *go* to a different doctor for his back pain. He's considering __*going*__ to a specialist.

2. Jim would rather walk than *drive* to work. Instead _____*of driving*_____, Jim walks along bike trails to his office.

3. I never *watch* commercials on TV. In fact, I can't stand _____ TV commercials, so I generally watch only shows that I've recorded.

4. Joanne's hobby is *cooking*. She loves _____ gourmet meals for friends and relatives.

5. Martina is nervous about *going* to the dentist for a filling. She has been afraid _____ to the dentist since she was a little girl.

6. Walter's dream is to *become* a doctor in a rural area. He has dreamed _____ a doctor since he was hospitalized as a child.

7. Nathan *has* a chocolate milkshake every afternoon for a snack. He often feels like _____ two, but he doesn't.

8. Every morning, rain or shine, Debbie rises early and stretches. Then she goes outside and *runs* for 30 minutes. Every morning, Debbie goes _____ for half an hour.

9. Mark *washes* all his clothes in hot water. Although his roommates tell him hot water could damage some clothes, he doesn't listen. He insists _____ all his clothes in hot water.

10. The little girl didn't see the car rolling slowly toward her. No one was in it, but fortunately a neighbor jumped into the car and stopped it before it could *hit* her. The neighbor stopped the car _____ the girl.

11. When Rita came to work, her eyes *were* red and she appeared upset, but she said everything was okay. Later, she was laughing and looked more relaxed. Rita seemed _____ better.

12. Tang has been studying medicine abroad for two years and hasn't *seen* his family in all that time. He is going home next week and is very excited _____ his family.

▶ **Practice 13. By + gerund.** (Chart 13-6)
Describe what the people did by using **by** + a gerund.

1. MARY: How did you comfort the child?
   SUE: I held him in my arms.
   Sue comforted the child _____*by holding*_____ him in her arms.

2. PAT: How did you improve your vocabulary?
   NADIA: I read a lot of books.
   Nadia improved her vocabulary _____ a lot of books.

3. KIRK: How did Grandma entertain the children?
   SALLY: She told them a story.
   Grandma entertained the children _____ them a story.

4. MASAKO: How did you improve your English?
   PEDRO: I watched TV a lot.
   Pedro improved his English _____ TV a lot.

5. JEFFREY: How did you catch up with the bus?
   JIM: I ran as fast as I could.
   Jim caught up with the bus _____ as fast as he could.

6. MR. LEE: How did you earn your children's respect?
   MR. COY: I treated them with respect at all times.
   Mr. Coy earned his children's respect _____ them with respect at all times.

▶ **Practice 14. By + gerund.** (Chart 13-6)
Complete the sentences with **by** + an appropriate verb from the list.

count	follow	look	pour	save	stretch	✓take	work

1. I arrived on time _____ *by taking* _____ a taxi instead of a bus.

2. I put out the fire _____ water on it.

3. Giraffes can reach the leaves at the tops of trees _____ their long necks.

4. I finished writing my final paper _____ all through the night.

5. Sylvia was able to buy an expensive condominium _____ her money for four years.

6. I cooked the noodles correctly _____ the directions on the package.

7. You can find out the temperature in any city in the world _____ it up on the Internet.

8. You can figure out how old a tree is _____ its rings.

CROSS-SECTION

20 RINGS
20 YEARS OLD

► **Practice 15. By vs. with.** (Chart 13-6)
Circle all the correct completions.

1. Ole went to Quebec by ____.
   a. bus
   b. a bus
   c. his feet
   d. plane
   e. taxi
   f. train

2. Kim ate dinner with ____.
   a. a fork
   b. a spoon
   c. chopsticks
   d. fork
   e. hand
   f. knife

3. Ali sent the information by ____.
   a. a phone
   b. email
   c. fax
   d. mistake
   e. his hand
   f. phone

4. Sid cleaned the kitchen with ____.
   a. a broom
   b. a mop
   c. hand
   d. soap and water
   e. disinfectant
   f. a cloth

► **Practice 16. Gerund as subject; *It* + infinitive.** (Chart 13-7)
Complete the sentences by using a gerund as the subject or *it* + infinitive. Add *is* where
appropriate. Use the verbs in the list.

complete	eat	live
drive	✓learn	swim

1. a. ____It is____ easy for anyone ____to learn____ how to cook an egg.

   b. ____Learning____ how to cook an egg _____is_____ easy for anyone.

2. a. _____ nutritious food _____ important for your health.

   b. _____ important for your health _____ nutritious food.

3. a. _____ on the wrong side of the road _____ against the law.

   b. _____ against the law _____ on the wrong side of the road.

4. a. _____ fun for both children and adults _____ in the warm sea.

   b. _____ in the warm sea _____ fun for both children and adults.

5. a. _____ expensive _____ in a dormitory?

   b. _____ in a dormitory expensive?

6. a. _____ difficult _____ these sentences correctly?

   b. _____ these sentences correctly difficult?

▶ **Practice 17. Purpose: *to* vs. *for.*** (Chart 13-8)
Rewrite the sentences. Use *it* . . . *for someone + an infinitive phrase.* Use the adjective in parentheses.

1. Shy people have a hard time meeting others at social events. (*difficult*)

   _____*It is difficult for shy people to meet*_____ others at social events.

2. In many cultures, young children sleep in the same room as their parents. (*customary*)

   In many cultures, _____
   in the same room as their parents.

3. Airline pilots need to have good eyesight. (*necessary*)

   _____ good eyesight.

4. Many teenagers can't wake up early. (*hard*)

   _____ early.

5. Elderly people need to keep their minds active. (*important*)

   _____ their minds active.

6. People don't like listening to monotone speakers. (*boring*)

   _____ to monotone speakers.

7. Scientists will never know the origin of every disease in the world. (*impossible*)

   _____ the origin of every disease in
   the world.

▶ **Practice 18. Purpose: *to* vs. *for.*** (Chart 13-9)
Complete the sentences with *to* or *for.*

1. Yesterday, I called the doctor's office . . .

   a. ___*for*___ an appointment.

   b. ___*to*___ make an appointment.

   c. _____ get a prescription.

   d. _____ a prescription.

   e. _____ ask a question.

   f. _____ get some advice.

   g. _____ some advice.

2. Yesterday, Chuck stayed after class . . .

   a. _____ talk with the teacher.

   b. _____ a talk with the teacher.

   c. _____ some extra help.

   d. _____ finish a project.

   e. _____ work with other students.

   f. _____ a meeting with other students.

   g. _____ help plan a class party.

▶ **Practice 19. Purpose: *to* vs. *for.*** (Chart 13-9)
Complete the sentences with *to* or *for.*

1. We wear coats in cold weather ___*to*___ keep warm.

2. We wear coats in cold weather ___*for*___ warmth.

3. Mark contacted a lawyer _____ legal advice.

4. Mark contacted a lawyer _____ discuss a legal problem.

5. Sam went to the hospital _____ an operation.

6. We hired a teenager _____ cut my grandmother's grass twice a month.

7. Frank went to the library _____ review for the test.

8. I play tennis twice a week _____ fun and exercise.

9. Jennifer used some medicine _____ cure an infection on her arm.

10. I lent Yvette some money _____ her school expenses.

11. I asked my manager _____ permission to take the rest of the day off.

▶ **Practice 20. _(In order) to._** (Chart 13-9)
Combine the given phrases in *italics* to create sentences using (*in order*) *to*.

1. *watch the news + turn on the TV*

   After he got home from work, Jack _____turned on the TV (in order) to watch the news._____

2. *wash his clothes + go to the laundromat*

   Every weekend Martin _____

   _____

3. *run + get to class on time*

   Every morning Jeannette _____

   _____

4. *let in some fresh air + open the bedroom windows*

   Every night I _____

5. *ask them for some money + call his parents*

   Sometimes Pierre _____

6. *listen to a baseball game + have the radio on*

   Some afternoons at work, my co-workers _____

   _____

7. *study in peace and quiet + go to the library*

   Some evenings, I _____

▶ **Practice 21. _Too_ vs. _enough._** (Chart 13-10)
Complete the sentences with the words in parentheses and **too** or **enough**.

1. I have a tight schedule tomorrow, so I can't go to the park.

   a. (*time*) I don't have _____enough time to go_____ to the park.

   b. (*busy*) I'm _____too busy to go_____ to the park.

2. I'm pretty short. I can't touch the ceiling.

   a. (*tall*) I'm not _____ to touch the ceiling.

   b. (*short*) I'm _____ to touch the ceiling.

3. Marcus has been out of work for months. He can't pay any of his bills.

   a. (*money*) Marcus doesn't have _____ to pay his bills.

   b. (*poor*) Marcus is _____ to pay his bills.

4. This tea is very hot. I need to wait a while until I can drink it.

   a. (*hot*) This tea is _____ to drink.

   b. (*cool*) This tea isn't _____ to drink.

5. I feel sick. I don't want to eat anything.

    a. (*sick*) I feel _____ to eat anything.

    b. (*well*) I don't feel _____ to eat anything.

6. Nora is only six years old. She can't stay home by herself.

    a. (*old*) Nora _____ to stay home by herself.

    b. (*young*) Nora _____ to stay home by herself.

▶ **Practice 22. Too vs. enough.** (Chart 13-10)
Complete the sentences with *too, enough*, or *Ø*.

1. I think this problem is _____*Ø*_____ important _____*enough*_____ to require our immediate attention.

2. Nina is not _____*too*_____ tired _____*Ø*_____ to finish the project before she goes home.

3. You can do this math problem by yourself. You're _____ smart _____ to figure it out.

4. Our company is _____ small _____ to start new branches overseas.

5. My niece doesn't drive yet. She's _____ young _____ to get a driver's license.

6. Robert is an amazing runner. His coach thinks he is _____ good _____ to begin training for an Olympic marathon.

7. Look at the children watching the clowns. They can't sit still. They're _____ excited _____ to stay in their chairs.

8. The heat outside is terrible! It's _____ hot _____ to fry an egg on the sidewalk!

▶ **Practice 23. Gerund vs. infinitive.** (Chapter 13)
Complete the passage with the correct form of the verbs in parentheses.

Generalizations About Extroverts and Introverts

An extrovert is someone who appears active and confident and who enjoys (*be*)

_____ with other people. This is the opposite of an introvert, who is quiet and
₁

shy and does not want (*spend*) _____ a lot of time with other people .
₂

An extrovert gets energy by (*be*) _____ around other people. An introvert
₃

gets energy from (*be*) _____ alone.
₄

Extroverts try (*find*) _____ social situations because they like interacting
₅

with people. Introverts often avoid (*be*) _____ in social situations because they
₆

are not comfortable in them.

An extrovert prefers (*talk*) _____ with someone else instead of (*sit*)

_____ alone and (*think*) _____. In fact, extroverts

sometimes seem (*think*) _____ and speak at the same time, unlike introverts

who think about their words before (*speak*) _____.

Extroverts, are often good at (*make*) _____ social conversation, while

introverts — who may be shy at first — would like (*discuss*) _____ ideas instead.

▶ **Practice 24. Gerund vs. infinitive.** (Chapter 13)
Complete the sentences with the gerund or infinitive form of the word in parentheses.

1. (*study*) _____*Studying*_____ English can be fun.

2. My boss makes a habit of (*write*) _____ nice emails to her employees when

   they've done a good job.

3. From the earth, the sun and the moon appear (*be*) _____ almost the same size.

4. A: I don't like airplanes.

   B: Why? Are you afraid of (*fly*) _____?

   A: No, I'm afraid of (*crash*) _____.

5. A: Let's quit (*argue*) _____. Let's just agree (*disagree*)

   _____. We can still be friends.

   B: Sounds good to me. And I apologize for (*raise*) _____ my voice. I

   didn't mean (*yell*) _____ at you.

   A: That's okay. I didn't intend (*get*) _____ angry at you either.

6. A: Do you think that it's important for children (*have*) _____ chores

   around the house?

   B: Yes, I do. I think it's essential for them (*learn*) _____ about

   responsibility that way.

7. A: What do you feel like (*do*) _____ this afternoon?

   B: I feel like (*go*) _____ (*shop*) _____ at the mall.

   What about you?

   A: I don't mind (*shop*) _____ at the mall when it's quiet, but there's a sale

   today and it will be too crowded.

8. A: Have you called Alexa yet?

   B: No, I keep (*put*) _____ it off?

   A: Why?

   B: She's mad at me for (*forget*) _____ (*send*) _____

   her a card on her birthday.

▶ **Practice 25. Editing.** (Chapter 13)
Correct the errors.

to buy
1. I decided not ~~buying~~ a new car.

2. The Johnsons are considering to sell their antique store.

3. Sam finally finished build his vacation home in the mountains.

4. My wife and I go to dancing at the community center every Saturday night.

5. Suddenly, it began to raining and the wind started to blew.

6. The baby is afraid be away from her mother for any length of time.

7. I am excited for start college this September.

8. You can send your application with fax.

9. My country is too beautiful.

10. Is exciting to drive a sports car.

11. My grandparents enjoy to traveling across the country in a motor home.

12. Elena made this sweater with her hands.

13. Running it is one of the sports we can participate in at school.

14. Swim with a group of people is more enjoyable than swim alone.

15. Meeting new people it is interesting.

► **Practice 26. Crossword puzzle.** (Chapter 13)
Complete the puzzle. Use the clues to find the correct words. All are grammar points from Chapter 13.

Across

2. The best way to eat pizza is _____ your fingers.
4. Sorry! I am _____ tired to go out tonight.
5. Would you mind _____ me up for work tomorrow? My car is being fixed.
6. Ben buys things at the mall on weekends when he goes _____.
9. We went to the lecture early in order to _____ good seats.
10. My family and I enjoy _____ together in our small sailboat.
11. The only way to get to the small island is _____ boat.
12. It's not difficult for Carlos to _____ the guitar because he is a professional guitarist.
13. Bob is 21. He is old _____ to vote.

Down

1. We are considering _____ our vacation plans. We may go in July instead of in June.
3. The Stein family is thinking about _____ to a larger house.
7. Margo expects to _____ from college next June.
8. I finished _____ at midnight and went right to bed.

Chapter 14
Noun Clauses

▶ **Practice 1. Questions vs. noun clauses.** (Chart 14-1)
If the sentence contains a noun clause, <u>underline</u> it and circle *noun clause*. If the question word introduces a question, circle *question*. Add appropriate final punctuation: a period (**.**) or a question mark (**?**).

1.	I don't know <u>where Yuri lives</u>**.**	(noun clause)	question
2.	Where does Yuri live**?**	noun clause	(question)
3.	I don't understand why Sofia left	noun clause	question
4.	Why did Sofia leave	noun clause	question
5.	When did Oliver leave	noun clause	question
6.	I don't know when Oliver left	noun clause	question
7.	What does "calm" mean	noun clause	question
8.	Tarik knows what "calm" means	noun clause	question
9.	I don't know how long the earth has existed	noun clause	question
10.	How long has the earth existed	noun clause	question
11.	Where is Patagonia	noun clause	question
12.	I don't know where Patagonia is	noun clause	question

▶ **Practice 2. Noun clauses that begin with a question word.** (Chart 14-2)
Answer the questions using noun clauses.

1. A: Where does Helen work?

   B: I don't know where _____*Helen works*_____.

2. A: What did Adam say?

   B: I didn't hear what _____.

3. Why are we doing this?

   I don't know why _____.

4. When does the new semester start?

   Tell me when _____.

5. Where did everyone go?

   I don't know where _____.

6. What do people believe?

   We don't know what _____.

7. Who believes that story?

I don't know who _____.

8. Whose cell phone is ringing?

I don't know whose _____.

▶ **Practice 3. Noun clauses that begin with a question word.** (Chart 14-2)
Complete the noun clauses.

1. Vince doesn't live near me. Do you know where _____*Vince lives*_____?

2. I don't know that woman. Do you know who _____*that woman is*_____?

3. Henri did something. Do you know what _____?

4. I don't know her phone number. Do you know what _____?

5. These are someone's keys. Do you know whose _____?

6. Clara met someone. Do you know who _____?

7. Carlo is absent today. Do you know why _____?

8. What time is it? Do you know what time _____?

9. Sam is studying something. Do you know what _____?

10. Someone called. Do you know who _____?

11. Ms. Gray will call later today. Do you know when _____?

12. The president is going to say something. Do you know what _____

_____?

13. Who is in that room? Do you know who _____?

14. What is in that drawer? Do you what _____?

15. A GPS system doesn't cost a lot of money, does it? Do you know how much _____

_____?

▶ **Practice 4. Information questions and noun clauses.** (Chart 14-2)
Complete the question and noun clause forms of the given sentences.

1. Marcos left at 11:00.

When _____*did Marcos leave?*_____

Could you tell me _____*when Marcos left?*_____

2. He said good-bye.

What _____

I didn't hear _____

3. The post office is on Second Street.

Where _____

Could you please tell me _____

4. It's half-past six.

What time _____

Could you please tell me _____

5. David arrived two days ago.

When _____

I don't know _____

6. Ana is from Peru.

What country _____

I'd like to know _____

7. Kathy was absent because she was ill.

Why _____ absent?

Do you know _____ absent?

8. Pedro lives next door.

Who _____ next door?

Do you know _____ next door?

9. Someone's car is in the driveway.

Whose _____ in the driveway?

Do you know _____ in the driveway?

10. These books are someone's.

Whose _____

Do you know _____

▶ **Practice 5. Noun clauses.** (Chart 14-2)
Complete each sentence with a noun clause made from the list. There is one extra word in each list.

1. *who, to, did, Helen, talked*

Who did Helen talk to? Do you know _____ *who Helen talked to* ____?

2. *does, who, lives*

Who lives in that apartment? Do you know _____ in that apartment?

3. *he, what, said, did*

What did he say? Tell me _____.

4. *has, Pat, does, what kind of car*

What kind of car does Pat have? I can't remember _____.

5. *how, their children, are, old, do*

How old are their children? I can't ever remember _____.

6. *why, did, you, said*

Why did you say that? I don't understand _____ that.

7. *I, do, can, catch, where*

Where can I catch the bus? Could you please tell me _____

the bus?

8. *does, what, this word, means*

What does this word mean? Could you please tell me _____?

► **Practice 6. Noun clauses.** (Chart 14-2)
Choose the correct completion.

1. Why _____ so late?
   a. you are   b. are you

2. I'd like to know why _____ so late.
   a. you are   b. are you

3. Tell us where _____ on your vacation, Pam.
   a. you went   b. did you go

4. I went sailing in the Bahamas. Where _____ on your vacation?
   a. you went   b. did you go

5. I couldn't understand the professor. What _____?
   a. she said   b. did she say

6. I couldn't understand her either. I have no idea what _____.
   a. she said   b. did she say

7. What _____?
   a. this word means   b. does this word mean

8. I don't know what _____.
   a. it means   b. does it mean

9. Do you know what _____?
   a. a bumblebee is   b. is a bumblebee

10. Ask Helen. She knows a lot of words. Hey, Helen. What _____?
    a. a bumblebee is   b. is a bumblebee

11. Who _____ on the phone?
    a. was that   b. that was

12. I don't know who _____. The person hung up.
    a. was that   b. that was

► **Practice 7. Noun clauses.** (Chart 14-2)
Read the email message. Choose the correct completion in each pair.

Hi Mom and Dad:

(1) Well, after one week in Mexico, I'm very glad to be here, but I also feel a little lost at times.
I thought that I knew some Spanish, but really, I can't understand what (*people are saying /
are people saying*). Even though I have a map, I can't read it very well, so I don't know where
(*are all the buildings / all the buildings are*). I know when (*my classes start / do my classes start*) — next
Monday — and where (*I register / do I register*). I know what classes (*am I taking / I am taking*), but,
of course, I don't know who (*my professors will be / will be my professors*).

(2) Last night I felt lonely. 😟 I don't know how long (*it will take / will it take*) to make new
friends, and I was wondering why (*did I come / I came*) here. But today I feel much better and I
know why (*am I / I am*) here: I'm going to study another language and learn about another culture,
and I'm going to be making new friends.

Love, Pat 😊

Change each *yes/no* question to a noun clause.

1. YES/NO QUESTION: Is Tom coming?

   NOUN CLAUSE: I wonder _____*if / whether Tom is coming*_____.

2. YES/NO QUESTION: Has Jin finished medical school yet?

   NOUN CLAUSE: I don't know _____.

3. YES/NO QUESTION: Does Daniel have any time off soon?

   NOUN CLAUSE: I don't know _____.

4. YES/NO QUESTION: Is the flight on time?

   NOUN CLAUSE: Can you tell me _____?

5. YES/NO QUESTION: Is there enough gas in the car?

   NOUN CLAUSE: Do you know _____?

6. YES/NO QUESTION: Is Yuki married?

   NOUN CLAUSE: I can't remember _____.

7. YES/NO QUESTION: Are the Nelsons going to move?

   NOUN CLAUSE: I wonder _____.

8. YES/NO QUESTION: Did Khaled change jobs?

   NOUN CLAUSE: I don't know _____.

▶ **Practice 9. Noun clauses.** (Chart 14-3)
Complete the sentences using noun clauses.

1. A: Are you going to need help moving furniture to your new apartment?

   B: I don't know _____*if I'm going to need*_____ help. Thanks for asking. I'll let you know.

2. A: What do you want for dinner tonight?

   B: I'm sorry. I couldn't hear you with the TV on.

   A: I want to know _____ for dinner tonight.

3. A: Is there going to be a movie on this flight?

   B: I'll ask the flight attendant. Excuse me, we're wondering _____

   _____ a movie on this flight.

4. A: Where do birds go in hurricanes?

   B: I have no idea _____ in hurricanes.

5. A: Can I borrow the car, Dad?

   B: I'll tell you later _____ the car.

6. A: Has Nasser already left the party?

   B: Sorry, it's so noisy here. I didn't catch that.

   A: I need to know _____ the party.

7. A: Why did Harold leave town so fast?

   B: I really don't know _____ town so fast.

► **Practice 10. Noun clauses.** (Chart 14-3)
Complete the sentences with the correct form of the verbs. Pay special attention to the use of final
-s/-es.

1. Does it rain a lot here?

    Could you tell me if it _____rains_____ a lot here?

2. How hot does it get in the summer?

    Could you tell me how hot it _____ in the summer?

3. What do people like to do here?

    Could you tell me what people _____ to do here?

4. Does bus number 10 run on holidays?

    Could you tell me if bus number 10 _____ on holidays?

5. Do the buses run on holidays?

    Could you tell me if the buses _____ on holidays?

6. How long does it take to get to the city?

    Could you tell me how long it _____ to get to the city?

7. What do people enjoy most about this area?

    Could you tell me what people _____ most about this area?

8. Does it seem like an expensive place to live?

    Could you tell me if it _____ like an expensive place to live?

► **Practice 11. *That*-clauses.** (Chart 14-4)
Choose the correct completion from Column B.

Column A

1. Johnny's hungry. I guess that _____.

2. Why are you afraid to fly on planes? Read this report. It proves that _____.

3. Our son has nightmares. He often dreams that _____.

4. The police assume that _____.

5. I have to get up very early tomorrow, so I suppose _____.

6. I always know when Paul is nervous. Have you ever noticed that _____?

7. I used to think that older people couldn't learn a new language, but now I realize that _____.

8. I'm not sure about the benefits of coffee, but I know that _____.

Column B

a. monsters are chasing him
b. he always twists his moustache when he is anxious
c. he didn't eat much lunch
d. they can
e. green tea has some healthy ingredients
f. flying is a lot safer than driving
g. an experienced thief stole the money
h. I should go to bed early tonight

► **Practice 12. *That*-clauses.** (Charts 14-4 and 14-5)
Add ***that*** to the sentences at the appropriate places to mark the beginning of a noun clause.

         that
1. I'm sorry ∧ you won't be here for Joe's party.

2. I predict Jim and Sue will get married before the end of the year.

3. I'm surprised you sold your car.

4. Are you certain Mr. McVay won't be here tomorrow?

5. Did you notice Marco shaved off his mustache?

6. It's a fact hot air rises.

7. A: How do you know it's going to be nice tomorrow?
   B: I heard the weather report.
   A: So? The weather report is often wrong, you know. I'm still worried it'll rain on our picnic.

8. A: I heard Professor Samson is leaving the university.
   B: Really? Why?
   A: Some people assume he is going to retire. But I doubt it. I think he is going to do research and writing.
   B: This is not good news! He's a great teacher.

► **Practice 13. *That*-clauses.** (Chart 14-5)
Write two sentences for each passage. Make noun clauses, and include the words in parentheses.

1. The Jensens celebrated the graduation of their granddaughter Alice from the university. After graduation, she was offered a good job in chemical research in a nearby town.

   The Jensens (*be pleased*) *are pleased that their granddaughter graduated from the university* .

   They (*be glad*) *are glad that she was offered a good job* .

2. One night on the news, Po's parents heard about a big fire at Po's university. All the students had to leave their dorms. Po's parents thought that maybe Po had been injured. When Po called them about an hour later, they felt relieved.

   At first, Po's parents (*be worried*)

       _____.

   Then, they (*be happy*) _____.

3. Kyle didn't study for his math exam. Afterward, he thought he had failed, but actually, he got one of the highest grades in the class. His teacher had known he would do well and praised him for earning such a high grade.

   Kyle (*be afraid*) _____.

   Kyle's teacher (*not, be surprised*) _____.

4. Karen lent her cousin Mark some money. He said that he needed it to pay the rent. Then she heard that he had left town. She feels upset that Mark lied to her. She regrets lending him money.

   Karen (*be angry*) _____.

   Karen (*be sorry*) _____.

5. People used to think that strenuous exercise was bad for the heart. However, now scientists have proven the opposite: strenuous exercise can be good for the heart. In addition, people used to think that eating a lot of red meat was good for the heart. Now doctors know that eating a lot of red meat is bad for the heart.

It is a fact (*exercise*) _____.

It is true (*eating a lot of red meat*) _____

_____.

▶ **Practice 14. Substituting *so* for a *that*-clause.** (Chart 14-6)
Give the meaning of *so* by writing a *that*-clause.

1. A: Does Alice have a car?

   B: I don't think **so**. (= I don't think _____ *that Alice has a car* ____.)

2. A: Is the library open on Sunday?

   B: I believe **so**. (= I believe _____.)

3. A: Does Ann speak Spanish?

   B: I don't think **so**. (= I don't think _____.)

4. A: Did Alex pass his French course?

   B: I think **so**. (= I think _____.)

5. A: Is Mr. Kozari going to be at the meeting?

   B: I hope **so**. (= I hope _____.)

6. A: Are these pants clean?

   B: I believe **so**. (= I believe _____.)

▶ **Practice 15. Quoted speech.** (Chart 14-7)
All of the sentences contain quoted speech. Punctuate them by adding quotation marks ("..."), commas (,), periods (.), and question marks (?). Use capital letters as necessary.

Example: My roommate said the door is open could you close it
My roommate said, "The door is open. Could you close it?"

1. Alex asked do you smell smoke

2. Something is burning he said

3. He asked do you smell smoke something is burning

4. Do you smell smoke he asked something is burning

5. Rachel said the game starts at seven

6. The game starts at seven we should leave here at six she said

7. She said the game starts at seven we should leave here at six can you be ready to leave then

> **Practice 16. Quoted speech.** (Charts 14-7 and 14-8)
Punctuate the quoted passage. Add quotation marks (". . ."), commas (,), periods (.), and question marks (?). Use capital letters as necessary.

One day my friend Laura and I were sitting in her apartment. We were having a cup of tea together and talking about the terrible earthquake that had just occurred in Iran. Laura asked me, "Have you ever been in an earthquake?"

Yes, I have I replied.

Was it a big earthquake she asked.

I've been in several earthquakes, and they've all been small ones I answered. Have you ever been in an earthquake?

There was an earthquake in my village five years ago Laura said. I was in my house. Suddenly the ground started shaking. I grabbed my little brother and ran outside. Everything was moving. I was scared to death. And then suddenly it was over.

I'm glad you and your brother weren't hurt I said.

Yes, we were very lucky. Has everyone in the world felt an earthquake sometime in their lives Laura wondered. Do earthquakes occur everywhere on the earth?

Those are interesting questions I said but I don't know the answers.

► **Practice 17. Reported speech: changing pronouns and possessive words.**
(Chart 14-8)
Complete the sentences with the correct pronouns or possessive words.

1. Mr. Lee said, "I'm not happy with my new assistant."

   Mr. Lee said that ____*he*____ wasn't happy with ____*his*____ new assistant.

2. Tom said to his wife, "My parents invited us over for dinner next weekend."

   Tom said that _____ parents had invited _____ over for dinner
   next weekend.

3. The little girl said, "I don't want to wear my good shoes to the party."

   The little girl said that _____ didn't want to wear _____ good
   shoes to the party.

4. Jim said, "A police officer gave Anna and me tickets for jaywalking and told us to cross the
   street with the traffic lights at the pedestrian crosswalk."

   Jim said that a police officer had given Anna and _____ tickets for jaywalking
   and told _____ to cross the street with the traffic lights at the crosswalk.

5. The Johnsons said to me, "We will send you an email when we arrive in Nepal."

   The Johnsons said that _____ would send _____ an email when
   _____ arrived in Nepal.

6. Jane said, "I want my daughter to feel good about herself."

   Jane said that _____ wanted _____ daughter to feel good about
   herself.

7. Mary and Jack said to me, "We are going to be out of town on the day of your party."

   Mary and Jack said that _____ were going to be out of town on the day of
   _____ party.

8. Bob said to us, "We will join you after we take my mother to the airport."

   Bob told us that _____ would join _____ after
   _____ took _____ mother to the airport.

► **Practice 18. Verb forms in reported speech.** (Chart 14-9)
Complete each sentence with the correct form of the verb.

1. Juan said, "I will meet you at the corner of Fifth and Broadway."

   Formal: Juan said (that) he ____*would meet*____ ⎫
   ⎬ us at the corner of Fifth and Broadway.
   Informal: Juan said (that) he ____*will meet*____ ⎭

2. Maria said, "I'm going to be about 15 minutes late for work."

   Formal: Maria said she _____ ⎫
   ⎬ about 15 minutes late for work.
   Informal: Maria said she _____ ⎭

3. Roberto said, "My new car has a dent."

   Formal: Roberto said his new car _____ ⎫
   ⎬ a dent.
   Informal: Roberto said his new car _____ ⎭

4. Phil said, "I need to borrow some money."

   Formal: Phil said he _____

   Informal: Phil said he _____ to borrow some money.

5. Sandy said, "I have flown on an airplane only once."

   Formal: Sandy said she _____

   Informal: Sandy said she _____ on an airplane only once.

6. Sami and Jun said, "We are planning a surprise party for Naoko."

   Formal: Sami and Jun said they _____

   Informal: Sami and Jun said they _____ a surprise party for Naoko.

7. Naoko said, "I don't want any gifts for my birthday."

   Formal: Naoko said she _____

   Informal: Naoko said she _____ any gifts for her birthday.

8. Ms. Wall said, "I can take care of your kids next weekend."

   Formal: Ms. Wall said she _____

   Informal: Ms. Wall said she _____ of my kids next weekend.

▶ **Practice 19. Verb forms in reported speech.** (Chart 14-9)
Complete the sentences. Write the opposite of the quoted speech. Use formal sequence of tenses.

1. A: I have a lot of time.
   B: Oh? I misunderstood you. I heard you say ____(that) you didn't have____ a lot of time.

2. A: I found my credit cards.
   B: I misunderstood you. I heard you say _____ your credit cards.

3. A: The Smiths didn't cancel their party.
   B: I misunderstood you. I heard you say _____ their party.

4. A: It will rain tomorrow.
   B: I misunderstood you. I heard you say _____ tomorrow.

5. A: The Whites didn't get a new car.
   B: I misunderstood you. I heard you say _____ a new car.

6. A: Mei exercises every day.
   B: I misunderstood you. I heard you say _____ every day.

7. A: My computer is working.
   B: I misunderstood you. I heard you say _____
   _____ .

8. A: Ali isn't coming on Friday.
   B: I misunderstood you. I heard you say _____ on Friday.

► **Practice 20. Reporting questions.** (Chart 14-10)
Change the quoted questions to reported questions. Use formal sequence of tenses.

1. Eric said to me, "How old are you?"

   Eric asked me _____*how old I was*_____.

2. Ms. Rush said to Mr. Long, "Are you going to be at the meeting?"

   Ms. Rush asked Mr. Long _____*if he was going to be*_____ at the meeting.

3. Larry said to Ms. Soo, "Do you have time to help me?"

   Larry asked Ms. Soo _____ time to help him.

4. Don said to Robert, "Did you change your mind about going to college?"

   Don asked Robert _____ mind about going to college.

5. Igor said to me, "How long have you been a teacher?"

   Igor asked me _____ a teacher.

6. I said to Tina, "Can you speak Swahili?"

   I asked Tina _____ Swahili.

7. Kathy said to Mr. May, "Will you be in your office around three?"

   Kathy asked Mr. May _____ around three.

8. The teacher said to Ms. Chang, "Why are you laughing?"

   The teacher asked Ms. Chang _____.

9. My uncle said to me, "Have you ever considered a career in business?"

   My uncle asked me _____ a career in business.

► **Practice 21. Quoting questions.** (Chart 14-10)
Change the reported speech to quotations.

1. Eric asked me if I had ever gone skydiving.

   Eric asked, _____*"Have you ever gone skydiving?"*_____

2. Chris wanted to know if I would be at the meeting.

   Chris asked, _____

3. Kate wondered whether I was going to quit my job.

   Kate asked, _____

4. Anna asked her friend where his car was.

   Anna asked, _____

5. Brian asked me what I had done after class yesterday.

   Brian asked, _____

6. Luigi asked me if I knew Italian.

   Luigi asked, _____

7. Debra wanted to know if I could pick up her daughter at school.

   Debra asked, _____

8. My boss wanted to know why I wasn't working at my desk.

   My boss asked me, _____

► **Practice 22. Reporting questions.** (Charts 14-9 → 14-10)
Look at the picture and complete the sentences with noun clauses. Use verbs that are appropriate for later reporting (rather than immediate reporting).

A new student, Mr. Sheko, joined an English class. The teacher asked the students to interview him. Later, Mr. Sheko told his friend about the interview.

1. They asked me _____ *why I had to come here.* _____

2. They asked me _____

3. They asked me _____

4. They asked me _____

5. They asked me _____

6. They asked me _____

7. They asked me _____

8. They asked me _____

9. They asked me _____

► **Practice 23. Reported speech.** (Charts 14-9 → 14-10)
Complete the reported speech sentences. Use formal sequence of tenses.

1. David said to me, "I'm going to call you on Friday."

   David said _____*(that) he was going to call me*_____

   on Friday.

2. John said to Ann, "I have to talk to you."

   John told Ann _____

   _____.

3. Diane said to me, "I can meet you after work."

   Diane said _____ after work.

4. Maria said to Bob, "I wrote you a note."

   Maria told Bob _____

   a note.

5. Anita asked Mike, "When will I see you again?"

Anita asked Mike when _____

_____ again.

6. Laura said to George, "What are you doing?"

Laura asked George _____

_____ .

▶ **Practice 24. *Say* vs. *tell* vs. *ask*.** (Chart 14-10)
Complete the sentences with *said*, *told*, or *asked*.

1. Ava _____*told*_____ me that she was hungry.

2. Ava _____*said*_____ that she was hungry.

3. Ava _____ me if I wanted to go out to lunch with her.

4. When the storm began, I _____ the children to come
into the house.

5. When I talked to Mr. Grant, he _____ he would be at the meeting.

6. Ali _____ his friends that he had won a scholarship to college. His friends
_____ they weren't surprised.

7. My supervisor _____ me if I could postpone my vacation. I _____ him
what the reason was. He _____ that our sales department needed me for a project.

8. My neighbor and I had a disagreement. I
_____ my neighbor that he was wrong. My
neighbor _____ me that I was wrong.

9. Fumiko _____ the teacher that Fatima wasn't
going to be in class.

10. Ellen _____ if I could join her for a movie.

I _____ I wasn't feeling well, but

I _____ her what movie she was going to.

The next day, Ellen _____ me she had enjoyed the movie.

► **Practice 25. Reported speech.** (Charts 14-1 → 14-10)
Complete the sentences by changing the quoted speech to reported speech. Use **said**, **told**, **asked**, or **replied**. Practice using the formal sequence of tenses.

1. Alex said, "Where do you live?" Alex _____asked me where I lived._____

2. He said, "Do you live in the dorm?" He _____ in the dorm.

3. I said, "I have my own apartment." I _____ my own apartment.

4. He said, "I'm looking for a new apartment." He _____ for a new apartment.

5. He said, "I don't like living in the dorm." He _____ in the dorm.

6. I said, "Do you want to move in with me?" I _____

7. He said, "Where is your apartment?" He _____

8. I said, "I live on Seventh Avenue." I _____ on Seventh Avenue.

9. He said, "But I can't move until the end of May." He _____ until the end of May.

10. He said, "I will cancel my dorm contract at the end of May." He _____ dorm contract at the end of May.

11. He said, "Is that okay?" He _____

12. I said, "I'm looking forward to having you as a roommate." I _____ as a roommate.

► **Practice 26. Reported speech.** (Charts 14-1 → 14-10)
Check (✓) <u>all</u> the correct sentences.

1. _____ a. The teacher asked are you finished?
   _✓_ b. The teacher asked if I was finished.
   _____ c. The teacher asked if was I finished?
   _____ d. The teacher asked that I was finished?
   _✓_ e. The teacher asked, "Are you finished?"

2. _____ a. Aki said he was finished.
   _____ b. Aki said that he was finished.
   _____ c. Aki replied that he was finished.
   _____ d. Aki answered that he was finished.
   _____ e. Aki said whether was he finished.

3. _____ a. Ann told Tom, she needed more time.
   _____ b. Ann told Tom she needed more time.
   _____ c. Ann told to Tom she needed more time.
   _____ d. Ann told she needed more time.
   _____ e. Ann said Tom she needed more time.
   _____ f. Ann said she needed more time.

4. _____ a. Donna answered that she was ready.

   _____ b. Donna answered was she ready.

   _____ c. Donna replied ready.

   _____ d. Donna answered, "I am ready."

   _____ e. Donna answered if she was ready.

5. _____ a. Mr. Wong wanted to know if Ted was coming.

   _____ b. Mr. Wong wanted to know is Ted coming?

   _____ c. Mr. Wong wondered if Ted was coming.

   _____ d. Mr. Wong wondered was Ted coming.

   _____ e. Mr. Wong wondered, "Is Ted coming?"

▶ **Practice 27. Reported speech.** (Charts 14-1 → 14-10)
Part I. Read the fable by Aesop.*

The Ant and the Grasshopper

(1–2) In a field one summer's day, a grasshopper was jumping around
and thinking to himself, "It's a beautiful day, and I love playing in the sun."

(3) An ant passed by. The Ant was carrying a heavy piece of corn.

(4–5) The Grasshopper asked the Ant, "What are you doing and
where are you going?"

(6) The Ant replied, "I am carrying food to my nest."

(7–8) The Grasshopper asked "Why are you working so hard in the
beautiful weather?"

(9) The Ant said, "If I bring food to the nest in the summer, I can have food in the winter."

(10–11) The Grasshopper asked the Ant, "Can you take a break now and play with me instead
of working?"

(12) The Ant answered, "I can't."

(13–14) The Ant said, "If I don't bring food to the nests in the summer, I won't have any food
for the winter."

(15) The Grasshopper said, "I'm not worried about the winter because I have plenty of food."

(16–17) The Ant continued walking. The Grasshopper saw many ants doing the same thing.
They were carrying heavy loads of food on their backs, and they were all going back to their nests.

(18) The Grasshopper wondered, "Do those ants ever have any fun?"

(19–22) The Grasshopper continued to play in the beautiful weather, and he played all summer
long. When winter came, the Grasshopper had no food. In fact, he was getting hungrier and
hungrier. The Grasshopper saw the ants. They were eating all the corn and grain that they had
collected during the summer.

(23–24) Then the Grasshopper thought to himself, "The ants are smart because they prepared
for the winter."

(25–26) And just before the Grasshopper died, he said to himself, "It is always a good idea to
prepare for the future."

---

*A fable teaches a lesson about right or wrong. Aesop was a Greek writer who wrote many fables.

Part II. Complete the sentences by changing the quoted speech to indirect speech. Use formal sequence of tenses.

1. (Lines 1–2) The Grasshopper was thinking to himself _____ *that it was a beautiful day, and*

    _____ *he loved playing in the sun* _____.

2. (Line 4) The Grasshopper asked the Ant _____ *what he was doing* _____

    and _____.

3. (Line 6) The Ant replied _____

    _____.

4. (Lines 7–8) The Grasshopper asked the Ant _____

    _____.

5. (Line 9) The Ant said _____

    _____.

6. (Lines 10–11) The Grasshopper asked the Ant _____

    _____.

7. (Line 12) The Ant answered _____.

8. (Lines 13–14) The Ant said _____

    _____.

9. (Line 15) The Grasshopper said _____

    _____.

10. (Line 18) The Grasshopper wondered _____

    _____.

11. (Lines 23–24) The Grasshopper thought _____

    _____.

12. (Lines 25–26) The Grasshopper said _____

    _____.

▶ **Practice 28. Editing.** (Chapter 14)
Correct the errors.

1. Excuse me. May I ask if how old are you?

2. I wonder did Rashed pick up something for dinner?

3. I'm unsure what does Lawrence do for a living.

4. Fernando said, "the best time for me to meet would be Thursday morning.

5. Eriko said to me was I coming to the graduation party. I say her that I wasn't.

6. I hope so that I will do well on my final exams.

7. I'm not sure if that the price includes the sales tax or not.

8. My mother said to me that, "How many hours did you spend on your homework?"

9. I told my brother, "Are you going to marry Paula?"

10. I'd like to know how do you do that.

11. My parents knew what did Sam and I do.

12. Is a fact that unexpected things happen in everyone's lives.

▶ **Practice 29. Word search puzzle.** (Chapter 14).
Circle the words that are the past tense forms of verbs often used to introduce noun clauses in reported speech. There are seven words in the puzzle.

The words may be horizontal, vertical, or diagonal. The first letter of each word is highlighted in gray.

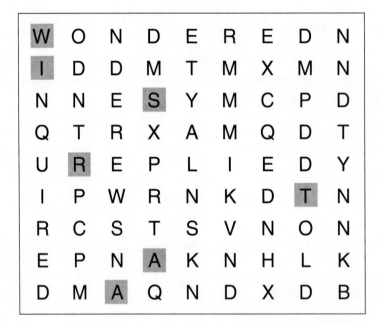

W	O	N	D	E	R	E	D	N
I	D	D	M	T	M	X	M	N
N	N	E	S	Y	M	C	P	D
Q	T	R	X	A	M	Q	D	T
U	R	E	P	L	I	E	D	Y
I	P	W	R	N	K	D	T	N
R	C	S	T	S	V	N	O	N
E	P	N	A	K	N	H	L	K
D	M	A	Q	N	D	X	D	B

Appendix **1**
Phrasal Verbs

▶ **Practice 1. Group A.***
Complete the examples for the chart.

Group A: Phrasal Verbs (separable)		
Verb	**Definition**	**Example**
figure out	find the solution to a problem	I *figured* ____*out*____ the answer.
hand in	give homework, papers, etc., to a teacher	We *handed* _____ our homework.
hand out	give something to this person, then that person, etc.	The teacher *handed* _____ the test papers to the class.
look up	look for information in a dictionary, phone book, online, etc.	I *looked* a word _____ in the dictionary.
make up	invent (a story)	Children like to *make* _____ stories.
pick up	lift	Tom *picked* _____ the baby.
put down	stop holding or carrying	I *put* _____ the heavy packages.
put off	postpone	We *put* _____ our trip until next summer.
put on	place clothes on one's body	I *put* _____ my coat before I left.
take off	remove clothes from one's body	I *took* _____ my coat when I arrived.
throw away ⎫ **throw out** ⎭	put in the trash, discard	I *threw* _____ my old notebooks. I *threw* _____ my old notebooks.
turn off	stop a machine or a light	I *turned* _____ the lights and went to bed.
turn on	start a machine or a light	I *turned* _____ the light so I could read.
wake up	stop sleeping	I *woke* _____ at six.
write down	write a note on a piece of paper	I *wrote* his phone number _____.

▶ **Practice 2. Group A**
Complete the sentences with particles from the list.

away	down	in	off	on	out	up

1. Johnny is all wet. I told him to take _____ his clothes and put _____ some dry ones.

2. Lilly made _____ a story. She didn't tell the truth.

---

*Appendix 1 presents phrasal verbs in small groups to be learned and practiced one group at a time. A complete reference list can found in the Student Book, pp. 399–400.

3. Alice used her online dictionary to look _____ a word. Then she wrote the definition _____.

4. Sometimes I postpone doing my homework. My parents get upset and tell me not to put it _____. They also get mad because I hand _____ some assignments late.

5. My arms hurt, so I put the baby _____ for a minute. But he started crying right away, so I picked him _____ again.

6. My roommate is messy. He never picks _____ his clothes.

7. My mother woke me _____ at 7:00, but I didn't get up until 7:30. I turned _____ the light and went back to sleep.

8. We don't need these receipts anymore. We can throw them _____.

9. When I got my physics test today, I realized that I couldn't figure _____ any of the answers. Our teacher had made a mistake and handed _____ the wrong test!

▶ **Practice 3. Group A.**
Choose all the correct completions for each sentence.

1. Akiko turned off   (the TV)   the butter   (the stove.)
2. I took off   my coat   my toys   my wedding ring.
3. Jonas put on   his shoes   a fire   the dishes.
4. Benjamin made up   a story   a fairy tale   an excuse.
5. Susanna threw out   some air   some rotten food   an old shirt.
6. Antonio put off   a doctor's appointment   a meeting   a trip.
7. Max figured out   a puzzle   a math problem   difficult.
8. Kyong handed in   some candy   a report   some late homework.
9. The secretary wrote down   a message   a pencil   a phone number.
10. The mail carrier put down   a box   the mail truck   a sack of mail.
11. Mustafa turned off   the light   the computer   the car engine.

▶ **Practice 4. Group B.**
Complete the examples for the chart.

Group B: Phrasal Verbs (nonseparable)		
Verb	**Definition**	**Example**
call on	ask (someone) to speak in class	The teacher *called* _____ Ali.
come from	originate	Where do these bananas *come* _____?
get over	recover from an illness or a shock	Sue *got* _____ her cold quickly.
get off	leave } a bus/airplane/train/subway	I *got* _____ the bus at First Street.
get on	enter }	I *got* _____ the bus at Fifth Street.
get in/into	enter } a car, a taxi	I *got* _____ the taxi at the airport.
get out of	leave }	I *got* _____ _____ the taxi at the hotel.
look into	investigate	The police are *looking* _____ the crime.
run into	meet by chance	I *ran* _____ Peter at the store.

▶ Practice 5. Group B.
Complete the sentences with particles from the list.

from	in	into	off	on	out of	over

1. When I raised my hand in class, the teacher called _____ me.

2. Fred feels okay today. He got _____ his cold.

3. Last week I flew from Chicago to Miami. I got _____ the plane in Chicago. I got _____ the plane in Miami.

4. Sally took a taxi to the airport. She got _____ the taxi in front of her apartment building. She got _____ the taxi at the airport.

5. I take the bus to school every day. I get _____ the bus at the corner of First Street and Sunset Boulevard. I get _____ the bus just a block away from the classroom building.

6. The receptionist at the power company didn't know why my bill was so high, but she said she would look _____ it.

7. I ran _____ Pierre at the mall. He's married and has ten kids!

▶ Practice 6. Group B.
Complete each sentence in Column A with the correct phrase from Column B.

Example: Annette speaks both French and English because she comes . . .
Annette speaks both French and English because she comes from Quebec.

Column A

1. Annette speaks both French and English because she comes . . . .

2. When Sylvia lost her job, it took her several weeks to get . . . .

3. Our office will need several days to look . . . .

4. When a plane lands, the first-class passengers get . . . .

5. While I was walking in the mall, I ran . . . .

6. When he left the hotel, David got . . . .

7. Mrs. Riley, our math teacher, often calls . . . .

Column B

a. into your request for medical records.

✓b. from Quebec.

c. over the shock.

d. into a taxi and went to the airport.

e. on unprepared students.

f. into several friends from high school.

g. off first.

► **Practice 7. Group C.**
Complete the examples for the chart.

Group C: Phrasal Verbs (separable)		
Verb	**Definition**	**Example**
ask out	ask (someone) to go on a date	Tom *asked* Sue _____. They went to a movie.
call back	return a telephone call	I'll *call* you _____ tomorrow.
call off	cancel	We *called* _____ the picnic because of the rain.
call up	make a telephone call	I *called* _____ my friend in New York.
give back	return something to someone	I borrowed Al's pen, then I *gave* it _____.
hang up	hang on a hanger or a hook	I *hung* my coat _____ in the closet.
pay back	return borrowed money to someone	Thanks for the loan. I'll *pay* you _____ soon.
put away	put something in its usual or proper place	I *put* the clean dishes _____.
put back	return something to its original place	I *put* my books _____ into my bag.
put out	extinguish (stop) a fire, a cigarette	We *put* _____ the campfire before we left.
shut off	stop a machine or light, turn off	I *shut* _____ my printer before I left the office.
try on	put on clothing to see if it fits	I *tried* _____ several pairs of shoes.
turn down	decrease the volume	Sue *turned* _____ the music. It was too loud.
turn up	increase the volume	Al *turned* _____ the radio. He likes loud music.

► **Practice 8. Group C.**
Complete the sentences with particles from the list.

away	back	down	off	on	out	up

1. You still owe me the money I lent you. When are you going to pay me _____?

2. Turn _____ the radio! It's too loud! I can't hear myself think.

3. Debra put _____ the fire in the oven with a fire extinguisher.

4. I'll wash and dry the dishes, and you can put them _____.

5. Before you buy shoes, you should try them _____ to see if they fit.

6. I can't hear the TV. Could you please turn it _____?

7. You took my toy! Give it _____.

8. I didn't hear anyone on the other end of the phone, so I hung _____.

9. You can look at these books, but please put them _____ on the shelf when you're finished.

10. Bob hasn't paid his electric bill for months, so the electric company shut his power
   _____.

11. A: I hear that Tom asked you _____ for next Saturday night.

   B: Yes, he did. He called me _____ a couple of hours ago and invited me to a dance.

   A: The dance has been called _____ because the musicians are on strike. Didn't you hear about it?

   B: No, I didn't. I'd better call Tom _____ and ask him what he wants to do instead.

▶ **Practice 9. Phrasal verbs: separable. (Groups A, B, C)**
Complete the sentences with a given particle where possible. If not possible, write "**X**."

1. *out*   a. Paulo asked _____*out*_____ one of his classmates.

   b. Paulo asked one of his classmates _____*out*_____.

2. *on*   a. The teacher called _____*on*_____ Ted for the answer.

   b. The teacher called Ted _____*X*_____ for the answer.

3. *into*   a. The police are looking _____ the murder, but need help from the public to solve it.

   b. The police are looking the murder _____, but need help from the public to solve it.

4. *into*   a. Khalifa ran his cousin _____ at the store.

   b. Khalifa ran _____ his cousin at the store.

5. *up*   a. Claire turned _____ the ringer on the phone.

   b. Claire turned the ringer on the phone _____.

6. *away*   a. Dr. Benson threw _____ a valuable coin by mistake.

   b. Dr. Benson threw a valuable coin _____ by mistake.

7. *down*   a. Yumi's baby cries whenever she puts him _____.

   b. Yumi's baby cries whenever she puts _____ him.

8. *up*   a. Would you please wake _____ me in one hour?

   b. Would you please wake me _____ in one hour?

9. *away*   a. You can leave the dishes. I'll put them _____ later.

   b. You can leave the dishes. I'll put _____ them later.

10. *up*   a. When Joan feels lonely, she calls _____ a friend and talks for a while.

   b. When Joan feels lonely, she calls a friend _____ and talks for a while.

11. *off*   a. The hill was so steep that I had to get _____ my bicycle and walk.

   b. The hill was so steep that I had to get my bicycle _____ and walk.

12. *from*   a. This fruit is very fresh. It came _____ my garden.

   b. This fruit is very fresh. It came my garden _____.

Complete the examples.

Group D: Phrasal Verbs (separable)		
Verb	**Definition**	**Example**
cross out	draw a line through	I *crossed* _____ the misspelled word.
fill in	complete by writing in a blank space	We *fill* _____ blanks in grammar exercises.
fill out	write information on a form	I *filled* _____ a job application.
fill up	fill completely with gas, water, coffee, etc.	We *filled* _____ the gas tank.
find out	discover information	I *found* _____ where he lives.
have on	wear	She *has* a blue blouse _____.
look over	examine carefully	*Look* _____ your paper for errors before you hand it in.
point out	call attention to	The teacher *pointed* _____ a misspelling.
print out	create a paper copy from a computer	I finished the letter and *printed* it _____.
tear down	destroy a building	They *tore* _____ the old house and built a new one.
tear out (of)	remove (paper) by tearing	I *tore* a page _____ _____ a magazine.
tear up	tear into small pieces	I *tore* _____ the secret note.
turn around **turn back** ⎫⎬⎭	change to the opposite direction	After a mile, we *turned* _____/_____.
turn over	turn the top side to the bottom	I *turned* the paper _____ and wrote on the back.

▶ **Practice 11. Group D.**
Complete the sentences with particles from the list.

around	back	down	in	of	out	over	up

1. When I finish writing on one side of the paper, I turn it _____*over*_____ and write on the back.

2. When the teacher finds a mistake in our writing, she points it _____ so we can correct it.

3. When I write words in this practice, I am filling _____ the blanks.

4. When I discover new information, I find something _____.

5. When I need to see information from my computer on paper, I print it _____.

6. When buildings are old and dangerous, we tear them _____.

7. When I turn and go in the opposite direction, I turn _____.

8. When I remove a piece of paper from a spiral notebook, I tear the paper _____ _____ my notebook.

9. When I write something that I don't want anybody else to see, I tear the paper into tiny pieces. I tear _____ the paper.

10. When I write information on an application form, I fill the form _____.

11. When I make a mistake in something I write, I erase the mistake if I'm using a pencil. If I'm using a pen, I cross the mistake _____ by drawing a line through it.

12. When my juice glass is empty, I fill it _____ again if I'm still thirsty.

13. When I check my homework carefully before I give it to the teacher, I look it _____ .

▶ **Practice 12. Groups A, B, C, D**
Complete the sentences with the particles in *italics*. The particles may be used more than once or not at all.

1. *out, away, back, down, off, on*

   Carol . . .

   a. put _____off_____ her vacation because she was sick.

   b. put _____ her boots to go out in the rain.

   c. put the phone _____ when she saw a spider crawling toward her.

   d. put her things _____ in her suitcase after the customs officer checked them.

   e. put _____ the stovetop fire with a small fire extinguisher.

   f. put _____ all the groceries she bought before she started dinner.

2. *out, in, up*

   James . . .

   a. handed _____ his financial report before the due date.

   b. handed _____ thank-you gifts to his staff for their hard work.

3. *into, off, on, up, over, out of*

   Linda . . .

   a. got _____ the flu in three days and felt wonderful.

   b. got _____ the bus and walked home.

   c. got _____ the bus and sat down behind the driver.

   d. got _____ a taxi to go to the airport.

   e. got _____ the taxi, paid the driver, and left a nice tip.

4. *in, down, up, out*

   a. This book has a few pages missing. The baby tore them _____ .

   b. Before I throw my credit card receipts away, I tear them _____ . I don't want anyone to read them.

   c. The building across the street will be torn _____ to make room for a parking garage.

5. *over, into, up*

   a. The neighbors asked the sheriff to look _____ a crime in their neighborhood.

   b. The sheriff looked _____ a suspect's address on the computer.

   c. The sheriff took the suspect's ID, looked it _____ slowly, and decided it was fake.

6. *off, down, up, back*

   a. I called Rita _____ several times, but got no answer. I'm a little worried.

   b. The meeting was called _____ because the chairperson was sick.

   c. Jack called and left a message. I'll call him _____ after dinner.

7. *over, up, in, off, back*

   a. You can't do your homework with the music on. Please turn it _____.

   b. It's cold, and I'm tired. Let's turn _____ and go home.

   c. Could I turn _____ the TV? I can't hear the news.

   d. Joe, the meat needs to be cooked on the other side. Would you turn it _____, please?

8. *in, out, up*

   a. I forgot to fill _____ a couple of blanks on the test. I hope I passed.

   b. Can I take this application home and fill it _____? I don't have much time now.

   c. Jack carries a thermos bottle to work. He fills _____ his cup when he gets thirsty.

   d. Gas is expensive. It costs a lot to fill _____ my tank.

► **Practice 13. Group E.**
Complete the examples for the chart.

Group E: Phrasal Verbs (separable)		
Verb	**Definition**	**Example**
blow out . . . . extinguish (a match, a candle)		He *blew* the candles _____.
bring back . . . . return		She *brought* my books _____ to me.
bring up . . . . (1) raise (children)		The Lees *brought* _____ six children.
	(2) mention, start to talk about	He *brought* the news _____ in conversation.
cheer up . . . . make happier		The good news *cheered* me _____.
clean up . . . . make neat and clean		I *cleaned* _____ my apartment.
give away . . . . donate, get rid of by giving		I didn't sell my old bike. I *gave* it _____.
help out . . . . assist (someone)		Could you please *help* me _____?
lay off . . . . stop employment		The company *laid* _____ 100 workers.
leave on . . . . (1) not turn off (a light, a machine)		Please *leave* the light _____. I can't see.
	(2) not take off (clothing)	I *left* my coat _____ during class.
take back . . . . return		She *took* a book _____ to the library.
take out . . . . invite out and pay		He *took* Mary _____. They went to a movie.
talk over . . . . discuss		We *talked* the problem _____.
think over . . . . consider		I *thought* the problem _____.
work out . . . . solve		We *worked* the problem _____.

Complete the sentences with particles from the list.

away	back	off	on	out	over	up

1. It's pretty chilly in here. You might want to leave your jacket _____ .

2. My father speaks with an Australian accent. He was brought _____ in Australia.

3. The Smiths have marriage problems but they are trying to work them _____ .

   They talk them _____ as soon as they occur.

4. After I lit the candles, I blew _____ the match.

5. My roommate gives _____ his old clothes to homeless people. He tries to help them _____ as often as possible.

6. I took my elderly parents _____ to a restaurant for their anniversary. Then I cleaned _____ their house the next day for them.

7. These are bad economic times. Businesses are laying _____ hundreds of workers.

8. The store's return policy is that you can bring clothes _____ within two weeks if you have a receipt.

9. I'm meeting with my supervisor later today. I'm going to bring _____ the idea of a raise.

10. I won't be home until midnight, so please leave some lights _____ .

11. When I'm sad, my friends try to cheer me _____ .

12. Are you sure you want to change jobs? Do you want to think it _____ some more?

13. I hate to bring this problem _____ , but we need to talk about it.

14. I can't sell this old table. I guess I'll give it _____ . Someone will be able to use it.

15. My parents usually help me _____ when I'm having trouble paying my bills.

16. You can borrow my tools, but when you finish, be sure to put them _____ .

Complete the examples for the chart.

Group F: Phrasal Verbs (intransitive)		
Verb	**Definition**	**Example**
break down	stop functioning properly	My car *broke* _____ on the highway.
break out	happen suddenly	War *broke* _____ between the two countries.
break up	separate, end a relationship	Ann and Tom *broke* _____ .
come in	enter a room or building	May I *come* _____ ?
dress up	put on nice clothes	People usually *dress* _____ for weddings.
eat out	eat outside of one's home	Would you like to *eat* _____ tonight?
fall down	fall to the ground	I *fell* _____ and hurt myself.
get up	get out of bed in the morning	What time did you *get* _____ this morning?
give up	quit doing something or quit trying	I can't do it. I *give* _____ .
go on	continue	Let's not stop. Let's *go* _____ .
go out	not stay home	Jane *went* _____ with her friends last night.
hang up	end a telephone conversation	When we finished talking, I *hung* _____ .
move in (**to**)	start living in a new home	Some people *moved* _____ next door to me.
move out (**of**)	stop living at a place	My roommate is *moving* _____ .
show up	come, appear	Jack *showed* _____ late for the meeting.
sit back	put one's back against a chair back	*Sit* _____ and relax. I'll get you a drink.
sit down	go from standing to sitting	Please *sit* _____ .
speak up	(1) speak louder (2) express one's opinion without fear	I can't hear you. You'll have to *speak* _____ .
stand up	go from sitting to standing	I *stood* _____ and walked to the door.
start over	begin again	I lost count, so I *started* _____ .
stay up	not go to bed	I *stayed* _____ late last night.
take off	ascend in an airplane	The plane *took* _____ 30 minutes late.

▶ **Practice 16. Group F.**
Complete the sentences with particles from the list.

back	down	in	off	on	out	over	up

1. The plane shook a little when it took _____ . It made me nervous.

2. I'm afraid we can't hear you in the back of the room. Could you please speak _____ ?

3. The computer teacher was so confusing. I didn't learn a thing! I think I'll just start _____ with a new teacher next term.

4. I was late to work. The bus broke _____, and we had to wait for another.

5. Mrs. Taylor is in the hospital again. She fell _____ and broke her hip.

6. Tim and Ann aren't getting married. They had a fight and broke _____ last night.

7. Julian's at the doctor's. He broke _____ in a rash last night, and he doesn't know what it is.

8. I'm very nervous when I fly. I can't just sit _____ and relax.

9. Sometimes when I stand _____ too fast, I get dizzy.

10. Someone keeps calling and hanging _____. It's very annoying.

11. Sorry, I didn't mean to interrupt you. Please go _____.

12. A: Professor Wilson, do you have a minute?

    B: Sure. Come _____ and sit _____.

▶ **Practice 17. Group F.**
Complete the sentences with particles from the list.

into	of	out	up

1. *Lazy Leo . . .*

    a. broke ___up___ with his girlfriend because she didn't want to wash his clothes.

    b. stayed _____ all night and didn't come home until morning.

    c. showed _____ late for class without his homework.

    d. goes _____ with friends to parties on school nights.

    e. eats _____ at restaurants because he doesn't like to cook.

    f. moved _____ _____ his apartment without telling the manager.

2. *Serious Sally . . .*

    a. goes to bed very early. She never stays _____ past 9:00.

    b. gets _____ at 5:00 every morning.

    c. speaks _____ in class when no one will answer.

    d. dresses _____ for school.

    e. moved _____ an apartment next to the library.

    f. never gives _____ when she gets frustrated.

3. *Independent Inga . . .*

    a. moved _____ _____ her parents' house when she was 16 and moved _____

    her own apartment.

    b. goes _____ by herself when her friends are busy.

    c. speaks _____ when she disagrees with someone.

► **Practice 18. Group G.**
Complete the examples for the chart.

Group G: Phrasal Verbs (three-word)		
Verb	**Definition**	**Example**
drop in (on)	visit without calling first or without an invitation	We *dropped* _____ _____ my aunt.
drop out (of)	stop attending (school)	Beth *dropped* _____ _____ graduate school.
fool around (with)	have fun while wasting time	My son likes to *fool* _____ _____ his friends on the weekends.
get along (with)	have a good relationship with	I *get* _____ well _____ my roommate.
get back (from)	return from (a trip)	When did you *get* _____ _____ Hawaii?
get through (with)	finish	I *got* _____ _____ my work before noon.
grow up (in)	become an adult	Anika *grew* _____ _____ Sweden.
look out (for)	be careful	*Look* _____ _____ that car!
run out (of)	finish the supply of (something)	We *ran* _____ _____ gas.
sign up (for)	put one's own name on a list	Did you *sign* _____ _____ the school trip?
watch out (for)	be careful	*Watch* _____ _____ that car!

► **Practice 19. Group G.**
Complete the phrasal verbs.

1. Look _____! There's a car coming! Look _____ _____ the truck too!

2. I grew up in New Zealand. Where did you grow _____?

3. If you want to be in the class, you have to sign _____ _____ it first.

4. I couldn't finish the examination. I ran _____ _____ time.

5. My cousin never does anything useful. He just fools _____ _____ his friends all day, wasting time.

6. Joe is really tired. He just got _____ _____ a 10-day mountain climbing trip.

7. Jack dropped _____ _____ school last week. His parents are upset.

8. Watch _____ _____ the truck! It has a loose wheel.

9. Joanne got _____ _____ her work early, so she's leaving for vacation today.

10. My neighbor likes to drop _____ _____ us during dinner. I think she's lonely.

11. A: I want to move to another dorm room.

    B: Why?

    A: I don't get _____ _____ my roommate. She's sloppy and plays loud music when I'm trying to study.

Complete each sentence with the correct word from the list.

assignment	✓gymnastics class	paint	snakes
cord	Hawaii	rocks	their neighbors

1. Martin signed up for a _____gymnastics class_____. It starts next week.

2. The Hansens get along well with _____. They even take vacations together.

3. I can't finish the living room walls because I've run out of _____.

4. The highway sign said to watch out for _____. They roll down the hills and sometimes hit cars.

5. As soon as I get through with this _____, we can go to lunch. I have just one more problem to figure out.

6. Don't fool around with that _____. You might get an electric shock.

7. You look very rested and relaxed. When did you get back from _____?

8. Look out for _____ on the path. They're not poisonous, but they might startle you.

► **Practice 21. Group H.**

Complete the examples.

Group H: Phrasal Verbs (three-word)		
Verb	**Definition**	**Example**
come along (with) .... accompany		Do you want to *come* _____ _____ us?
come over (to) .... visit the speaker's place		Some friends are *coming* _____ tonight.
cut out (of) .... remove with scissors or knife		I *cut* an article _____ _____ today's paper.
find out (about) .... discover information about		When did you *find* _____ _____ the problem?
get together (with) .... join, meet		Let's *get* _____ after work today.
go back (to) .... return to a place		I *went* _____ _____ work after my illness.
go over (to) .... (1) approach (2) visit another's home		I *went* _____ _____ the window. Let's *go* _____ _____ Jim's tonight.
hang around (with) ⎫ **hang out (with)** ⎬ ..... spend time relaxing		John likes to *hang* _____ the coffee shop. Kids like to *hang* _____ _____ each other.
keep away (from) .... not give to		*Keep* matches _____ _____ children.
set out (for) .... begin a trip		We *set* _____ _____ the mountain at sunrise.
sit around (with) .... sit and do nothing		Don't *sit* _____ all day. Do something!

► **Practice 22. Group H.**
Complete each sentence with <u>two</u> particles.

1. Before we consider buying a home in this area, we'd like to find __*out*__ more __*about*__ the schools.

2. The mountain climbers set _____ _____ the summit at dawn and reached it by lunchtime.

3. When my grandma was 65, she decided to go _____ _____ school and get a college degree.

4. Some teenagers like to hang _____ _____ friends at the mall, but the management doesn't approve.

5. Susie needs to keep _____ _____ the dog. She's allergic to the fur.

6. I'm going shopping. Do you want to come _____ _____ me?

7. I invited my class to come _____ _____ our beach house on Saturday.

8. Oh, no. Tommy cut several pictures _____ _____ his new storybook.

9. A: Did you go _____ _____ Brian's last night?
   B: No, he wasn't home, so I sat _____ my apartment _____ my cat.

► **Practice 23. Group H.**
Complete the sentences with particles that will give the same meanings as the <u>underlined</u> words.

1. I'd like to <u>get information</u> about the company. I want to find __*out*__ __*about*__ it before I apply for a job there.

2. The two brothers <u>began their</u> fishing <u>trip</u> to the lake before sunrise. They set _____ early because they wanted to be the first ones there.

3. What time is the supervisor <u>returning</u>? I'd like to talk to him when he gets _____.

4. Mark won't be home for dinner. He plans to <u>join</u> his co-workers for a party.
   They only get _____ once a year, so Mark is looking forward to it.

5. The dog was growling when the dog catcher <u>approached</u> him. The dog catcher went _____ _____ him very carefully.

► **Practice 24. Review: Appendix 1**
Choose the correct particle.

1. Professor Brown always calls ____ the students who sit in the back of the class to answer.
   a. on   b. off   c. out   d. back

2. Tommy takes other children's toys and doesn't want to give them ____.
   a. away   b. back   c. in   d. to

3. My computer printer isn't working. I can't print ____ any of my work.
   a. out   b. in   c. over   d. back

4. Bobby, let's take a few minutes and pick ____ the toys in your room. They're all over the floor.
   a. over   b. on   c. up   d. away

5. Not enough people signed up ____ the math class, so it had to be canceled.
   a. for   b. in   c. into   d. with

6. This cold has lasted too long. I feel like I'll never get _____ it.
    a. with   b. over   c. away   d. back

7. Aren't you going to try _____ these shoes before you buy them?
    a. in   b. of   c. up   d. on

8. Keep away _____ the stove! It's still hot.
    a. off   b. from   c. out   d. of

9. Look how nice Jenny's bedroom looks! She spent all morning cleaning it _____.
    a. over   b. back   c. up   d. away

10. Steven had problems early in his career, but he seems to have worked them _____.
    a. up   b. over   c. off   d. out

11. Do you have a fire extinguisher in your house to put _____ fires?
    a. off   b. out   c. back   d. down

12. It took Tim only 20 minutes to figure _____ the answer to the puzzle.
    a. on   b. in   c. up   d. out

13. Mr. Beem is very wealthy and generous. He wants to give _____ all his money before he dies.
    a. away   b. in   c. into   d. from

14. I cut your picture out _____ the newspaper today. Did you know you were going to be in it?
    a. in   b. off   c. of   d. from

15. Some friends came _____ last night. We talked and listened to music.
    a. over   b. about   c. into   d. from

16. This hike is pretty exhausting. I don't think I can go _____. I need to rest.
    a. out   b. in   c. to   d. on

17. There's a gas station. I'll wash the windows while you fill _____ the tank.
    a. on   b. in   c. up   d. out

18. A fight broke _____ among students after school. Fortunately, no one was injured.
    a. out   b. down   c. in   d. off

19. I'm sorry, but you wrote about the wrong topic. You'll need to start _____.
    a. over   b. to   c. with   d. back

20. Tim didn't finish college. He dropped _____ after two years.
    a. in   b. off   c. of   d. out

21. Mr. Robinson is happy to lend his adult children money as long as they pay it _____.
    a. up   b. back   c. down   d. for

Appendix 2
Preposition Combinations

▶ **Practice 1. Group A.**[*]

Test yourself and practice the preposition combinations. Follow these steps:

(1) **Cover** the ANSWERS column with a piece of paper.
(2) Complete the SENTENCES.
(3) Then remove the paper and check your answers.
(4) Then **cover** both the ANSWERS and the SENTENCES to complete your own REFERENCE LIST.

(5) Again check your answers.

Preposition Combinations: Group A		
Answers	**Sentences**	**Reference List**
from	He was absent ____*from*____ work.	**be absent** ____*from*____ s.t.[**]
of	I'm afraid ____*of*____ rats.	**be afraid** ____*of*____ s.t./s.o.[**]
about	I'm angry ____*about*____ it.	**be angry** _____ s.t.
at / with	I'm angry _____ you.	**be angry** _____ s.o.
about	I'm curious _____ many things.	**be curious** _____ s.t./s.o.
to	This is equal _____ that.	**be equal** _____ s.t./s.o.
with	I'm familiar _____ that book.	**be familiar** _____ s.t./s.o.
of	The room is full _____ people.	**be full** _____ (*people/things*)
for	I'm happy _____ you.	**be happy** _____ s.o.
about	I'm happy _____ your good luck	**be happy** _____ s.t.
to	He's kind _____ people and animals.	**be kind** _____ s.o.
to	She's always nice _____ me.	**be nice** _____ s.o.
to	Are you polite _____ strangers?	**be polite** _____ s.o.
for	I'm ready _____ my trip.	**be ready** _____ s.t.
for	She's thirsty _____ lemonade.	**be thirsty** _____ s.t.

[**]s.t. = "something"; s.o. = "someone"

---

[*]Appendix 2 presents preposition combinations in small groups to be learned and practiced one group at a time.

▶ Practice 2. Group A.
Match each phrase in Column A with a phrase in Column B. Use each phrase only once.

Column A

1. Our dog is afraid _b_.

2. The class is curious ____.

3. Mr. White is angry ____.

4. Several nurses have been absent ____.

5. After gardening all day, Helen was thirsty ____.

6. The workers are angry ____.

7. The baseball coach was happy ____.

8. The kitchen cupboard is full ____.

9. I'm not ready ____.

10. It's important to be kind ____.

Column B

a. about his team's win

✓b. of cats

c. for a glass of lemonade

d. for the start of school

e. from work due to illness

f. about the snake in the cage

g. to everyone

h. of canned foods

i. about their low pay

j. at his dog for chewing his slippers

▶ Practice 3. Group A.
Complete the sentences with prepositions.

1. Mr. Porter is nice _____ everyone.

2. One inch is equal _____ 2.54 centimeters.

3. Joe has good manners. He's always polite _____ everyone.

4. I'm not familiar _____ that book. Who wrote it?

5. Anna got a good job that pays well. I'm very happy _____ her.

6. Anna is very happy _____ getting a new job.

7. Jack's thermos bottle is full _____ coffee.

8. The workers were angry _____ the decrease in their pay.

9. Half the students were absent _____ class yesterday. There is a flu virus going around.

10. I'm not familiar _____ that movie. Who is in it?

11. Children ask "Why" a lot. They are curious _____ everything.

12. William has been afraid _____ spiders since he was a child.

▶ Practice 4. Group B.

The prepositions in the column on the left are the correct completions for the blanks. Follow the same steps you used for Group A on page 270.

Preposition Combinations: Group B		
Answers	**Sentences**	**Reference List**
for	I admire you _____ your honesty.	**admire** s.o. _____ s.t.
for	He applied _____ a job.	**apply** _____ s.t.
with	I argued _____ my husband.	**argue** _____ s.o.
about / over	We argued _____ money.	**argue** _____ s.t.
in	My parents believe _____ me.	**believe** _____ s.o./s.t.
from	I borrowed a book _____ Oscar.	**borrow** s.t. _____ s.o.
with	I discussed the problem _____ Jane.	**discuss** s.t. _____ s.o.
with	Please help me _____ this.	**help** s.o. _____ s.t.
to	I introduced Sam _____ Helen.	**introduce** s.o. _____ s.o./s.t.
at	I laughed _____ the joke.	**laugh** _____ s.t./s.o.
for	I'm leaving _____ Rome next week.	**leave** _____ (*a place*)
at	Don't stare _____ me.	**stare** _____ s.o./s.t.

▶ Practice 5. Group B.

Complete the sentences with prepositions.

1. I borrowed this dictionary _____ Pedro.

2. Could you please help me _____ these heavy suitcases?

3. Sue, I'd like to introduce you _____ Ed Jones.

4. You shouldn't stare _____ other people. It's not polite.

5. Do you believe _____ ghosts?

6. Are you laughing _____ my mistake?

7. I admire my father _____ his honesty and intelligence.

8. I argued _____ Elena _____ politics.

9. I discussed my educational plans _____ my parents.

10. I applied _____ admission to the university.

11. We're leaving _____ Cairo next week.

▶ Practice 6. Groups A and B.

Complete the sentences with prepositions.

1. Dan is always nice _____ everyone.

2. A: How long do you need to keep the Spanish book you borrowed _____ me?

   B: I'd like to keep it until I'm ready _____ the exam next week.

3. A: Why weren't you more polite _____ Alan's friend?

   B: Because he kept staring _____ me all evening. He made me nervous.

4. $\frac{5}{10}$ is equal _____ $\frac{1}{2}$.

5. You did a lot of shopping. The refrigerator is full _____ food.

6. May I please borrow some money _____ you? I'm thirsty _____ an ice cream soda, and we're walking right by the ice cream shop.

7. A: Mike, I really admire you _____ your ability to remember names. Will you help me _____ the introductions?

   B: Sure. Ellen, let me introduce you _____ Pat, Andy, Olga, and Ramon.

▶ Practice 7. Group C.

The prepositions in the column on the left are the correct completions for the blanks. Follow the same steps you used for Group A on page 270.

	Preposition Combinations: Group C	
Answers	**Sentences**	**Reference List**
of	I'm aware _____ the problem.	**be aware** _____ s.t./s.o.
for	Smoking is bad _____ you.	**be bad** _____ s.o./s.t.
to	The solution is clear _____ me.	**be clear** _____ s.o
about	Alex is crazy _____ football.	**be crazy** _____ s.t.
from	Jane is very different _____ me.	**be different** _____ s.o./s.t.
for	Venice is famous _____ its canals.	**be famous** _____ s.t.
to / with	She's friendly _____ everyone.	**be friendly** _____ s.o.
for	Fresh fruit is good _____ you.	**be good** _____ s.o.
for	I'm hungry _____ some chocolate.	**be hungry** _____ s.t.
in	I'm interested _____ art.	**be interested** _____ s.t.
about	I'm nervous _____ my test scores.	**be nervous** _____ s.t.
with	I'm patient _____ children.	**be patient** _____ s.o.
of	My parents are proud _____ me.	**be proud** _____ s.o./s.t.
for	Who's responsible _____ this?	**be responsible** _____ s.t./s.o.
about	I'm sad _____ losing my job.	**be sad** _____ s.t.
to	A lemon is similar _____ a lime.	**be similar** _____ s.o./s.t.
of / about	I'm sure _____ the facts.	**be sure** _____ s.t.

▶ Practice 8. Group C.

Complete the sentences with prepositions.

1. I don't understand that sentence. It isn't clear _____ me.

2. Mark Twain is famous _____ his novels about life on the Mississippi River.

3. I'm hungry _____ some chocolate ice cream.

4. Our daughter graduated from the university. We're very proud _____ her.

5. A lot of sugar isn't good _____ you. It is bad _____ your teeth.

6. Who was responsible _____ the accident?

7. My coat is similar _____ yours, but different _____ Ben's.

8. Some people aren't friendly _____ strangers.

9. My daughter is crazy _____ horses. She is very interested _____ them.

10. Sara knows what she's talking about. She's sure _____ her facts.

▶ Practice 9. Groups A and C.
Complete the sentences with prepositions.

1. Dr. Nelson, a heart specialist, is . . . .

   a. proud _____ her work.

   b. famous _____ her medical expertise.

   c. sure _____ her skills.

   d. familiar _____ the latest techniques.

   e. patient _____ her patients.

   f. aware _____ the stresses of her job.

   g. interested _____ her patients' lives.

   h. kind _____ her patients' families.

2. Her patient, Mrs. Green, is . . . .

   a. sad _____ her illness.

   b. nervous _____ an upcoming surgery.

   c. aware _____ her chances for survival.

   d. full _____ hope.

   e. not afraid _____ dying.

   f. curious _____ alternative medicines.

   g. ready _____ unexpected side effects.

   h. hungry _____ a home-cooked meal.

▶ Practice 10. Group D.
The prepositions in the column on the left are the correct completions for the blanks. Follow the same steps you used for Group A on page 270.

Preposition Combinations: Group D		
Answers	**Sentences**	**Reference List**
with	I agree _____ you.	**agree** _____ s.o.
about	I agree with you _____ that.	**agree with** s.o. _____ s.t.
in	We arrived _____ Toronto at six.	**arrive** _____ (*a city/country*)
at	We arrived _____ the hotel.	**arrive** _____ (*a building/room*)
about	We all complain _____ the weather.	**complain** _____ s.t./s.o.
of	A book consists _____ printed pages.	**consist** _____ s.t.
with	I disagree _____ you.	**disagree** _____ s.o.
about	I disagree with you _____ that.	**disagree with** s.o. _____ s.t.
from	She graduated _____ Reed College.	**graduate** _____ (*a place*)
to	Ted invited me _____ a picnic.	**invite** s.o. _____ s.t.
to	We listened _____ some music.	**listen** _____ s.t./s.o.
for	Jack paid _____ my dinner.	**pay** _____ s.t.
to	I talked _____ Lisa on the phone.	**talk** _____ s.o.
about	We talked _____ her problem.	**talk** _____ s.t.
on	A salesman waited _____ a customer.	**wait** _____ s.o.
for	We waited _____ the bus.	**wait** _____ s.t.
about	Sally complained to me _____ my dog.	**complain to** s.o. _____ s.t.

Complete the sentences with prepositions.

1. Tom paid _____ his airplane ticket in cash.

2. Joan graduated _____ high school two years ago.

3. I waited _____ the bus.

4. Jim is a waiter. He waits _____ customers at a restaurant.

5. I have a different opinion. I don't agree _____ you.

6. I arrived _____ this city last month.

7. I arrived _____ the airport around eight.

8. I listened _____ the news on TV last night.

9. The supervisor agreed _____ the employees' decision to work longer days and shorter weeks.

10. This practice consists _____ verbs that are followed by certain prepositions.

11. Jack invited me _____ his party.

12. I complained _____ the landlord _____ the leaky faucet in the kitchen.

13. Annie disagreed _____ her father _____ the amount of her weekly allowance.

14. Did you talk _____ Professor Adams _____ your grades?

► **Practice 12. Groups A, B, and D.**
Complete the sentences with prepositions.

1. Everyone is talking _____ the explosion in the high school chemistry lab.

2. Carlos was absent _____ class six times last term.

3. Fruit consists mostly _____ water.

4. Our children are very polite _____ adults.

5. Three centimeters is equal _____ approximately one and a half inches.

6. I borrowed some clothes _____ my best friend.

7. Are you familiar _____ ancient Greek history?

8. I discussed my problem _____ my uncle.

9. I admire you _____ your ability to laugh _____ yourself when you make a silly mistake.

10. A: Are you two arguing _____ each other _____ money again?

    B: Yeah, listen _____ this.

    A: Shhh. I don't want to hear any of this. Stop complaining _____ me _____ your finances. I don't agree with either of you.

▶ Practice 13. Group E.

The prepositions in the column on the left are the correct completions for the blanks. Follow the same steps you used for Group A on page 270.

Preposition Combinations: Group E		
Answers	**Sentences**	**Reference List**
about	She asked me _____ my trip.	**ask** s.o. _____ s.t. (inquire)
for	She asked me _____ my advice.	**ask** s.o. _____ s.t. (request)
to	This book belongs _____ me.	**belong** _____ s.o.
about / of	I dreamed _____ my girlfriend.	**dream** _____ s.o./s.t.
about	Do you know anything _____ jazz?	**know** _____ s.t.
at	I'm looking _____ this page.	**look** _____ s.t./s.o.
for	I'm looking _____ my lost keys.	**look** _____ s.t./s.o. (search)
like	Anna looks _____ her sister.	**look** _____ s.o. (resemble)
to	I'm looking forward _____ vacation.	**look forward** _____ s.t.
to	Your opinion doesn't matter _____ me.	**matter** _____ s.o.
with	Something is the matter _____ the cat.	**be the matter** _____ s.t./s.o.
for	I'm searching _____ my lost keys.	**search** _____ s.t./s.o.
from	She separated the boys _____ the girls.	**separate** (*this*) _____ (*that*)
about / of	I warned them _____ the danger.	**warn** s.o. _____ s.t.

▶ Practice 14. Group E.

Complete the sentences with prepositions.

1. What's the matter _____ Billy? Is he hurt?

2. We can go out for dinner, or we can eat at home. It doesn't matter _____ me.

3. To make this recipe, you have to separate the egg whites _____ the yolks.

4. I don't know anything _____ astrology.

5. I'm looking forward _____ my vacation next month.

6. Dennis dreamed _____ his girlfriend last night.

7. Right now I'm doing a practice. I'm looking _____ my book.

8. Jim can't find his book. He's looking _____ it.

9. Jim is searching _____ his book.

10. I asked the waitress _____ another cup of coffee.

11. I asked Rebecca _____ her trip to Japan.

12. Does this pen belong _____ you?

13. The city was warned _____ the hurricane in advance.

14. Do you think Jon looks _____ his father or his mother?

15. Magda is always looking _____ her keys. She seems pretty disorganized.

16. Look _____ those clouds. It's going to rain.

► **Practice 15. Group E.**

Make sentences by matching each phrase in Column A with a phrase in Column B. Use each phrase only once.

Column A

1. The sheriff is searching _____.

2. The baby keeps looking _____.

3. Once again, Rita is looking _____.

4. In this picture, Paula looks _____.

5. The Browns are looking forward _____.

6. Before you do the wash, you need to separate the darks _____.

7. Sometimes Joey is afraid to sleep. He often dreams _____.

8. Something's the matter _____.

9. The sign on the highway warned drivers _____.

10. We're planning to move here. Do you know much _____?

Column B

a. about monsters and dragons

b. to their 20th wedding anniversary

c. for her glasses. She always misplaces them

d. about the schools in this area

e. about high winds on the bridge

f. with this car. It's making strange noises

g. for the escaped prisoner

h. from the whites

i. at the TV screen. It has bright colors

j. like her mother. The resemblance is very strong

► **Practice 16. Group F.**

The prepositions in the column on the left are the correct completions for the blanks. Follow the same steps you used for Group A on page 270.

	Preposition Combinations: Group F	
Answers	**Sentences**	**Reference List**
to	I apologized _____ my friend.	**apologize** _____ s.o.
for	I apologized _____ my behavior.	**apologize** _____ s.t.
of	I don't approve _____ Al's behavior.	**approve** _____ s.t.
to / with	I compared this book _____ that book.	**compare** (*this*) _____ (*that*)*
on	I depend _____ my family.	**depend** _____ s.o./s.t.
of / from	He died _____ heart disease.	**die** _____ s.t.
from	The teacher excused me _____ class.	**excuse** s.o. _____ s.t.
for	I excused him _____ his mistake.	**excuse** s.o. _____ s.t. (forgive)
for	I forgave him _____ his mistake.	**forgive** s.o. _____ s.t.
of	I got rid _____ my old clothes.	**get rid** _____ s.t./s.o.
to	What happened _____ your car?	**happen** _____ s.t./s.o.
on	I insist _____ the truth.	**insist** _____ s.t.
from	I protected my eyes _____ the sun.	**protect** s.t./s.o. _____ s.t./s.o.
on	I am relying _____ you to help me.	**rely** _____ s.o./s.t.
of	Mr. Lee took care _____ the problem.	**take care** _____ s.t./s.o.
for	Thank you _____ your help.	**thank** s.o. _____ s.t.

*Also possible: *I compared this **and** that.* (**And** is not a preposition. A parallel structure with **and** may follow **compare**.)

▶ Practice 17. Group F.

Complete the sentences with prepositions.

1. I apologized _____ Ann _____ stepping on her toe.

2. I thanked Sam _____ helping me fix my car.

3. My grandfather doesn't approve _____ gambling.

4. Please forgive me _____ forgetting your birthday.

5. My friend insisted _____ taking me to the airport.

6. Please excuse me _____ being late.

7. Children depend _____ their parents for love and support.

8. In my composition, I compared this city _____ my hometown.

9. Umbrellas protect people _____ rain.

10. We're relying _____ Jason to help us move into our new apartment.

11. We had mice in the house, so we set some traps to get rid _____ them.

12. Who is taking care _____ the children while you are gone?

13. What happened _____ your finger? Did you cut it?

14. My boss excused me _____ the meeting when I became ill.

15. What did Mr. Hill die _____?

▶ Practice 18. Group F.

Write "C" beside the correct sentences. Write "I" beside those that are incorrect. In some cases, both may be correct.

1. a. ___C___ John needs to be excused from the meeting.

   b. ___C___ John excused his co-worker for the accounting error.

2. a. ___C___ Do you approve of your government's international policies?

   b. ___I___ Do you approve on the new seat-belt law?

3. a. _____ I apologized for the car accident.

   b. _____ I apologized to Mary's parents.

4. a. _____ Why did you get rid over your truck? It was in great condition.

   b. _____ I got rid of several boxes of old magazines.

5. a. _____ Pierre died of a heart attack.

   b. _____ Pierre's father also died from heart problems.

6. a. _____ It's not a good idea to compare one student to another.

   b. _____ I wish my parents wouldn't compare me with my brother.

7. a. _____ We can rely on Lesley to keep a secret.

   b. _____ There are several people whom my elderly parents rely in for assistance.

8. a. _____ You can relax. I took care about your problem.

   b. _____ The nurses take wonderful care of their patients at Valley Hospital.

► **Practice 19. Group G.**
The prepositions in the column on the left are the correct completions for the blanks. Follow the same steps you used for Group A on page 270.

	Preposition Combinations: Group G	
Answers	**Sentences**	**Reference List**
to	I'm accustomed _____ hot weather.	**be accustomed** _____ s.t.
to	I added a name _____ my address book.	**add** (*this*) _____ (*that*)
on	I'm concentrating _____ this Practice.	**concentrate** _____ s.t.
into	I divided the cookie _____ two pieces.	**divide** (*this*) _____ (*that*)
from	They escaped _____ prison.	**escape** _____ (*a place*)
about	I heard _____ the prison escape.	**hear** _____ s.t./s.o.
from	I heard about it _____ my cousin.	**hear about** s.t. _____ s.o.
from	The escapees hid _____ the police.	**hide** (s.t.) _____ s.o.
for	We're hoping _____ good weather.	**hope** _____ s.t.
by	I multiplied 8 _____ 2.	**multiply** (*this*) _____ (*that*)
to / with	I spoke _____ the teacher.	**speak** _____ s.o.
about	We spoke to Dr. Carter _____ my problem.	**speak to/with** _____ s.t.
about	I told the teacher _____ my problem.	**tell** s.o. _____ s.t.
from	I subtracted 7 _____ 16.	**subtract** (*this*) _____ (*that*)
about	I wonder _____ lots of curious things.	**wonder** _____ s.t.

► **Practice 20. Group G.**
Complete the sentences with prepositions.

1. Shhh. I'm trying to concentrate _____ this math problem.

2. How did the bank robbers escape _____ jail?

3. Did you tell your parents _____ the dent in their new car?

4. We're hoping _____ good weather tomorrow so we can go sailing.

5. Did you hear _____ the earthquake in Turkey?

6. I heard _____ my sister last week. She sent me an email.

7. I spoke _____ Dr. Rice _____ my problem.

8. I'm not accustomed _____ cold weather.

9. When you divide 6 _____ 2, the answer is 3.

10. When you subtract 1 _____ 6, the answer is 5.

11. When you multiply 6 _____ 3, the answer is 18.★

12. When you add 6 _____ 4, the answer is 10.★★

13. George wondered _____ his team's chances of winning the tennis tournament.

14. Sally hid her journal _____ her younger sister.

★Also possible: *multiply 6 **times** 3*

★★Also possible: add 6 ***and*** 4; add 6 ***plus*** 4

► **Practice 21. Groups E, F, and G.**
Complete the sentences with prepositions.

1. My father insisted _____ knowing the truth.

2. I was wondering _____ your birthday. What do you want to do?

3. What's the matter _____ you today?

4. He hid the money _____ his wife.

5. We separated the younger kids _____ the teenagers.

6. I apologized _____ my boss _____ my mistake.

7. We got rid _____ the insects in our apartment.

8. Who does this book belong _____?

9. The prisoners escaped _____ their guards.

10. Does it matter _____ you what time I call this evening?

11. We're looking forward _____ your visit.

12. Fresh vegetables are good _____ you.

13. Parents protect their children _____ harm.

14. Shhh. I'm trying to concentrate _____ my work.

15. I rely _____ my friends for their help.

16. I don't approve _____ Bob's lifestyle.

17. The official warned us _____ the danger of traveling in the countryside alone.

► **Practice 22. Review: Appendix 2.**
Choose the correct preposition.

1. What time do you need to be ready _____ work?
   a. at   b. about   c. on   d. for

2. One pound is equal _____ 2.2 kilos.
   a. for   b. to   c. in   d. on

3. Too many vitamins may be bad _____ your health.
   a. in   b. about   c. for   d. with

4. That box looks very heavy. Can I help you _____ it?
   a. with   b. in   c. about   d. on

5. Our cat got rid _____ all the mice in our basement.
   a. about   b. off   c. in   d. of

6. Everyone admires Mr. Kim _____ his generosity with his time and money.
   a. for   b. from   c. with   d. about

7. What happened _____ your hand? It's swollen.
   a. on   b. to   c. in   d. about

8. Paul is so smart. He graduated _____ the university in just three years.
   a. of   b. at   c. from   d. to

9. Angela has applied _____ several jobs in the airline industry, but she hasn't gotten an interview yet.
   a. to   b. with   c. of   d. for

10. This car can't belong _____ Mike. It's too nice!
     a. about   b. with   c. to   d. at

11. Monica loves vegetables, but she's not crazy _____ fruit.
     a. over   b. in   c. at   d. about

12. Jack paid _____ my dinner.
     a. with   b. for   c. on   d. in

13. I tried to tell Jessica _____ my trip, but she didn't seem interested. I wonder if she was jealous.
     a. to   b. about   c. with   d. off

14. We're really happy _____ Professor James. He just received an award for excellence in teaching.
     a. for   b. to   c. over   d. in

15. People say I shouldn't care what other students think, but their opinions matter _____ me.
     a. on   b. for   c. with   d. to

16. Annie eats vegetables only if they are separated _____ the other foods on her plate.
     a. between   b. from   c. with   d. to

17. Kristi forgave her twin sister _____ taking her cell phone without asking.
     a. about   b. from   c. for   d. with

18. Doctors say that even ten minutes of exercise a day is good _____ you.
     a. at   b. for   c. with   d. about

19. I'm sorry. Your explanation still isn't clear _____ me.
     a. to   b. with   c. about   d. in

20. My sister complained _____ the manager.
     a. for   b. with   c. at   d. to

21. She complained _____ the slow service in the restaurant.
     a. about   b. for   c. over   d. by

22. The problem with your answer is that you multiplied six _____ eight instead of subtracting it.
     a. to   b. from   c. by   d. over

Index

Not (SEE Negatives)
Not as . . . as, 155
Noun clauses, 237–254
    with *if/whether,* 241
    with question words (*what he said*), 237–240
    reported speech, sequence of tenses, 246–247
    with *that* (*I think that . . .*), 242–244
    with yes/no questions, 241–242
Nouns:
    count/noncount (*chairs/furniture*), 191–206
    plural forms, 94–95, 104
    possessive (*Tom's*), 107–108
    as subjects and objects, 96
    used as adjectives (*a flower garden*), 103

O

Object pronouns, personal (*him, them*), 105–107
    in adjective clauses (*whom I met*), 209–211
Objects:
    of a preposition (*on the desk*), 97–99
    of a verb (*is reading a book*), 96–97
On, as time preposition (*on Monday*), 100–101
One, much, many, 194
Or, 136–137
Other, 112–113
Ought to, 122

P

Parallel structure with *and, but, or,* 133
    with verbs (*walks and talks, is walking and talking*), 51
Particles, in phrasal verbs (*put away*), 255–269
Participial adjectives (*interested* vs. *interesting*), 184, 243
Partitives (SEE Units of measure)
Passive (*It was mailed by Bob*), 170–190
    vs. active, 175
    by-phrase, use of, 178–180
    modal auxiliaries (*should be mailed*), 181
    stative (*is married*), 183
    summary of forms, 172–173, 182
Past habit (*I used to live in . . .*), 29
Past participles, 22
    as adjectives (*be tired, be surprised*), 183
        following *get* (*get tired*), 186
        vs. *-ing* (*interested* vs. *interesting*), 184
    of irregular verbs, 23
    in passive, 170–176
Past perfect (*had left*), 67
Past progressive (*was eating*), 26–28
Past time, 16–32 (SEE ALSO Tenses)
Period, 133–134, 140
Personal pronouns (*she, him, they*), 105–107

Phrasal verbs, 255–269
    intransitive, 264–265
    nonseparable, 256–257
    separable, 255–256, 258–260, 262–263
    three-word, 266–268
Please, 119–120
Plural nouns, 94–95, 104 (SEE ALSO Singular and plural)
Polite questions using modals (*May I? Would you?*), 127
Possessive:
    in adjective clauses (*whose*), 216–217
    nouns (*Tom's*), 107
    pronouns and adjectives (*mine* and *my*), 108–109
Prefer, 129
Prepositional phrases (*on the desk*), 97–99
Prepositions (*at, from, under*), 97–100
    combinations with verbs and adjectives, 270–281
    followed by gerunds, 225–226
    objects of, 97–99
    of place, 98–99
        vs. time, word order, 100–101
    placement in adjective clauses, 215–216
    placement in information questions, 75–78
    in stative passive (*be married to*), 183
    of time (*in, on, at*), 100–101
    used as particle in phrasal verbs (*put off, put on*), 255–269
Present participle (*eating*), 22
    as adjective (*interesting*), 183–184
    vs. gerund, 221
Present perfect (*have eaten*), 55–70
    vs. present perfect progressive, 64–65
    vs. simple past, 62–63
Present time, 1–15 (SEE ALSO Tenses)
Principal parts of a verb (*eat, ate, eaten, eating*), 22
Probably, 39
Progressive verbs (*be* + *-ing*), 5–7, 12–13
    vs. non-action (*I am thinking* vs. *I think*), 12
    past (*was doing*), 26–28
    present (*is doing*), 2, 5–7, 12–13
    present perfect (*has been doing*), 64–65
Pronouns:
    in adjective clauses (*who, which*), 209–213
    in comparisons, 154
    contractions with (SEE Contractions of Verbs)
    personal (*I, them*), 105–107
    possessive (*mine, theirs*), 108–109
    reflexive (*myself, themselves*), 109–110
    used as expressions of quantity (*many, some*), 199–200
Punctuation:
    apostrophe (*Tom's*), 107–108

Answer Key

CHAPTER 1: PRESENT TIME

PRACTICE 1, p. 1
1. is
2. name
3. is
4. am
5. am
6. meet
7. are
8. you
9. am
10. are
11. you
12. from
13. am
14. from
15. are
16. you
17. am
18. are
19. is
20. do
21. play OR meet
22. do
23. do
24. write
25. do
26. like
27. write
28. do
29. you
30. is
31. is
32. Is
33. is
34. is
35. is
36. is

PRACTICE 2, p. 2
1. am sitting
2. sit
3. do
4. am doing
5. am looking
6. am writing
7. is sitting
8. is working
9. works
10. is checking
11. checks
12. writes

PRACTICE 3, p. 3
Part I
1. speak
2. speak
3. speaks
4. speak
5. speaks

Part II
6. do not / don't speak
7. do not / don't speak
8. does not / doesn't speak
9. do not / don't speak
10. does not / doesn't speak

Part III
11. Do . . . speak
12. Do . . . speak
13. Does . . . speak
14. Do . . . speak
15. Does . . . speak

PRACTICE 4, p. 3
1. plays
2. conducts
3. collect
4. programs
5. trains
6. run
7. cooks
8. work
9. drives
10. write

PRACTICE 5, p. 4
1. doesn't point . . . points
2. doesn't come . . . comes
3. doesn't snow . . . snows
4. don't grow . . . grow
5. doesn't follow . . . follows
6. don't fly . . . fly
7. doesn't revolve . . . revolves
8. don't turn . . . turn

PRACTICE 6, p. 4
1. do
2. Ø
3. does
4. Ø
5. do
6. Ø
7. Ø . . . does
8. Ø
9. Ø
10. do
11. Do

PRACTICE 7, p. 5
Part I
1. am speaking
2. are speaking
3. is speaking
4. are speaking
5. is speaking

Part II
6. am not speaking
7. are not speaking
8. is not speaking
9. are not speaking
10. is not speaking

Part III
11. Are . . . speaking
12. Is . . . speaking
13. Are . . . speaking
14. Are . . . speaking
15. Is . . . speaking

PRACTICE 8, p. 5

1. is looking
2. is staring
3. are texting
4. is filing
5. are listening
6. is moving
7. is drawing
8. is sleeping
9. am trying
10. is speaking
11. is losing
12. is falling

PRACTICE 9, p. 6

Group 1
1. c
2. a
3. b

Group 2
1. c
2. b
3. a

Group 3
1. b
2. c
3. a

Group 4
1. b
2. a
3. c

PRACTICE 10, p. 6

1. Is he
2. Does he
3. Is he
4. Is he
5. Does he
6. Is he
7. Is he
8. Does he
9. Does he
10. Does he

PRACTICE 11, p. 7

1. Is she
2. Does she
3. Is she
4. Is she
5. Does she
6. Does she
7. Is she
8. Is she
9. Does she
10. Is she

PRACTICE 12, p. 7

1. b
2. a
3. a
4. c
5. b
6. b
7. a
8. a
9. a
10. c
11. c
12. c

PRACTICE 13, p. 8

1. usually . . . Ø
2. Ø . . . usually
3. always . . . Ø
4. Ø . . . always
5. usually . . . Ø
6. Ø . . . always
7. sometimes . . . Ø
8. never . . . Ø
9. Ø . . . never
10. Ø . . . usually . . . Ø
11. Ø . . . always . . . Ø
12. Ø . . . always

PRACTICE 14, p. 8

1. a. usually doesn't come
   b. doesn't ever come
   c. seldom comes
   d. sometimes doesn't come
   e. doesn't always come
   f. occasionally doesn't come
   g. never comes
   h. hardly ever comes
2. a. isn't usually
   b. is rarely
   c. isn't always
   d. isn't frequently
   e. is never
   f. isn't ever
   g. is seldom

PRACTICE 15, p. 9

1. always wakes
2. sometimes skips
3. frequently visits
4. is usually
5. seldom surfs
6. usually cleans
7. rarely does
8. is never

PRACTICE 16, p. 9

Part I
Verbs: are, form, have, call, are, occur, travel, cause, like, is coming
Frequency adverbs: Usually, often, never

Part II
1. T
2. F
3. F
4. F
5. T
6. F
7. F
8. T

PRACTICE 17, p. 10

1. Plural
2. Singular
3. Plural
4. Singular
5. Singular
6. Plural
7. Plural
8. Singular
9. Singular
10. Plural

PRACTICE 18, p. 10

1. eats
2. gets
3. teaches
4. works
5. does
6. studies
7. pays
8. has
9. buys
10. goes

PRACTICE 19, p. 11

Underlined verbs:
1. hops
2. live (No change.)
3. carries . . . watches
4. tastes . . . comes
5. are . . . contain (No change.)
6. bakes . . . cuts . . . puts
7. is . . . fixes
8. works . . . fries . . . serves
9. go . . . Fred goes

PRACTICE 20, p. 11

1. leaves
2. He walks
3. catches
4. he transfers
5. He arrives
6. He stays
7. he leaves
8. He attends
9. He
10. studies
11. tries
12. he goes
13. He has

PRACTICE 21, p. 12

1. a
2. a
3. b
4. b
5. a
6. a
7. b
8. a
9. b
10. a

PRACTICE 22, p. 12

1. is snowing
2. takes
3. drive
4. am watching
5. prefer
6. need
7. understand
8. belongs
9. is raining . . . is shining

PRACTICE 23, p. 13

1. usually doesn't take
2. needs
3. is enjoying
4. are
5. are eating
6. are drinking
7. (are) reading
8. is working
9. is feeding
10. are playing
11. knows
12. love
13. has
14. play
15. is smiling
16. relaxing
17. usually takes
18. is

PRACTICE 24, p. 13

1. Don **is** not working now.
2. Florida doesn't **have** mountains.
3. This train **is always** late.
4. Does Marta usually **go** to bed early?
5. Mr. Chin always come**s** to work on time.
6. Shh! The concert **is** starting now.
7. The refrigerator **does not (doesn't)** work.
8. **Does** Catherine **have** a car?
9. Pam and Bob are getting married. They **love** each other.
10. Anne **does** not understand this subject.
11. Jessica **sometimes asks** her parents for advice.
12. **Do** you do your laundry at the laundromat on the corner?
13. When the color blue mixe**s** with the color yellow, the result is green.
14. Boris **fries** two eggs for breakfast every morning.
15. We are **studying** English.

PRACTICE 25, p. 14

1. A: Are
   B: I am OR I'm not
2. A: Do
   B: they do OR they don't
3. A: Do
   B: I do OR I don't
4. A: Does
   B: she does OR she doesn't
5. A: Are
   B: they are OR they aren't
6. A: Do
   B: they do OR they don't
7. A: Is
   B: he is OR he isn't
8. A: Are
   B: I am OR I'm not
9. A: Is
   B: it is OR it isn't
10. A: Do
    B: we do OR we don't

PRACTICE 26, p. 15

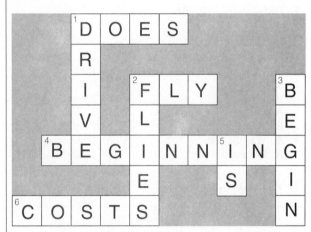

CHAPTER 2: PAST TIME

PRACTICE 1, p. 16

1. Did it start early? — It didn't start early.
2. Did Bob arrive late? — Bob didn't arrive late.
3. Was Hal here? — Hal wasn't here.
4. Did Dad plant roses? — Dad didn't plant roses.
5. Did Mom like the game? — Mom didn't like the game.
6. Did Kim cook dinner? — Kim didn't cook dinner.
7. Did Nat play tennis? — Nat didn't play tennis.
8. Were they late? — They weren't late.
9. Did Sam invite Ann? — Sam didn't invite Ann.
10. Did we do our work? — We didn't do our work.

PRACTICE 2, p. 16

Statement	Question	Negative
1.	Do you work	
2.	Did you work	You didn't work
3. She works	Does she work	
4.	Did she work	She didn't work
5. They work		They don't work
6.	Did they work	They didn't work
7. He works	Does he work	
8.	Did he work	He didn't work

PRACTICE 3, p. 17

1. A: Is
   B: isn't
2. A: Was
   B: was
3. A: Did
   B: did
4. A: Was
   B: wasn't
5. A: Was
   B: was
6. A: Was
   B: was
7. A: Was
   B: was
8. A: Did
   B: did
9. A: Is
   B: is
10. A: Did
    B: did

PRACTICE 4, p. 17

1. Did he study
2. Was he sick
3. Was she sad
4. Did they eat
5. Were they hungry
6. Did you go
7. Did she understand
8. Did he forget

PRACTICE 5, p. 18

1. Did
2. Was
3. Was
4. Were
5. Did
6. Did
7. Did
8. Were
9. Were
10. Are

PRACTICE 6, p. 18

1. A: Did you pass
   B: I did
2. A: Were you
   B: I wasn't
3. A: Did you practice
   B: I did
4. A: Was the test
   B: it wasn't
5. A: Did you make
   B: I didn't
6. A: Was the car
   B: it was
7. A: Did you put
   B: I did
8. A: Did you go
   B: I didn't

PRACTICE 7, p. 19

PRACTICE 8, p. 20

Double the consonant.	Drop the –e.	Just add -ing.
hitting	coming	learning
beginning	hoping	listening
cutting	smiling	raining
hopping	taking	staying
winning	writing	studying

PRACTICE 9, p. 20

1. waiting, wait
2. petting, pet
3. biting, bite
4. sitting, sit
5. writing, write
6. fighting, fight
7. waiting, wait
8. getting, get
9. starting, start
10. permitting, permit
11. lifting, lift
12. eating, eat
13. tasting, taste
14. cutting, cut
15. meeting, meet
16. visiting, visit

PRACTICE 10, p. 21

Part I
1. is beginning
2. are broadcasting
3. are running
4. are competing
5. are racing
6. is starting
7. are getting
8. are trying
9. are speeding
10. isn't raining
11. are worrying

Part II
1. cheered
2. shouted
3. enjoyed
4. raced
5. crossed
6. finished
7. occurred
8. crashed
9. needed
10. started
11. completed
12. happened

End of verb	Double the consonant?	Simple form	-ing	-ed
-e	No	live	living	lived
		race	racing	raced
Two Consonants	No	work	working	worked
		start	starting	started
Two Vowels + One Consonant	No	shout	shouting	shouted
		wait	waiting	waited
One Vowel + One Consonant	Yes	ONE-SYLLABLE VERBS		
		pat	patting	patted
		shop	shopping	shopped
	No	TWO-SYLLABLE VERBS: STRESS ON FIRST SYLLABLE		
		listen	listening	listened
		happen	happening	happened
	Yes	TWO-SYLLABLE VERBS: STRESS ON SECOND SYLLABLE		
		occur	occurring	occurred
		refer	referring	referred
-y	No	play	playing	played
		reply	replying	replied
		study	studying	studied
-ie		die	dying	died
		tie	tying	tied

PRACTICE 11, p. 22

1. stopped
2. picked
3. arrive
4. crying
5. walk, walking
6. went
7. practiced
8. referred
9. made
10. hopped
11. hoped, hoping
12. put
13. eating
14. sing
15. listened, listening

PRACTICE 12, p. 23

Part I	Part III	Part V
bought	blew	hit
brought	drew	hurt
fought	flew	read
thought	grew	shut
taught	knew	cost
caught	threw	put
found		quit

Part II	Part IV	Part VI
swam	broke	paid
drank	wrote	said
sang	froze	
rang	rode	
	sold	
	stole	

PRACTICE 13, p. 23

1. was . . . flew . . . spent
2. came . . . took . . . put . . . lost
3. began . . . sang . . . became . . . knew . . . wore

PRACTICE 14, p. 24

1. walked . . . yesterday
2. talked . . . last
3. opened . . . yesterday
4. went . . . last
5. met . . . last
6. Yesterday . . . made . . . took
7. paid . . . last
8. Yesterday . . . fell
9. left . . . last

PRACTICE 15, p. 25

1. didn't fly . . . rode
2. aren't . . . are
3. wasn't . . . was (answers will vary)
4. didn't come . . . came
5. doesn't come . . . comes
6. didn't sleep . . . slept
7. isn't . . . is
8. didn't disappear . . . disappeared
9. don't make . . . make

PRACTICE 16, p. 26

1. | | is | was |
2. think | | thought
3. | are playing | played
4. drink | am drinking | |
5. teaches | | taught
6. swims | is swimming | |
7. | are sleeping | slept
8. reads | | read
9. try | are trying | |
10. | are eating | ate

1.		is	was
2.	think		thought
3.		are playing	played
4.	drink	am drinking	
5.	teaches		taught
6.	swims	is swimming	
7.		are sleeping	slept
8.	reads		read
9.	try	are trying	
10.		are eating	ate

PRACTICE 17, p. 26

1. were hiding
2. were singing
3. was watching
4. were talking
5. were reading . . . were sitting . . . looking

PRACTICE 18, p. 27

1. was playing . . . broke
2. scored . . . was playing
3. hurt . . . was playing
4. was hiking . . . found
5. saw . . . was hiking
6. picked up . . . was hiking
7. tripped . . . fell . . . was dancing
8. was dancing . . . met
9. was dancing . . . got

PRACTICE 19, p. 27

1. were walking
2. was washing . . . dropped . . . broke
3. saw . . . was eating . . . was talking . . . joined
4. was singing . . . did not hear
5. A: Did your lights go out
   B: was taking . . . found . . . ate . . . went . . . slept

PRACTICE 20, p. 28

1. d   5. g
2. c   6. h
3. b   7. f
4. a   8. e

PRACTICE 21, p. 28

        1   2

1. The fire alarm sounded. Everyone left the building.
   When the fire alarm sounded, everyone left the building.

        1   2

2. They left the building. They stood outside in the rain.
   After they left the building, they stood outside in the rain.

        2   1

3. Everyone started to dance. The music began.
   As soon as the music began, everyone started to dance.

        2   1

4. The music ended. They danced to all the songs.
   They danced to all the songs until the music ended.

5. The fans in the stadium applauded and cheered.
2
1
The soccer player scored a goal.
When the soccer player scored a goal, the fans in the stadium applauded and cheered.
2   1

6. Everyone left the stadium. The game was over.
Everyone left the stadium as soon as the game was over.
1   2

7. I looked up her phone number. I called her.
Before I called her, I looked up her phone number.
1   2

8. The phone rang 10 times. I hung up.
I hung up after the phone rang 10 times.

PRACTICE 22, p. 29

1. used to hate school
2. used to be a secretary
3. used to play tennis
4. used to have fresh eggs
5. used to crawl under his bed . . . put his hands over his ears
6. used to go
7. used to wear
8. used to hate
9. used to eat

PRACTICE 23, p. 30

Part I

Underlined verbs: Do . . . orbit, do . . . orbit, orbit, is, is means, orbit.
Circled verbs: used to orbit, Did . . . disappear, did . . . disappear, changed, decided, reclassified, put, reclassified, orbited.

Part II

1. T
2. T
3. F
4. T
5. F
6. T
7. F

PRACTICE 24, p. 30

1. We **didn't visit** my cousins last weekend.
2. They **walked** to school yesterday.
3. I **understood** all the teacher's questions yesterday.
4. Matt and I were **talking** on the phone when the lights went out.
5. When Flora **heard** the news, she didn't **know** what to say.
6. David and Carol **went** to Italy last month.
7. I didn't **drive** a car when I **was** a teenager.
8. Carmen didn't **use(d)** to eat fish, but now she does.
9. Ms. Pepper didn't **die** in the accident.
10. **Did** you **see** that red light? You didn't **stop**!
11. I used to **live** in a big city when I was a child. Now I live in a small town.
12. Last night at about seven we **ate** a delicious pizza. Howard **made** the pizza in his new oven.
13. Sally **broke** her right foot last year. After that, she **hopped** on her left foot for three weeks.

PRACTICE 25, p. 31

1. was preparing
2. was playing
3. rang
4. was boiling
5. turned
6. answered
7. opened
8. saw
9. was holding
10. needed
11. screamed
12. fell
13. hurt
14. slammed
15. ran
16. heard
17. was waiting
18. opened
19. took
20. thanked
21. signed

PRACTICE 26, p. 31

1. a
2. b
3. b
4. a
5. c
6. c
7. b
8. b
9. c
10. b
11. a
12. a
13. c

PRACTICE 27, p. 32

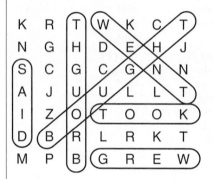

CHAPTER **3**: FUTURE TIME

PRACTICE 1, p. 33

1. is going to be
4. will finish
5. will design
8. is going to live
10. 'll be

PRACTICE 2, p. 33

1. am going to leave
2. is going to leave
3. isn't going to leave
4. Are . . . going to leave
5. is going to be
6. are going to be
7. am not going to be
8. Is . . . going to be
9. is going to rain
10. isn't going to snow
11. isn't going to shine
12. Is . . . going to rain

PRACTICE 3, p. 34
1. is going to wake up
2. is going to catch
3. is going to jump
4. are going to fall

PRACTICE 4, p. 34

am going to	will
are going to	will
is going to	will
are going to	will
are going to	will
are not going to	will not / won't
is not going to	will not / won't
am not going to	will not / won't

PRACTICE 5, p. 35
The Smiths **will** celebrate their 50th wedding anniversary on December 1st of this year. Their children are planning a party for them at a local hotel. Their family and friends **will** join them for the celebration.

Mr. and Mrs. Smith have three children and five grandchildren. The Smiths know that two of their children **will** be at the party, but the third child, their youngest daughter, is far away in Africa, where she is doing medical research. They believe she **will** not come home for the party.

The Smiths don't know it, but their youngest daughter **will** be at the party. She is planning to surprise them. It **will** be a wonderful surprise for them! They **will** be very happy to see her. The whole family **will** enjoy being together for this special occasion.

PRACTICE 6, p. 35
1. Will Nick start
   Is Nick going to start
2. Will Mr. Jones give
   Is Mr. Jones going to give
3. Will Jacob quit
   Is Jacob going to quit
4. Will Mr. and Mrs. Kono adopt
   Are Mr. and Mrs. Kono going to adopt
5. Will the Johnsons move
   Are the Johnsons going to move
6. Will Dr. Johnson retire
   Is Dr. Johnson going to retire

PRACTICE 7, p. 36
1. Tomorrow will be
2. Will we have
3. we will have
4. Will the test be
5. will not be
6. Will I pass
7. You will pass
8. will not pass

PRACTICE 8, p. 36
1. a. arrives
   b. arrived
   c. is going to arrive
   d. will arrive
2. a. eats
   b. ate
   c. is going to eat
   d. will eat
3. a. doesn't arrive
   b. didn't arrive
   c. isn't going to arrive
   d. will not arrive
4. a. Do . . . eat
   b. Did . . . eat
   c. Are . . . going to eat
   d. Will . . . eat
5. a. don't eat
   b. didn't eat
   c. am not going to eat
   d. will not eat

PRACTICE 9, p. 37
1. 'll enjoy . . . 'll begin . . . 'll teach
2. 'll be . . . 'll call
3. 'll start . . . 'll ride . . . 'll drive

PRACTICE 10, p. 37
1. A: Will you / Are you going to help
   B: I will / am OR I won't / I'm not
2. A: Will Paul / Is Paul going to lend
   B: he will / is OR he won't / isn't
3. A: Will Jane / Is Jane going to graduate
   B: she will / is OR she won't / isn't
4. A: Will her parents / Are her parents going to be
   B: they will / are OR they won't / aren't
5. A: Will you / Are you going to answer
   B: I will / am OR I won't / I'm not
6. A: Will Jill / Is Jill going to text
   B: she will / is OR she won't / isn't

PRACTICE 11, p. 38

Part I
1. I'll probably go
2. she probably won't come
3. he'll probably go
4. he probably won't hand
5. they'll probably have

Part II
6. I'm probably going to watch
7. I'm probably not going to be
8. they probably aren't going to come
9. she probably isn't going to ride
10. it is probably going to be

PRACTICE 12, p. 39

	100% Certain	About 90% Certain	About 50% Certain
1.		✓	
2.			✓
3.			✓
4.		✓	
5.			✓
6.	✓		
7.	✓		
8.		✓	
9.			✓
10.		✓	
11.			✓
12.		✓	

PRACTICE 13, p. 39
1. are probably going to have
2. are probably not going to invite
3. may have . . . Maybe . . . will have
4. may rent
5. will probably decide
6. may not be . . . may be
7. will go
8. probably won't go

PRACTICE 14, p. 40
1. a
2. a
3. c
4. b
5. a
6. a
7. c
8. a
9. c
10. b
11. b

PRACTICE 15, p. 41

Part I
1. 'm going to work
2. 'm going to watch
3. 're going to move
4. 'm going to get

Part II
1. 'll answer
2. 'll ask
3. 'll clean
4. 'll pay

PRACTICE 16, p. 42
1. 'm going to
2. 'll
3. 'm going to
4. 'll
5. 'm going to . . . 'll

PRACTICE 17, p. 42
1. will
2. are going to
3. are going to
4. are going to
5. am going to
6. am going to
7. will

PRACTICE 18, p. 43
Underlined clauses:
1. Before Bill met Maggie
2. until he met Maggie.
3. When he met Maggie
4. after he met her
5. After they dated for a year
6. As soon as Bill gets a better job
7. before they buy a house
8. when they have enough money
9. After they get married
10. until they die

PRACTICE 19, p. 43
1. After I finish . . . I'm going to go
2. I'm not going to go . . . until I finish
3. Before Ann watches . . . she will finish
4. Jim is going to read . . . after he gets
5. When I call . . . I'll ask
6. Ms. Torres will stay . . . until she finishes
7. As soon as I get . . . I'm going to take

PRACTICE 20, p. 44
1. If it rains tomorrow,
2. If it is hot tomorrow,
3. if he has enough time
4. If I don't get a check tomorrow,
5. if I get a raise soon
6. If Gina doesn't study for her test,
7. if I have enough money
8. If I don't study tonight,

PRACTICE 21, p. 45
Sam and I are going to leave on a road trip tomorrow. We'll pack our suitcases and put everything in the car before we **go** to bed tonight. We'll leave tomorrow morning at dawn, as soon as the sun **comes** up. We'll drive for a couple of hours on the interstate highway while we **talk** and **listen** to our favorite music. When we **see** a nice rest area, we'll stop for coffee. After we **walk** around the rest area a little bit, we'll get back in the car and drive a little longer. We'll stay on that highway until we **come** to Highway 44. Then we'll turn off and drive on scenic country roads. If Sam **gets** tired, I'll drive. Then when I **drive,** he'll probably take a little nap. We'll keep going until it **gets** dark.

PRACTICE 22, p. 45
1. e
2. g
3. a
4. f
5. b
6. c
7. d

PRACTICE 23, p. 46
1. <u>When Sue has enough money,</u> she is going to buy an apartment. OR
   Sue is going to buy an apartment <u>when she has enough money</u>.
2. <u>Before my friends come over,</u> I'm going to clean up my apartment. OR
   I'm going to clean up my apartment <u>before my friends come over</u>.
3. <u>When the storm is over,</u> I'm going to do some errands. OR
   I'm going to do some errands <u>when the storm is over</u>.
4. <u>If you don't learn how to use a computer,</u> you will have trouble finding a job. OR
   You will have trouble finding a job <u>if you don't learn how to use a computer</u>.
5. <u>As soon as Joe finishes his report,</u> he is going to meet us at the coffee shop. OR
   Joe is going to meet us at the coffee shop <u>as soon as he finishes his report</u>.
6. <u>After Lesley washes and dries the dishes,</u> she will put them away. OR
   Lesley will put away the dishes <u>after she washes and dries them</u>.
7. <u>If they don't leave at seven,</u> they won't get to the theater on time. OR
   They won't get to the theater on time <u>if they don't leave at seven</u>.

PRACTICE 24, p. 46

1. will be
2. 'll get
3. 'll wash
4. brush
5. 'll put
7. 'll go
8. turn on
9. 'll walk
10. see
11. 'll watch
12. make
13. destroys
14. get
15. 'll pour
16. open
17. will come
18. 'll talk
19. 'll have
20. 'll make
21. say
22. 'll finish
23. 'll go
24. is
25. has
26. 'll work
27. will ring
28. 'll talk
29. 'll go
30. make
21. will be

PRACTICE 25, p. 48

1. I'm going to stay . . . I'm staying
2. They're going to travel . . . They're traveling
3. We're going to get . . . We're getting
4. He's going to start . . . He's starting
5. She's going to go . . . She's going
6. My neighbors are going to build . . . My neighbors are building

PRACTICE 26, p. 48

1. is traveling
2. is leaving
3. is speaking
4. are having
5. is . . . taking
6. are coming
7. am meeting
8. am graduating

PRACTICE 27, p. 49

1. b
2. a
3. a
4. b
5. b
6. a
7. b
8. a

PRACTICE 28, p. 49

1. a
2. a, b
3. a, b
4. a, b
5. a
6. a, b
7. a
8. a, b
9. a
10. a, b

PRACTICE 29, p. 50

1. A: does . . . begin / start
   B: begins / starts
2. opens
3. arrives / gets in
4. begins / starts
5. A: do . . . close
   B: closes
6. open . . . starts / begins . . . . arrive . . . ends / finishes
7. A: does . . . depart / leave
   B: leaves / departs
   B: does . . . arrive (get in)

PRACTICE 30, p. 51

1. d
2. f
3. a
4. h
5. b
6. c
7. g
8. e

PRACTICE 31, p. 51

1. study
2. set
3. doing
4. go
5. fell
6. is writing . . . is waiting
7. takes . . . buys
8. go . . . tell
9. am taking . . . forgetting
10. will discover . . . (will) apologize

PRACTICE 32, p. 52

1. My friends **will** join us after work.
2. Maybe the party **will end / is going to end** soon. OR The party **may end** soon.
3. On Friday, our school **will close / is going to close** early so teachers can go to a workshop.
4. It **will rain / is going to rain** tomorrow.
5. Our company is going to **sell** computer equipment to schools.
6. Give grandpa a hug. He's about to **leave.**
7. Mr. Scott is going to retire and **move** to a warmer climate.
8. If your soccer team **wins** the championship tomorrow, we'll have a big celebration for you.
9. I bought this cloth because **I'm going to / am going to** make some curtains for my bedroom.
10. I moving to London when I **finish** my education here.
11. Are you going **to go** to the meeting? OR Are you **going to** the meeting?
12. I opened the door and **walked** to the front of the room.
13. When **are** you going to move into your new apartment?
14. Maybe I **will** celebrate my 30th birthday with my friends at a restaurant. OR **I may** celebrate . . .

PRACTICE 33, p. 52

1. am working
2. need
3. go
4. am going to finish
5. write
6. stayed
7. was reading
8. heard
9. went
10. didn't see
11. went
12. found
13. made
14. is watching
15. always watches
16. is
17. is going to mow
18. am making
19. is cooking
20. were
21. used to make
22. got
23. are gong to go / are going
24. are
25. are going to see
26. bought
27. always buy
28. leave
29. usually stay
30. are
31. are not going to stay
32. tried
33. was
34. may stay
35. will stay
36. plays
37. skips
38. isn't doing
39. doesn't study
40. go
41. will / is going to flunk
42. saw
43. ran
44. caught
45. knocked
46. called
47. was waiting / waited
48. got
49. understood
50. put
51. took
52. ended
53. woke

PRACTICE 34, p. 54

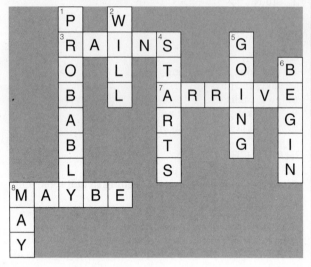

CHAPTER 4: THE PRESENT PERFECT AND THE PAST PERFECT

PRACTICE 1, p. 55
1. finished
2. stopped
3. put
4. known
5. been
6. wanted
7. said
8. had
9. gone
10. taken

PRACTICE 2, p. 55

Group I

Simple form	Simple past	Past participle
hurt	hurt	hurt
put	put	put
quit	quit	quit
upset	upset	upset
cut	cut	cut
shut	shut	shut
let	let	let
set	set	set

Group II

Simple form	Simple past	Past participle
ring	rang	rung
drink	drank	drunk
swim	swam	swum
sing	sang	sung
sink	sank	sunk

Group III

Simple Form	Simple Past	Past Participle
win	won	won
feed	fed	fed
weep	wept	wept
stand	stood	stood
keep	kept	kept
sit	sat	sat
stick	stuck	stuck
meet	met	met
have	had	had
find	found	found
buy	bought	bought
catch	caught	caught
fight	fought	fought
teach	taught	taught
pay	paid	paid
bring	brought	brought
think	thought	thought

PRACTICE 3, p. 56
1. has taught
2. has sold
3. has loved
4. have had
5. have known
6. have played
7. have gotten
8. have gone
9. have been
10. has been

PRACTICE 4, p. 57
1. since
2. for
3. since
4. for
5. for
6. since
7. since
8. since
9. since
10. for

PRACTICE 5, p. 57
1. I have been in this class **for** a month.
2. I have known my teacher **since** September.
3. Sam has wanted a dog **for** two years.
4. Sara has needed a new car **since** last year / **for** a year.
5. Our professor has been sick **for** a week / **since** last week.
6. My parents have lived in Canada **since** December.
7. I have known Mrs. Brown **since** 1999.
8. Tom has worked at a fast-food restaurant **for** three weeks.

PRACTICE 6, p. 57
1. A: Have you ever eaten
   B: have . . . have eaten OR haven't . . . have never eaten
2. A: Have you ever talked
   B: have . . . have talked OR haven't . . . have never talked
3. A: Has Erica ever rented
   B: has . . . has rented OR hasn't . . . has never rented
4. A: Have you ever seen
   B: have . . . have seen OR haven't . . . have never seen
5. A: Has Joe ever caught
   B: has . . . has caught OR hasn't . . . has never caught
6. A: Have you ever had
   B: have . . . have had OR haven't . . . have never had
7. A: Have I ever met
   B: have . . . have met OR haven't . . . have never met
8. A: Have the boys ever been
   B: have . . . have been OR haven't . . . have never been

PRACTICE 7, p. 58

1. have you been
2. have you made
3. Have you always enjoyed
4. have
5. have you traveled
6. have been
7. have never wanted
8. Have you ever thought
9. haven't
10. haven't met

PRACTICE 8, p. 59

1. b   5. b
2. a   6. a, b
3. a, b   7. a
4. a   8. a

PRACTICE 9, p. 60

1. has not started school yet
2. has already learned the alphabet
3. has already corrected our tests
4. has not returned the tests yet
5. has not cooked dinner yet
6. has already cooked dinner

PRACTICE 10, p. 60

1. haven't met all my neighbors yet
2. has traveled
3. has already changed
4. has already given
5. hasn't invited
6. have just retired
7. haven't seen
8. haven't picked
9. has lived
10. have already spent

PRACTICE 11, p. 61

1. has . . . put   5. have met
2. has drunk   6. have . . . found
3. has . . . begun   7. have . . . paid
4. has won   8. have bought

PRACTICE 12, p. 62

1. C   8. F
2. F   9. C
3. F   10. C
4. F   11. F
5. C   12. F
6. F   13. C
7. F   14. F

PRACTICE 13, p. 62

1. a, c, d, e, g, h
2. c, e, f, i

PRACTICE 14, p. 63

1. c, i   4. j, d
2. k, e   5. l, f
3. a, g   6. b, h

PRACTICE 15, p. 63

(1) started, was, had, has become, has been
(2) has led, has made, took, went, have gone, hasn't ended

PRACTICE 16, p. 64

1. have been waiting . . . twenty minutes
2. has been watching . . . two hours
3. has been working . . . 7:00 this morning
4. has been driving . . . six hours
5. has been writing . . . three years
6. have been arguing . . . Jim brought home a stray cat
7. has been raining . . . two days
8. has been losing . . . she began her diet OR her birthday

PRACTICE 17, p. 64

1. F   3. T   5. T
2. F   4. F   6. F

PRACTICE 18, p. 64

1. b   5. a
2. b   6. a
3. a   7. b
4. b   8. a

PRACTICE 19, p. 65

1. has been getting
2. have known
3. have been studying
4. have collected / have been collecting
5. have risen
6. has become

PRACTICE 20, p. 66

1. need
2. is
3. Have you ever worked
4. have worked / 've worked
5. had
6. did you work
7. have worked / 've worked
8. have never had
9. did you like
10. did not like / didn't like
11. was
12. are you working
13. do not have / don't have
14. have not had / haven't had
15. quit
16. Are you looking
17. am going to go / 'm going
18. is looking
19. will do / 'll do
20. have never looked / 've never looked
21. will be / is
22. do not know / don't know
23. will find / 'll find
24. go

PRACTICE 21, p. 67

1. 2 Larry called Jane.
   1 Jane went out.
2. 2 I opened the door.
   1 Someone knocked on the door.

3. 1 Her boyfriend called.
   2 My sister was happy.
4. 1 He saw me putting on my coat.
   2 Our dog stood at the front door.
5. 2 Ken laughed at my joke.
   1 Ken heard the joke many times.
6. 2 Don opened his car door with a wire hanger.
   1 Don lost his keys.

PRACTICE 22, p. 67

Underlined words:
(1) had always watched
(2) had always read
(3) had never let . . . had always listened
(4) had always left
(5) 'd never put
(6) had never shared

1. had always watched
2. had always read
3. had never let
4. had always left
5. had never put
6. had never shared

PRACTICE 23, p. 68

1. c	4. d
2. f	5. b
3. e	6. a

PRACTICE 24, p. 68

1. A: Did you enjoy
   B: enjoyed
2. A: Did you see
   B: was . . . hadn't seen
3. A: haven't seen
   B: is . . . haven't seen
4. A: Did you get
   B: got . . . had already begun
5. had already gone
6. have painted
7. have you painted
8. A: were painting . . . walked
   B: have been painting

PRACTICE 25, p. 69

1. Where were you? I **have been** waiting for you for an hour.
2. Anna **has** been a soccer fan **for** a long time.
3. Since I **was** a child, I have liked to solve puzzles.
4. Have you ever **wanted** to travel around the world?
5. The family **has been** at the hospital since they **heard** about the accident.
6. My sister is only 30 years old, but her hair has **begun** to turn gray.
7. Jake has been working as a volunteer at the children's hospital **for** several years.
8. Steve has worn his black suit only once since he **bought** it.
9. My cousin **has been** studying for medical school exams since last month.
10. I don't know the results of my medical tests **yet.** I'll find out soon.
11. The phone **had** already stopped ringing when Michelle entered her apartment.

PRACTICE 26, p. 70

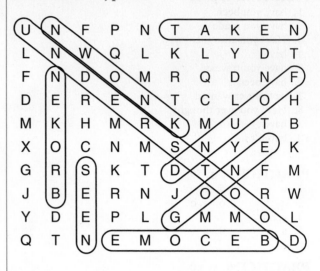

CHAPTER 5: ASKING QUESTIONS

PRACTICE 1, p. 71

1. c	4. c, a
2. b	5. b
3. a	6. b

PRACTICE 2, p. 72

1. Do you like coffee?
2. Does Tom like coffee?
3. Is Pietro watching TV?
4. Are you having lunch with Raja?
5. Did Rafael walk to school?
6. Was Clarita taking a nap?
7. Will Ted come to the meeting?
8. Is Ingrid a good artist?
9. Were you at the wedding?

PRACTICE 3, p. 73

1. A: Is	5: A: Have
B: is	B: haven't
2. A: Is	6. A: Did
B: isn't	B: didn't
3. A: Does	7. A: Are
B: does	B: am
4. A: Do	8. A: Will
B: do	B: will

PRACTICE 4, p. 73

1. A: Do	6. A: Does
B: don't	B: does
2. A: Are	7. A: Is
B: aren't	B: is
3. A: Is	8. A: Does
B: isn't	B: doesn't
4. A: Do	9. A: Will
B: do	B: won't
5. A: Do	
B: don't	

PRACTICE 5, p. 74

1. A: Does Jane
   B: she does
2. A: Does George
   B: he doesn't
3. A: Did Jane and Anna
   B: they did
4. A: Did Jane
   B: she didn't
5. A: Did George
   B: he did
6. A: Did Jane and Anna
   B: they didn't
7. A: Did George and John
   B: they did
8. A: Will Jane
   B: she will
9. A: Will George and Anna
   B: they will
10. A: Will John
    B: he won't

PRACTICE 6, p. 75

1. does Phil work
2. does Phil work
3. is Marta making
4. did she say
5. did Jean and Don visit
6. did they visit her

PRACTICE 7, p. 75

1. Does
2. Where
3. Is
4. When
5. Will
6. When
7. Are
8. Where
9. Is
10. Where
11. Did
12. When

PRACTICE 8, p. 76

Question word	Helping verb	Subject	Main verb	Rest of sentence
1. Ø	Did	you	hear	the news yesterday?
2. When	did	you	hear	the news?
3. Ø	Is	Eric	traveling	in South America?
4. Where	is	Eric	traveling?	
5. Ø	Will	the class	end	in December?
6. When	will	the class	end?	
7. Ø	Did	the teacher	help	a student?
8. Who(m)	did	the teacher	help?	
9. Ø	Will	the chef	cook	his special chicken dinner tonight?
10. What	will	the chef	cook	tonight?

PRACTICE 9, p. 77

1. Where did apple trees originate (b)
2. Where do apple trees grow (b)
3. Do they grow (a)
4. Do the trees produce apples (a)
5. When do they produce (b)
6. What do you find (b)
7. Will some of the seeds become (a)

PRACTICE 10, p. 78

1. d
2. e
3. c
4. b
5. f
6. a

PRACTICE 11, p. 78

1. a. you are going downtown
   b. are you going downtown
2. a. did Paul leave early for
   b. Paul left early
3. a. are your clothes on the floor
   b. are your clothes on the floor for
4. a. Mira needs money
   b. does Mira need money

PRACTICE 12, p. 78

1. Why are you waiting
2. When does Rachel start
3. Why did you miss
4. When are you leaving
5. When do you expect
6. Where did you eat lunch
7. What time did you eat
8. Why do you eat lunch
9. Where does the bullet train go
10. When will they build a bullet train
11. Where did you study
12. Why did you study

PRACTICE 13, p. 79

1. S Who is talking
2. O Who(m) do we hear
3. O Who(m) do you know . . .
4. S Who was on TV . . .
5. S What is happening . . .
6. O What does Jason know
7. O Who(m) did Gilda call
8. S Who answered the phone
9. O What did you say
10. S What is important

PRACTICE 14, p. 80

Part I
1. What
2. Who
3. Who
4. What
5. Who
6. What

Part II
1. Who(m)
2. Who
3. What
4. What
5. What
6. What

PRACTICE 15, p. 80
1. Who knows Julio?
2. Who(m) does Julio know?
3. Who will help us?
4. Who(m) will you ask?
5. Who(m) is Eric talking to?
6. Who is knocking on the door?
7. What surprised them?
8. What did Jack say?
9. What did Sue talk about?
10. Who(m) did Rosa talk about?

PRACTICE 16, p. 81
1. Who taught . . .
2. What did Robert see
3. Who got . . .
4. What are you making
5. Who(m) does that cell phone belong . . .
6. What is . . .

PRACTICE 17, p. 81

Answers will vary.
1. What does *abroad* mean
   It means in a foreign country
2. What does *underneath* mean
   It means directly under another object
3. What does *mild* mean
   It means fairly warm, not cold (when you are talking about the weather)
4. What does *cool* mean
   It means very attractive, fashionable, and interesting (when you are talking about a person)
5. What does *industrious* mean
   It means hard-working

PRACTICE 18, p. 82
1. What is Alex doing . . .
2. What did you do . . .
3. What do astronauts do . . .
4. What are you going to do . . .
5. What did Sara do . . .
6. What is Emily going to do . . .
7. What do you want to do . . .
8. What does Nick do . . .

PRACTICE 19, p. 82
1. Which
2. What
3. What
4. Which . . . which
5. What
6. which
7. What
8. What . . . which

PRACTICE 20, p. 83
1. What kind of music . . .
2. What kind of clothes . . .
3. What kind of Italian food . . .
4. What kind of books . . .
5. What kind of car . . .
6. What kind of government . . .
7. What kind of job . . .
8. What kind of person . . .

PRACTICE 21, p. 83
1. Who
2. Whose
3. Whose
4. Who
5. Who
6. Who
7. Whose

PRACTICE 22, p. 84
1. Whose house is that?
2. Who's living in that house?
3. Whose umbrella did you borrow?
4. Whose book did you use?
5. Whose book is on the table?
6. Who's on the phone?
7. Who's that?
8. Whose is that?

PRACTICE 23, p. 84
1. hot . . . hot
2. soon
3. expensive
4. busy . . . busy
5. serious . . . serious
6. safe
7. fresh . . . fresh
8. well . . . well

PRACTICE 24, p. 85
1. How often
2. How many times
3. How many times
4. How often
5. How often
6. How many times

PRACTICE 25, p. 85
1. How far is it
   How many miles is it
   How long does it take
2. How high is Mount Everest
   How many meters is Mount Everest
   How long did it take . . .
   How many days did it take . . .
3. How long is . . .
   How many miles is . . .
   How many days does it take . . .

PRACTICE 26, p. 86
1. far
2. long
3. often
4. far
5. far
6. long
7. high
8. long
9. often
10. far
11. long
12. often

PRACTICE 27, p. 87
1. How do you spell your name
2. How do you like . . .
3. How do you say . . .
4. How do you pronounce . . .
5. How do you feel . . .

PRACTICE 28, p. 87

1. a
2. b
3. c
4. a
5. b
6. c

PRACTICE 29, p. 88

1. will the clothes be dry
2. did you do
3. book did you download
4. long did it take
5. bread do you like
6. are you calling me
7. are you meeting
8. is taking you
9. you are leaving

PRACTICE 30, p. 89

1. What is Jack doing . . .
2. Who(m) is he playing . . .
3. What is Anna doing
4. What is she throwing . . .
5. What are Anna and Jack holding
6. What is . . .
7. Where are they
8. How long have they been playing
9. Who is winning . . .
10. Who won . . .

PRACTICE 31, p. 90

1. a. don't
   b. doesn't
   c. don't
   d. doesn't
   e. aren't
   f. doesn't
   g. do
   h. is
   i. am
2. a. didn't
   b. didn't
   c. wasn't
   d. did
   e. didn't
3. a. aren't
   b. is
   c. isn't
   d. wasn't
   e. wasn't
   f. were
4. a. hasn't
   b. haven't
   c. have
   d. hasn't
   e. has
   f. have

PRACTICE 32, p. 90

1. A: haven't you
   B: Yes, I have
2. A: has he
   B: No, he hasn't
3. A: didn't you
   B: Yes, I did
4. A: don't you
   B: Yes, I do
5. a. haven't they
   b. Yes, they have
6. a. hasn't she
   b. Yes, she has
7. a. is it
   b. No, it isn't
8. A: doesn't he
   B: Yes, he does

9. A: is it
   B: No, it isn't
10. A: is it
    B: No, it isn't
11. A: weren't they
    B: Yes, they were
12. A: will she
    B: No, she won't

PRACTICE 33, p. 91

1. **Who** saw the car accident?
2. How about **asking** Julie and Tim to come for dinner Friday night?
3. What time **does class begin** today?
4. Where **do** people go to get a driver's license in this city?
5. How long **does it take** to get to the beach from here?
6. She is working late tonight, **isn't** she?
7. **Whose** glasses are those?
8. **How tall is** your father?
9. Who **did you talk / have you talked** to about registration for next term?
10. How come **you are** here so early today?

PRACTICE 34, p. 92

1. When are you going to buy
2. How are you going to pay
3. How long have you had
4. How often do you ride
5. How do you usually get
6. Did you ride
7. Who gave
8. Did you ride
9. How far did you ride
10. Does your bike have
11. What kind of bike do you have
12. When did Jason get
13. Who broke
14. How did he break it
15. Did Billy get hurt
16. Did the bike have a lot of damage
17. Which wheel fell off
18. Has Jason fixed the bike yet

PRACTICE 35, p. 93

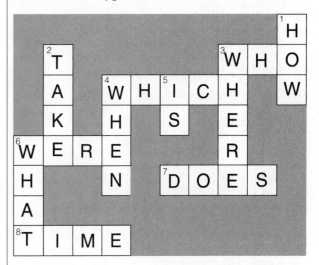

CHAPTER 6: NOUNS AND PRONOUNS

PRACTICE 1, p. 94

A (shark) is a (fish). Sharks live in oceans all over the (world). Some types are very large. The largest (shark) is the (size) of a (bus). It has 3,000 teeth, in five rows in its (mouth). When one (tooth) falls out, a new (tooth) grows in quickly. Many sharks are dangerous, and people try to avoid them.

PRACTICE 2, p. 94

Living things that breathe	Furniture	Places on a map	Fruits and Vegetables
children	beds	cities	apples
foxes	lamps	countries	cherries
men	shelves	lakes	carrots
mice	tables	oceans	peaches
cats		rivers	tomatoes
tigers			

PRACTICE 3, p. 95

1. houses
2. door
3. boxes
4. shelf
5. copies
6. families
7. woman
8. children
9. fish
10. fly
11. dishes
12. glasses
13. dollar
14. euros
15. roof
16. lives
17. radios

PRACTICE 4, p. 95

Underlined nouns:
1. Airplane**s** . . . wing**s**
2. bab**ies** . . . **teeth**
3. Child**ren** . . . swing**s**
4. No change.
5. potato**es**, bean**s**, pea**s**, . . . tomato**es**
6. No change.
7. animal**s** . . . zoo**s**
8. Human**s** . . . **feet**
9. No change.
10. Government**s** . . . tax**es**

PRACTICE 5, p. 96

       S   V   O
1. Caroline dropped a dish.
       S   V
2. The dish fell.
       S   V   O
3. The noise woke her baby.
       S   V
4. The baby cried.
       S   V   O
5. Caroline rocked her baby.
       S   V
6. The phone rang.
       S   V
7. A man came to the door.
       S   V
8. The dog barked loudly
       S   V   O
9. Caroline answered the door.

PRACTICE 6, p. 96

	subject	verb	object of verb
1.	Children	play	Ø
2.	Children	like	ice cream
3.	A package	arrived	Ø
4.	The mail carrier	delivered	the package
5.	My mother	sent	the package
6.	The passengers	boarded	the airplane
7.	The plane	left	the gate
8.	The plane	left	Ø

PRACTICE 7, p. 97

1. N
2. V
3. N
4. V
5. V
6. N
7. N
8. V
9. N
10. V
11. V
12. N

PRACTICE 8, p. 97

1. in
2. on
3. on
4. beside
5. above
6. below
7. behind
8. at
9. into
10. out

PRACTICE 9, p. 98

1. f
2. e
3. d
4. c
5. b
6. a

PRACTICE 10, p. 98

1. in / into . . . on
2. in . . . of
3. near . . . to
4. above . . . below
5. of
6. through . . . on
7. from

PRACTICE 11, p. 99

Part I
Circled words:
(1) in, in, over, through, on, under, into
(2) after, around, across, on, against, near
(3) behind, beneath

Underlined words:
(1) Jamaica, sky, beaches, trees, roof, door, house
(2) storm, neighborhood, street, ground, house, house
(3) clouds, sun

Part II
1. Dark clouds appeared in the sky.
2. The water came in under the door.
3. After the storm, the people walked around the neighborhood.
4. The tree had fallen on the ground/ across the street.
5. The sun had been behind the clouds.
6. The neighbors felt happy and grateful when they were standing beneath the hot Jamaican sun.

PRACTICE 12, p. 100
1. in
2. in
3. on
4. on
5. at
6. at
7. in
8. on
9. at
10. at
11. in
12. on
13. in
14. in
15. on

PRACTICE 13, p. 100
1. at . . . in . . . in . . . on . . . on
2. on . . . At . . . at . . . in . . . In

PRACTICE 14, p. 100
1. to the airport tomorrow morning
2. a new job last month
3. skis in the mountains in January
4. has breakfast at the coffee shop in the morning
5. jogged in the park last Sunday
6. bought a house in the suburbs last year

PRACTICE 15, p. 101
1. 1 the driver.
   2 at a busy intersection.
   3 at midnight.
2. 2 on the lake.
   3 last summer.
   1 a sailboat.
3. 2 in the river.
   1 several fish.
   3 last weekend.
4. 3 at noon.
   1 our lunch.
   2 in the park.
5. 1 a magazine.
   2 at the corner newsstand.
   3 after work yesterday.

PRACTICE 16, p. 101
1. are
2. are
3. is
4. is
5. are
6. is
7. are
8. is
9. are
10. are
11. is

PRACTICE 17, p. 101
1. make
2. need
3. Do
4. are
5. are
6. comes
7. is
8. pay
9. are
10. needs
11. go
12. work
13. are

PRACTICE 18, p. 102
1. loud → voice
2. sweet → sugar
3. easy → test
4. free → air
5. delicious → food . . . Mexican → restaurant
6. sick → child
7. sick → child . . . warm → bed . . . hot → tea

PRACTICE 19, p. 102
1. old
2. old
3. bad
4. easy
5. hard
6. narrow
7. clean
8. empty
9. safe
10. light
11. light
12. public
13. right
14. right
15. long

PRACTICE 20, p. 103
1. page numbers
2. paper money
3. apartment buildings
4. rose gardens
5. key chains
6. city governments
7. brick walls
8. egg cartons
9. mountain views
10. traffic lights
11. apple pies
12. steel bridges

PRACTICE 21, p. 103
1. b
2. c
3. a
4. b
5. b
6. a

PRACTICE 22, p. 104
1. T
2. T
3. T
4. T
5. F

PRACTICE 23, p. 104
1. The **mountains** in Chile are beautiful.
2. **Cats** hunt **mice**
3. **Mosquitos** are small **insects**.
4. Everyone has **eyelashes**.
5. Do you listen to any podcasts when you take plane **trips**?
6. **Forests** sometimes have **fires**. Forest **fires** endanger wild **animals**.

7. Sharp kitchen **knives** can be dangerous.
8. I couldn't get **concert** tickets for Friday. The **tickets** were all sold out.
9. There are approximately 250,000 different **kinds** of **flowers** in the world.
10. I applied to several foreign **universities** because I want to study in a different **country**.
11. Ted lives with three other university **students**.
12. In the past one hundred **years**, our daily **lives** have changed in many **ways**. We no longer need to use oil **lamps** or **candles** in our **houses**, raise our own **chickens**, or build daily **fires** for cooking.

PRACTICE 24, p. 105
1. a. her → Dr. Gupta
   b. She → Dr. Gupta
   c. them → students
   d. They → students
   e. they → classes
2. a. him → Dr. Reynolds
   b. He → Dr. Reynolds
   c. them → patients
   d. he → Dr. Reynolds
   e. him → Dr. Reynolds
3. a. It → my hometown
   b. I → Beth
   c. They → the people
   d. me → Beth
   e. They → the people
   f. you → you (the reader of this passage)
   g. they → the people
   h. you → you (the reader of this passage)

PRACTICE 25, p. 106
1. O
2. S
3. S
4. O
5. S
6. O
7. S
8. S
9. O
10. S
11. O
12. O
13. S
14. O

PRACTICE 26, p. 106
1. me, them, us, you, her, him
2. He, You, I, She, They, We
3. him and me, you and me, her and me, them and us
4. He and I, She and I, You and I

PRACTICE 27, p. 107
1. me
2. me
3. I
4. She
5. she . . . her
6. he . . . him
7. us . . . us
8. them . . . They

PRACTICE 28, p. 107
1. a
2. b
3. b
4. a
5. a
6. b
7. a
8. b
9. a
10. a

PRACTICE 29, p. 108
1. friend's
2. friends'
3. parents'
4. mother's
5. Carl's
6. Carl's
7. baby's
8. baby's
9. babies'
10. Ann's
11. Bob's
12. James's / James'

PRACTICE 30, p. 108
1. I met **Dan's** sister yesterday.
2. No change.
3. I know **Jack's** roommates.
4. No change.
5. I have one roommate. My **roommate's** desk is always messy.
6. You have two roommates. Your **roommates'** desks are always neat.
7. No change.
8. Jo Ann is **Betty's** sister. My **sister's** name is Sonya.
9. My name is Richard. I have two sisters. My **sisters'** names are Jo Ann and Betty.
10. I read a book about the changes in **women's** roles and **men's** roles in modern society.

PRACTICE 31, p. 108
1. your . . . yours
2. her, hers
3. his, his
4. your, yours
5. their, our, theirs, ours

PRACTICE 32, p. 109
1. her
2. hers
3. Our
4. theirs
5. your
6. mine . . . my . . . yours
7. their . . . theirs
8. mine . . . yours

PRACTICE 33, p. 109
1. myself
2. ourselves
3. himself
4. herself
5. themselves
6. yourself
7. yourselves
8. itself

PRACTICE 34, p. 110
1. cut myself
2. be proud of yourself
3. talks to himself
4. taught myself
5. blamed herself
6. help yourselves
7. takes care of himself
8. enjoyed themselves
9. worked for himself
10. introduce themselves

PRACTICE 35, p. 110
1. me . . . him
2. yourselves
3. itself
4. its . . . its
5. hers
6. him
7. yourself . . . your
8. our . . . our
9. ours
10. themselves
11. itself
12. himself

PRACTICE 36, p. 111

(1)
1. his
2. He
3. himself
4. he
5. him

(2)
1. Her
2. her
3. She
4. Our
5. We
6. It
7. her
8. mine
9. hers
10. I

(3)
1. He
2. his
3. his
4. Her
5. They
6. themselves
7. them
8. my
9. theirs
10. their

PRACTICE 37, p. 112

1. one . . . another . . . another . . . the other
2. one . . . another . . . the other
3. one . . . another . . . another . . . another . . . the other
4. one . . . the other
5. one . . . another . . . another . . . another . . . another . . . the other

PRACTICE 38, p. 112

1. The other
2. Another
3. The other
4. a. Another
   b. the other
5. a. another
   b. another
   c. another
   d. another
   e. another

PRACTICE 39, p. 113

1. The others
2. The others
3. Others
4. others
5. other
6. Others
7. Other
8. The others
9. The other

PRACTICE 40, p. 113

1. a
2. a
3. c
4. d
5. b
6. b
7. a
8. d
9. b

PRACTICE 41, p. 114

1. are
2. potatoes
3. by myself
4. on . . . at
5. vacation
6. us
7. its
8. our . . . yours
9. himself
10. the others

PRACTICE 42, p. 114

1. Look at those **beautiful** mountains!
2. The children played **a game** on Saturday afternoon at the park.
3. There are two **horses**, several **sheep**, and a cow in the **farmer's** field.
4. The owner of the store is busy **at** the moment.
5. The teacher met **her** students at the park after school.
6. Everyone **wants** peace in the world.
7. I grew up in a **very large city**.
8. This apple tastes sour. There are more, so let's try **another** one.
9. Some **trees** lose their **leaves** in the winter.
10. I am going to wear my **blue shirt** to the party.
11. People may hurt **themselves** if they use this machine.
12. Our neighbors invited my friend and **me** to visit **them**.
13. My **husband's** boss works for twelve **hours** every **day**.
14. The students couldn't find **their** books.
15. I always read **magazine** articles while I'm in the waiting room at my **dentist's** office.

PRACTICE 43, p. 115

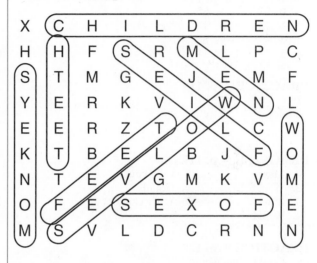

CHAPTER 7: MODAL AUXILIARIES

PRACTICE 1, p. 116

1. Ø
2. to
3. Ø
4. Ø
5. to
6. Ø
7. to
8. Ø
9. Ø . . . Ø
10. Ø . . . to
11. Ø . . . Ø

PRACTICE 2, p. 116

1. zebra
2. cat
3. Elephants
4. Monkeys
5. camels
6. cow
7. horse
8. donkey
9. squirrel
10. ants

PRACTICE 3, p. 117

1. possibility
2. possibility
3. permission
4. possibility
5. possibility
6. permission
7. possibility
8. permission
9. possibility
10. permission

PRACTICE 4, p. 117
1. I might take a nap.
2. Maybe she is sick.
3. Maybe there will be time later.
4. Our team may win.
5. You might be right.
6. We may hear soon.
7. It may rain.
8. It might snow.
9. Maybe she will come tomorrow.
10. Maybe she is at home right now.

PRACTICE 5, p. 118
1. b   4. a
2. c   5. b
3. c   6. a

PRACTICE 6, p. 118
1. b   5. b
2. b   6. a
3. a   7. b
4. a   8. a

PRACTICE 7, p. 119
1. e   4. b
2. d   5. c
3. f   6. a

PRACTICE 8, p. 119
1. May   5. will / could
2. Would   6. Could
3. May   7. Will / Could
4. Would

PRACTICE 9, p. 120
1. Could, Can, Would
2. Could, May, Can
3. Would, Could, Will
4. Can, May, Could
5. Will, Can, Could

PRACTICE 10, p. 120
1. shouldn't drive a long distance
2. should quit
3. should drive the speed limit
4. shouldn't give too much homework
5. should attend all classes
6. shouldn't be cruel to animals
7. should always be on time for an appointment
8. shouldn't throw trash out of your car window

PRACTICE 11, p. 121
1. j . . . i
2. e . . . f
3. b . . . g
4. h . . . d
5. a . . . c

PRACTICE 12, p. 122
1. a   6. c
2. c   7. a
3. b   8. c
4. a   9. b
5. b   10. c

PRACTICE 13, p. 122
1. have   5. have
2. must   6. have
3. has   7. had
4. had   8. have

PRACTICE 14, p. 123
1. had to   5. have to
2. had to   6. had to
3. have to   7. have got to . . . have to
4. had to   8. must

PRACTICE 15, p. 123
1. had to study
2. had to turn off
3. Did . . . have to work
4. had to see
5. had to be
6. had to close

PRACTICE 16, p. 124
1. You didn't stop at the red light. You have to stop at red lights.
2. You've got to be more responsible.
3. You have to send them back and get the right ones.
4. Okay. Everyone must fill out an application. Here it is.
5. No. He just has to stay in bed for a couple of days and drink plenty of water.

PRACTICE 17, p. 124
1. must   7. must not
2. don't have to   8. don't have to
3. must not   9. must not
4. don't have to   10. don't have to
5. don't have to   11. must not
6. must not

PRACTICE 18, p. 125
People have to / must
eat and drink in order to live
pay taxes
stop when they see a police car's lights behind them

People must not
fall asleep while driving
drive without a license
take other people's belongings

People don't have to
cook every meal themselves
say "sir" or "madam" to others
stay in their homes in the evening

PRACTICE 19, p. 126
1. c   4. a
2. d   5. b
3. e

PRACTICE 20, p. 126
1. 2   5. 2
2. 1   6. 2
3. 2   7. 2
4. 1   8. 1

PRACTICE 21, p. 126

1. will	7. should
2. can't	8. won't
3. wouldn't	9. could
4. wouldn't	10. shouldn't
5. can	11. doesn't
6. do	12. shouldn't

PRACTICE 22, p. 127

1. Wait
2. Don't wait
3. Read
4. Don't put
5. Come in . . . have

PRACTICE 23, p. 127

1. 1, 3, 2
2. 2, 1, 4, 3
3. 4, 2, 1, 3

PRACTICE 24, p. 128

Part I	*Part II*	*Part III*
1. fly	5. go	8. have
2. sail	6. shop	9. do
3. walk	7. see	10. plan
4. listen		11. tell

PRACTICE 25, p. 129

1. prefer
2. like
3. would rather
4. would rather
5. A: prefer
   B: likes . . . would rather
6. B: prefer
   A: like

PRACTICE 26, p. 129

1. Alex prefers swimming to jogging.
2. My son would rather eat fish than beef.
3. Kim prefers salad to dessert
4. In general, Nicole likes coffee better than tea.
5. Bill would rather teach history than work as a business executive.
6. When considering a pet, Sam likes dogs better than cats.
7. On a long trip, Susie prefers driving to riding in the back seat.
8. I would rather study in a noisy room than study in a quiet room.
9. Alex would rather play soccer than baseball.

PRACTICE 27, p. 130

1. must	7. might
2. has to	8. wasn't able to
3. might	9. Would you
4. could	10. must
5. must	11. ought to
6. isn't able to	12. should

PRACTICE 28, p. 131

1. Before I left on my trip last month, I **had to** get a passport.

2. Could **you bring** us more coffee, please?
3. Ben can **drive**, but he prefers **to** take the bus.
4. A few of our classmates can't **come** to the school picnic.
5. **Could / Would / Will / Can** you take our picture, please?
6. Come in, come in! It's so cold outside. You **must be** freezing!
7. Jim would rather **have** Fridays off in the summer than a long vacation.
8. I must **read** several long books for my literature class.
9. Take your warm clothes with you. It **may / might /** snow. OR Maybe **it will** snow.
10. It's such a gorgeous day. Why **don't we** go to a park or the beach?

PRACTICE 29, p. 132

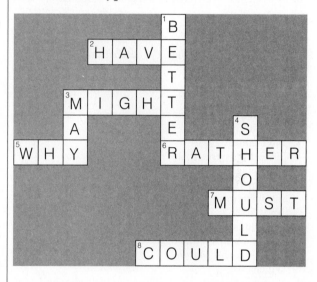

CHAPTER 8: CONNECTING IDEAS

PRACTICE 1, p. 133

               noun + noun + noun
1. My kitchen has a new <u>sink</u>, <u>refrigerator</u>, and <u>oven</u>.

         adjective + adjective
2. Danny is a <u>bright</u> and <u>happy</u> child.

   verb   +   verb
3. I <u>picked</u> up the telephone and <u>dialed</u> Steve's number.

       noun + noun + noun
4. I have a <u>computer</u>, a <u>printer</u>, and a <u>scanner</u> in my home office.

       verb   +   verb
5. The cook <u>washed</u> the vegetables and <u>put</u> them in boiling water.

      adj. + adj.
6. My feet were <u>cold</u> and <u>wet</u>.

      adj. + adj.   +   adj.
7. Anita is <u>responsible</u>, <u>considerate</u>, and <u>trustworthy</u>.

                 noun +
8. The three largest land animals are the <u>elephant</u>, the

  noun   +   noun
<u>rhinoceros</u>, and the <u>hippopotamus</u>.

9. A hippopotamus <u>rests</u> in water during the day and <u>feeds</u> on land at night.

PRACTICE 2, p. 134

1. S V S V
   Birds fly, and fish swim.
2. Birds fly. Fish swim.
3. Dogs bark. Lions roar.
4. Dogs bark, and lions roar.
5. A week has seven days. A year has 365 days.
6. A week has seven days, and a year has 365 days.
7. Ahmed raised his hand, and the teacher pointed at him.
8. Ahmed raised his hand. The teacher pointed at him.

PRACTICE 3, p. 134

1. No change.
2. I opened the door, walked into the room, and sat down at my desk.
3. No change.
4. Their flag is green, black, and yellow.
5. No change.
6. Tom made a sandwich, poured a glass of juice, and sat down to eat his lunch.
7. Ms. Parker is intelligent, friendly, and kind.
8. No change.
9. Did you bring copies of the annual report for Sue, Dan, Joe, and Mary?
10. No change.
11. Can you watch television, listen to the radio, and read the newspaper at the same time?

PRACTICE 4, p. 134

1. I Amy jogged along the road. I road my bicycle.
2. C
3. C
4. I My mother trained our dog to get the newspaper. My father trained it to bark at strangers.
5. I The river rose. It flooded the towns in the valley.
6. C
7. C
8. C
9. I Sharon's children don't believe in astrology. They dismiss the information she gives them.

PRACTICE 5, p. 135

Answers may vary.

1. The twins' first names mean **silver** and **gold**.
2. In Japan, many people **live** a long time and **receive** respect when they are old.
3. The twins were **old** and **healthy**.
4. The twins **often** laughed and smiled.
5. The twins **always** had a simple lifestyle and always **walked** everywhere.
6. They **enjoyed** people, and they **enjoyed** each other.
7. Kin and Gin **had many** children **and** grandchildren.
8. When they died, Kin and Gin **weren't** together.

PRACTICE 6, p. 136

1. I talked to Amy for a long time, but she didn't listen.
2. No change.
3. No change.
4. No change.
5. Please call Jane, Ted, or Anna.
6. Please call Jane, Ted, and Anna.
7. No change.
8. I didn't call Leo, Sarah, or Hugo.
9. I waved at my friend, but she didn't see me.
10. I waved at my friend, and she waved back.

PRACTICE 7, p. 136

1. a
2. d
3. g
4. h
5. e
6. f
7. b
8. c

PRACTICE 8, p. 136

1. c
2. b
3. a
4. c
5. b
6. c
7. a
8. c

PRACTICE 9, p. 137

1. C
2. C
3. C
4. I I bought some apples, peaches, and bananas.
5. I I was hungry, so I ate an apple.
6. C
7. C
8. I My daughter is affectionate, shy, independent, and smart.

PRACTICE 10, p. 137

1. James has a cold. He needs to rest and drink plenty of fluids, so he should go to bed and drink water, fruit juices, or soda pop. He needs to sleep a lot, so he shouldn't drink fluids with caffeine, such as tea or coffee.
2. The normal pulse for an adult is between 60 and 80 beats per minute, but exercise, nervousness, excitement, and a fever will all make a pulse beat faster. The normal pulse for a child is around 80 to 90.
3. Edward Fox was a park ranger for 35 years. During that time, he was hit by lightning eight times. The lightning never killed him, but it severely burned his skin and damaged his hearing.

PRACTICE 11, p. 137

Gina wants a job as an air traffic controller. Every air traffic controller worldwide uses English, so it is important for her to become fluent in the language. She has decided to take some intensive English courses at a private language institute, but she isn't sure which one to attend. There are many schools available, and they offer many different kinds of classes. She has also heard of air traffic control schools that include English as part of their coursework, but she needs to have a fairly high level of English to attend. She has to decide soon, or the classes will be full. She's planning to visit her top three choices this summer and decide on the best one for her.

PRACTICE 12, p. 138

1. did	7. will
2. does	8. am
3. didn't	9. won't
4. do	10. has
5. wasn't	11. don't
6. is	12. doesn't

PRACTICE 13, p. 138

1. does	7. would
2. doesn't	8. does
3. isn't	9. can't
4. are	10. is
5. will	11. does
6. can	12. did

PRACTICE 14, p. 138

1. does Tom Tom does	5. did Jason Jason didn't
2. does Brian Brian doesn't	6. can Rick Rick can't
3. was I I was	7. does Laura Laura does
4. did Jean Jean did	8. does Alice Alice doesn't

PRACTICE 15, p. 139

Part I
1. can't either
2. doesn't either
3. did too
4. did too
5. couldn't either
6. would too

Part II
7. so is
8. neither did
9. neither is
10. neither have
11. so did
12. so does

PRACTICE 16, p. 139

1. h	5. g
2. c	6. d
3. b	7. a
4. f	8. e

PRACTICE 17, p. 140

1. Because his coffee was cold, Jack didn't finish it. **H**e left it on the table and walked away.
2. I opened the window because the room was hot. **A** nice breeze came in.
3. Because the weather was bad, we canceled our trip into the city. **W**e stayed home and watched TV.
4. Debbie loves gymnastics. **B**ecause she hopes to be on an Olympic team, she practices hard every day.
5. Francisco is very good in math. **B**ecause several colleges want him to attend, they are offering him full scholarships.

PRACTICE 18, p. 140

1. *lose weight*—Eric went on a diet because he wanted to lose weight.
2. *didn't have money*—The family couldn't buy food because they didn't have money.
3. *have several children*—Our neighbors are very busy because they have several children.
4. *be tired*—Because I am tired, I am going to bed.
5. *exercise every day*—Because Susan exercises every day, she is in great shape.
6. *have a high fever*—Because Jennifer has a high fever, she is going to the doctor.

PRACTICE 19, p. 140

1. a. He was hungry**, so** he ate a sandwich.
   b. **Because** he was hungry**,** he ate a sandwich.
   c. He ate a sandwich **because** he was hungry.
2. a. **Because** my sister was tired**,** she went to bed.
   b. My sister went to bed **because** she was tired.
   c. My sister was tired**, so** she went to bed.
3. a. Schoolchildren can usually identify Italy easily on a world map **because** it is shaped like a boot.
   b. **Because** Italy has the distinctive shape of a boot**,** schoolchildren can usually identify it easily.
   c. Italy has the distinctive shape of a boot**, so** schoolchildren can usually identify it easily on a map.

PRACTICE 20, p. 141

1. like	5. didn't change
2. don't like	6. didn't pass
3. is	7. ate
4. stayed	8. were

PRACTICE 21, p. 142

1. b	5. a
2. a	6. a
3. a	7. b
4. b	8. b

PRACTICE 22, p. 142

1. because	6. Even though
2. even though	7. Because
3. even though	8. Because
4. even though	9. Even though
5. because	

PRACTICE 23, p. 143

1. because
2. because
3. although
4. Because
5. Although
6. although
7. because

PRACTICE 24, p. 144

1. c	6. c
2. a	7. b
3. c	8. b
4. b	9. a
5. b	10. c

PRACTICE 25, p. 145

1. I don't drink coffee, and my roommate **doesn't** either.
2. The flight was overbooked, **so** I had to fly on another airline. OR **Because** the flight was overbooked, I had to fly on another airline.
3. Many people use computers for email**,** the Internet, and word processing.
4. Even **though** my father works two jobs, he always has time to play soccer or baseball on weekends with his family.
5. I saw a bad accident**,** and my sister **did** too.
6. Oscar always pays his bills on time**,** but his brother **doesn't**.
7. **Although / Even though** my mother is afraid of heights, I took her up to the observation deck at the top of the building. OR Because . . . I **didn't take** her . . .
8. Janey doesn't like to get up early**,** and **Joe doesn't either / neither does Joe**.
9. My mother and my father **immigrated** to this country 30 years ago.
10. **Because** Maya is very intelligent, her parents want to put her in an advanced program at school.

PRACTICE 26, p. 146

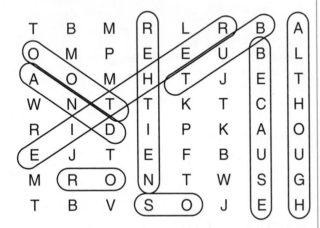

CHAPTER 9: COMPARISONS

PRACTICE 1, p. 147

1. (just) as busy as Jason (is).
2. (nearly) as busy as Jason (is)
3. (nearly) as tired as Susan (was).
4. (nearly) as tired as Susan (was).
5. (just) as lazy as her sister Amanda (is)
6. (nearly) as lazy as Alan (is)

PRACTICE 2, p. 147

1. aren't as strong as
2. is as tall as
3. isn't as wealthy as
4. isn't as polluted as
5. isn't as studious as
6. aren't as difficult as

PRACTICE 3, p. 148

Part I

1. not nearly as
2. almost as / not quite as
3. not nearly as
4. just as

Part II

5. just as
6. not nearly as
7. almost as / not quite as
8. not nearly as

Part III

9. just as
10. not nearly as
11. almost as / not quite as

Part IV

12. just as
13. almost as
14. just as
15. not nearly as
16. almost as / not quite as

PRACTICE 4, p. 149

Part I

1. as snow
2. as ice
3. as a picture
4. as a bat
5. as a bone
6. as a pillow
7. as a wink
8. as a mouse
9. as a bird
10. as pie

Part II

11. cold as ice
12. quick as a wink
13. blind as a bat
14. white as snow
15. quiet as a mouse
16. pretty as a picture
17. easy as pie
18. free as a bird
19. soft as a pillow
20. dry as a bone

PRACTICE 5, p. 150

1. stronger . . . the strongest
2. more important . . . the most important
3. softer . . . the softest
4. lazier . . . the laziest
5. more wonderful . . . the most wonderful
6. calmer . . . the calmest
7. tamer . . . the tamest
8. dimmer . . . the dimmest
9. more convenient . . . the most convenient
10. more clever / cleverer . . . the most clever / the cleverest
11. better . . . the best
12. worse . . . the worst
13. farther / further . . . the farthest / the furthest
14. slower . . . the slowest
15. more slowly . . . the most slowly

PRACTICE 6, p. 151

1. older than
2. more expensive than
3. larger
4. hotter than
5. slower than
6. creamier than
7. worse than
8. faster than
9. more important
10. quicker than

11. heavier
12. safer than
13. more difficult than

PRACTICE 7, p. 151
1. colder than . . . higher
2. foggier . . . sunnier
3. drier . . . healthier
4. more international . . .
   more expensive . . . cheaper

PRACTICE 8, p. 152
1. prettier
2. more careful
3. more energetic
4. more comfortable
5. more generous
6. richer
7. quietly . . . quiet
8. quiet . . . noisier . . . more noisily . . . more noisily . . .
   more noisily

PRACTICE 9, p. 153
1. the worst
2. worse
3. the best
4. better
5. the worst
6. worse
7. the worst
8. better

PRACTICE 10, p. 153
1. a, b
2. b
3. a, b
4. b
5. b
6. a, b

PRACTICE 11, p. 153
1. more slowly (adv)
2. slower (adj)
3. more serious (adj)
4. more seriously (adv)
5. more politely (adv)
6. more polite (adj)
7. more careful (adj)
8. more carefully (adv)
9. more clearly (adv)
10. clearer (adj)

PRACTICE 12, p. 154
1. I did / me
2. she is / her
3. she did / her
4. I was / me
5. he will / him
6. he has / him
7. I am / me
8. he is / him
9. I am / me
10. she is / her

PRACTICE 13, p. 155
1. a
2. b, c, d
3. a
4. b, c, d
5. b, c, d
6. a
7. b, c, d
8. a
9. b, c, d

PRACTICE 14, p. 155
2. not as friendly as → less friendly than
   not as interesting as → less interesting than
   not as difficult → less difficult
3. not as convenient as → less convenient than
   not as close . . . as (No change.)
   not as exciting as → less exciting than
4. not as comfortable . . . as → less comfortable . . . than
   not as unhappy as → less unhappy than
   not as bad as (No change.)

PRACTICE 15, p. 156
1. a, b, c
2. a, c
3. a, b, c
4. b, c
5. a, b
6. a

PRACTICE 16, p. 157
1. Sam enjoys football more than his best friend **does**.
2. No change.
3. The coach helped Anna more than Nancy **did**. OR
   The coach helped Anna more than **she** / **he helped**
   Nancy.
4. Sara likes tennis more than her husband **does**.
5. No change.
6. No change.
7. Charles knows Judy better than Kevin **does**. OR
   Charles knows Judy better than **he knows** Kevin.

PRACTICE 17, p. 157
1. more books
2. more enjoyment
3. more news
4. more readers
5. more cell phones
6. more things

PRACTICE 18, p. 158
Part I. Adjectives
1. more pleasant
2. louder
3. more difficult

Part II. Adverbs
4. more clearly
5. more carefully
6. faster

Part III. Nouns
7. more homework
8. more snow
9. more friends
10. more problems
11. more cars
12. more money

PRACTICE 19, p. 159
1. better and better
2. bigger and bigger
3. warmer and warmer
4. noisier and noisier
5. madder and madder
6. longer and longer
7. more and more expensive
8. friendlier and friendlier / more and more friendly
9. worse and worse

PRACTICE 20, p. 159
1. more . . . stronger
2. softer . . . easier
3. simpler . . . more relaxed
4. longer . . . more tired
5. harder . . . more

PRACTICE 21, p. 160
1. more she talked, the more excited she got
2. more he talked, the hungrier I got
3. the older you are, the more you understand
4. faster he talked, the more confused I became
5. the more the fans clapped and cheered, the better
   their team played

PRACTICE 22, p. 160
1. the tallest mountain
2. the biggest organ
3. the most common word
4. the farthest planet
5. The most popular sport
6. the most intelligent animals
7. the worst flood . . . the highest level
8. the best policy

PRACTICE 23, p. 161

Part I
1. the most difficult . . . ever
2. the easiest . . . ever
3. the most interesting . . . in
4. the best . . . of
5. the wisest . . . ever
6. the fastest . . . of
7. the most artistic of
8. the most brilliant . . . in
9. the most successful . . . in
10. the busiest . . . in
11. the most generous . . . ever
12. the most important . . . in

Part II
13. the least ambitious of
14. the least expensive . . . ever
15. the least populated . . . in
16. the least anxious . . . ever

PRACTICE 24, p. 162

Part I
1. A pencil . . . a phone
2. A diamond ring . . . a paper clip
3. A cup of coffee . . . a bag of coffee beans
4. Radios . . . MP3 players . . . big screen TVs
5. A compact car . . . a house
6. Footballs, soccer balls, . . . basketballs . . . table-tennis balls

Part II
7. Angel Falls . . . than Niagara Falls
8. Giessbach Falls . . . as Cuquenán Falls
9. Angel Falls . . . of all
10. Niagara Falls . . . as Angel Falls
11. Giessbach Falls . . . as Cuquenán Falls

Part III
12. Air . . . than iron
13. Iron . . . than wood
14. iron . . . of all
15. Air . . . as water
16. air . . . of all
17. Water . . . as air
18. Water . . . iron . . . than wood

PRACTICE 25, p. 163
1. a   5. a
2. b   6. b
3. b   7. a
4. a   8. b

PRACTICE 26, p. 164
1. the funniest . . . funnier
2. sadder . . . the saddest

3. the best . . . better
4. more exhausting . . . the most exhausting
5. happier . . . the happiest
6. more entertaining . . . the most entertaining
7. harder . . . the hardest
8. hotter . . . the hottest

PRACTICE 27, p. 164
1. c   6. a
2. c   7. b
3. c   8. c
4. a   9. a
5. b   10. c

PRACTICE 28, p. 165
1. more intelligent than . . . the smartest . . . in
2. the most popular . . . in
3. smaller than
4. More potatoes . . . than
5. the closest . . . faster than
6. the largest . . . in . . . the smallest . . . of
7. more information
8. kinder . . . more generous
9. more honest . . . than
10. the worst
11. the safest
12. faster . . . than
13. bigger than

PRACTICE 29, p. 166
1. alike   6. like
2. like   7. alike
3. alike   8. like
4. alike   9. like
5. like   10. alike

PRACTICE 30, p. 166
1. different from   7. the same as
2. similar to   8. the same as
3. the same as   9. different from
4. different from   10. similar to
5. the same as   11. different from
6. similar to

PRACTICE 31, p. 167

Part I
1. A is like D.
2. A and D are alike.
3. C is similar to A and D.
4. B is different from A, C, and D.

Part II
5. similar to
6. the same as
7. different
8. the same as
9. different from

PRACTICE 32, p. 167
1. like
2. like
3. alike
4. A: alike
   B: the same . . . the same . . . the same
5. like

6. A: like
   B: similar
7. alike . . . alike . . . different
8. the same . . . the same . . . different

PRACTICE 33, p. 168
1. My brother is older **than** me.
2. A sea is **deeper** than a lake.
3. A donkey isn't as big **as** a horse.
4. Ellen is **the** happiest person I've ever met.
5. When I feel embarrassed, my face gets **hotter and hotter**.
6. One of **the** largest **animals** in the world is the hippopotamus.
7. The traffic on the highway is **worse** than it used to be.
8. Jack is the same **age as** Jerry / **as old as** Jerry.
9. Peas are similar **to** beans, but they have several differences.
10. Last winter was pretty mild. This winter is cold and rainy. It's much **rainier** than last winter.
11. Mrs. Peters, the substitute teacher, is **friendlier** than the regular instructor.
12. Although alligators and crocodiles are similar, alligators are **not as big as** / **smaller than** crocodiles.
13. Mohammed and Tarek come from different countries, but they became friends easily because they speak **the** same language, Arabic.

PRACTICE 34, p. 169

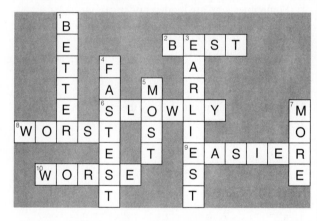

CHAPTER 10: THE PASSIVE

PRACTICE 1, p. 170
1. active, grow
2. passive, is grown
3. active, wrote
4. passive, was written
5. active, explained
6. passive, was explained
7. passive, are designed
8. active, design
9. active, are fixing
10. passive, is being fixed

PRACTICE 2, p. 170
1. is delivered
2. is being delivered
3. has been delivered
4. was delivered
5. was being delivered
6. is going to be delivered
7. will be delivered

PRACTICE 3, p. 171

Present		Present perfect	
1.	c	13.	p
2.	a	14.	n
3.	b	15.	m
4.	d	16.	o

Past		Progressive	
5.	e	17.	r
6.	g	18.	q
7.	h	19.	s
8.	f	20.	t

Future
9. k
10. i
11. l
12. j

PRACTICE 4, p. 172
1. brought
2. built
3. bought
4. carried
5. done
6. eaten
7. found
8. given
9. gone
10. grown
11. hit
12. hurt
13. left
14. lost
15. made
16. planned
17. played
18. pulled
19. read
20. saved
21. sent
22. spoken
23. spent
24. taken
25. taught
26. visited
27. worn
28. written

PRACTICE 5, p. 172
1. is spoken
2. are written
3. are read
4. was built
5. were found
6. has been eaten
7. is going to be visited
8. will be played
9. are going to be taken
10. have been grown
11. are being worn
12. was being carried

PRACTICE 6, p. 173
Part I
1. are collected
2. are written
3. is grown
4. are eaten
5. am paid
6. is understood

Part II
7. were collected
8. was built
9. were written
10. was destroyed

Part III
11. have been visited
12. has been spoken
13. has been read
14. has been worn

Part IV
15. will be discovered
16. will be visited
17. will be saved

Part V
18. is going to be hurt
19. are going to be offered
20. is going to be chosen

Part VI
21. is being announced
22. are being covered
23. am being treated
24. was being followed
25. were being washed

PRACTICE 7, p. 175
1. a
2. b
3. b
4. a
5. b
6. a
7. b

PRACTICE 8, p. 175
1. Was the game seen by many people?
2. Will Pat be shocked by the news?
3. Is lunch being served by the restaurant now?
4. Are the rules understood by everyone?
5. Is the solution going to be explained by the professor?
6. Have you been accepted by the university?
7. Has the contract been signed by both the buyer and the seller?
8. Was the thief found by the police?

PRACTICE 9, p. 176
1. collect taxes
2. use the tax money
3. provides many services
4. use these services
5. build and repair roads
6. train police forces
7. operates the fire department
8. pays teachers
9. issues professional licenses
10. runs the postal system
11. maintain armies
12. manage health care

PRACTICE 10, p. 176
1. The City Film Society will show a new film from India, *Falling Rocks*.
2. Movie critics have reviewed the film.
3. Audiences gave the movie good ratings.
4. Did a famous writer write the movie?
5. A new actress plays the main female part.
6. Does someone commit a murder in the movie?
7. Does a spy kill the main character?
8. Will many people see the movie?
9. Is the movie going to win an award?

PRACTICE 11, p. 177
1. transitive — letter
2. intransitive — No object.
3. intransitive — No object.
4. intransitive — No object.
5. transitive — the ball
6. intransitive — No object.
7. intransitive — No object.
8. transitive — the vase
9. transitive — the book
10. intransitive — No object.

PRACTICE 12, p. 177
1. No change.
2. me; I was awakened by loud sounds around midnight.
3. a tree; A tree was struck by lightning.
4. No change.
5. my neighbor's car; My neighbor's car was hit by the tree.
6. the car alarm; The car alarm was activated by the impact.
7. No change.
8. the roof of the car; The roof of the car was damaged by the tree.
9. No change.
10. my neighbor; My neighbor is going to be upset by the damage.

PRACTICE 13, p. 178
Checked sentences: 2, 4, 6, 9

PRACTICE 14, p. 178

	passive verb	action performed by
1.	are used	unknown
2.	was opened	Shelley
3.	will be translated	unknown
4.	was stolen	unknown
5.	was designed	a famous architect
6.	is going to be built	unknown
7.	has been rented	a young family with two small children
8.	has also been rented.	unknown

PRACTICE 15, p. 179
1. The soccer game has been canceled
2. The meeting has been canceled by the president.
3. Ethnic dishes are served at that restaurant.
4. I was confused in class yesterday.
5. I was confused by the teacher's directions.
6. The dishes haven't been washed yet.
7. They should be washed soon.
8. Was this sweater washed in hot water?
9. I was invited to the party by Luis.
10. Have you been invited to the party?

PRACTICE 16, p. 179
1. Sometimes keys are hidden under cars.
2. Cats hide under cars.
3. Students are taught by teachers.
4. Students study a lot.
5. Cereal is often eaten at breakfast.
6. Cats eat cat food.
7. Mice are eaten by cats.
8. Songs are sung to children by their mothers.
9. Thai food is cooked in Thai restaurants.
10. Chefs cook in restaurants.

PRACTICE 17, p. 180
1. b
2. b
3. a
4. b
5. b
6. a
7. b
8. a

PRACTICE 18, p. 180
1. I — It **happened** many years ago.
2. C — (No change.)
3. I — I **went** to school yesterday.
4. I — Two firefighters **were injured** while they were fighting the fire.
5. I — Sara **accidentally broke** the window.
6. C — (No change.)
7. I — Timmy was **eating** when the phone rang.
8. I — I **agree** with you.
9. I — The little boy **fell** down while he was running in the park.
10. I — The swimmer **died** from a shark attack.
11. C — (No change.)
12. I — I **slept** for nine hours last night.

PRACTICE 19, p. 181

1. has to be returned
2. should be returned
3. must be sent
4. could be sent
5. should be sent
6. can be put away
7. may be thrown away
8. might be picked up
9. will be cleaned up

PRACTICE 20, p. 182

1. a. The animal should be treated by a veterinarian.
   b. The animal will be given medicine.
2. a. No, the last paragraph has to be changed.
   b. No, it must be signed by Mr. Hayes.
3. a. It might be bought by a famous hockey star.
   b. It may be converted into apartments.
4. a. The credit card company should be called immediately.
   b. The mistake ought to be fixed right away.
5. a. It should be read by everyone.
   b. A movie of the book will be made.
6. a. It should be shortened.
   b. It has to be done soon.

PRACTICE 21, p. 182

1. were used . . . appeared . . . were made . . . were worn . . . began . . . were called . . . became . . . remained . . . were put . . . wore . . . have been manufactured
2. are being sold . . . is displayed . . . aren't needed . . . have never worn . . . may disappear . . . will be considered

PRACTICE 22, p. 183

Part I

1. to
2. about
3. from
4. of
5. in / with
6. of
7. with
8. in / with
9. about
10. with

Part II

11. in
12. with
13. of
14. to
15. to
16. with
17. from

Part III

18. of
19. in
20. with
21. for

PRACTICE 23, p. 183

1. The little girl is **excited about** her birthday party.
2. Mr. and Mrs. Rose **are devoted to** each other.
3. Could you please help me? I need directions. I **am** lost.
4. The students are **bored with** their chemistry project.
5. The paper bags at this store **are composed of** recycled products.
6. Your friend needs a doctor. He **is** hurt.
7. How well are you **prepared for** the driver's license test?
8. Mary has been **engaged to** Paul for five years. Will they ever get married?

PRACTICE 24, p. 184

1. interesting
2. interested
3. exciting
4. excited
5. fascinated
6. fascinating
7. boring . . . confusing
8. bored . . . confused
9. interesting
10. fascinating . . . surprising

PRACTICE 25, p. 184

1. interested
2. confusing . . . confused
3. excited . . . exciting
4. surprising . . . surprised
5. embarrassing . . . embarrassed
6. fascinating . . . fascinated
7. satisfying . . . satisfying
8. inspiring . . . inspired

PRACTICE 26, p. 185

1. confusing
2. frustrated
3. confusing
4. embarrassed
5. embarrassing
6. interested
7. interesting
8. exhausting . . . tired
9. frightening
10. frightened

PRACTICE 27, p. 185

1. c
2. a
3. b
4. a
5. c

PRACTICE 28, p. 186

1. g
2. c
3. a
4. h
5. b
6. f
7. d
8. e

PRACTICE 29, p. 186

1. Get
2. got
3. am getting
4. got
5. Get
6. get
7. got
8. get
9. am getting
10. am getting

PRACTICE 30, p. 187

1. b, c
2. a
3. b, c
4. a
5. a
6. b, c
7. b, c
8. a

PRACTICE 31, p. 187

1. Ø
2. is
3. are . . . am
4. Ø
5. is
6. Ø
7. Ø
8. is
9. is
10. Ø

PRACTICE 32, p. 188

1. used to get
2. is used to working
3. used to play
4. used to be
5. is used to working
6. is used to eating

PRACTICE 33, p. 188

1. I was supposed to return this book to the library.
2. We are supposed to read Chapter 9 before class tomorrow.
3. I was supposed to go to a party last night, but I stayed home.
4. We are supposed to do Exercise 10 for homework.
5. It is supposed to rain tomorrow.
6. I am / you are supposed to take one pill every six hours.
7. I am supposed to dust the furniture and vacuum the carpet.

PRACTICE 34, p. 189

1. The moving boxes **were** packed by Pierre.
2. My uncle **died** in the war.
3. Miami **is** located in Florida.
4. I was very wor**ried** about my son.
5. Mr. Rivera **is** interested in finding a new career.
6. Did you tell everyone the **shocking** news?
7. After ten years, I **am** finally used to this wet and rainy climate.
8. The newspaper **is supposed** to come every morning before eight.
9. The Millers have been marr**ied to** each other for 60 years.
10. I **used** to drink coffee with cream, but now I drink it black.
11. What happen**ed** at the party last night?
12. Several people almost **got killed** when the fireworks exploded over them.
13. A new parking garage **is** being **built** for our office.
14. I have been living in England for several years, so I **am accustomed to** driving on the left side of the road.

PRACTICE 35, p. 190

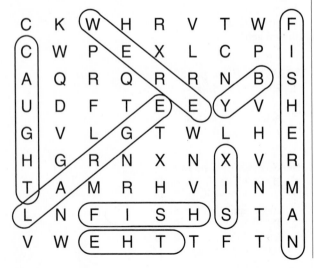

CHAPTER 11: COUNT/NONCOUNT NOUNS AND ARTICLES

PRACTICE 1, p. 191

1. a	9. an	16. a
2. an	10. an	17. an
3. a	11. an	18. a
4. an	12. a	19. an
5. a	13. a	20. a
6. a	14. an	21. a
7. an	15. a	22. an
8. a		

PRACTICE 2, p. 191

1. a chair
2. chairs
3. chairs
4. chair
5. furniture
6. Some
7. Furniture
8. some
9. desk
10. desks

PRACTICE 3, p. 192

Mail	Fruit	Jewelry	Furniture
bills	apples	bracelets	beds
checks	bananas	earrings	chairs
letters	oranges	necklaces	sofas
packages	strawberries	rings	tables

PRACTICE 4, p. 192

1. water
2. light
3. thunder
4. gold
5. help
6. fun

PRACTICE 5, p. 192

1. Ø . . . Ø
2. Ø . . . **boots** . . . **socks**
3. **cookies** . . . Ø
4. Ø . . . Ø . . . Ø
5. Ø . . . **bones**
6. Ø . . . Ø
7. Ø . . . Ø

PRACTICE 6, p. 193

1. word	word**s**
2. Ø	vocabulary
3. Ø	slang
4. Ø	homework
5. assignment	assignment**s**
6. dress	dress**es**
7. Ø	clothing
8. family	famil**ies**
9. Ø	knowledge
10. Ø	information
11. fact	fact**s**
12. Ø	luck

PRACTICE 7, p. 193

1. Tom lived in <u>a</u> big city for many years. However, three years ago he left the city. It had Ø pollution and Ø smog, and he couldn't breathe well. Now he lives in <u>a</u> small town in the mountains. He breathes Ø clean air and drinks Ø fresh water. He knows that it was <u>a</u> good idea to leave the city because his health is better.

2. Cornell University is named for Ezra Cornell. Ezra Cornell was a philanthropist who lived in Ithaca, New York. He loved the area and wanted to improve it. People there didn't have a library, and so he built one for them. Then, he wanted to build a university where people could gain Ø knowledge in Ø practical subjects, such as farming, as well as in Ø history, Ø literature, and Ø science. Cornell owned a large farm in the area, and in an act of generosity, he donated it as the site for the new university. Cornell University opened in 1865, and today it is known as an excellent university — one of the best universities in the world.

PRACTICE 8, p. 194
1. bread, corn, peas, and rice.
2. apple trees, grass, lakes, mountains, and scenery.
3. bracelets, jewels, jewelry, and rings.
4. equipment, machines, machinery, and tools.

PRACTICE 9, p. 194
1. one
2. much
3. many
4. much
5. much
6. much
7. much
8. many
9. one
10. much
11. many
12. much
13. much
14. one
15. many
16. many

PRACTICE 10, p. 194
1. a. apples, vegetables
   b. coffee, fruit, sugar
2. a. answers, persons (OR people), things
   b. English, slang
3. a. ideas, suggestions
   b. homework, information, work
4. a. police officers
   b. crime, garbage, traffic, violence

PRACTICE 11, p. 195
1. many letters are
2. much mail Ø
3. many men have
4. much English literature Ø
5. many English words
6. much gasoline Ø
7. much petrol Ø
8. many grandchild**ren**
9. much fun Ø
10. many islands are
11. many people Ø
12. many zero**es** / zeros are

PRACTICE 12, p. 195
1. a
2. some, many
3. a
4. some, much
5. some, many
6. some, much
7. an
8. a
9. an
10. some, many
11. a
12. an
13. some, many
14. some, much
15. a
16. some, much
17. a
18. an
19. some, much
20. some, many

PRACTICE 13, p. 196
1. a little . . . Ø
2. a little . . . Ø
3. a few orange**s**
4. a little . . . Ø
5. a little . . . Ø
6. a few suggestion**s**
7. a few question**s**
8. a few . . . Ø
9. a few . . . minute**s**
10. a little . . . Ø
11. a little . . . Ø
12. a little . . . Ø

PRACTICE 14, p. 196
1. d, f, g, h
2. c, e
3. c, d
4. c
5. a, c, f, h
6. d, g

PRACTICE 15, p. 197
(1) Scientists . . . animals . . . plants . . . place
(2) flowers . . . trees . . . deserts . . . oceans . . . mountains
(3) Rice . . . crop . . . world . . . crops . . . weather . . . fields
(4) Plants . . . health . . . air . . . trees . . . earth . . . air

PRACTICE 16, p. 198
1. e
2. a
3. g
4. i
5. j
6. h
7. b
8. f
9. c
10. d

PRACTICE 17, p. 198
1. jar
2. bottle
3. box
4. jar
5. can / tin
6. bag / box
7. jar
8. bottle
9. bag / box
10. can / tin

PRACTICE 18, p. 198
1. cup
2. pounds / kilos
3. glass
4. gallons
5. bottle / carton
6. piece
7. pieces
8. piece
9. sheets / pieces
10. loaf
11. piece
12. piece

PRACTICE 19, p. 199
1. many suitcases
2. much sunscreen
3. many pairs of sandals
4. much toothpaste
5. much luggage
6. much money
7. many days

PRACTICE 20, p. 199

1.	a	9.	some
2.	some	10.	an
3.	some	11.	some
4.	a	12.	a
5.	some	13.	some
6.	an	14.	a
7.	some	15.	some
8.	a		

PRACTICE 21, p. 200

1. a . . . some . . . a . . . some . . . some
2. some . . . some . . . some . . . some
3. some . . . some . . . a . . . a . . . some

PRACTICE 22, p. 200

1. A
2. the
3. a . . . a . . . a
4. the . . . the
5. the
6. a
7. a . . . a
8. the . . . the
9. a
10. the
11. a . . . a
12. The . . . the . . . the
13. a
14. the

PRACTICE 23, p. 201

1. some . . . a . . . The . . . the
2. some . . . a . . . a . . . a . . . The . . . The . . . the
3. A: an
   A: A . . . a . . . a
   B: the
   A: The . . . the . . . the
4. a . . . a . . . an . . . The . . . the . . . the . . . the . . . the

PRACTICE 24, p. 201

1.	a	11.	a
2.	a	12.	the
3.	a	13.	the
4.	The	14.	the
5.	a	15.	the
6.	the	16.	a
7.	the	17.	the
8.	the	18.	the
9.	the	19.	the
10.	the		

PRACTICE 25, p. 202

1. a . . . Ø . . . Ø
2. Ø
3. The
4. The . . . a . . . the . . . Ø . . . Ø . . . Ø
5. A: the
   B: the
6. the . . . the
7. Ø . . . Ø . . . Ø
8. A: the
   B: the . . . the
9. an . . . A . . . a . . . a . . . Ø . . . the . . . the . . . the

PRACTICE 26, p. 203

1. Ø
2. Ø
3. Ø . . . the
4. The . . . Ø
5. Ø . . . Ø
6. Ø . . . Ø
7. Ø
8. The . . . Ø . . . Ø
9. Ø
10. Ø . . . Ø . . . Ø
11. The
12. The . . . Ø . . . The . . . the

PRACTICE 27, p. 204

1. **the** Dead Sea
2. **the** Amazon River
3. Shanghai
4. **the** Sahara Desert
5. **the** Thames River
6. Europe
7. **the** Alps
8. Lake Tanganyika
9. North America
10. **the** Indian Ocean
11. **the** Netherlands
12. North America
13. Nepal
14. **the** Urals
15. Lagos
16. **the** United Arab Emirates

PRACTICE 28, p. 204

1. I'm taking **B**iology 101 this semester.
2. I'm taking history, biology, **E**nglish, and calculus this semester.
3. Some lab classes meet on **S**aturday.
4. My roommate likes **V**ietnamese food, and **I** like **T**hai food.
5. Shelia works for the **X**erox corporation. **I**t is a very large corporation.
6. Pedro is from **L**atin **A**merica. He speaks **S**panish.
7. My favorite park is **C**entral **P**ark in **N**ew **Y**ork.
8. No change.
9. I like Uncle **J**oe and Aunt **S**ara.
10. **S**usan **W**. Miller is a professor.
11. I am in **P**rof. **M**iller's class.
12. In January, it's winter in **C**anada and summer in **A**rgentina.
13. I would like to visit **L**os **A**ngeles.
14. It's the largest city in **C**alifornia.

PRACTICE 29, p. 205

Correct the errors.
1. The mail carrier brought only one **letter** today.
2. Mr. Dale gave his class **a** long history assignment for the weekend.
3. Tariq speaks several language**s**, including Arabic and German.
4. I usually have **a** glass **of** water with my lunch.
5. A helpful police officer gave us (**some**) **information** about the city.
6. This recipe calls for two cup**s** of nut**s**.
7. **Many** vegetable**s** are believed to have cancer-fighting ingredients.

8. Only applicants with the necessary **experience** should apply for the computer position.
9. When Vicki likes a movie, she sees it several time**s**.
10. No change.
11. Is it possible to stop all **violence** in the world?
12. Some of the **homework** for my English class was easy, but many of the assignment**s** were unclear.
13. Diane has been to Rome several time**s** recently. She always has **a** wonderful time.
14. Many parents need **advice** about raising children.
15. A person doesn't need **much** equipment to play baseball: just **a** ball and a bat.

PRACTICE 30, p. 206

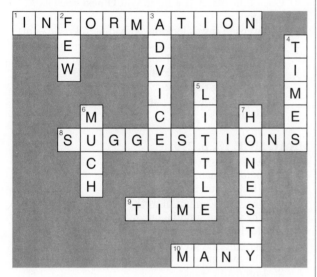

CHAPTER **12**: ADJECTIVE CLAUSES

PRACTICE 1, p. 207

1. who helped me move the refrigerator
   1: I thanked
   2: He helped
2. who was wearing a gray suit
   1: A woman asked
   2: She was wearing
3. that was wearing a blue coat
   1: I saw
   2: He was wearing
4. who had pulled his brother from the icy river
   1: The parents hugged
   2: He had pulled
5. that broke the vase
   1: The girl apologized
   2: She broke

PRACTICE 2, p. 208

Adjective clauses:
     S V
1. who live next to me
     S V
2. who live across the street
     S V
3. that is from India
     S V
4. who have children

     S   V
5. who teaches at the university
     S   V
6. who is training to play basketball in the Special Olympics.

PRACTICE 3, p. 208

1. *Long sentence 1:* The woman who answered the phone was polite.
   Long sentence 2: The woman that answered the phone was polite.
2. *Long sentence 1:* The man who played the guitar is also a singer.
   Long sentence 2: The man that played the guitar is also a singer.
3. *Long sentence 1:* I read about the soccer player who was injured yesterday.
   Long sentence 2: I read about the soccer player that was injured yesterday.
4. *Long sentence 1:* I know a man who has sailed around the world.
   Long sentence 2: I know a man that has sailed around the world.

PRACTICE 4, p. 209

1. who / that cuts hair
2. who / that makes pizza
3. who / that plays tennis
4. who / that teaches English
5. who / that trains horses
6. who / that eats meat
7. who / that drink tea
8. who / that fight fires

PRACTICE 5, p. 209

1. The woman that Jack met was polite.
2. The woman Jack saw was very tall.
3. The woman that Jack knows is a professor.
4. The student that the teacher helped was thankful.
5. The student I helped was happy about the exam.
6. The student who I just met won a scholarship.
7. The student whom you see over there is the class president.

PRACTICE 6, p. 210

1. S
2. O that
3. S
4. O that
5. S
6. S
7. O who
8. O who
9. S
10. O that
11. S

PRACTICE 7, p. 210

1. a, b, c, d
2. c, d
3. a, b, c, d
4. c, d
5. b, d
6. a, b, c

PRACTICE 8, p. 211

1. who / that
2. that / Ø / who / whom
3. that / Ø / who / whom
4. who / that
5. who / that
6. that / Ø / who / whom

PRACTICE 9, p. 211

1. b
2. a
3. b
4. b
5. a
6. a
7. b
8. b

PRACTICE 10, p. 212

1. O ~~which~~
2. S
3. O ~~that~~
4. O ~~which~~
5. S
6. S
7. S
8. O ~~that~~

PRACTICE 11, p. 212

1. that / which / Ø
2. that / which
3. that / which / Ø
4. that / which / Ø
5. that / which

PRACTICE 12, p. 213

1. I visited
2. that I drank
3. I was wearing
4. that I've known and loved
5. who I married
6. that we have had
7. which we bought

PRACTICE 13, p. 213

1. a, b, d, e
2. a, d
3. c, d
4. c, d, e
5. a, d
6. c, d, e
7. a, b, d, e
8. c, d, e
9. a, d
10. c, d

PRACTICE 14, p. 214

1. students . . . are
2. people . . . are
3. compound . . . consists
4. students . . . speak
5. people . . . know
6. student . . . is
7. people . . . live
8. person . . . makes
9. artists . . . make

PRACTICE 15, p. 215

1. a. we went to
   b. we went to
2. a. you introduced me to
   b. you introduced me to
3. a. I am quite familiar with
   b. which I am quite familiar
4. a. you should talk with
   b. whom you should talk
5. a. we are waiting for
   b. we are waiting for
6. a. I'm interested in
   b. I'm interested in

PRACTICE 16, p. 215

1. a. that . . . for
   b. which . . . for
   c. Ø . . . for
   d. which . . . Ø
2. a. that . . . to
   b. which . . . to
   c. Ø . . . to
   d. which . . . Ø
3. a. that . . . in
   b. which . . . in
   c. Ø . . . in
   d. which . . . Ø
4. a. that . . . with
   b. Ø . . . with
   c. who . . . with
   d. that . . . with
   e. whom . . . Ø

PRACTICE 17, p. 216

1. I enjoyed the CD [we listened **to** at Sara's apartment.]
2. I paid the shopkeeper for the glass cup [I accidentally broke **Ø**.]
3. The bus [we were waiting **for**] was only three minutes late.
4. Mrs. Chan is someone [I always enjoy talking **to** about politics.]
5. I showed my roommate the letter [I got from a co-worker **Ø**.]
6. One of the subjects [I've been interested **in** for a long time] is astronomy.
7. The people [I talked **to** at the reception] were interesting.
8. One of the places [I want to visit **Ø** next year] is Mexico City.
9. The website [I was looking **at**] had useful reviews of new computers.
10. The book [I wanted **Ø**] wasn't available at the library.
11. English grammar is one of the subjects [**Ø** which I enjoy studying the most.]
12. The friend [I waved **to** / **at**] didn't wave back. Maybe he just didn't see me.

PRACTICE 18, p. 216

1. whose daughter is a test-pilot
   1: I know a man.
   2: His daughter is a test-pilot.
2. whose husband is out of work
   1: The woman found a job at Mel's Diner.
   2: Her husband is out of work.
3. whose wallet I found
   1: The man gave me a reward.
   2: I found his wallet.

PRACTICE 19, p. 217

1. The firefighters are very brave. Their department has won many awards.
   → The firefighters whose department has won many awards are very brave.
2. I talked to the boy. His kite was caught in a tree.
   → I talked to the boy whose kite was caught in a tree.
3. The family is staying in a motel. Their house burned down.
   → The family whose house burned down is staying in a motel.
4. I watched a little girl. Her dog was chasing a ball in the park.
   → I watched a little girl whose dog was chasing a ball in the park.
5. The reporter won an award. Her articles explained global warming.
   → The reporter whose articles explained global warming won an award.
6. I know a man. His daughter entered college at the age of 14.
   → I know a man whose daughter entered college at the age of 14.
7. We observed a language teacher. Her teaching methods included role-playing.
   → We observed a language teacher whose teaching methods included role-playing.

8. The teachers are very popular. <u>Their</u> methods include role-playing.
   → The teachers whose methods include role-playing are very popular.

PRACTICE 20, p. 217

True (checked) answers:
1. a, c
2. c
3. b, c
4. c
5. a
6. a, c

PRACTICE 21, p. 218

1. who / that
2. who / that
3. that / which / Ø
4. whose
5. that / which
6. Ø / that / who / whom
7. whose
8. that / which
9. who / that
10. Ø / that / who / whom
11. who / that . . . Ø / that / who / whom . . . whom

PRACTICE 22, p. 218

1. a
2. b
3. b
4. b
5. a
6. a
7. a
8. b

PRACTICE 23, p. 219

1. A movie that **looks** interesting opens tomorrow.
2. My family lived in a house **that / which was** built in 1900.
3. There's the man that we **saw** on TV.
4. I don't know people **whose** lives are carefree.
5. It is important to help people who **have** no money.
6. At the airport, I was waiting for friends **Ø / that / who / whom** I hadn't **seen** for a long time.
7. The woman **who / that** lives next door likes to relax by doing crossword puzzles every evening.
8. My teacher has two cats **whose** names are Ping and Pong.
9. I enjoyed the songs which we **sang**.
10. The person to **whom** you should speak is Gary Green.

PRACTICE 24, p. 220

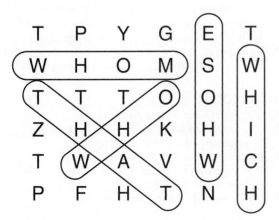

CHAPTER 13: GERUNDS AND INFINITIVES

PRACTICE 1, p. 221

1. moving
2. living
3. taking
4. buying
5. giving
6. doing
7. reviewing
8. finding
9. driving
10. retiring
11. getting married
12. working

PRACTICE 2, p. 221

1. went dancing
2. is going to go hiking
3. went shopping
4. go swimming
5. goes fishing
6. go sightseeing
7. go camping
8. go sailing
9. go skiing
10. went skydiving

PRACTICE 3, p. 222

1. to wait   INF
2. walking   GER
3. to help   INF
4. cleaning   GER
5. to order   INF
6. quitting   GER
7. to work   INF
8. to grow   INF

PRACTICE 4, p. 222

1. to invite
2. being
3. to pay
4. mailing
5. to pass
6. to consider
7. accepting
8. reading
9. visiting
10. to hurt
11. asking
12. to look
13. to try
14. to enjoy
15. opening
16. to keep
17. to give
18. to support
19. to finish

PRACTICE 5, p. 223

1. b
2. a, b
3. a, b
4. b
5. a, b
6. a, b
7. a, b
8. b
9. a
10. a, b
11. a, b
12. a, b
13. b
14. a
15. b

PRACTICE 6, p. 224

1. to go . . . to pay . . . to get . . . to apply . . . to receive
2. to take . . to go . . . to go . . . being . . . to go . . . skiing . . . swimming . . . sailing
3. getting . . . to tell . . . leaving . . . to have . . . to create . . . to take

PRACTICE 7, p. 224

Part I

1. to work
2. working
3. to work
4. working
5. to work
6. to work / working
7. to work
8. to work
9. working
10. to work
11. to work
12. working

Part II

13. to leave
14. to leave
15. leaving
16. leaving
17. leaving
18. leaving
19. to leave
20. to leave
21. leaving
22. to leave

Part III

23. to know
24. to know
25. to know
26. knowing
27. to know
28. to know
29. to know / knowing
30. to know
31. to know
32. to know / knowing

PRACTICE 8, p. 225

Part I

1. of <u>flying</u>
2. for <u>hurting</u>
3. in <u>helping</u>
4. at <u>listening</u>
5. of <u>working</u>
6. about <u>walking</u>
7. of / about <u>owning</u>
8. about <u>buying</u>

Part II

9. for <u>closing</u>
10. for <u>lending</u>
11. on <u>becoming</u>
12. for <u>taking</u>
13. on <u>eating</u>
14. to <u>finishing</u>
15. from <u>making</u>
16. about . . . <u>having</u>

PRACTICE 9, p. 226

1. for . . . for interrupting
2. in . . . in learning
3. for . . . for helping
4. on . . . on walking
5. for . . . for losing
6. like . . . like going
7. at . . . at drawing
8. in . . . in saving
9. about . . . about forgetting
10. about . . . about going
11. to . . . to going
12. of . . . of staying

PRACTICE 10, p. 226

Part I

1. e
2. f
3. a
4. b
5. c
6. d

Part II

7. j
8. k
9. l
10. g
11. h
12. i

PRACTICE 11, p. 227

(1) doing . . . doing / to do . . . to do
(2) to write . . . doing . . . thinking
(3) for being . . . to thank . . . sending . . . wearing . . . to wear
(4) to seeing . . . for taking

PRACTICE 12, p. 228

1. going
2. of driving
3. watching
4. cooking / to cook
5. of going
6. about becoming
7. having
8. running
9. on washing
10. from hitting
11. to be
12. about seeing

PRACTICE 13, p. 228

1. by holding
2. by reading
3. by telling
4. by watching
5. by running
6. by treating

PRACTICE 14, p. 229

1. by taking
2. by pouring
3. by stretching
4. by working
5. by saving
6. by following
7. by looking
8. by counting

PRACTICE 15, p. 230

1. a, d, e, f
2. a, b, c
3. b, c, d, f
4. a, b, d, e, f

PRACTICE 16, p. 230

1. a. It is . . . to learn
   b. Learning . . . is
2. a. Eating . . . is
   b. It is . . . to eat
3. a. Driving . . . is
   b. It is . . . to drive
4. a. It is . . . to swim
   b. Swimming . . . is
5. a. Is it . . . to live
   b. Is living
6. a. Is it . . . to complete
   b. Is completing

PRACTICE 17, p. 231

1. It is difficult for shy people to meet . . .
2. it is customary for young children to sleep . . .
3. It is necessary for airline pilots to have . . .
4. It is hard for many teenagers to wake up . . .
5. It is important for elderly people to keep . . .
6. It is boring for people to listen . . .
7. It is impossible for scientists to know . . .

PRACTICE 18, p. 231

1. a. for
   b. to
   c. to
   d. for
   e. to
   f. to
   g. for
2. a. to
   b. for
   c. for
   d. to
   e. to
   f. for
   g. to

PRACTICE 19, p. 231

1. to
2. for
3. for
4. to
5. for
6. to
7. to
8. for
9. to
10. for
11. for

PRACTICE 20, p. 232

1. turned on the TV (in order) to watch the news.
2. goes to the laundromat (in order) to wash his clothes.
3. runs (in order) to get to class on time.
4. open the bedroom windows (in order) to let in some fresh air.
5. calls his parents (in order) to ask them for some money.
6. have the radio on (in order) to listen to a baseball game.
7. go to the library (in order) to study in peace and quiet.

PRACTICE 21, p. 232

1. a. enough time to go
   b. too busy to go
2. a. tall enough
   b. too short
3. a. enough money
   b. too poor
4. a. too hot
   b. cool enough
5. a. too sick
   b. well enough
6. a. isn't old enough
   b. is too young

PRACTICE 22, p. 233

1. Ø . . . enough
2. too . . . Ø
3. Ø . . . enough
4. too . . . Ø
5. too . . . Ø
6. Ø . . . enough
7. too . . . Ø
8. Ø . . . enough

PRACTICE 23, p. 233

1. being
2. to spend
3. being
4. being
5. to find
6. being
7. to talk / talking
8. sitting
9. thinking
10. to think
11. speaking
12. making
13. to discuss

PRACTICE 24, p. 234

1. Studying
2. writing
3. to be
4. B: flying
   A: crashing
5. A: arguing . . . to disagree
   B: raising . . . to yell
   A: to get
6. A: to have
   B: to learn
7. A: doing
   B: going shopping
   A: shopping
8. A: putting
   B: forgetting to send

PRACTICE 25, p. 235

1. I decided not **to buy** a new car.
2. The Johnsons are considering **selling** their antique store.
3. Sam finally finished **building** his vacation home in the mountains.
4. My wife and I **go dancing** at the community center every Saturday night.
5. Suddenly, it began to **rain** and the wind started to **blow**.
6. The baby is afraid **of being** away from her mother for any length of time.
7. I am excited **about starting** college this September.
8. You can send your application **by** fax.
9. My country is **very** beautiful.
10. **It is** exciting to drive a sports car.
11. My grandparents enjoy **traveling** across the country in a motor home.
12. Elena made this sweater **by hand**.
13. Running **is** one of the sports we can participate in at school.
14. **Swimming** with a group of people is more enjoyable than **swimming** alone.
15. Meeting new people **is** interesting.

PRACTICE 26, p. 236

CHAPTER 14: NOUN CLAUSES

PRACTICE 1, p. 237

1. . noun clause
2. ? question
3. . noun clause
4. ? question
5. ? question
6. . noun clause
7. ? question
8. . noun clause
9. . noun clause
10. ? question
11. ? question
12. . noun clause

PRACTICE 2, p. 237

1. Helen works
2. Adam said
3. we are doing this
4. the new semester starts
5. everyone went
6. people believe
7. believes that story
8. cell phone is ringing

PRACTICE 3, p. 238

1. Vince lives
2. that woman is
3. Henri did
4. her phone number is
5. keys these are
6. Clara met
7. Carlo is absent
8. it is
9. Sam is studying
10. called
11. Ms. Gray will call
12. the president is going to say
13. is in that room
14. is in that drawer
15. a GPS system costs

PRACTICE 4, p. 238

1. did Marcos leave? . . . when Marcos left?
2. did he say? . . . what he said.
3. is the post office? . . . where the post office is?
4. is it? . . . what time it is?
5. did David arrive? . . . when David arrived.
6. is Ana from? . . . what country Ana is from.
7. was Kathy . . . why Kathy was . . .
8. lives . . . who lives . . .
9. car is . . . whose car is . . .
10. books are these? . . . whose books these are?

PRACTICE 5, p. 239

1. who Helen talked to
2. who lives
3. what he said
4. what kind of car Pat has
5. how old their children are
6. why you said
7. where I can catch
8. what this word means

PRACTICE 6, p. 240

1. b
2. a
3. a
4. b
5. b
6. a
7. b
8. a
9. a
10. b
11. a
12. b

PRACTICE 7, p. 240

1. people are saying . . . all the buildings are . . . my classes start . . . I register . . . I am taking . . . my professors will be
2. it will take . . . I came . . . I am

PRACTICE 8, p. 241

1. if / whether Tom is coming
2. if / whether Jin has finished medical school yet
3. if / whether Daniel has any time off soon
4. if / whether the flight is on time
5. if / whether there is enough gas in the car
6. if / whether Yuki is married
7. if / whether the Nelsons are going to move
8. if / whether Khaled changed jobs

PRACTICE 9, p. 241

1. if I'm going to need
2. what you want
3. if there is going to be
4. where birds go
5. if you can borrow
6. if Nasser has already left
7. why Harold left

PRACTICE 10, p. 242

1. rains
2. gets
3. like
4. runs
5. run
6. takes
7. enjoy
8. seems

PRACTICE 11, p. 242

1. c
2. f
3. a
4. g
5. h
6. b
7. d
8. e

PRACTICE 12, p. 243

1. I'm sorry that . . .
2. I predict that . . .
3. I'm surprised that . . .
4. Are you certain that . . .
5. Did you notice that . . .
6. It's a fact that . . .
7. A: How do you know that . . .
   A: I'm still worried that . . .
8. A: I heard that . . .
   A: Some people assume that. . . I think that . . .

PRACTICE 13, p. 243

1. are pleased that their granddaughter graduated from the university
   are glad that she was offered a good job
2. were worried that Po had been injured
   they were happy when Po called
3. was afraid that he had failed
   was not surprised that he had done well
4. was angry that Mark lied to her
   is sorry that she lent him money
5. that exercise can be good for the heart
   that eating a lot of red meat is bad for the heart

PRACTICE 14, p. 244

1. that Alice has a car
2. that the library is open on Sunday
3. that Ann speaks Spanish
4. that Alex passed his French course
5. that Mr. Kozari is going to be at the meeting
6. that these pants are clean

PRACTICE 15, p. 244

1. Alex asked, **"D**o you smell smoke**?"**
2. **"S**omething is burning**,"** he said**.**
3. **H**e asked, **"D**o you smell smoke**? S**omething is burning**."**
4. **"D**o you smell smoke**?"** he asked. **"S**omething is burning**."**
5. **R**achel said,**"T**he game starts at seven**."**
6. **"T**he game starts at seven**. W**e should leave here at six**,"** she said**.**
7. She said**, "T**he game starts at seven**. W**e should leave here at six**. C**an you be ready to leave then**?"**

PRACTICE 16, p. 245

One day my friend Laura and I were sitting in her apartment**.** We were having a cup of tea together and talking about the terrible earthquake that had just occurred in Iran**.** Laura asked me, **"**Have you ever been in an earthquake**?"**

"Yes, I have,**"** I replied**.**

"Was it a big earthquake**?"** she asked**.**

"I've been in several earthquakes, and they've all been small ones,**"** I answered**. "**Have you ever been in an earthquake**?"**

"There was an earthquake in my village five years ago,**"** Laura said**. "**I was in my house**. S**uddenly the ground started shaking**. I** grabbed my little brother and ran outside**. E**verything was moving**. I** was scared to death**. A**nd then suddenly it was over**."**

"I'm glad you and your brother weren't hurt,**"** I said**.**

"Yes, we were very lucky**. H**as everyone in the world felt an earthquake sometime in their lives**?"** Laura wondered**. "**Do earthquakes occur everywhere on the earth**?"**

"Those are interesting questions,**"** I said, **"**but I don't know the answers**."**

PRACTICE 17, p. 246

1. he . . . his
2. his . . . them
3. she . . . her
4. him . . . them
5. they . . . me . . . they
6. she . . . her
7. they . . . my
8. he . . . us . . . they . . . his

PRACTICE 18, p. 246

	Formal	*Informal*
1.	would meet	will meet
2.	was going to be	is going to be
3.	had	has
4.	needed	needs
5.	had flown	has flown
6.	were planning	are planning
7.	didn't want	doesn't want
8.	could take care of	can take care of

PRACTICE 19, p. 247

1. (that) you didn't have
2. (that) you hadn't found
3. (that) the Smiths had canceled
4. (that) it wouldn't rain
5. (that) the Whites had gotten
6. (that) Mei didn't exercise
7. (that) your computer wasn't working
8. (that) Ali was coming

PRACTICE 20, p. 248

1. how old I was
2. if he was going to be
3. if she had
4. if he had changed his
5. how long I had been
6. if she could speak
7. if he would be in his office
8. why she was laughing
9. if I had ever considered

PRACTICE 21, p. 248

1. "Have you ever gone skydiving?"
2. "Will you be at the meeting?"
3. "Are you going to quit your job?"
4. "Where is your car?"
5. "What did you do after class yesterday?"
6. "Do you know Italian?"
7. "Can you pick up my daughter at school?"
8. "Why aren't you working at your desk?"

PRACTICE 22, p. 249

1. why I had come here
2. if I had met many people
3. what I was going to study
4. how long I would stay
5. how I liked it here
6. where I was from
7. if the local people were friendly to me
8. how I had chosen this school
9. if I liked the weather here

PRACTICE 23, p. 249

1. (that) he was going to call me
2. (that) he had to talk to her
3. (that) she could meet me
4. (that) she wrote / had written him
5. she would see him
6. what he was doing

PRACTICE 24, p. 250

1. told
2. said
3. asked
4. told
5. said
6. told . . . said
7. asked . . . told . . . said
8. told . . . told
9. told
10. asked . . . said . . . asked . . . told

PRACTICE 25, p. 251

1. asked me where I lived.
2. asked me if / whether I lived
3. told him / replied / said that I had
4. told me / said that he was looking
5. told me / said that he didn't like living
6. asked him if / whether he wanted to move in with me.
7. asked me where my apartment was.
8. replied / told him / said that I lived
9. told me / said that he couldn't move
10. told me / said that he would cancel his
11. asked me if / whether that was okay.
12. told him / replied / said that I was looking forward to having him

PRACTICE 26, p. 251

1. b, e
2. a, b, c, d
3. b, f
4. a, d
5. a, c, e

PRACTICE 27, p. 252

1. that it was a beautiful day and he loved playing in the sun
2. what he was doing . . . where he was going
3. that he was carrying food to the nest
4. why he was working so hard in the beautiful summer weather
5. that if he brought food to the nest in the summer, he could have food in the winter
6. if he could take a break then, and play with him instead of working
7. that he couldn't
8. that if he didn't bring food to the nests in the summer, he wouldn't have any food for the winter
9. that he wasn't worried about the winter because he had plenty of food
10. if those ants ever had any fun
11. that the ants were smart because they had prepared for the winter
12. that it was always a good idea to prepare for the future

PRACTICE 28, p. 253

1. Excuse me. May I ask how old **you are**?
2. I wonder **if** Rashed **picked** up something for dinner.
3. I'm unsure what Lawrence **does** for a living.
4. Fernando said, **"The** best time for me to meet would be Thursday morning."
5. Eriko **asked** me **if I was** coming to the graduation party. I **told** her that I wasn't.
6. I **hope that** I will do well on my final exams.
7. I'm not sure **if the** price includes the sales tax or not.
8. My mother **asked me**, "How many hours did you spend on your homework?"
9. I **asked** my brother, "Are **you** going to marry Paula?"
10. I'd like to know **how you** do that.
11. My parents knew what Sam and I **did.**
12. **It is** a fact that unexpected things happen in everyone's lives.

PRACTICE 29, p. 254

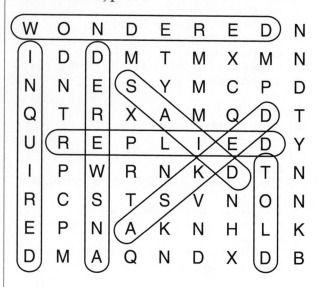

APPENDIX 1: PHRASAL VERBS

PRACTICE 2, p. 255

1. off . . . on
2. up
3. up . . . down
4. off . . . in
5. down . . . up
6. up
7. up . . . off
8. away
9. out . . . out

PRACTICE 3, p. 256

1. the TV, the stove
2. my coat, my wedding ring
3. his shoes
4. a story, a fairy tale, an excuse
5. some rotten food, an old shirt
6. a doctor's appointment, a meeting, a trip
7. a puzzle, a math problem
8. a report, some late homework
9. a message, a phone number
10. a box, a sack of mail
11. the light, the computer, the car engine

PRACTICE 5, p. 257

1. on
2. over
3. on . . . off
4. into / in . . . out of
5. on . . . off
6. into
7. into

PRACTICE 6, p. 257

1. b
2. c
3. a
4. g
5. f
6. d
7. e

PRACTICE 8, p. 258
1. back
2. down
3. out
4. away
5. on
6. up
7. back
8. up
9. back
10. off
11. out . . . up . . . off . . . back

PRACTICE 9, p. 259
1. out . . . out
2. on . . . X
3. into . . . X
4. X . . . into
5. up . . . up
6. away . . . away
7. down . . . X
8. X . . . up
9. away . . . X
10. up . . . up
11. off . . . X
12. from . . . X

PRACTICE 11, p. 260
1. over
2. out
3. in
4. out
5. out
6. down
7. around
8. out of
9. up
10. out
11. out
12. up
13. over

PRACTICE 12, p. 261
1. a. off
   b. on
   c. down
   d. back
   e. out
   f. away
2. a. in
   b. out
3. a. over
   b. off
   c. on
   d. into
   e. out of
4. a. up
   b. up
   c. down
5. a. into
   b. up
   c. over
6. a. up
   b. off
   c. back
7. a. off
   b. back
   c. up
   d. over
8. a. in
   b. out
   c. up
   d. up

PRACTICE 14, p. 263
1. on
2. up
3. out
4. over
5. out
6. away . . . out
7. out . . . up
8. off
9. up
10. on
11. up
12. over
13. up
14. away
15. out
16. away

PRACTICE 16, p. 264
1. off
2. up
3. over
4. down
5. down
6. up
7. out
8. back
9. up
10. up
11. on
12. in . . . down

PRACTICE 17, p. 265
1. a. up
   b. up
   c. up
   d. out
   e. out
   f. out of
2. a. up
   b. up
   c. up
   d. up
   e. into
   f. up
3. a. out of . . . into
   b. out
   c. up

PRACTICE 19, p. 266
1. out . . . out for
2. up
3. up for
4. out of
5. around with
6. back from
7. out of
8. out for
9. through with
10. in on
11. along with

PRACTICE 20, p. 267
1. gymnastics class
2. their neighbors
3. paint
4. rocks
5. assignment
6. cord
7. Hawaii
8. snakes

PRACTICE 22, p. 268
1. out . . . about
2. out for
3. back to
4. out with
5. away from
6. along with
7. over to
8. out of
9. A: over to
   B: around . . . with

PRACTICE 23, p. 268
1. out about
2. out
3. back
4. together
5. up to

PRACTICE 24, p. 268
1. a
2. b
3. a
4. c
5. a
6. b
7. d
8. b
9. c
10. d
11. b
12. d
13. a
14. c
15. a
16. d
17. c
18. a
19. a
20. d
21. b

APPENDIX 2: PREPOSITION COMBINATIONS

PRACTICE 2, p. 271
1. b
2. f
3. j
4. e
5. c
6. i
7. a
8. h
9. d
10. g

PRACTICE 3, p. 271
1. to
2. to
3. to
4. with
5. for
6. about
7. of
8. about
9. from
10. with
11. about
12. of

PRACTICE 5, p. 272

1. from
2. with
3. to
4. at
5. in
6. at
7. for
8. with . . . about / over
9. with
10. for
11. for

PRACTICE 6, p. 272

1. to
2. A: from
   B: for
3. A: to
   B: at
4. to
5. of
6. from . . . for
7. A: for . . . with
   B: to

PRACTICE 8, p. 273

1. to
2. for
3. for
4. of
5. for . . . for
6. for
7. to . . . from
8. to / with
9. about . . . in
10. of / about

PRACTICE 9, p. 274

1. a. of
   b. for
   c. of / about
   d. with
   e. with
   f. of
   g. in
   h. to
2. a. about
   b. about
   c. of
   d. of
   e. of
   f. about
   g. for
   h. for

PRACTICE 11, p. 275

1. for
2. from
3. for
4. on
5. with
6. in
7. at
8. to
9. with
10. of
11. to
12. to . . . about
13. with . . . about
14. to . . . about

PRACTICE 12, p. 275

1. about
2. from
3. of
4. to
5. to
6. from
7. with
8. with
9. for . . . at
10. A: with . . . about
    B: to
    A: to . . . about

PRACTICE 14, p. 276

1. with
2. to
3. from
4. about
5. to
6. about / of
7. at
8. for
9. for
10. for
11. about
12. to
13. about / of
14. like
15. for
16. at

PRACTICE 15, p. 277

1. g
2. i
3. c
4. j
5. b
6. h
7. a
8. f
9. e
10. d

PRACTICE 17, p. 278

1. to . . . for
2. for
3. of
4. for
5. on
6. for
7. on
8. to / with
9. from
10. on
11. of
12. of
13. to
14. from
15. of / from

PRACTICE 18, p. 278

Correct sentences:

1. a, b
2. a
3. a, b
4. b
5. a, b
6. a, b
7. a
8. b

PRACTICE 20, p. 279

1. on
2. from
3. about
4. for
5. about
6. from
7. to / with . . . about
8. to
9. by
10. from
11. by
12. to
13. about
14. from

PRACTICE 21, p. 280

1. on
2. about
3. with
4. from
5. from
6. to . . . for
7. of
8. to
9. from
10. to
11. to
12. for
13. from
14. on
15. on
16. of
17. about

PRACTICE 22, p. 280

1. d
2. b
3. c
4. a
5. d
6. a
7. b
8. c
9. d
10. c
11. d
12. b
13. b
14. a
15. d
16. b
17. c
18. b
19. a
20. d
21. a
22. c

NOTES

NOTES

NOTES

NOTES

NOTES

NOTES

NOTES

NOTES

NOTES

NOTES